IMMORTAL REBELS

IMMORTAL REBELS

Freedom for the Individual
in the Bible

by

ISRAEL J. GERBER, Ph.D.

JONATHAN DAVID : *PUBLISHERS*
New York

"TEMPLE ISRAEL"

IMMORTAL REBELS

Library of Congress Catalogue Card No. 63-21528

PRINTED IN THE UNITED STATES OF AMERICA

TABLE OF CONTENTS

To

My Children
BARBARA JANE
SHARON MAY
AND
WAYNE SCOTT

"A Heritage of the Lord"

Introduction

No matter how familiar one may be with the contents of the Bible, it presents a challenge to the mind and imagination. "Turn it, and turn it again, for everything is in it," wrote Ben Bag Bag in the *Ethics of the Fathers*. Extracting new insights from the Bible is a never ending process, for it documents every facet of the life of man. Human problems are its subject, and the Pentateuch, especially Genesis, presents them through the family situations it describes.

Having read and studied the Pentateuch numerous times, along with Midrashic interpretations and elaborations of the events narrated in it, I have become increasingly aware of an obvious, yet unexplored, pattern throughout its first book. Genesis is devoted almost entirely to family relationships, presenting every conceivable aspect of sibling strife, and rebellion in the parent-child association. The individual *vis-a-vis* other individuals is its substance; the meaning of their conflicting inter-relationships is its essence. There are struggles between parents, brothers, half-brothers, twins, and sisters, each seeking to utilize his freedom to realize the self. Though it is an ancient book, Genesis contains insights into the human personality as penetrating as any being written today.

In the beginning, God created Adam and then Eve. Heeding the Lord's command to be fruitful and multiply, these two human beings created a new phenomenon—the family. Already confronted by pain and the difficulties of earning a living by sweat and toil, they unsuspectingly initiated the new relationship. The family became a source of pleasure to them and an irritating perplexity.

Ever since this initial record of a family, the problems of parent-child and sibling relationships have interested man immensely. Few, if any, have not experienced problems either as child or parent. Underlying all human relationships is one basic question—how to effect a meaningful rapport with one's fellow creatures with a minimum of distress. Man's constant quest of an appropriate response to this challenge leads him to maturity, and to the greatest possible happiness in life.

It is incumbent to assess both the individual and the group within which he lives. How does he affect the family? And how does the family affect him? Just as the individual influences the environment, so is he shaped by the environment.

In Genesis we observe the reactions of siblings to this chronic problem. They act upon their impulses in an effort to cope with rivals. And it is most discouraging. Cain killed Abel; Abraham disowned Ishmael; Jacob fled from home; his brothers sold Joseph into slavery. Similar interpersonal crises occur in modern society.

Freud compartmentalized the family, describing the mother as the giver and depriver of love and approval; the father as the authority who protects and menaces. Freud saw each family member as a separate entity. His view is dated, however; today the family is viewed as a whole. This volume deals with the interwoven complex of individuals who comprise the dynamic family unit.

We are not concerned with biblical criticism—whether the characters really lived or whether the incidents described actually occurred—but with the insights of the early Hebrew authors who perceived the true nature of man's struggle for a meaningful existence. Psychological analysis of the characterizations found in the biblical narratives and in the abundant commentaries of ancient Jewish scholars, reflects profound perception of human behavior. These writings tersely and succinctly define the underlying dynamic factors of human personality.

How the biblical characters coped with the realities of their existence, or failed to cope with them, relates to an understanding of modern man. Modern man also begins life within the family structure, pursues the fulfillment of his potential self throughout life in an inescapable relation to others, and faces the absolute certainty that "death is the portion of us all." But until he dies, he lives—and how he will live is his daily burden. Like his biblical counterpart, modern man chooses his course of action and bears the responsibility for his choice; he is ever the judge of himself. With this in mind, the personality problems of the biblical characters will be analyzed in the chapters ahead.

In gathering the data from the early Hebrew writings, numerous contradictory statements were encountered. It was necessary to shed those interpretations and hypothetical situations that are beyond the realm of rationality and do not coincide with the main theme of the book. All biblical references that do not include the name of the book, unless otherwise indicated, refer to Genesis.

I am grateful and indebted to all those, too many to enumerate, who shared this journey with me. Some, however, I wish to thank by name. For his penetrating analysis of the psychological material, I am deeply grateful to my good friend, Dr. Marshall L. Fisher. He scrutinized the manuscript with discernment, and the insights he conveyed at seminars conducted for the clergy as Director of the Charlotte Mental Health Clinic were of immeasurable benefit to me.

I feel most fortunate that many capable people within the membership of my congregation generously placed their talents at my disposal. I am especially grateful to Mrs. Stanley S. Slesinger whose keen perception in editing the manuscript gave clarity to the salient ideas of this volume. My sincerest thanks to Mrs. Nathan Ades, who made valuable suggestions as the manuscript emerged from notes, to Miss Judy Frazier, who graciously typed the manuscript in its entirety as often as the writer requested it, and to Mrs. Irving Richek, who also helped in committing my writing to the printed page.

Not to be overlooked are the members of my family who made their contributions wittingly and unwittingly. For her encouragement despite the many hours spent alone due to this "competitor," my most profound love and affection to Sydelle, my dear wife.

ISRAEL J. GERBER

Charlotte, North Carolina
Chanukah 5723

CHAPTER ONE

The Eyes of Both of Them Were Opened

(Genesis 3:7)

THE prime factor in all human progress is rebellion. Revolutionary thought in the social and physical sciences, in religion, education, the arts, and government has provided the impetus for mankind's tortuous climb toward realization of his capabilities.

As an historical record of the early development of the Jewish people, the Bible portrays their dissatisfaction with the *status quo* and their striving to attain a superior mode of living. Abraham, the first recorded rebel and heretic, rejected man's tendency to fashion the future in the pattern of the present. Not content to merely improve upon what already existed, he discarded paganism in its entirety. If the future would continue to repeat the past, civilization could not improve—at best it could retain its defects; or, what seemed more certain to Abraham, civilized life as he knew it would disintegrate. Abraham refused to settle for mere survival—to "sit under his vine and under his fig tree"—to play a waiting game with oblivion. He rebelled against the degradation of consigning man's fate to idols, and began anew. He conceived and fostered monotheism, a concept of One God utterly foreign to the Mesopotamians of that era, but which has captured the minds of men and is widely accepted throughout the world today. Thus Abraham personifies the ever-continuing process of rebellion and change that has characterized his descendants throughout almost four millennia of existence.

The spark struck by Abraham inflamed Moses to rebel against slavery and the belief that slaves were preordained to remain forever in servitude. His successful challenge to the might of Egypt engraved the right to rebel in the memory of his people—a right future generations exercised to promote their freedom.

1

The pages of the Bible also portray the earliest recorded resistance to conquest of the mind. The Bible relates in part the continuous rebellion of individuals and groups that propelled the development of the Jewish people. Subjugated people customarily abandoned their idols and adopted the deities of their masters, reasoning that their own gods were weak and ineffectual while those of the victors must wield great power. Although enslaved and deprived of the most fundamental human rights, the Hebrew slaves not only refused to embrace the idols of the Pharaoh, but dared to maintain a religious belief utterly opposed to that of the Egyptians. They demonstrated that the Lord is God under all circumstances, good or bad. Centuries of enslavement could not erase this idea. So it has been in every period of Jewish history wherever Jews have lived, and what is true of one people is generally true of all mankind: When every other right is gone, the mind and spirit still demand their freedom.

Psychological analysis and existential interpretation of the family portraits in the Bible bring another rebellion into focus—the rebellion against the principle of primogeniture, and, by implication, of predetermination. Primogeniture established the life-long superiority of the first-born and the permanent inferiority of the other off-spring. In contrast, analysis of the biblical families reveals constant rebellion against this custom and continuous striving to promote freedom-for-the-individual.

The conception of freedom-for-the-individual as the basis of civilized society is the underlying theme of the Pentateuch. With "the breath of life" man was conceived as a "living soul," not as a creature shackled by supernatural powers to a static existence, as he was in primitive cultures. The first book of the Bible, especially, depicts man as a free spirit striving to break the fetters of predetermination. When Adam and Eve ate from the Tree of Knowledge, "the eyes of them both were opened" (3:7) and they came face to face with reality. The future was theirs to decide; their choice between good and evil would determine their fate.

Genesis shows man endowed with a mind with which to plumb the depths of his capabilities, and with a spirit with which to overcome his limitations. He has the inner freedom to accept his own impulse, to evaluate its worth to himself, and to initiate his own act. Without this inner freedom, man would remain inanimate clay. If man rejects his instinct, if he judges himself evil, if he is the instrument of another will, man cannot live in the vacuum of outer freedom. For freedom implies an inner honesty—to understand oneself, to accept oneself, and to have the will to refine the alloy of one's nature. Man eventually faces death, and every moment of his life poses the need to choose his course of action and to bear the responsibility for his deeds. The outer freedom accorded him in the social environment traps the man who lacks the inner freedom to become himself.

This is not to ignore the determinism to which each person is always subjected. Prevailing factors which the individual had no part in creating are determined. Consequently, each individual confronts both determinism and freedom. Each story in Genesis suggests that the accident of birth should no longer limit man in his potential growth. His position in society is based upon the quality of equality—how well he utilizes his inner freedom. His thoughts and actions portray his true self and impart meaning to his existence.

Via the family settings within its pages, the Pentateuch as a whole, and Genesis in particular, presents the existential right of all individuals to freedom. The early development of democratic patterns conveyed through these Scriptural episodes began within the family, extended subsequently to the tribe, and ultimately to the nation. Thus the purpose of the Pentateuch takes on new dimensions of meaning and value.

"Why did God choose to create mankind from one man instead of from many?" asks the Talmud. And the Rabbis reply, "So that no man might boast that his father is descended from better ancestry, although no two men are alike." The ultimate equality of all men is portrayed in the act of creation, and the Book of Genesis attributes this evolution to the Lord Himself. God is no respecter of persons. By accepting the younger Abel's sacrifice over that of the older Cain, the Lord showed that the worth of an individual is not rooted in prescribed divine law, but in the discriminating self-knowledge with which man utilizes the divine power within him. Deeds and their meaning to the doer are the measure of the individual's beneficence to himself and to mankind.

This is the unique and consistent thread that runs through the familial relationships in the Torah. From the birth of the first brothers, Cain and Abel, through the final sibling relationship of Miriam, Aaron and Moses, there is a consistent revolt against the assumption of power and leadership based upon the order of birth. With Cain and Abel, the Lord established the pattern. Mankind, perceiving the wisdom of this procedure, followed suit. Noah favored his youngest son, Shem, over his brothers. The younger Isaac, not the older Ishmael, carried forward his father's religious idea, as did Jacob instead of Esau. This theme continues with unvaried regularity. Jacob loved Rachel, the younger sister, not the older Leah. Jacob favored Joseph, the youngest of the four first-born of their mothers, over his brothers. The younger Ephraim took precedence over his older brother Manasseh, and the younger Moses rose above the older Aaron to liberate the Jewish people from Egyptian bondage. Throughout, the younger child came out ahead of his older sibling. Again, when Jacob blessed his sons before he died, he blessed the younger Zebulun before the older Issachar and the younger Asher before the older Naphtali. In each instance, the older child was dethroned. Occurring with such consistent regularity in these writings, it is difficult to view this emphasis as mere coincidence. It reflects a calculated intention to portray man as the authors understood him.

In a society where the oldest son enjoyed the right of primogeniture, where the position of the first-born was highly valued, showing preference to a younger sibling would inevitably precipitate a crisis among the children. Yet these families flouted the accepted practice with unconditional regularity, as though they intended to promote hostility. It would seem that there would have been at least one family in which the older sibling retained his position. That this did not occur in Genesis strongly indicates adherence to a strict editorial policy in the writing of these stories. Why emphasize this reversal of the accepted custom?

In the patriarchal society, the head of the family was the recognized absolute authority. He could do whatever he wished with his children. Thus, Abraham could banish Ishmael and decide to sacrifice Isaac. And therein lies the substance of the familial conflict and individual suffering of the personalities portrayed in Genesis. Whereas there was no judgment or choice involved under the system of primogeniture—the first-born was considered superior by virtue of forces beyond any man's control— the exercise of judgment and choice carried with it a new burden of responsibility. A double-edged sword, the freedom of choice held forth both great promise and great risk. The choice of a patriarch who selected a fledgling son to succeed him might prove wise, if that son displayed leadership qualities. On the other hand, if disaster followed the choice of the wrong son, the patriarch had no one to blame but himself. No doubt this deterred many fathers from interfering with the operation of primogeniture. This, too, represented a choice—in some cases a bad one— but one for which the patriarch could rationalize that he was not responsible. King Jehoshaphat apparently knew that his oldest son Jehoram lacked the merit to succeed him, yet he allowed him to become king simply because he was the first-born (II Chronicles 21:3). The bloody murders of his brothers by which Jehoram attempted to maintain the position for which he was so poorly equipped, testify to his father's cowardly choice. As the paternal authority, however, Jehoshaphat exercised his prerogative. Such an environment promoted sibling rivalry. The future of the offspring depended upon the whims of the patriarch. He could disown them or name any one of them as his heir or successor, despite the favored position of the first-born. He could even relegate future generations to inferior status, as Noah did to Ham's children. With such broad and unlimited powers, it was only natural that the sons vied with each other to occupy a favored position with the all-powerful patriarch.

This helps to explain the rivalries which existed among the families and between the brothers who dominate the Book of Genesis, as will be seen in the succeeding chapters of this book. They strove with each other as they competed for the good graces of their father, who could either bless them or curse them. This type of sibling rivalry has persisted in the Middle East throughout the ages.

In *Sex and Family in the Bible and the Middle East,* Raphael Patai elaborates upon this phenomenon. He tells of a psychological study of childhood in an Egyptian village. The families there utilized sibling rivalry as a means of developing their children and helping them mature. Certain parents overtly provoked sibling rivalry if it was not evident enough among their children. The theory behind this practice is that sibling strife develops within the child the fortitude to meet rivals upon attaining adulthood. In this particular village, sibling conflict has become so interwoven with the cultural pattern that brothers actually avoid each other. Friction appears especially among the offspring of one father and different mothers, as among the twelve sons of Jacob. Proverbs still circulating in that area are: "I and my cousins against the world; I and my brothers against my cousins; I against my brothers;" "They who are from one back and two different wombs do not love each other;" and, "He who has not suckled my mother's breasts is not my brother." A concomitant value of this type of conflict is that it may mitigate or displace the father-son or oedipal conflict. By concentrating upon their brothers, the sons have little opportunity to view their father as a competitor for the love of the mother.

Patai's empirical findings and observations help us appreciate the background against which we should view the biblical narratives of sibling rivalry. Undoubtedly, it was a consciously fostered pattern of behavior in the Hebrew patriarchal family. The biblical parents might have felt that exposure to competitive stress within the family was the best way to prepare their sons for life—a life which depended largely on their ability to compete with their peers and their enemies. By utilizing this approach, they promoted a greater concern for individual growth among their children and fostered the principle of individual freedom.

Although the head of the family in the patriarchal society, or the leader of the tribe, was in full control and made all decisions affecting the welfare of the group, the patriarchs in Genesis nevertheless encouraged the growth of the individual personality. While they advocated regulating the individual and compelling him to conform to the traditional patterns when survival of the group depended upon convention, at the same time they granted a degree of freedom to everyone. They regarded freedom of choice, with its accompanying risk, as the surest method of developing talents and attaining potential growth. They concluded that man can utilize freedom; that regardless of his position, he has the God-given right to work out his own destiny; that the individual has status in his own right. Combining patriarchal control with a modicum of personal freedom, they believed, offered the most favorable condition for individual and group progress. They understood that free men can strive and progress while they accept limitations within themselves and within the social structure. Such a framework negates the domination of the autocrat and fosters tolerance of diversity. Young men who were permitted to test their capabilities and fortitude in promoting their individual welfare fulfilled their dignity as human beings. The patriarchs placed a premium upon individuality; without it they saw man stripped of his dignity.

In the Pentateuch we observe man emerging with personal rights, shaking himself free from complete domination by the group. When the Lord made His covenant with the Hebrews at Mt. Sinai, He made it with each individual present, not only with the group as a whole. The Ten Commandments, in fact, are addressed to the individual, implying that each man is free to obey or to disobey and is responsible for his acts. The Jewish people refused to accept the concept of Original Sin because it condemned man at birth. They could not condone a moral condition thrust upon man unaware, through no act of his own. To adjudge oneself guilty before one sees the light of day, to accept predetermined meanings, is to refuse to make use of one's freedom and is, therefore, immoral. It is to alienate one's freedom and to resign oneself to fatalism. The early Hebrews understood this and refused to countenance it. To them, freedom meant that man must realize his predicament, and either accept it, or complain about it, or try to change it. They set the pattern for their descendants. The early Hebrews protested against primogeniture and instituted changes, transforming the moral concept of man and giving life the meaning they have chosen. In a world that still clings to the concept of predetermination, the record of the Jews for non-conformity remains unbroken.

What a stir Abraham must have made among the people when he returned from Mount Moriah with a living Isaac. Abraham challenged the prevailing practice of human sacrifice and dared regard himself a religious person, yet the gods did not destroy him. What images were shattered by the escape of the Jews from Egyptian bondage. They realized their condition, protested it, and changed it, visibly demonstrating the impotence of Egyptian idolatry. Through the biblical and other accounts of such behavior, the literature of the Jewish people asserts that no person should be wholly submerged in the social mass. By concentrating upon the individual's development, stimulating the growth of a mature personality, the patriarchs provided for superior leadership. They recognized that the potential strides of the group were limited only by the opportunities available to the individual for his personal growth. Providing the individual with the freedom to exploit these opportunities to the best of his abilities is the essence of true democracy. And, in turn, the individual's full development and affirmation of self were regarded as his responsibility to society.

The Pentateuch portrays women, too, with distinct individuality. Few women ever had greater power over a man than the outspoken Sarah wielded over Abraham. She contributed to his greatness, yet it is clear she sought her own fulfillment. The independent Rebekah was a positive force in Isaac's life. Even passive Rachel and stoic Leah commanded Jacob's respect and consideration; he would not move his family without their consent. The daughters of Zelophehad demanded their right of inheritance, which was granted them, a practice unheard of in those years. No mere chattels, biblical women articulated and actively pursued their life goals.

The role of the early Hebrew women contrasts sharply with that of women in other cultures. As primitive societies developed and war became a means of settling disputes, physical strength acquired great importance. Women were a liability to men at war; they were unable to fight. War-like societies, consequently, relegated women to an inferior status. The Hebrews, however, sought a peaceful existence. They would fight when necessary, but their concept of justice and righteousness demanded the preservation of human life. Their treatment of their women reflected the emphasis on peace. A Hebrew woman's rights in marriage included food, clothing, and conjugal relationship. In the absence of these she could demand recourse. In early Hebrew culture the concept of freedom-for-the-individual applied equally to women.

Romantic love first flowered, not in medieval ballads or nineteenth century literature, but in Genesis. The love story of Jacob and Rachel in complete simplicity acknowledges the reality of physical love. To see Rachel was to desire her, and Jacob loved even her memory with passion. For Rachel, loving Jacob was the singular fact of her life, and bearing his son gave meaning to her existence. Genesis depicted the free choice of a mate and the expression of physical love in marriage as the highest good.

The promotion of individuality appears in another sphere as well. Names have always had great significance to the Jewish people. The name of a child commemorated an important event in the life of the tribe or the family or the individual. The use of names in the Bible also underscores the theme of freedom-for-the-individual. No person need retain the same name throughout life. Nor should the designation made by his parents at birth hamper him. Rather, if he progressed and matured, or achieved some great accomplishment, he could, indeed should, make note of it by varying his original name or by adopting a new one altogether. He had the latitude to make his name more meaningful. Thus, as Abram and Sarai assumed new responsibilities, their names were altered to Abraham and Sarah (17:5,15). When Eve became a bearer of children, a duty she apparently did not have in the Garden of Eden since death was not then a concomitant of life, she was given the name "Chavah" because she became "the mother of all living" (3:20). Jacob's name was changed to Israel when he won a victory of the spirit; Esau acquired the additional name of "Edom" (25:30), and Hoshea's name became Joshua (Numbers 13:16). Freedom-for-the-individual—growth, change, evolution—operated in every circumstance in the Bible.

In each familial relationship analyzed in the succeeding chapters, a younger child was encouraged to challenge the position of the first-born, even to purchasing the birthright as did Jacob. Although primogeniture remained the accepted mode of providing leadership in the patriarchal society, it did not operate with automatic precision in the exceptional families. Rather, primogeniture functioned side by side with the new freedom of action advocated by the early Jewish patriarchs. A practice so deeply ingrained in a culture does not give way in one generation, nor in three. In time, the courageous example of the patriarchs justified the displacement of older children for others. A fuller appreciation of individual worth blossomed into an ideal which later took root in reality. With

the assumption of judgment and responsibility, Genesis established the
individual as the cornerstone of society and expressed the deep conviction
that the greatest resource of society is its people. In maintaining that the
merit of individual action should earn the leadership role, Genesis acknowledged that the greatness of every nation rests on the accomplishments of
individual men.

Just as Genesis denied favor to the first-born merely because he was
older, so did it deny special recognition to the younger son merely because
he was younger. Only when the older and younger sons were of like caliber
was the former to be given preference (Deuteronomy 21:15-17). In every
other case, primogeniture was shelved. Judah became the leader of his
brothers although he was born fourth; Levi earned the rights of priesthood,
although third in the order of birth. Beyond the infancy of the Hebrew
people, David, youngest of Jesse's eight sons, slew Goliath, and ascended
the throne of Israel. And while he was still alive, David crowned Solomon,
his youngest son. This theme appeared again when the Prophet Amos
said that he was not the son of a prophet, yet he was able to become
a spokesman of God in his own right. In the Apocrypha, Mattathias
designated Judah Maccabee, the third of his five sons, to assume the
leadership of the revolt against the Greco-Syrians after his death. Beginning with Genesis, the Bible and other Hebrew writings advocated that
each individual possesses a potential which must not be repressed or belittled or ignored. He must not be restrained from reaching out to attain
greater heights. The accident of birth is finite; man's potential infinite.

God's call, "Go, get thee out," summoned Abraham to make an entirely new start. Abraham founded a new group, different theologically,
sociologically, and politically from its contemporaries. Abraham's new
idea of God created the climate for the sibling relationship depicted in
Genesis and for the fuller development of the individual that followed.
Monotheism, the belief in the existence of One God who is the Creator
and Sustainer of the Universe, established the foundation for the democratic idea. Since there is but One God, and since He created man in
His own image, then all men are equally His children. Each human being
has a divine spark within him. The concept of One God embraces the
equality of all men. Regardless of station, all men deserve equally fair
treatment. From its inception, the Jewish people has held as basic concerns
the dignity of the individual, protection of his rights, and development
of his abilities. Monotheism, the daringly new and purified insight into
God, also carried a new concept of man's relationship to his fellow man
and has had a permanent effect upon the history and thinking of mankind.

The religious idea of the ancient Hebrews, which elevated man to individual responsibility, also conveyed the concept of mutual responsibility. It obligated the individual to concern himself with the needs and rights of others by telling him, "Yes, you are your brother's keeper."

Abraham's revolt against the Mesopotamian way of life marked the beginning of protest against the enervating *status quo*. Happily, the social protest of the Jewish people has ever propelled mankind in its thrust toward a higher, more sublime morality. To extract individual freedom from domination by the group, they ran counter to the accepted social order, though fully aware that man flounders and suffers in confusion when social order crumbles. They produced the dilemma of existential freedom for a purpose—to enable man to dominate the environment rather than submit to domination. In freeing the individual from the chains of predetermination and establishing him in a mutual relationship with his fellow man, Abraham's rebellion paved the way for the ultimate evolution of self-government. Man's assumption of responsibility to himself and to society foreshadowed democratic government. The Book of Exodus records the first application of this principle when Moses called seventy elders into counsel with him. Having escaped from slavery into freedom, the first responsibility of free men was self-administration. Pursuant to the acceptance of the Ten Commandments, all subsequent legislation of a democratic nature develops this principle. Like the American Declaration of Independence, all expressions of the right of the individual to freedom grew out of the revolt of Abraham. The vote in our democratic society extends the early Hebraic view that every human being has the right to express his preference on the basis of his own interpretation and understanding of the law. Not predetermined, his course of action follows the free exercise of his mind and discretion and choice. The imperative from the Book of Leviticus, "Proclaim liberty throughout the land unto all the inhabitants thereof," conveys in its original Hebrew wording the existential meaning of freedom. "D'ror," the Hebrew word for "liberty," comes from the root word which means "to live"[1]—to live in every dimension. The inscription on the Liberty Bell is the heritage of all mankind. And today, in every part of the world, heirs to the biblical conception of freedom-for-the-individual continue to emerge from the darkness of predetermination into an awareness of the spiritual freedom inherent in living.

CHAPTER TWO

Bring Forth Children

(Genesis 3:16)

ALMOST every parent meets the problem of "sibling rivalry," or "sibling jealousy," upon the arrival of the second offspring, and finds that it becomes even more acute as the number of children increases. As a rule, the younger child receives more love and attention, merely because he is younger, and engenders jealousy in his older sibling. The world's first family as portrayed in Genesis, that of Adam and Eve and their sons, ran headlong into this problem without prior warning or understanding. The story of their experience reveals profound insight into the dynamics of human behavior.

Abel's arrival marked the onset of a strained relationship in the household of Adam and Eve. Cain experienced the first major problem of growing up in a dispassionate world. With envy he observed the love and attention which had once been his alone showered upon his younger brother. To him, Abel was another competitor for his mother's love, Adam having already deprived him of much of Eve's time and affection. The Rabbis well surmised that such competition existed among the boys when they suggested that the brothers "quarrelled about the first Eve."[1] They recognized that such a complication can lead to serious consequences. Children vie with each other for the mother's attention, which to them is synonymous with love, for the mother is the most essential person during childhood, spending most of her time with them. She makes the child feel wanted and loved, and is the one upon whom he depends for security. It is not unusual to hear the male child state that he wishes to marry his mother, as the female child often desires to marry her father. Expressing subconscious incestuous strivings,[2] each child regards the parent of the opposite sex as existing for him or her alone, and resents the existence of the other parent. This has been labelled the Oedipus Complex.

In the Oedipus situation, the child really hates both parents. He hates his father because he regards him as his rival, and hates his mother because she denies herself to him. The traumatic element in the Oedipus Complex consists not so much in the child's sexual attraction toward the parent of the opposite sex, as in the hostility he feels toward the parent of the same sex, and the aggression engendered by his jealousy.

The intensity of a younger brother's hostility, however, surpasses that of an only child. Awakening to the attraction of his mother, the younger son regards his older brother as more of an adversary than his father.[3] We must conclude that Abel as well as Cain entertained incestuous feelings toward their mother.

According to the Genesis story, Cain and Abel were not only attracted to their mother, but actually populated the world in this fashion. Striving for their mother's love was therefore more than a desire for affection. Mothers frequently act as seductresses, inviting their sons' affections. This is especially evident in homes where there is no father, or where he is a weak character, as was Adam. Such parents encourage the son to maintain a possessive attitude toward his mother, while she simultaneously derives pleasure from him. This accounts for some men remaining bachelors, men with mother fixations, and for women with strong father attachments who evolve into spinsterhood. They refuse to leave their parents because they feel no one is capable of replacing them. Sometimes parents unwittingly encourage this emotional tie in their children. They are flattered by the child's attention and affection and they unconsciously seek to preserve the relationship by holding on to their offspring. When such strong parental attachment is carried over into adulthood, the immature personality finds it impossible to enter into a satisfactory marriage. Or, if he does marry, he experiences an unsatisfactory relationship. It is an attempt to love two women, or two men.

Cain was understandably antagonistic toward his sibling. Abel deprived him of indulgences and pleasures that he felt were justly his. In addition, he could no longer talk to his father or mother and was hardly even noticed. Abel only had to cry and they would hasten to his side, trying to please him. All at once his sibling had usurped his position. He concluded that Abel was superior to him, to merit so much attention. Cain felt alone and rejected, unsure of his parents' love. He did not understand that parents have an inexhaustible supply of love, enough for all their children. All his efforts to recapture his former position in the household failed. Since he was less desirable to his mother, he felt that he was bad. She would never admit that he was better than Abel. Cain attempted drastic measures to regain her love, but when he was unable to compete with Abel successfully, he felt he had proved to his parents that they were right—that he was bad. Like all children, the problem Cain faced with relation to his parents largely determined his relationship with his brother. In addition to responding to Abel's demands, his parents labored from sun-up to sun-down to wrest a living from the unwilling earth, while they coped with the general problem of marital adjustment and parenthood. Cain felt ignored, deprived of the attention he deserved. Nor did Adam and Eve sufficiently reassure him of their love, which is the bedrock of every child's security. Even when they tried to divide their attention between their sons, their affection for Cain appeared to lack spontaneous sincerity. Their interest in him, regardless of its intensiveness, seemed unreal. Cain felt his parents were not concerned with his well-being,[4] and he never regained his self-esteem.

Cain resented Abel's intrusion and made his enmity evident. He showed his hostility by tattling on Abel and on occasion gave vent to his feelings by injuring the "intruder." Cain must have uttered the derogatory remarks common to all children and he must have suggested that his parents send Abel away, a veiled expression of the wish that his brother would die. Very early in their relationship, Cain wished Abel dead, and his destructive wishes never left him.[5] Unconsciously, he regarded them as equivalent to the actual destruction of his brother, producing a need for punishment that remained with him throughout life.

Eve was aware that Cain harbored resentment toward his brother, but she was unwilling to accept the inevitable existence of such feelings between her sons. She felt they had to love each other at all times; friendship would not suffice. Her unrealistic behavior made it impossible to deal with tensions as they arose. She tried to repress her knowledge of the truth, but only succeeded in distorting it. Her repressions found subconscious expression in her dreams. She visualized Cain drinking Abel's blood with avidity, though Abel begged him not to gulp it all down.[6] When she informed Adam of her dream, he was concerned and he took precautions to prevent such an occurrence. He manipulated the environment by separating the two lads, giving each boy a home of his own, and teaching each of them a different occupation so that their paths would not cross.[7] Abel became a keeper of sheep; Cain a tiller of the soil.

At first Cain was pleased and satisfied with his work, but he gradually grew to detest it. Nomadic people regarded the shepherd as superior to the farmer. Sheep raising carried with it social prestige because it was regarded as skillful work, while farming was viewed as a lowly occupation. The Midrash depicts farmers unfavorably. "Three had a great desire for agriculture, and no good was found in them; Cain, Noah, and Uzziah."[8] Cain became a murderer, Noah a drunkard, and Uzziah agitated against the priesthood. Because he was beneath his brother in social status, this class distinction engendered feelings of inferiority in Cain. Adopting the attitude of his environment toward his occupation, which modern psychology terms introjection or internalization, Cain felt himself diminished in prestige, developed a poor opinion of himself, and experienced feelings of self-hatred.

When the time arrived for the brothers to marry, the problem of finding brides arose. Perhaps they argued as to who should marry their mother. To eliminate the possibility of incest (which is an acknowledgement of the subconscious desire for it), the Rabbis explain that each brother was born with a twin sister whom he was to wed. But a most peculiar thing had happened. Cain was born with one twin sister; Abel with two. Cain wanted one of Abel's twin sisters, an exquisite beauty,[9] and he claimed that, since he was the older brother, he should take precedence and have two wives. Besides his own sister, Cain wanted to marry Abel's beautiful sister. Possessing her would inflate his ego and settle the question of who would dominate whom. Cain felt that winning Abel's sister away from him would display his strength and put his younger brother in his proper place, but Abel also felt compelled to test his power to dominate. Cain strove passionately to achieve his two-fold aim, but failed because Abel was physically stronger than he.[10] When Abel married both sisters with whom he was born, Cain construed it a slur against himself and proof that he was not good enough to have two wives, that he was sexually inferior to his younger brother. Sex, the highest and strongest expression of love, exerts so powerful an influence that it can induce murder, and the Sages of Israel apparently acknowledged it as a dominant motivating force long before psychology defined it. Cain was confronted by a compound feeling of insufficiency: the fact that he met with defeat was more damaging than that he did not meet with success.

The debilitating effect of this blow to Cain's ego soon became evident. In years to come, Adam told his sons, the Jewish people would offer sacrifices in observance of a holiday. In anticipation of that occasion, Adam requested them to make a sacrifice to God.[11] Abel readily consented, but Cain acquiesced only after an argument with Adam. Cain then offered of "the fruit of the ground," the worst of the crop, while Abel sacrificed from the firstlings of his flock, sheep that had not been shorn. Cain offered his sacrifice haughtily; Abel with humility. Greedily, Cain brought *shelomim,* a sacrifice of which the owner consumes the greater part, while

Abel sacrificed an *olah,* the entire oblation, without taking any portion of it home. Aware that he was not behaving maturely, Cain felt a sullen-ness and moroseness settle upon him, instead of the expected sense of joy.[12] Also, a flame descended from heaven and consumed Abel's sacrifice, but Cain's refused to burn. It smoked until it almost choked him.[13] Even God loved Abel more! Cain was bitterly disappointed and dejected. Piqued by this slight, his anger mounted because Abel was now extolled as a prototype of goodness.

Ancient Hebrew literature gives us insight into Cain's and Abel's personalities by reporting or conjecturing about a dispute that took place between them. The Rabbis[14] tell that they debated between them-selves the nature of the universe. Cain maintained that the world was not created with mercy; that there is neither law nor judge, neither re-ward nor punishment. Good deeds bear no fruit, he averred, because God rules the world with arbitrary power. Otherwise He would have accepted his offering. Abel maintained that God rewards good deeds irrespective of persons. God graciously accepted his sacrifice because his deeds were better. They debated this point heatedly, adding further strain to their frayed relationship.

The offerings tendered by the brothers reflect their emotional growth and character development. With his parents' love and attention withheld from him, except for infrequent moments, Cain aped their behavior and was niggardly in his contribution to the Lord. He therefore brought of "the fruit of the ground," those that had fallen off the branches and lain on the ground, the bruised and inferior fruit, the surplus of his produce. It was not that he lacked good agricultural products of which to make an offering. He had more than enough, but he behaved like a miser. His "gift" was symptomatic of a kind of fear to which stingy people are generally subject. They dare not give, even when they have more than they need, for fear that they may deprive themselves.[15] Cain was stingy with his wares, as his parents were stingy with their most precious com-modity—love for him. If he had to part with something, even where the Lord was concerned, it would be with left-overs. After all, wasn't he receiving from his parents what was left over from Abel? His need to attain superior status to Abel rendered Cain incapable of giving pleasure and happiness to anyone else. He kept as much as he could for himself. If his possessions were greater, he felt greater.

Conversely, Cain might have considered his offering of left-overs the most valuable thing he possessed. He still wanted to win approval and acceptance and his only examples were his parents. He identified with them, using their behavior as a guide. He reasoned that left-overs were good because this was what his parents gave him. Like a miser, Cain hoarded what he loved and felt that giving even a little was an expression of love. Such behavior leads to deterioration in human relationships, to isolation and loneliness such as Cain soon came to know.

Abel, on the other hand, having enjoyed his parents' lavish show of love, developed a different type of personality. As he had received freely, so did he give freely. He stood ready to contribute of the best that he owned, just as he had received the best of others. He felt secure in the knowledge that he was loved, which engendered within him a confident, optimistic outlook upon life. By comparison, Cain grew insecure and anxious. He was pessimistic, suspicious, and subject to moods. By their example, Adam and Eve created the characters of their sons. Not born one "good" and one "bad," they developed different personalities in response to different conditions, for no two human beings experience identical conditions.

Adam and Eve apparently failed to instill within Cain the same secure feeling they had given Abel. One should not condemn them, however, because as new parents they were learning. They relied solely upon their own experiences, having no available body of knowledge on which to draw nor examples to follow. Young people today can better prepare themselves for marriage and parenthood. They can educate themselves to avoid the pitfalls of selfishness and irresponsibility. If they do not, they perform a great disservice to themselves and their offspring. Unlike the first parents, they must bear a heavy responsibility for whatever personality deficiencies ensue.

Adam and Eve set poor examples for their sons. The Bible relates that the serpent approached Eve, not Adam, to eat the fruit of the Tree of Knowledge of Good and Evil, because it is the woman who runs the household. When man returns from the day's labor, he eats what his wife has prepared for him. If Eve were successfully beguiled, Adam would fall easy prey. At first, Eve refused. She believed that death would overtake her if she touched the Tree. The serpent insisted that this was not true. To prove his contention, he shook the Tree violently, and ate from the fruit that fell. Demonstrating that he did not die, the serpent assured Eve that she would not die. Unsure now of her former belief, Eve determined to do as the serpent had suggested. Since her conscience bothered her, however, she compromised with herself. She would eat only the skin of the fruit. When she saw that no harm befell her, she ate the fruit itself. As soon as she had swallowed it, the Angel of Death appeared before her. She expected death momentarily. Selfishly, she resolved to make Adam eat of the forbidden fruit too, lest he marry another woman after her death. If she died, she did not wish him to survive either.[16] A humorous story told about them reflects this attitude. One night Adam stayed out late and Eve became worried. When he returned, Eve accused him of having been out with another woman. Adam argued that it was impossible because they were the only two people on earth, but Eve was not convinced. That night, when Adam fell asleep, Eve silently stole over to him and counted his ribs!

When Adam refused to submit to Eve's urging, she resorted to weeping and harangued him until he finally yielded. But even this did not satisfy her. She insisted upon giving the fruit to all living beings so that they would also be subject to death. Eve behaved like an aggressive, dominating, forceful personality, imposing her will upon everyone.

Confronted by what they had done, both Adam and Eve exhibited infantile behavior, refusing to assume responsibility for their deeds. When asked for an explanation, Adam hurled the burden of his guilt upon Eve. "The woman whom Thou gavest to be with me, she gave me of the tree, and I did eat." The Lord rejected this evasion, however, and chastised him, saying that he had no business obeying her. He was the head of the family, not she.[17] Adam manifested a passive, weak personality. Eve, in turn, cast the blame upon the serpent. "The serpent beguiled me, and I did eat." Neither Adam nor Eve displayed traits of character that would affect their children beneficially. To absolve themselves, they were ready to wield whatever argument they could muster, rather than admit the truth. We may well assume that they later exhibited this pattern before their sons.

The narrative of Adam's death indicates that Eve suffered from a severe guilt-complex. When Adam became severely ill, Eve asked that she bear half his pain because she was responsible for his illness. When he died, she spent all her time weeping, and when her end drew near she prayed that she would be buried beside Adam.[18] There were occasions when Adam and Eve were solicitous toward each other, as when Eve pleaded that Adam should not die, since she sinned by leading him astray, and when she suggested that Adam slay her and return to Paradise. Adam came to Eve's assistance when she suffered extreme pain in childbirth,[19] but an inner resentment remained. Adam's last words to his wife before he died cut through the veneer of compatibility. He flung the final accusation at Eve, "What misfortune didst thou bring upon us . . . death is the portion of all."[20] Early Hebrew scholars obviously recognized that a home without love provides the worst possible environment for growing

children. The manner in which parents display their love for each other,
as well as for their children, determines the emotional climate of the
family. "When the parents love one another, the child loves both parents;
when the parents hate one another, the child is compelled to side with
one against the other. This induces fear since he must then lose the love
of the parent he rejects in favor of the other one."[21]

We may assume the absence of love affected Cain adversely from the
beginning. The lack of loyalty and harmony colored everything that transpired within the family and disturbed him deeply. The emotional climate
of the family was unstable, fraught with tensions and conflicts. The unwholesome quality of their emotional expression blocked the development
of well-integrated, creative children. Due to the faulty guidance of their
parents, Cain and Abel were continually at loggerheads with each other,
which corroborates the adage, "scratch a problem child and you may find
a problem parent."

Despite the hostility that festered within him, Cain heard the God-
impelled question repeating itself within him. "Why art thou wroth?
And why is thy countenance fallen?" Why did he persist in carrying this
chip on his shoulder? Why was he constantly so angry? Why was he so
depressed and moody? "If thou doest well, shall it not be lifted up? And
if thou doest not well, sin croucheth at the door; and unto thee is its
desire, but thou mayest rule over it." Cain gained sufficient insight to
realize that man is not only capable of choosing between good and evil,
but he must. Man must train and discipline himself to make the correct
decisions. When man gains this mastery, life's reward follows. Cain admitted to himself that blaming Abel and his parents for his inadequacies
demeaned him. He recognized that anger, envy and hatred possessed him,
and for no valid reason. The cause of his hostility lay within him. He
accepted his hostility as a part of his equipment as a human being.
External experiences vexed him, but he perceived that if he could alter his
response he could alter his mode of life. He could strive to perfect
his behavior; he had hope for his future. If he turned to God in sincerity
to effect reconciliation, he could expect Heavenly aid. If he should persist
in his imperfection, however, he would wallow hopelessly in evil.

This burst of intellectual lucidity did not console Cain. The assurance
that he possessed the power to regain God's favor as well as his own self-
respect had little meaning for him. His hatred of his brother was too
intense and overpowering. He could not free himself of it.[22] The desire
to do away with his brother obsessed him, and the opportunity soon
presented itself.

Cain and Abel, the sole offspring of Adam and Eve, fell heir to the entire world. They both recognized this fact, but the details of the will had not been determined. They argued about the division of the inheritance. Cain wanted the double share due the oldest son; Abel objected. They finally agreed that Cain would take the immovable property, the real estate, and Abel the movable goods.

As soon as they concluded this agreement, Cain shouted to Abel, "You are standing on my land."

"Whatever you are wearing belongs to me," Abel retorted.

"Do not stand on my property," Cain demanded. "Fly in the air."

"You are wearing my goods," Abel countered. "Take them off. Strip!"

Soon thereafter, one of Abel's sheep trampled a field Cain had planted. He raged at Abel, "You have no right to live on my land and allow your sheep to pasture there."

"Then you have no right to use the wool of my sheep to make clothing for yourself," Abel retaliated. "If you will take off the wool you are wearing, and will pay me for the meat of my flocks which you have eaten, then I will do as you request. I will fly in the air—if I can."

"I could kill you," Cain rejoined. "Who would demand your blood of me?"

"God!" Abel flashed back. "He will avenge me. He brought us into the world. He is the Judge who visits the wicked deeds upon the wicked, and the evil deeds upon the evil. Should you kill me, God will know your secret, and He will punish you."[23]

Although quarrels are ordinarily a means of communication among children, clearing the air and acting as a safety valve, this dispute heightened Cain's already burning hostility. He harassed Abel, taunted and mistreated him. Thoroughly unhappy and dissatisfied with himself, he suffered pangs of self-hatred and turned these feelings outward. He rationalized that by harming Abel he would really punish himself. He attacked Abel, expressing his resentment in physical aggression. Abel, the stronger of the two, overpowered him and Cain saw death staring him in the face. To extricate himself from his predicament, he cried out, "Abel, my brother, do me no harm. We are the only two children in the world. What will you tell our father if you kill me?" Abel was filled with pity and compassion when Cain called him "my brother" and freed him. Seizing the opportunity, Cain leaped up and grabbed a weapon.[24] In a frenzy of anger he beat Abel brutally, finally striking him in the neck and slaying him. Cain accidentally stumbled onto murder. The compulsion was not to kill, but to hurt. Meyer Levin aptly entitled his description

of the Leopold-Loeb case "Compulsion." Leopold and Loeb had not originally desired to kill the Frank boy, but that was how it ended. This is
often true of murder.

Once Cain picked up the weapon and struck the first blow, he was
committed to direct aggression. The accumulated tensions within him,
released by his initial physical response, burst out of control. He beat
Abel mercilessly, having lost all sense of proportion. Oblivious to his
own actions, Cain was temporarily out of contact with reality, or in
common usage, temporarily insane. He stopped beating him only when
Abel lay lifeless and unresponsive at his feet; and then, with the cessation
of violent physical action, consciousness returned. Cain gasped, "My
God, what have I done?"

Cain's repressed jealousy, resentment and hatred of his sibling, all
at once vaulted to the fore and he could no longer restrain himself from
killing Abel. The supposed favoritism of Adam and Eve toward Abel,
the rivalry between the brothers for Eve's affection, the apparent superiority
of Abel in everything from occupation to social standing, to marriage, to
acceptable holy sacrifices, all combined to motivate Cain's actions. His
unquenchable desire to retaliate for all the injustices he presumed had
been perpetrated against him could no longer be stayed. Cain's criminality,
like all types of behavior now classified as delinquent, was a spontaneous
reaction, but experience had nourished it from childhood. Unfortunately,
his aggressive behavior did not alert his parents to his need for their love
and approval. Instead, it further alienated them. It is no surprise, therefore,
that Cain turned out the way he did, for aggression against rival siblings
as well as parents, in impulse and fantasy, does at times result in murder.[25]

Cain's major inadequacy was a conflict over feelings of superiority-
inferiority. When a child is born, he is helpless and thoroughly insufficient
compared to those around him. Living in an adult environment, he regards
himself as weak and small. This engenders within him feelings of inferiority,
inadequacy and insecurity. As he grows, so does the list of his inferiorities.
He can neither stand, walk, nor run; nor feed himself; nor defend himself.
He depends upon others for his survival. Without the interest of his
parents or other adults he could not exist. He must wait, sometimes for
a protracted period, for attention. Only then, perhaps after having utilized
various pantomimic devices, does he get what he wants. At the same time
the child feels omnipotent, for his antics almost always achieve results,
leading him to conclude that his mother and he are one. This condition
exists throughout life, with variations—in school, at work, at play, and
so forth. He wants to be like others, which is a paramount factor in the

continuous shaping of his character. In addition to the normal everyday inferiorities Cain experienced, Abel's arrival relegated him to a back seat. As they grew, Cain's inferiority to his new brother grew. He felt physically, intellectually and socially inferior, and in the degree to which he adopted this attitude his thinking and actions were affected.

As the process of growth unfolds, the child absolutely must relinquish some of his superior feelings. No longer omnipotent, he develops an inferior appraisal of himself. To compensate for the loss of his superior feelings, he will attempt to prove himself a real man. He will strive to attain a condition in life which will give him a feeling of strength, of completeness, of security, whether by acceptable or unacceptable means. An urge to go upward and forward, to attain perfection, motivates him. This feeling begins in childhood and remains throughout life an intrinsic necessity of his existence.

All people, whether so-called socially "adjusted" or so-called socially "maladjusted," pursue this aim of self-perfection. Although society regards the direction of the latter as improper, their goal and purpose exist no less. Cain sought to achieve his goal by socially unacceptable means: by conflict, by attempting to dominate his brother, by catering to his narcissistic ego strivings. The solution he chose did not solve his inner problem. It left him with the same unstable character.

Due to the normal inferior feelings of childhood, aggravated by the tensions engendered by Abel's presence, abilities and social status, Cain especially needed to enhance his self-esteem. He had endured the feeling of inferiority for too long a time and he was unable to relinquish his feelings of superiority. In relation to Abel his feelings conflicted. Such debilitating insecure feelings, which could be equated with femininity, usually evoke an attitude of hostility and aggression to overcome them. The person fears the loss of a valuable part of self, his masculinity. He longs for protection and is unable to cooperate with others. He expects to take and has no desire to give.

People who are especially sensitive to feelings of disparagement develop "safeguarding tendencies," or defense mechanisms, by which they seek to protect the ego. By means of these devices or fictions, they aim to rid themselves of their inferior feelings and elevate their self-esteem. Striving for a higher level exerts an enormous influence and draws all available psychological forces in this direction. The stronger the inferiority feeling on the part of the individual, the more attention does he give to becoming superior. He attempts to overcome his strong feelings of inferiority or deficiency through over-compensation. He strives to achieve esteem and prestige among his fellowmen, and if he fails, these feelings frequently lead to criminal behavior.

To compensate for his inherent inferiority, the child adopts a model. He imitates the qualities he feels will help him overcome this insecurity, such as voice, posture and gestures; he adopts his model's attitudes, ideas and goals, as well. He even strives to outstrip his model, and gain complete mastery of his situation. This singleness of purpose leads to hoarding possessions, striving for power and influence, and to the illusory self-aggrandizement that accompanies disparagement and cheating of others.

Unfortunately, Cain found no strong person to serve as his model. His father was weak, and there were no other men in his environment. He wanted to possess more than his brother. He wanted his mother's love, but she thwarted him. He wanted to have two wives, and again he was rebuked. He did manage to get all the real estate, in title, but not in fact. Neither could he malign his brother to elevate himself. Who would listen to him? His father? His mother? Abel's wives? Cheating was out of the question. Everyone would know the culprit. Cain felt cornered. Overpowered by his life-long resentment of his brother,[26] he could find no means by which to build up his self-esteem and assert his manliness.

Cain did not realize that concentrating on himself reduced his benefits to society. Only when one's interests are not self-centered, when one desires to make a contribution to society as a whole, can one compensate for whatever defects he may have. Fighting only to free oneself of limitations actually fortifies and solidifies them into an insurmountable barrier to progress. Had Cain striven for goals outside himself, based on interest in others, he would have been able to overcome his inner difficulties and build a more useful life.

Inferiority feelings appear in anxiety states which produce shyness, shame, embarrassment, and the like. The degree of such feeling depends mainly on the person's interpretation of the situation in which he finds himself. This interpretation fluctuates frequently until it hardens within his mind and manifests itself as a self-appraisal, or as an appraisal of others. As an example, the Nazis developed a theory that other people are actually inferior, and they proclaimed the Aryan race superior to all other races. When man is unsure of his own status, he feels impelled to belittle others to elevate his own self-esteem, or attributes inferiority to them because he views them as a threat. Here lies the root of prejudice. To retard the progress of the Negro, Caucasians employ the notion that the hue of a person's skin determines his status. The white male also generally regards the Negro as sexually superior, and he holds it against him.[27] To overcome their assumed inferiority, the whites thrust the Negro into a subservient position. The claim that Negroes are more promiscuous sexually, compounded by statistics of illegitimate births, further serves to elevate the self-image of the non-Negroes. In their minds, the socially unacceptable is equated with inferiority.

Inferiority feelings do not, in themselves, indicate abnormality. On the contrary, they initiate all the progress of mankind. Without the feeling of ignorance, or the desire to improve his situation, or to know more of the universe and how to control it, man would not move forward. It would seem that civilization rests upon feelings of inferiority.

Nevertheless, since feelings of inferiority are a shameful indication of weakness to most people, a determined effort is made to conceal them. Preoccupied with the consequences of his inferiority, man may avoid self-appraisal so successfully that it remains outside his awareness. Cain resorted to physical aggression, and by brute force removed the source of his irritation. Eliminating Abel achieved the two-fold aim of removing the source of his inferiority and displaying his greatness. Through murder Cain emphasized his masculine sovereignty and denied his inferiority.[28] In addition to his chronic personality patterns, Cain's solution to his predicament manifested psychopathological behavior.

Cain's behavior paralleled the general pattern found operating among a dozen criminals analyzed by Menninger. All of them wanted to remain dependent children and greatly resented those forces which denied them this satisfaction. They harbored mixed feelings of revenge, self-assertion and guilt. Like them, Cain wanted to remain close to his parents as a dependent child, but Abel thwarted this gratification. He subconsciously resolved that some day he would quit himself of his brother, and at the same time punish his parents. Cain judged them as guilty as Abel because they encouraged Abel in his behavior. Through murder Cain fulfilled his need for gratification. As David acquired the strength of the giant when he killed Goliath, Cain displayed his own greatness and took upon himself the mantle of Abel's greatness. Through the same act, Cain also envisioned the destruction of his father and mother. He finished them as a force in his life; he would take over now. They brought him into the world, but he could lead them out of it.

As soon as his brother was dead, Cain felt that his act of murder would not and should not go unrequited. A sense of guilt with a corresponding need for punishment accompanied his aggressive action.[29] Subconsciously, Cain expected some form of punishment to atone for the wrong he had committed. Like most acts of criminality, Cain's act of murder was also motivated by an urge for self-destruction. The ancient Rabbis,[30] who commented that Cain was resigned to his guilt being visited upon him, recognized the self-destructive element in his anti-social behavior.

It is interesting to note that Cain's behavior after the murder was identical to that of his parents after they had eaten the forbidden fruit. Parental influence again predominated. Like them, Cain attempted deception. They hid, at first, and then blamed one another for their transgression; Cain denied any knowledge of his brother's whereabouts. When he called Abel "my brother" and then slew him, he exhibited their insincerity; and when he assumed that now he would inherit the whole world, he was as selfish as they. A megalomaniac, Cain imagined himself alone in the world. With Abel gone and Adam too old to have any more children, he would share the limelight with no one.

But after committing the murder, Cain was bewildered. He had no voice in selecting the brother with whom he had been forced to live in constant intimacy and incessant competition. He resented him and wanted to hurt him, but he had never consciously wanted to kill him. Abel's offenses no longer seemed so great. If anyone else had overshadowed him in the same way, Cain would have taken it lightly, or even overlooked it. Cain felt wrong and uncomfortably guilty—his sense of relief outweighed by the fear of his parents' reactions. What would he tell them? He decided to run away, but how could he escape his conscience? Abel could have killed him, but he attacked when Abel's back was turned. And although he could not remember how it happened, he knew that he had killed his brother. Even when committed unintentionally, defiance of authority tweaks the conscience unawares. Guilt enveloped and oppressed Cain, until he found a device to assuage it. He gradually adopted an attitude of self-magnification,[31] convincing himself that he was invulnerable and that the murder would not be detected.

One day as he walked smugly in the field, however, he heard the voice of the Lord ask, "Where is Abel, thy brother?" Cain was caught unawares. He had persuaded himself that the incident had passed and was completely forgotten, but now it cropped up all over again. The question had been put to him gently, affording him the opportunity to reflect calmly upon his deed, admit his blunder, and repent. But Cain lied about knowing Abel's whereabouts, asking "Am I my brother's keeper?" He hoped to escape the anticipated and deserved punishment, but he had misjudged the situation. Confronted by what he had done, he questioned how the Lord knew about it. No one saw him do it. When the Lord reminded him that Abel had already informed him that He was aware of everything, Cain reverted to the displacement mechanism, again shifting the blame onto Abel. If Abel had never been born, he would not have had to share his parents, nor to compete with Abel. He would have had no sister to covet; he would have inherited everything. He would have made an acceptable offering, if Abel had not made one with which to compare it. Furthermore, his parents must share in his guilt.

The Lord rejected Cain's explanation and asked, "What hast thou done? The voice of thy brother's blood crieth . . . from the ground." Then Cain blamed the Lord for the murder. If God had accepted his sacrifice and not created the evil inclination within him,[32] he would never have thought of killing Abel. Moreover, Cain argued, he had never seen a human being killed. How was he to know that striking Abel would result in his death? Like his parents, Cain sought scapegoats, rationalizing that the origin of his acts lay outside himself, not within.

When he was sentenced to become "a fugitive and wanderer . . . in the earth," Cain protested the penalty as unfair and too harsh. Instead of a banishing God, Cain hoped for a forgiving God. He had expelled his parents from the Garden of Eden, but He did not condemn them to live alone. Cain prayed that the Lord would forgive and pardon his iniquity.[33] The Lord thereupon reduced his sentence; Cain would still be a fugitive, but not forever. He settled in the land of Nod, and proceeded to immortalize his name by erecting cities and naming them after his offspring. As a means of atonement, he buried Abel. Abel's body had lain exposed for a long time because Cain did not know what to do with it. One day he observed a bird bury in the ground another bird it had killed. Following this example, he dug a grave for Abel and interred him.[34]

In spite of his atonement, Cain's behavior did not alter. "He augmented his household substance with much wealth, by rapine and violence; he excited his acquaintances to procure pleasure and spoils by robbery, and he became a great leader of men into wicked causes. He also introduced a change in that way of simplicity wherein men lived before; and was the author of measures and weights; and whereas they lived innocently and generously while they knew nothing of such acts, he changed the world into cunning craftiness."[35] As one might expect, the sages attribute similar character traits to Cain's descendants.[36] To the extent that the child attempts to identify himself with a father figure, Cain's children were compelled to model themselves after him for no one else was available. Consciously and unconsciously, growing children attempt to identify with or pattern themselves after the father figure or the culturally accepted model. This is a most important factor in the development of character and personality in the offspring, and in the molding of the maturing child's ego-ideal. Like his parents, Cain also set a poor example for his family. In this sense, the "iniquities of the fathers" are visited "upon the children unto the third and fourth generation." But each generation has its unique opportunity to overcome its environment and to transcend the limitations of its forebears. Indeed, Cain's descendants eventually became the bene-factors of mankind. Those born after the fifth generation introduced metal work, music and cattle-breeding (4:20-22).

Throughout, Cain was a colorful figure, more vivid and far more in-teresting than Abel. The latter departs from the biblical scene without uttering a word. Cain, however, coined the timeless phrases:

"Am I my brother's keeper?"

"Fugitive and wanderer in the earth."

"My punishment is greater than I can bear."

"The mark of Cain" originated in this story, and also the expression "Cain complex," which refers to the conflict among siblings to win and hold the affection of the parents.

It may seem ironic that the evil-doer became immortal, while the righteous one paled into insignificance. But Cain bore a greater resemblance to men throughout the centuries than Abel. Cain's awareness of himself and others gave him the vitality to act. Although he was limited by the example of unloving and irresponsible parents, Cain strove to achieve an identity acceptable to himself. The fact that he did not fail completely underscores biblical insight into the dynamic quality of man.

CHAPTER THREE

The Nakedness of His Father

(Genesis 9:22)

NOAH was in his generation a man righteous and wholehearted"
(6:9), Scripture states. He was a man of merit, whose actions set him
apart from his contemporaries. The generation of Noah lived during a
troubled period in the development of group living and Noah was a
troubled man. Through the personification of Noah and his three sons,
the Bible portrays the struggle of man to re-form himself and society.

At a time when the social structure had grown from the lone patriarchal tribe into a loose confederation of autocratic family groups number-
ing in the tens of thousands, communal life was chaotic. Lacking effective
leadership and law, the people of Noah's day were malevolent, steeped
in idolatry, robbery, incest and murder.[1] Tribal feuds raged with inter-
necine ferocity. Violent destruction was the order of the day. But Noah
stood alone among his own generation, "a righteous man who found grace
in the eyes of the Lord" (6:8).

To stand alone, and to stand for change, is to suffer. The story of
Noah's family relationships, as told in Genesis and amplified in other
Hebrew literature, reveals the evolution of his personality and that of
each of his three sons, Shem, Ham and Japheth. The Bible almost wholly
ignores the distaff side of the family, except for the few references to
Noah's wife and daughters-in-law entering and leaving the ark, although
the Midrash does comment on Noah's wife. The inter-action of Noah
and his sons, especially Ham, reveals that the early Hebrew writers had
acquired penetrating insight into the dynamics of personality.

As many Rabbis have argued, Noah's behavior certainly was not altogether admirable. Yes, they maintained, Noah was a righteous man in
his generation. Judged in accordance with the moral standards of his day,
he was the best. But he was selfish, and a drunkard. He was spiteful and
lacked compassion. Had he lived in the time of Moses or Samuel, he
would have been found wanting.[2]

In the biblical narrative, God told Noah to construct an ark in order
to save himself and his family from an impending flood that would inun-
date the entire earth. Why was Noah, of all men, the only one who
anticipated impending disaster? And why was he alone able to conceive
a way to avert total destruction?

A man of many God-given talents, Noah possessed great intelligence.
He was capable of designing and building the ark with only the help of
his youngest son, Shem.[3] He provided a twelve-month food supply for all
the humans and animals brought aboard—thirty-two species of birds and
three hundred and sixty-five species of reptiles[4]—a tremendous operation.
Just before entering the ark, Noah chose wives for his sons in order to
repopulate the world after the flood.[5] He thought of everything. Hebrew
literature also attributes to Noah the invention of the plough, the scythe,
the hoe, and other implements used in cultivating the soil, whereas it was
believed that men who lived before Noah worked the soil with their bare
hands.[6] Until the time of Noah, the Midrash states, neither the cow nor
the furrow obeyed the ploughman, and the human hand was of one
piece, without separate fingers.[7] Ever since the curse in Adam's day, the
Rabbis explain, oats or thorns had sprouted where wheat was sown, but
for Noah and his descendants the earth bore the crops that they planted.[8]

Noah, then, had the intelligence to appraise a problem, the imagination
to hypothesize a solution, and the energy and will to accomplish the task.
With a singleness of purpose, he constructed the ark that would save
him and his family from the doom he foresaw. He saw that the individual
and collective behavior patterns of his day were leading to destruction.
So, without a word of protest, Noah obeyed the injunction to save his
family. Unlike Abraham and Moses, who came after him, Noah showed
no interest in the fate of humanity. When Abraham learned that Sodom
and Gomorrah were doomed, he challenged the Lord with the searing
question, "Shall not the Judge of all the earth do justly?" (18:25). At
the risk of incurring the Lord's displeasure, Abraham tried to dissuade
Him from destroying the cities, but Noah maintained a complete and
self-preserving silence when faced with the destruction of the world. In
a similar situation, Moses also challenged the Lord. God told Moses He
would destroy the Hebrews for worshipping the Golden Calf, and offered
to make Moses the first patriarch of a new people. Moses refused and
said: "Yet now, if Thou wilt forgive their sin—; and if not, blot me,
I pray Thee, out of Thy book which Thou hast written" (Exodus 32:32).
In no sense did Noah approach such nobility. As long as he and his

family were spared, Noah was content to let the people drown. The destruction of others did not, on the surface, disturb him.

True, he took his time in constructing the ark, one hundred and twenty years in all, first planting the trees and then hewing them down. While the people continued in their violent way of life, Noah went about his preparations for the flood without warning them. Only when they asked what he was doing, did Noah advise them that he was preparing to avoid destruction.

"Old man," they derided him, "what is this ark for?"

Noah turned on them with a threat. "Unless you repent of your evil ways," he told them, "the Lord will destroy you in a flood."[9]

They mocked him and Noah retorted in anger, "Repent, for if not, the Holy One, blessed be He, will bring a deluge upon you and cause your bodies to float upon the earth like gourds. Moreover, you shall be taken as a curse for all future generations." Noah declared they had only as many days in which to save themselves as Methuselah would live. Even then they laughed at his harsh warnings and defied their fate. "We will not turn aside from our perversions."[10]

Finally, Noah's prediction came true. As the flood waters rose, God instructed Noah and his family to enter the ark. "And thou and thy sons, and thy wife and thy sons' wives with thee" (6:18). Outside, seven hundred thousand people, men and women, gathered around the ark. When the flood broke loose, they begged Noah to give them shelter and rescue them. The ark could not hold them all, yet Noah could not readily reject them. He argued, "Behold, you have rebelled against God, saying, 'He is not God.' Therefore He has brought this ruin upon you, to annihilate you from the face of the earth." Without bitterness Noah recalled his warnings and their blatant refusal to help themselves. "One hundred and twenty years have I labored before you, to show you the way, and you would not hearken unto the voice of God. Yet now you desire to be kept alive!" Noah felt that his example should have been sufficient, that they should have imitated his righteousness. Instead, they had laughed at him.

The people then cried out, "Behold, we are ready now to return to God. Open the ark to receive us, that we may live and not die."

Noah wavered. He still hoped to prove the accuracy of his prediction and the correctness of his remedy for the evils of his society, but to admit even a few to the ark might endanger the survival of his family and the animals in his charge. And if he were willing to take the risk, how could he select those who should survive? In ignoring his advice

and ridiculing him, they had all rejected him. Now that the power of
life and death rested in his hands, Noah rejected all of the people. They
could drown, he decided, and they would not have the opportunity to
pull him under with them. "Now you seek God, when your need presses
upon you. One hundred and twenty years the Lord appointed unto you
as the term of repentance, and you did not return unto Him. Naught
will you accomplish with your words today. The Lord will not hearken
unto you, nor give you ear." Unyielding and unforgiving, Noah bolted
the ark doors.

The people saw that all was lost. Some tried to storm the entrance
to the ark and then tried to overturn it, but the fury of the rain and
the confusion of panic-stricken people and wild beasts prevented them
from doing so.[11] In their struggle against death, they were unable to
suppress their desire to live; they used their little children to dam up
the waters streaming out of the springs.[12] Noah witnessed the final agony
of the people. Like a splinter in the eye, the horror of the destruction of
mankind imbedded itself in his mind and his consciousness could not close
over it. At that moment, when Noah rejected the multitudes, he suffered
the irretrievable loss of their love and his self-image became distorted—
he set himself apart from mankind. But urgent problems forced Noah's
attention to the practical matters of living on the ark.

In addition to existing behavior problems in Noah's family, the situation on the ark applied strict limitations to the freedom of all four couples.
The duration of their confinement on the ark was uncertain and they
could not increase or replace the provisions. The first and most significant
discipline Noah imposed was sexual continence. Perhaps his purpose was
to avoid having more mouths to feed. He may have realized that living
conditions on the ark might endanger the survival of mothers and infants,
and that pregnant women would be unable to do their share of work. The
sons had little opportunity to cohabit with their wives before embarking.
If they did live together, it was for a very limited period of time. Now
they were forbidden to do so for the entire first year of their marriages.

Noah may have considered it unseemly to indulge in sexual activity
during a general calamity. When so many had died, this was a suitable
sacrifice on the part of those left unscathed.[13] The manner in which they
embarked, the men by themselves and the women by themselves (6:18),
reflected this discipline, and the manner in which they disembarked inferred
that the ban was lifted. "Go forth from the ark, thou, and thy wife,
and thy sons, and thy sons' wives with thee" (8:16). They left in pairs.
A second support for this type of behavior is the verse, "And unto

Joseph were born two sons before the year of famine came" (41:50). Since it is superfluous to indicate that these births occurred before the famine, the intent is obvious. "They are gaunt with want and famine" (Job 30:3) is also interpreted to mean that one should regard his wife as though she were lonely, that is, menstruous, when want and famine occur.[14]

In addition to the sexual ban, Noah must have also suspended the use of wine, as did Joseph and his brothers during their separation. This was no time for celebration. Besides, to let their guard down in their circumstances would court disaster. Hundreds of helpless creatures aboard depended for survival on only eight people. Noah must have supervised the close control of their food, for without some form of rationing they might have escaped drowning only to starve to death. And Noah must have divided the work, delegating the responsibility of preparing the food to the women and the task of feeding the animals to his sons. Those animals accustomed to eating by day, they fed during the day; and those that normally ate by night, they fed during the night.[15] At times Noah was puzzled, not knowing what type of food the animals ate[16] but he dealt adequately with the problem. Strict compliance to standards of sanitation was also necessary, or they would have died of disease.

The response of the sons to this tension-producing situation, as described in the Bible and the Midrash, reveals much about their relationships with each other and with their father. Of the three sons, Ham is far more interesting, and more stories concern him than the others. His behavior was socially acceptable until the time he entered the ark; otherwise Noah would not have permitted him to remain alive. His subsequent antisocial and perverse sexual behavior, however, indicates that Ham already harbored strong neurotic tendencies and conflicts rooted in factors which disturbed his early emotional development.[17]

One factor in the evolution of Ham's personality was his relationship with Noah. As the head of the household, with all the connotations inherent in this role, Noah personified authority to Ham. A "pleasure-bent anarchist," like all children, Ham saw his father as opposed to his desires. At opposite poles where enjoyment was concerned, Noah repressed Ham's pursuit of pleasure. Although it may be untrue, a child often feels dominated by one or both of his parents, attributing to them super-natural powers for controlling him and reading his thoughts. Ham may have felt that Noah overpowered him at every turn, for Noah was a forceful leader. To construct an ark large enough to house his family and pairs of every species of the animal world, and to provide and store supplies for all of them for about a year—which he did most capably, since none of it spoiled[18]—required a strong individual. Rather than a benign leader compelled to act with unequivocal authority to assure the survival of all, Noah must have appeared to Ham as an irrational tyrant.

Another factor which contributed to Ham's early emotional develop-ment was the personality of his mother. The little written about Noah's wife suggests that possibly she was neurotic. During Noah's long preoccu-pation with the impending disaster and his determined preparations for it, she must have smarted under his overbearing domination. She, too, was someone to reckon with, and the Midrash states that she did assert herself with good deeds that equaled Noah's.[19] Not to be ignored, she gave every evidence that she was his peer, or perhaps even better. If she could not impress Noah, she could solicit the recognition she needed from her sons. Of the three, Ham was most inclined to fill her need because of his own emotional problems. To satisfy her narcissistic strivings, Noah's wife un-doubtedly provoked competition between Noah and Ham for her affection. Ham's subsequent behavior with Noah revealed that he had a strong Oedipus complex; he needed a mother, a role his real mother was unable to fill.

Apparently Ham's brothers did not suffer from the same oppressive feelings. More secure emotionally, they did not consider their father dic-tatorial and they were not used by their mother. Both Scripture and the Midrash portray them as respectful sons. Their hostility was not directed at Noah.

Under normal circumstances, Ham's latent neurotic tendencies might have made him merely unhappy, but under the tensions, stresses and anxieties to which he was subject on the ark, his behavior altered sharply. Like the others, he suffered from fear of the unknown. Everything about the flood was without precedent in his experience except his relationship within the family. His father's unyielding authority he knew, and reckoned with; his brothers' privilege he knew, and envied; his mother at once attracted and repelled him. On the ark, Ham's position within the family became intolerable.

According to the Bible, Shem was the oldest son, Ham the middle son, and Japheth the youngest (5:32; 6:10; 7:13; 9:18). The generally accepted version in the Midrash reverses the order, claiming that Japheth was the oldest and Shem the youngest.[20] Regardless of which is the proper chronological order, Ham was the middle child, and one may assume that he encountered the inconsistencies and frustrations that are the lot of a middle child to a greater degree than he enjoyed the rewards and pleasures of childhood.

As a middle child Ham occupied a peculiar position from birth and was never secure in relation to his brothers or his parents. Japheth, the older brother, was automatically a third adult in the household—a parent, junior grade. At least until Ham was born, Japheth had enjoyed the security of an only child and he knew where he stood. He was not compelled to work out a pattern for his life. He only had to imitate Noah, for by right of primogeniture Japheth would step into Noah's role in the course of time. Ham's younger brother, Shem, was the "baby" or pet of the household. His presence diverted the attention of the parents from Ham, and Shem retained his special niche throughout his childhood, since his right of prior domain was never displaced. Ham, however, figuratively hovered in mid-air, never on sure ground. The privileges accorded Japheth, the first-born, were denied him because he was too young, yet he was constantly compared with him, both positively and negatively. Neither was he given the latitude of Shem, the "baby"—he was old enough to know better. Ham received neither the recognition of the oldest nor the attention of the youngest, and consequently drifted into the background of parental notice and affection. The insecurity of his position may have led him to become more competitive than his brothers and less concerned with authority and responsibility. Because of his family experience, Ham may have developed an inferiority complex.[21]

Whereas Ham harbored hostile feelings against his brothers before they entered the ark, the daily irritations of living in close quarters soon resulted in overt aggression. Ham was reminded constantly of Japheth's superior status. When there was work to do, the more menial tasks were assigned to Ham. Furthermore, Japheth gave Ham orders, and Noah expected Ham to comply. There was no justice to it, Ham felt. Just because he was the oldest, Japheth already exercised authority over him, and he would automatically become the head of the family when their father died. Why not he? Ham felt as deserving as Japheth. He visualized himself in the coveted role. Given the opportunity, he could become a strong, powerful leader like his father. Ham attempted to show off his ability to his father, but Japheth, suspecting his purpose, drew Shem into a coalition with him to put Ham in a bad light and effectively nullified Ham's efforts. Struggling under a heavy burden of responsibility, Noah took no notice of Ham's achievements. On the contrary, when he saw Japheth irritated, Noah must have considered Ham a trouble maker.

Utterly confused as to what was expected of him, Ham resented his awkward position, and his parents who had created it. He had no desire to be pampered, like Shem; he wanted to assert his masculinity and assume the leadership some day. Noah's rigid application of the principle of primogeniture, however, vitiated this aim. Every avenue of self-expression was closed to him, preventing him from becoming the man he wanted to be. He was unable to identify with his father; he gave love, but did not receive it from his mother; his brothers oppressed him; and conjugal relations with his wife were forbidden. Ham felt cornered, blocked in every direction in which he turned to assert himself. It was too much for him. Ham rebelled against each of the forces holding him in check, and against the entire microcosm of society on the ark. To get even with them, he jeopardized their very survival. He defied the rule of continence on the ark, and a Midrashic statement might be interpreted to mean that he also became a sexual deviate by copulating with the dog.[22] His personality development would justify this conclusion.

The anti-social nature of Ham's sexual perversion represented an unconscious self-assertive effort to escape from rigid, life-long compliance to authority without any corresponding gratification.[23] It was an act of defiance and rebellion. Frustrated in satisfying his passive-dependent needs and thwarted in every aspect of his life situation, Ham's overwhelming anxiety severed his control of his impulses.[24] Like other sex offenders who commit their offenses in an effort to free themselves of tension and regain self-esteem, Ham regressed to less complex sex patterns. Unable to comply with the socially acceptable standard of behavior for his chronological age, Ham reverted to behavior that was emotionally satisfying on an infantile level.

Indulging in bestiality represented a fixation at a low stage of psychosexual development, a stunting of his emotional growth. Since he was denied security and affection by his parents and since other satisfactions were unattainable, Ham reacted with a display of hostility and resentment against authority. He became rebellious and noncooperative at a time when conformity to rules was vital. Because his curiosity regarding sex had never been adequately satisfied, Ham attached disproportionate importance to it, allowing it to become the center of his interest. Outright prohibition of the sex act directed Ham's attention to it. Ham became a "libertine," regarding sexual gratification as the dominant need of his life, and compulsively seeking new ways to achieve it.[25] Hungry for new sexual excitement, he moved from one type of gratification to another, even exposing himself to possible destruction in quest of sex objects.[26] Since it is generally agreed that man prefers intercourse with a willing adult female for his sexual gratification, and since he did have relations with his wife, Ham's deviation denotes the severity of his personality problem. He was a sexual psychopath, in that he indulged in patterns of sexual deviation characterized by socially prohibited aggressiveness and compulsiveness.[27]

Zoophilia seldom represents more than a few episodes in the entire life of an individual, most of them more or less experimental in nature. Sex relations with animals usually occur in rural communities,[28] and the ark was a comparable environment. Emotionally maladjusted, Ham may have rationalized that he did not violate the proscription against intercourse with a human female, but merely indulged in a form of masturbation. At one time, when Christian lawgivers adopted the Jewish code against intercourse with animals, they applied another misinterpretation. Regarding cohabitation between a Christian and a Jewess, or vice versa, as equivalent to zooerasty, they ruled that both participants were subject to burning because "coition with a Jewess is precisely the same as if a man should copulate with a dog."[29] The fact that Turks and Saracens were also compared to dogs may have eased the painful irony for the Jews.

In any case, it is reasonably certain that Ham's behavior provoked Noah's wrath and further removed him from the position he sought. Ham's low opinion of himself motivated his perverted behavior, and justified his subsequent chastisement. When a pervert is unhappy in his sexual behavior or has strong aggressive tendencies against society, he allows himself gratification only if he expects punishment to follow.[30] Through this punishment he obtains relief from his severe sense of guilt.

As their stay on the ark lengthened, Noah began to suffer from a profound sense of personal inadequacy. The destruction of all mankind remained impaled in his memory, cutting a deep wound of personal guilt. He brooded that he had rejected humanity and that he was in great measure responsible for their deaths. Perhaps he could have saved a few, but he sealed their doom when he shut them out of the ark. Perhaps he should have joined them in death; if he had been more humble God might have spared them all. Noah consumed himself with unresolved self-condemnation. His inferiority feelings were compounded by lack of sleep[31] and physical exhaustion; he coughed up blood as a result of the cold he endured on the ark.[32] When the flood tossed the ark from side to side, his difficulties mounted. The lions roared, the oxen lowed, the wolves howled, and all the other animals gave vent to their agony. At times it seemed the ark would break asunder. The members of his family were all afraid death was near, and probably blamed him for their plight. Stress, anxiety and guilt took their toll of Noah's physical and emotional resources. Despairing, he prayed, "O Lord, help us, for we do not possess the strength to bear the evil that encompasses us . . . Death stares us in the face . . . Redeem us and save us."[33]

Physically weakened, Noah lost his grip on the powerful forces he attempted to control. Perhaps through carelessness, or through a desire to atone for his guilt, he exposed himself to danger and was severely maimed by a lion he had neglected to feed.[34] The beast rendered Noah incapable of conjugal relations.[35] His wounds, combined with his run-down physical condition and distraught emotional state, further diminished Noah's capacity to exert a masculine and controlling influence.[36] Although his sons did not know the full extent of his injuries, Noah's declining strength and masculinity intensified the competition among them. Ham challenged Japheth's rights and again found himself at a disadvantage in relation to his brothers.

Noah's sexual impotence must have aggravated the prevailing competition between himself and his wife. Although they did not sleep together, she may have learned, when she nursed him, that the lion had rendered him incapable of sexual relations. Now she could look down on him; she was a whole woman, and he was something less than a man. Ham then became the object of his father's unsatisfied love needs, as he was for his mother. Due to his physical condition, Noah felt that he would never again fulfill his love experience with his wife. In such circumstances, the father may require from his child an exaggerated show of affection. He may demand from him the love he cannot elicit from his wife, becoming actively seductive toward the child. When the child becomes the object of the father's unsatisfied love needs, tremendous tensions may ensue because of the jealousy and competitiveness aroused.[37] Noah must have used Ham for the satisfaction of his emotional needs, and Ham could not fail to sense that he was used by each of his parents for their own satisfaction, as well as to make the other jealous. However much he enjoyed proximity to his mother, Ham felt she was not primarily concerned with him. However satisfying his father's belated interest, Ham knew he could never replace Japheth. Used as a pawn for the release of his parents' conflicting emotional tensions, Ham developed explosive conflicts of his own.

Finally, as the waters subsided, Noah and his family could look forward to release from the confinement of the ark. The frightful tensions under which they had lived would at last come to an end, they thought, and they could return to the life they had known before. But when Noah stepped out of the ark and witnessed the destruction of life wrought by the flood, he wept bitterly and cried out to God. "O Lord of the world, Thou art called merciful! Thou shouldst have had mercy upon Thy creatures!"

God replied, "Thou fool, now thou speakest this way. But not when I addressed kind words unto thee."

And Noah remembered the words of God. "I saw thee as a righteous man before Me in this generation, and I will bring the flood upon the earth to destroy all flesh. Make an ark for thyself of gopher wood."

"All this I conveyed to thee," God continued, "telling thee all these circumstances, that thou mayest entreat mercy for the earth. But didst thou concern thyself that ruin would cover the earth? When thou heard that thou would be rescued, thou did build an ark, and thou wast saved. Now that the earth is wasted, thou openest thy mouth to supplicate and pray."[38]

Upon hearing this rebuke from God, Noah fell sullen. He brooded, and his guilt-feelings intensified. He realized his folly. If the people had failed to repent, the fault was his. He had not shared his knowledge soon enough. And when he did, he spoke to them too harshly threatening them with words like fiery flints. He had judged them too rigidly, for now he knew they were not altogether evil. Even though God had called him a "righteous man," Noah knew he was not altogether righteous. There was no doubt in his mind now that he should not have turned his back on mankind, and that he had been responsible for their deaths. No punishment could equal Noah's burden of guilt, yet he attempted to propitiate God.

After descending from the ark, Noah erected an altar to express his gratitude to God. Crippled, and oppressed by guilt for the ruin of the earth and the destruction of its inhabitants, he was still thankful that he and his family were spared. His offering and his prayers assuaged his guilt somewhat and provided a familiar pattern he could follow until he might find a way to reconstruct his life.

Noah's next moves, according to the Bible, are less easily understood. He "planted a vineyard. And he drank of the wine, and was drunken; and he was uncovered within his tent" (9:20-21). It is not surprising that Noah planted a vineyard, since they were common possessions of the inhabitants of Palestine, and "wine maketh glad the heart of man" (Psalms 104:15). A gardener, Noah probably took a vine with him when he entered the ark, and planted it after the flood.[39] But was it more urgent than growing food for his family? That Noah took to drink soon after leaving the ark is supported by a story in the Midrash that the vines sprang up over night and bore fruit. Or he may have drunk wine left untouched during the period of abstinence on the ark. But why did Noah become intoxicated? Was he a sick and compulsive alcoholic?

The only recorded instance of Noah's resorting to strong drink, he
may be likened to the dipsomaniac who drinks excessively only periodically
or sporadically, as a reaction to situations of stress, experiencing complete
amnesia of weeks or months prior to inebriation.[40]

Noah was no longer the confident man who had built the ark, for
his experiences affected him physically, emotionally and spiritually. The
past was painful to remember, and the present incomprehensible. Alcohol
served as a palliative, enabling him to forget for a time the overbearing
sense of guilt under which he struggled and his oppressive fears and
anxieties. Scripture advises, "Give . . . wine unto the bitter in soul"
(Proverbs 31:6). Pleasure derived through the use of the mouth and
taste must have compensated for other satisfactions Noah was unable
to attain.

Noah's alcoholism also indicates that he suffered the unconscious conflict of the desire to destroy the mother and yet remain dependent upon
her.[41] In the light of present knowledge, it would thus seem that Noah
was anxious to destroy the object upon whom he was too dependent. Since
his real mother had died before the flood,[42] someone else served as his
substitute mother. Noah's wife might have played a dual role. She was
like a mother to him, and also his competitor. Drinking fortified him with
the courage to hate her although he wanted to love her. Through alcohol
Noah felt that he was destroying her by torturing her, and at the same
time destroying himself—concurrent murder and suicide.

Drinking further served as a substitute for identification with his
wife-mother. To him, she and the alcoholic beverage were the same. He
sought to resume his former existence in that sheltered area where the
rivalries of love and hate do not exist. Drinking himself into unconsciousness, Noah approximated the prenatal condition of complete serenity, the
absence of tensions. He regarded his emergence from the unconscious state
as being born again, delivered into the loving care of a mother who would
nurse him back to complete health. Noah's alcoholism was in reality an
unconscious regression. Drowning himself in a pool of alcohol symbolized
an unconscious desire to be one with her.[43]

Noah derived euphoria from alcohol—a kind of "degenitalized sexu-
ality." It reestablished the orgastic sensation denied to him.[44] Incapable of
sexual activity, Noah may have used alcohol as a means of attaining sexual
satisfaction no longer available to him through natural means.

Alcohol had still another effect, one Noah needed: It artificially raised
his self-esteem. Wine made him feel important, an attitude he had not
enjoyed since before the lion maimed him. Alcohol relieved his inferiority

feelings in relation to his wife and helped him convince himself that he was better than she. His alienation from his contemporaries also left him with severe inferiority feelings. True, he had believed himself better than others before the flood, but now that he alone survived, he realized that he was not worthy to be saved on his own merits.[45] In Noah's mind, being apart from mankind was equivalent to being inferior to mankind. Alcohol temporarily restored his self-esteem—the feeling that he was an important individual in his own right.

Alcohol also enabled Noah to express some of his pent-up hostility against authority, perhaps the authority of God Himself. Although God had called him "righteous" and had selected him from all men to live, Noah had some reason to feel the Lord had treated him unfairly. He had followed God's instructions, and God allowed the lion to cripple him—God's selected one! Furthermore, God commanded him to "be fruit-ful, and multiply, and replenish the earth" (9:1), and now he was im-potent! How could God suggest this to him? Alcohol reduced his inhibi-tions and enabled Noah to express rebellion against his Heavenly Creator. When he was sober he might have regarded God as so oppressive, domineer-ing and unapproachable that he was afraid to talk with Him. He therefore got drunk in order to express his rebellion against God.

While on the one hand strong drink served as rebellion, on the other hand it served as a means of withdrawing from the world. Noah felt unfulfilled in his marital relations and he could not face the humiliation that accompanied his physical condition. He escaped to the vineyard. Drinking enabled him to flee from himself and from his wife and children; a devious yet adequate manner of rejecting them.

Though Noah felt that the multitudes deserved their fate, he might have identified himself with the "generation of the flood." By losing himself in strong drink he became part of that generation, experiencing oblivion as they had. It helped him to forget the people who drowned when he shut the ark doors in their faces.

Alcohol gave Noah feelings of elation which he had been unable to attain in the ark. In supervising the logistics of the huge operation, he had labored for years under a constant strain. Now wine enabled him to exclude from his mind the world with all its difficulties.

Alcoholism is also a form of self-destruction.[46] We sometimes read or hear of people who drink themselves to death. Rev. Joseph L. Kellerman of the Charlotte (N.C.) Alcohol Information Center has told the author of solitary drinkers who have said: "I didn't have the courage to commit suicide, so I drank myself into oblivion." A personality defect, aggravated by a tension-producing life situation, underlies this manifestation. Seeking escape from himself, from the situation, and from self-inflicted neurotic misery, an individual caught in this circular turmoil frequently uses alcohol to effect his release. While less acceptable socially, drugs serve the same purpose. In essence, their purpose is to escape from the pain of living— a form of suicide. Like others who utilize alcohol or narcotics when faced with unhappiness, anxieties or conflicts, Noah attempted to ameliorate his problems in the same fashion.

Whenever an individual drinks enough alcohol for it to have deleterious effects, his anxieties can be considered pathological.[47] A basic understanding of this fact is inherent in a legend[48] which tells that Noah's assistant in cultivating the vine was Satan, or the demon Shimadon, who fertilized the vine by draining the blood of a lamb, a lion, a pig and a monkey, in that order, onto the soil in which it was planted. He thus conveyed to Noah the qualities of wine: Before a man drinks it, he is innocent as a lamb; if he drinks of it moderately, he feels strong as a lion; if he drinks more of it than he can stand, he resembles a pig; and, if he drinks to the point of intoxication, he behaves like a monkey and knows not what he is doing.

Any or all of the personality defects deduced above, combined with Noah's unique relationship with God and mankind, could have caused him to turn to alcohol. His dependency on alcohol also suggests still other unconscious manifestations. Through the imbibing of wine, Noah indicated a desire to remain unconscious not only of his own suffering but also of the pain and suffering that still existed in the world despite the flood. He desired to remain unconscious of the responsibility that lay upon him to help set the world in order again, to face a situation that had not existed prior to the flood. He desired to remain unconscious of the new adjustment that he had to make regarding his person and his relationship with his family. Alcohol relieved him of this burden of growth, of adopting a new evaluation of himself and a new understanding of his responsibilities. In this sense, Noah remained "once-born," using William James' terminology, which refers to a person whose "world is a sort of rectilinear or one-storied affair, whose accounts are kept in one denomination, whose parts have only the values which they appear to have."[49] Noah tried to retreat or withdraw from the process of growth through strong drink. He actually had the same rectilinear dimension as the people of his day, and thus was not much better than they. Like them, he wanted to remain static, to hold unchanging values and to act only in conventionally accepted patterns. God's grace was his, but Noah was oblivious to it.

To experience the process of rebirth, or to be "twice-born," it is necessary to make continuous sacrifices on behalf of higher values. The affirmation of good, not merely the evasion of evil, would have enabled Noah to discard his lower self and to become his higher, or more mature, self. In no sense would this have been a repudiation of the self; rather, a fuller awareness and acceptance of the possibilities now available to him would have enabled Noah to exploit his capabilities in spite of his limitations. This is the underlying concept of spiritual growth. By deadening his faculties with alcohol, Noah not only denied his impotence but also his physical and mental capabilities. It was a sort of repression, an imitation of death. Because of the ordeal he had recently endured, Noah was perhaps too tired to search for a changing or evolving truth; this would demand a greater degree of consciousness. Old ideas of himself and of the world no longer represented reality. New situations demanded new attitudes, but Noah was not ready to accept anything which had as its concomitant greater responsibility. Unwilling to go forward, Noah retreated. Lacking the courage to accept consciousness of himself and of the world he was privileged to reconstruct, Noah lost himself in drink.

In an over-compensating attempt to prove his masculinity,[50] Noah peeled off his clothes while he was under the influence of alcohol. By exhibiting himself he denied that he was sexually incompetent, and at the same time compensated for the stress resulting from his sexual inadequacy. The act of exposing himself expressed his subconscious plea, "Reassure me that I have a penis, that I need not be afraid."[51] Noah must have derived some satisfaction from this anti-social behavior, in that it restored a certain degree of masculine status and, therefore, assurance against being impotent. That Noah sought these satisfactions is a further indication that he had a mother attachment.[52]

It would seem that Noah was the type of exhibitionist who only feels the abnormal impulse to expose himself while under the influence of alcohol. Experience proves that even small doses of liquor can adversely affect those whose morality derives only from training and not from an inner acceptance of good living. When relieved of their inhibitions by alcohol, such people discard their thin cover of morals and lose their sexual discernment.[53]

When Ham stumbled upon the scene, he found his father naked and in a drunken stupor. In a few verses the Bible presents a dynamic interplay between them. "And Ham, the father of Canaan, saw the nakedness of his father, and told his two brethren without" (9:22); "And Noah awoke from his wine, and knew what his youngest son had done unto him"

(9:24); and then Noah cursed Canaan, Ham's son (9:25, 26, 27). Revealing a profound insight into motivational psychology, the ancient sages
elaborate upon this scene, stating that Ham abused his father sexually and
castrated him. Because Ham is referred to in this instance as the youngest
son and because Canaan bore Noah's curse, it is believed that Canaan
came upon Noah and called Ham's attention to his father's condition.

Ham's first impulse was to commit sodomy upon his father. For the
first time he saw his father helpless; the dominant authority lay before
him like a woman. Ham knew the danger. Noah would be enraged if he
awoke and learned that Ham had used his body; his brothers would surely
punish him for degrading their father. Yet he could not deny this opportunity to satisfy his craving. His unfulfilled desires mingled in his mind
with fear and memories of rejection. Finally, his aggressiveness overcame
his fear and confusion—Ham ravished Noah's body.

By indulging in sodomy, Ham finally expressed his homosexual tendencies. Some might contend that he was bisexual in that he was married
and was able to make adjustments alternating between homosexuality and
heterosexuality. Bergler,[54] however, disagrees with this reasoning, holding
the opinion that there is no condition properly described as bisexual. He
feels that such a person is really a homosexual who possesses some rem-
nants of heterosexuality. In any event, it appears that Ham did possess
many subconscious traits that are invariably present in male homosexuals.[55]

Ham was an "injustice collector." He created situations in which he
found himself at the short end of things, subconsciously seeking defeat,
humiliation and rejection. Violating the code of the ark regarding sexual
behavior and calling his brothers' attention to their father's condition are
two examples. It seems that he had a masochistic or self-punishing craving
for danger, and that he was not averse to taking advantage of a person
in a weak position. It was when Noah was helpless that Ham ravaged his
body, thus femininizing the male leader and reducing him in status to
that of the weaker sex. He also lowered his own masculine status by
practicing sodomy, which served as an atonement through his own denigra-
tion. Indulging in zooerasty, and then using a male as his sex object, would
indicate that he was a fugitive from women, and that these acts served to
mitigate his fear of women. We must assume that Ham suffered deep
inner guilt as a result of his perversion, which is also part of the homosexual
structure.

Ham could be termed an aggressive sexual deviate.[56] Although he
lived in a promiscuous generation when unnatural sexual passion abounded,[57]
and Ham undoubtedly had knowledge of such experiences, at the time of

his perverted behavior Ham was subject to the social structure established for living in the ark. He was old enough to recognize the need for social limitations to behavior, but he committed atypical and compulsive sex acts which were inconsistent with his supposed state of maturity. By displaying tendencies toward antisocial character formations, Ham revealed that he was mentally ill, overwhelmed by anxiety derived from frustrated passive-dependent needs and thwarting life situations.

An aggressive personality usually over-reacts to blows dealt him by reality because he resents the passive role of a victim. He develops an "instinct of retaliation,"[58] which is observable in his attitudes. His goal is to adjust the environment to his needs and demands, rather than to adjust himself to the requirements of the environment. With Noah assuming the image of a dominant father, Ham felt himself attacked by him, so he counter-attacked.

Under certain conditions, the natural aggressiveness of such an individual becomes excessive. Affects of the external world—when one must measure himself against a more powerful person, such as Noah—create these conditions. This inequality of forces, this inadmissible injustice, can lead the weaker individual toward sadism and inspire criminal desires, like castrating the powerful one. Ham's desire to castrate the omnipotent authority was actually a desire to mutilate the threatening power before Noah had an opportunity to castrate him.

Excessive aggressiveness might also manifest itself in other anti-social behavior, and the Midrash[59] does relate that Ham was a thief. When he left the ark, he stole the clothes of skin that the Lord had made for Adam and Eve. Methuselah had given them to Noah, who brought them into the ark. Ham gave them to his son, Cush, who in turn gave them to Nimrod. Conceivably, Ham had homosexual desires for Noah while in the ark, but was unable to express them. Thwarted in this conquest, Ham robbed him instead[60] and the clothes served as a totem.

Now that Ham had momentarily dominated his father by committing sodomy on him, the realization came that his victory was only temporary. When Noah awoke, he would resume his role of dominance, forever removing the possibility that Ham could assert his manliness. Ham would remain irreparably alien and inferior, and his already intolerable position might even become worse. Now that the ban on intercourse was lifted, his parents might have more children, further removing him from the intimacy he craved with both his mother and his father. And his continuous disadvantage in relation to his brothers would intensify with the appearance of additional children. Ham must have phantasied a way to overcome this anxiety; he could castrate his father and assure himself that there would be no more siblings. This thought also augured relief from his other frustrations. The desire to castrate his father denotes Ham's subconscious desire to have intercourse with his mother.[61] Ham had hungered for her sexually, but she was unobtainable. Apparently he needed a mother, for she had been unable to satisfy him. By converting Noah into a female, Ham felt that Noah would serve as his mother and gratify his longing.

Although Ham knew that his brothers were not far from Noah's tent, and he had reason to fear them, the opportunity to destroy Noah and relieve his anxiety was irresistible. Unaware that Noah was already impotent after being attacked by the lion,[62] Ham compulsively acted out his phantasy. He castrated Noah. Emasculation was tantamount to destroying Noah; it was symbolic murder, a sign of victory over the symbol of authority. Ham knew that their society recognized only one leader— only one "real man." When the father holds this position, the son does not assume leadership until after the father's death.[63] Ham degraded Noah from the position of authority that fathers generally occupy to the role of a lesser person.[64] For that moment, Japheth did not exist for him, and Ham stepped into the position of father.

Ham's next move was motivated by his masochistic craving for punishment. His perverted act of aggression had brought his self-esteem to a new low and he must have suffered an inner depression. To ward off the masochistic depression, Ham unconsciously employed the technique of pseudo-euphoric camouflage. According to a story in the Midrash, Ham told his brothers about Noah with flippant hilarity, using every device to ridicule and further humiliate him before his sons. "The first man had but two sons," he said, "and one slew the other; this man Noah has three sons, yet he desires to beget a fourth."[65] Underlying Ham's jesting words in this story is the Rabbis' perception of his real motivation—the desire to prevent the birth of more siblings, and to demote Noah from his position of dominance.

When Shem and Japheth learned of Noah's compromising situation, the Bible states that they covered him, and did so in such a way that they did not view him in his wretched condition. They paid him the homage due a parent by his children, and at the same time joined forces again in opposition to Ham. Stories in the Midrash, however, add overtones to this act, indicating that Shem initiated the move to cover Noah in this fashion, and that Japheth simply joined him.[66]

Sober again, Noah recalled what had transpired. Ashamed, embarrassed and angry at himself, Noah experienced feelings of guilt and despair, a form of melancholia or clinical depression which usually follows the alcoholic mania.[67] Unable to face or tolerate himself, he was therefore unable to face or tolerate anyone else. He condemned himself, and Ham's treatment confirmed Noah in his attitude toward himself. He sought to cause himself discomfort and suffering; he sought punishment, as alcoholics generally do. Ham obliged Noah, which was the wrong thing to do. Shem and Japheth used good therapeutic technique, however, in not rebuking or condemning him. They ignored him and his condition completely. But Noah was incensed with Ham. The thought of castration was terrifying. He hated himself, and this bred hatred of his son.

Noah was confirmed in his earlier belief that he should have remained celibate. He had decided not to marry because he knew that mankind was destined for destruction. But the Lord commanded him: "Take a wife and sire children, for you are a righteous man before Me in this generation. And thou and thy children with thee shall live in the midst of the earth." Noah had obeyed and married Naamah, the daughter of Enoch,[68] but now he felt this had been a mistake. If he hadn't complied, Ham would never have been born and he would not have suffered at his hand.

Impotence, to a man who is always anxious, signifies weakness and an undesired femininity. It deeply offends his self-esteem. His position as the leader of the family is shaky, and feelings of insecurity envelop him—he needs reassurance. He feels more vulnerable than before and vastly inferior —his ego is shattered. But impotence produces reactions of protection and dynamic healing against these denigrating effects. Noah felt that he must repay Ham for dethroning him; he must hurt Ham as badly as he had been hurt. Throughout life, man endeavors to win status by demonstrating his worth as a man.[69] Depriving Noah of his masculinity impaired the fulfillment of his paternal function—earning prestige and authority within the family. No longer sure of himself, Noah was unable to be a good father. Fearful and anxious, he blurted out: "Cursed by Canaan; a servant of servants shall he be unto his brethren" (9:25), and repeated it two more times, "And let Canaan be their servant" (9:26, 27). Knowing that a parent is most vulnerable in respect to his children, Noah cursed Ham's son. On the surface the curse does not appear excessively cruel, but its harshness is quite evident upon reflection. Bondage in any form is a cruel fate. Noah condemned Ham to double pain, in that Canaan would suffer in servitude, and Ham would look on helplessly.

Since the Lord Himself blessed Ham when they left the ark (9:1),[70] Noah did not curse him directly, for he could do him no harm. He there-fore cursed Ham in the person of his son, Canaan.[71] Noah felt that Ham

had behaved abominably and should not go unpunished. He thereupon
resorted to a subterfuge that is still practiced today. A common Yiddish
expression is *sollst nor nicht derstickt veren*—"you should only *not* get
choked." Cursing the child directly is repugnant to the parent, so he
inserts the word "not" though he means the opposite. By cursing Canaan,
Noah felt that he really cursed Ham. Another common Yiddish expression,
ah rieach in dein taten's taten, means "may an evil spirit befall your
father's father." This, obviously, is not a direct curse. As angry as parents
may become, they do not wish to curse their children directly. Instead, they
use the grandfather, who may have already died, and they do not designate
whether the paternal or maternal ancestor is the scapegoat. Some punishment was due Canaan, however, because when he came upon Noah in
a drunken stupor he drew Ham's attention to it.[72] If he had not, none
of this would have occurred. Noah reasoned, therefore, that Canaan was
as evil as his father.

Stories in the Midrash imply another psychological motivation for
Noah's reaction to Ham's behavior. The Lord wanted Noah to have four
sons among whom to divide the world.[73] In the ark, Noah grieved because
he had no young son to wait on him. When the ban on intercourse would
be lifted, he resolved he would sire other children,[74] and he would make
them servants to his sons as well.[75] Though he had become lame, he felt
that he would still be able to procreate, because a physical injury which
eliminates real sexual intercourse does not impair sexual desire. But when
Ham castrated him, he destroyed Noah's dwindling hope of impregnating
his wife. Noah reasoned that Ham had prevented him from begetting a
fourth son, so he cursed Ham's fourth son, Canaan (10:6).[76]

That Canaan deserved punishment is borne out in later events. He
refused to go to the land Noah allotted to Ham and his descendants,
and appropriated instead the territory assigned to Shem and his children.
When he saw that the land extending from Lebanon to the Nile River
was good, he settled on it. In its breadth, it extended from the Jordanian
border to the Mediterranean Sea. His father and brothers warned him
that the land did not belong to him. If he persisted, they told him, he
and his children would fall accursed in the land in a rebellion, because
he was violating an oath made before God and Noah. But nothing could
persuade Canaan to reverse his stand.[77] In justifying the curse on Canaan,
some ancient commentators suggest that Canaan actually castrated Noah,
but that Ham divulged the secret.[78]

Noah inveighed against Ham and Canaan because he saw himself in
them. They reflected his own anxieties, obsessions, rigidities and compen-

satory need for aggrandizement.[79] Ham was as selfish as he had been. Noah thought only of his own safety when mankind was destroyed; Ham thought of his own pleasures—even risked the safety of his family by copulating on the ark when it was forbidden. Perhaps Ham acted more willfully, but neither father nor son displayed a concern for others. Noah's disregard for the feelings of other people redounded to his own harm. That Ham could commit sodomy and castrate his own father demonstrated how well he had learned cruelty.

Ham's behavior forced Noah to admit that he set a less than ideal example for his sons. He gave no thought to the effect his actions might have on his children and exposed himself to the consequences of his ill-considered behavior. One cannot exonerate Ham, however, because under Hebrew law children are required to honor and respect their parents under all circumstances, even when they behave objectionably.[80] Without doubt, Shem and Japheth deserved Noah's blessing. But how could Noah curse a misguided son when he was a misguided father?

If others regarded Noah as righteous, then his sons regarded him as more than that. Fathers are gallant heroes to their children, and Noah certainly deserved this recognition from his sons because he had saved them from death in the flood. When Noah constructed the altar and praised God, his sons undoubtedly joined him in prayer. But when their model went astray, one could expect little else of his children. With how much justification could Noah point an accusing finger at Ham?

With the curse directed against Ham and his descendants, an already existing pattern in Noah's relationship with Shem and Japheth came to the fore. As Noah punished Ham, he rewarded Shem and Japheth for their respect. In the Bible and other ancient writings, Shem, rather than Japheth, now appears as Noah's distinct favorite.[81] By his deeds Shem overturned the rights of the first-born. Noah recognized that Shem deserved greater commendation because he took the initiative and led Japheth in covering him.[82] As his spiritual reward, therefore, he gave Shem the *talis* (prayershawl) and *tephillin* (phylacteries), while he gave Japheth the *arba kanfos* (a four-cornered garment like a toga) and granted him burial in Palestine.[83] The Bible also mentions Shem's name with the Lord's, "Blessed be the Lord, the God of Shem" (9:26), an honor not generally accorded living persons.

Shem was the youngest of the children, another factor that contributed to Noah's favoritism. Noah showered his affections upon the "baby" of the household and pampered him. The Midrash[84] contends, long before the birth of psychology, that the third or the youngest child is most loved.

Adam had three sons, Cain, Abel and Seth, and Seth was the most beloved. "And Adam lived a hundred and thirty years, and begot a son in his own likeness, after his image; and called his name Seth" (5:3). This language was not used with Cain or Abel. Amram also had three children, Miriam, Aaron and Moses, and according to the Psalmist, Moses was the chosen one (106:23). The same holds true with Noah's three sons. Although Shem was youngest, the authors of Scripture listed him first because they regarded him as the most important and most righteous of the three, and because he possessed distinguishing characteristics and features.[85] When Noah became physically deformed and therefore unfit to serve as priest, he selected Shem to offer sacrifices in his stead.[86] Further displaying favoritism, Noah transmitted Raphael's Torah to Shem, as well as medical remedies derived from plants which Raphael had taught him.[87] And, just before his death, Noah transferred the robes of honor to Shem.[88] Like Noah, Shem was also born circumcized,[89] and they shared in joint experiences. They hid Abraham for an entire month when he fled from Nimrod, and helped to persuade his father, Terach, to leave their country.[90]

Jewish tradition also regards Shem highly. He is identified with Melchizadek, the priest (14:19);[91] it is said that he helped Abraham with prayers (14:19-20);[92] it was through him (25:23) that Rebekah learned that she would give birth to twins;[93] and Isaac and Jacob were supposed to have studied in a school that Shem had established.[94]

Noah continued to favor Shem. In Noah's symbolic division of the world among his sons,[95] Shem fared better than Japheth, the oldest. Noah bequeathed the middle of the earth to Shem, which included Mt. Sinai, Mt. Zion, and the Holy of Holies in the Temple—the choicest bits of "real estate." Japheth received the North, the cold continent; Ham, the hot continent to the South. (This legend may account for the popular belief that all colored peoples descended from Ham.)

Noah's blessings and curse affected each of his sons. Ham took his family and established a city some distance away which he named Neelatamuck, after his wife. His own self-hatred, combined with the contempt in which he was held by his father and his brothers, forced Ham to leave home and to achieve emotional maturity. By removing himself from the pattern that had produced and nurtured his infantile behavior, Ham was able to regain his self-esteem and assume responsibility for his own acts.

Surprisingly enough, Japheth reacted in similar fashion. He also took his family away, and built a city which he named after his wife, Adatanesses. It is quite possible that he was jealous of Ham.[96] If Ham could do it, so could he. As a result of Noah's change of attitude with respect to primogeniture, Japheth began to test his strength. Japheth must have been deeply hurt when he did not receive treatment at least equal to Shem. From childhood, Noah led him to believe that he would be given primary consideration. Noah accorded him the prestige and honor of the first-born, pushed him to special attainments, and expected him to grow up quickly in all respects. Having served as the pathfinder for his brothers, Japheth was chagrined when he did not replace his father as priest. And it must have irked him that the *Shechinah*, the holy spirit, was to rest only in the tents of Shem.[97] The painful shock of his demotion precipitated his flight, but it also gave Japheth a reason, for the first time, to become his best self.

As the first-born, he had never been required to judge his own behavior. He had always assumed that his birth alone assured him superior status. But now Japheth experienced rebirth in self-knowledge. He could continually expand his existence through a greater awareness of the possibilities open to him. Now he realized that he must choose his actions and be judged, by himself and by others, in accordance with their worth. For Japheth, his loss of a fixed status, even a superior one, marked the beginning of freedom.

The departure of Ham and Japheth is comparable to the child who runs away from home. Every parent hears this threat at one time or another. The child's primary purpose in forewarning his parents is to hurt them. It is his way of saying they do not appreciate him. When a child resorts to such a threat, he actually asks his parents to tell him not to leave. A good response at that time is "I love you, I want you to remain. But, if you insist on leaving, it is up to you." At that moment, the child will usually express his grievance.

The same technique operates when a child debases himself by making such remarks as: "I'm ugly," or "I'm stupid." He is really telling his parents: "Please reassure me that I am not ugly; that I am not stupid." Children belittle themselves when their parents do not praise them sufficiently. They feel insecure and they want their parents to bolster their ego.

Although it is regarded today as wholesome for children to move away and assert their independence, it was not the accepted pattern in biblical days. The patriarchal society expected sons to remain with their father in the clan. Shem did just that. He did not abandon his father. He also built his own city, which he named after his wife, Zedektelbab, but he established it in the vicinity of his father's house. And so it developed that Shem, the "baby," manifested the deep inner strength to assume the mantle of leadership. His personality was forged in the constant warmth of his father's love and shaped by the hammer of sibling rivalry. Of the three brothers, Shem alone did not live a static existence. He was neither accepted in advance, like Japheth, nor rejected, like Ham. Rather, by having the opportunity to express his true self, and by doing so, he earned the rights and the responsibilities that otherwise would have been granted to the first-born.

When Noah saw that his sons had separated and lived apart from one another, he reproached them because he feared their jealousies might result in murder. He manifested a concern for them and displayed a fatherly interest in their welfare. Despite his poor example, Noah had endeavored to give his sons a proper education for life as he knew it. He had attempted to teach his children and grandchildren the laws and commandments that he knew,[98] but, like many parents, he made mistakes for which his children suffered. Noah's mistakes, however, were not wilfull or intentional. Like many misguided parents today whose children become delinquents, Noah tried his best, but he was not an unqualified success.

There is no agreement among the ancient sages as to whether Noah was a man of faith at the beginning of the narrative. Some say that he was not, because he did not enter the ark until the waters reached his knees.[99] Others maintain that only a man of faith would enter the ark at the height of day, as Noah did, so that the people could not claim ignorance of what was happening. Because he was a righteous man (7:13),[100] Noah trusted God to save him, both from the flood and from the people who might have destroyed him and the ark. The Rabbis do agree, however, that Noah changed as a result of his experience, and that change can best be described as a spiritual one.

At the outset, Noah believed that his generation was beyond redemption; he had no faith in the power of repentance, in man's capacity to change, in the eventual triumph of man's innate goodness over his destructive inclinations. He readily abandoned hope for his own son, Ham, as he did for society. Through suffering, however, he learned compassion and became reconciled to his own limitations and to the limitations of all mankind. Like Abraham and Moses, he pleaded with God for the sake of future generations, refusing to leave the ark until God promised that he would not bring another flood to destroy the earth.[101] As Noah's self-appraisal evolved from self-righteousness to self-hatred to self-acceptance, he was able to conceive of all mankind as capable of change.

Noah learned that his righteousness was not a predetermined and immutable fact, but that he could only regard himself as righteous relative to his responsibility. On the other hand, his guilt as a result of his failure to meet his responsibility, emphasized to him that he was fallible—he was not God. In the flux between the two extremes, Noah discovered his true humanity and that of mankind. His spiritual growth as a result of the experiences described in Genesis apparently gave him the flexibility so necessary for group living. He lived out his days at one with his fellow man, and never again severed himself from society.

CHAPTER FOUR

Father of a Multitude

(Genesis 17:4)

M ANY problems complicated life in the household of Abraham. It was a polygynous marriage in which the two wives, Sarah and Hagar, vied with each other for the coveted role of the lady of the house, and their sons, the half-brothers Isaac and Ishmael, were caught up in a rivalry involving their father and his legacy to them. Abraham, the husband and father, was compelled to appease and mediate among them in order to keep his family together.

The first problem encountered in the Biblical narrative of these five people is the rivalry between Sarah and Hagar. After many years of marriage, Sarah remained barren and therefore unable to fulfill the conventional image of family life. In a desperate attempt to dispel the appearance of inadequacy and total failure as a woman,[1] she requested Abraham to marry her servant, Hagar, so that she could adopt and rear as her own any children Hagar would bear (16:2). Sarah must have felt she owed this to Abraham for his understanding and faithfulness throughout the long years of their married life. She would volunteer this plan out of love and devotion to her husband. To admit her failure must have cost Sarah dearly in self-respect; to suggest that her husband marry another woman took courage, for risks were clearly involved.

To compensate for the indignities she suffered at his hand, the Egyptian Pharaoh presented his daughter, Hagar, to Sarah as a gift.[2] Although Sarah could have ordered Hagar to marry Abraham, since she was a chattel, she rejected this approach. Any arrangement to produce an heir to Abraham would require the full consent of all concerned. To persuade Hagar to agree to this arrangement without coercion, Sarah made a sweeping concession. Sarah told Hagar that she would not assume the role of concubine, but would become a true wife of Abraham, with all privileges.[3]

Why was Sarah so anxious that Hagar be chosen for this task? Perhaps because Hagar's royal ancestry, like Sarah's,[4] would assure regal status to the child that would be born. Perhaps Sarah feared that Abraham was already thinking of marrying someone else. She would act first. Hagar was "safe"; she would never dethrone her no matter how many children she would have. Sarah thought she would never be jealous of her. Merely a convenient tool to fulfill a particular need, Hagar would serve as a defense against the break-up of her marriage.

Although custom in that era permitted a childless wife to provide her husband with a handmaid who would bear him children,[5] Abraham did not welcome Sarah's proposal. Obviously a man of greater faith than his wife, Abraham succumbed to Sarah's insistence in order to satisfy her profound longing for a child (16:2). He had never displayed scorn or reproached Sarah for her barrenness. Nor did he entertain the thought of marrying another woman even though polygamy was the norm of the day. In fact, when he realized that his nephew, Lot, was unworthy to inherit his estate, Abraham had resigned himself to leaving his wealth to his trusted and faithful steward, Eliezer of Damascus (15:2).[6] He took particular care not to make Sarah feel inadequate and he gave her no indication of his disappointment. Only in his private devotions did he express his unhappiness and indulge in self-pity, lamenting "And I go childless" (15:2). On the other hand, Sarah never complained of her barrenness, either. Since she had never resigned herself to it, she must have stifled her complaints, for Abraham could have blamed her, and there was always the possibility that he might divorce her.

Strained relations soon developed between Sarah and Hagar, because Hagar pointed a finger at Sarah's inadequacy. By becoming pregnant, and so quickly, Hagar laid the blame for Sarah's barrenness at her own feet. Abraham, obviously, was virile. Having already sustained a blow to her ego in suggesting that Abraham marry another woman, Sarah's self-esteem now suffffered a more decisive blow. Her influence upon Abraham, she felt, affected him like castration, while Hagar rescued him from infertility, a mark of shame in that era. With her self-esteem at low ebb, Sarah brooded. Would Hagar actually fulfill God's promise? If so, then what role would she play in founding this new people Abraham talked about? Sarah felt like excess baggage.

Hagar must have hated Sarah from the beginning. Sarah had a husband of her own and enjoyed the prestige of being lady of the house, the things Hagar wanted most. A princess who had lived in a palace, Hagar was reduced now to the status of a slave. Sarah had everything, everything *she* would have had if Sarah had not deceived her father about her marital status (12:13). If Sarah had not lied, she would have joined Pharaoh's harem, Abraham would be dead, and Hagar would have remained a splendid princess enjoying the comforts and luxury of home, the love of her parents, and the association of her friends at court. Now Sarah's proposal gave her the opportunity to retaliate and Hagar could not resist it. To plummet from the proud position of a royal princess to the level of a slave required too great an adjustment. She became vicious and spiteful. Although deemed worthy to serve in the divine plan to found a great nation from Abraham, Hagar was not prepared to accept her circumstances, and behaved in a manner beneath the dignity of this role.

Upon becoming pregnant, Hagar assumed an air of superiority, regarding herself as much better than her mistress. She was going to have a child; Sarah could not become pregnant. Yet when women came to call on Sarah, she suggested that they visit with Hagar since she was expecting a child. And when they did, Hagar told them: "My mistress Sarah is not inwardly what she is outwardly. She appears to be a righteous woman, but she is not. If she were, so many years would not have elapsed without her conceiving, whereas I conceived in one night."[7] She lacked sympathy for Sarah's feelings. The closer she came to her day of delivery, the more spiteful and antagonistic Hagar became toward Sarah.

As a result, Sarah was disgruntled with herself for insisting that Abraham marry Hagar. Her plan had backfired. She suffered humiliation, developed feelings of insecurity, and behaved like a fearful woman. She became jealous of her erstwhile slave, the "safe little maiden," and she visualized her husband slipping away from her. Her coveted role as mistress of the house was in jeopardy, for Abraham might be drawn to the woman who was carrying his child. It all seemed so unfair. She was a princess who had sacrificed power, wealth, family and homeland to go with Abraham into the unknown to spread the teachings of the one true God. Yes, she had faith,[8] but it did not warrant uprooting herself, for she had nothing to gain from this adventure. Yet she joined in his work, converting women to Abraham's ideal while he converted the men.[9] She even saved his life when she stretched a point on his behalf by telling the Egyptians and Abimelech of Gerar that he was her brother (12:13; 20:5), and she almost lost her virtue doing so.[10] Furthermore, Abraham owed his wealth to her, because Pharaoh and Abimelech gave him many flocks and servants after these incidents (12:16; 20:14). Now Abraham rejected her. In spite of all that she had done for him, Sarah felt that she was in peril, her years of devotion and consecration to his ideal forgotten. She was losing her husband and her cherished position hung in the balance. To win back her mate, to restore her confidence and to bolster her ego, Sarah felt compelled to do something.

Sarah devised a scheme—and a daring one at that—to put Abraham to the test. She initiated the first step of her plan immediately, confronting him with the charge, "My wrong be upon thee . . . the Lord judge between me and thee" (16:5). She blamed him for her present plight, and scratched his face.[11] It was his fault, she said, that Hagar was so arrogant toward her. Why didn't he speak up in her behalf? Although it was her plan that he marry Hagar, Sarah placed the responsibility for it squarely upon Abraham. She convinced herself that Abraham was to blame, a most common reaction. Using Abraham for an *azazel,* a goat upon whom to vent her wrath, she blamed him for her own failure and shortcoming. She implied, "You made me do it. I am not responsible for my actions." Sarah attempted to absolve herself of all blame, rationalizing that the decision, made to meet the realities of the situation, was not hers.

The law of the land at that time gave the first wife the right to punish insolence on the part of the second wife. When Sarah complained to Abraham of Hagar's haughtiness, he told her, "Behold, thy maid is in thy hand; do to her that which is good in thine eyes" (16:6). He reminded Sarah that the law was on her side, that he had no voice in the matter. Abraham could have become enraged, as many men would, and said that the whole affair was her idea, that she had made her bed and now she could lie in it. He could have retorted that Hagar was giving him what she could not, and that if she didn't like it she could leave. He could have become indignant that she doubted his love, after he had spoken of her beauty (12:11). Instead, Abraham remained calm. Undoubtedly, beneath his air of understanding for Sarah, he felt an uneasy sensation of guilt. Perhaps he was to blame for Sarah's barrenness. Perhaps he could never fulfill the mission entrusted to him by God. Perhaps he was a failure. In any event, Abraham saw the future of his family at stake. If his marriage was to remain intact, one of them must maintain an even disposition. While Sarah stormed, Abraham exercised a measure of restraint. He ignored the scratch she had inflicted on his face and replied mildly, "Thy maid is in thy hand."

One would hardly expect Abraham to reply in such a manner. He was a forceful, dynamic personality, with tremendous qualities of leader-ship. Instead of putting the matter in Sarah's hands, he could have easily disposed of the problem himself. But this was typical of his behavior. Al-though he was to found a new faith, he did not have definite goals and objectives. Instead, Scripture tells us, he left home with nothing specific in mind. He wandered aimlessly throughout Canaan, and groped his way through difficult situations. Unlike the realistic, practical leader whose plans are all worked out in advance, Abraham followed an inner impulse. But far from weakness,[12] this was Abraham's great strength.

The cultural level of the people in his native land could not permit Abraham to attain his ideal. With implicit faith in their familiar way of life, his countrymen clung to their antiquated ideas and were content to perpetuate what was handed down to them. Unlike his neighbors, Abraham was dissatisfied with the *status quo*. His home town offered his restive spirit no hope. When he realized that he could never establish an ethically superior way of life in Ur, he left home. In leaving, Abraham displayed the qualities that made him a truly great man. He was dynamic, a spirit on the move, a pioneer who broke with tradition and struck out for the new.

His capacity for spiritual change propelled Abraham into the unknown, and his creature-feeling, his dependence upon the Almighty fortified him for his journey.[13] Instead of following an established or familiar route, he led his camp into the untracked desert, knowing that they might endure hardship and long periods of loneliness. Abraham was unconcerned. He was ready to take his chances.

Through it all, Abraham did not seek the best for himself. When they parted company, he gave Lot the opportunity to select the pasturage he wanted, knowing full well that his nephew would choose the fertile plains of Sodom (13:8-9). And when Sarah died, he did not even own a burial plot. Yet this did not diminish Abraham's stature, nor did the fact that he had no definite goal in mind. His willingness to risk danger added to the excitement of the trip and made each forward step more gratifying.

Abraham's mild response to Sarah, "Thy maid is in thy hand," was foreshadowed by the evident quality of his character. Whenever they pitched camp, he set up Sarah's tent before his own.[14] Even though he and Lot had parted ways after a dispute, Abraham risked his life to rescue Lot when he was captured by a huge force (14:14-17). And later, when gossip was rampant that Sarah became pregnant as a result of her experience with Abimelech,[15] he displayed no signs of agitation. Above all, Abraham was a man of justice. He dared to argue with the Lord Himself when he felt that even a few people might be treated unfairly (18:23-33). He gave Sarah *carte blanche* in dealing with Hagar, and referred to Hagar as a "maid," not as a wife, indicating that she meant nothing to him. Sarah need have no fears because of Hagar. She was still his beloved; he had no intention of shifting his affection.

Sarah had triumphed! Although she was sorry she had reproached Abraham, she had needed reassurance. And now that she had regained a measure of security, Sarah lost no time in pressing her advantage. She dealt harshly with Hagar. She restrained her from cohabiting with Abraham, slapped her face with a slipper, and compelled her to carry water buckets and towels to the baths,[16] a task relegated to a slave. Out of the depths of her jealousy and fear of Hagar, Sarah violated her agreement with her. Disregarding Hagar's status as a true wife of Abraham, she compelled her to do the most ignominious tasks, making her life so difficult and miserable that Hagar finally ran away. How Sarah must have rejoiced when she learned that Hagar was gone. Thank goodness, she must have sighed with relief, she was rid of a thorn in her side.

Sarah's respite was short-lived, however. After losing her unborn child,[17] Hagar returned. She conceived again and resigned herself to a life of hardship under Sarah. Hagar took pride in her fortitude and managed to achieve a sense of personal worth and purpose which gave her inner peace. At last Hagar grasped the value of her existence. No matter what Sarah would do to her, she was immune. She suffered emotional turmoil, but she reconciled herself with life, and became sufficient unto herself.[18]

Imagine the happiness with which Abraham greeted the birth of his son, Ishmael, a most wanted child! Now he had a son, an heir, who would carry on his new way of life. Delighted with his son, Abraham was thoroughly satisfied with the outcome of Sarah's plan. And when the Lord continued to promise him that Sarah would yet give birth to a son, he replied: "Oh that Ishmael might live before Thee" (17:18). Despite her feelings toward Hagar, Sarah must have been devoted to Ishmael and personally interested in him. After all, if not for her, Ishmael would never have been born. Sarah must have taken him from Hagar at birth to train him in the proper manners, to implant in him Abraham's ideals, and to prepare him to assume the role of Abraham's son. At the same time, imagine the emotional torment of Hagar. The woman whom she despised was rearing and educating her son. Hagar must have wondered if Ishmael was getting the proper care, or if Sarah was venting on him her hatred for his mother. Seeing her son run around the camp, Hagar must have longed to hug him, kiss him, or even touch him. Her only consolation was that Abraham would not allow anyone to mistreat him. Again, her infinite resignation stood Hagar in good stead.

Throughout the next dozen years, an undertone persisted that Sarah would give birth to a son. Though it was difficult for her to believe that such an event might occur, the prediction kept a spark of hope alive in Abraham and Sarah. And then, when a stranger told Abraham that Sarah would give birth in one year's time, Sarah laughed at this far-fetched presumption (18:10-12). She masked her despair with a display of humor, saying that Abraham was too old. Not she, but Abraham was too old. What a staunch spirit! Instead of breaking down at hearing the words of the stranger, and bewailing her wasted life, Sarah laughed. It enabled her to release tension and to maintain control of herself. Much to her surprise, she did become pregnant; and when she conceived, she became a woman fulfilled. Out of her despair came jubilation, but it must have been tempered by doubts. Even if she should bear a living child, it might be a girl. At her advanced age, could she expect to survive the ordeal of childbirth? At these moments, Sarah's child was unwanted, except that if it were a male it would even her score with Hagar. When Isaac was born, new life coursed through her veins. He, too, was a most welcome child. He rescued her from shame and restored her to the standing which she had never actually lost. Isaac's birth entrenched her position. Her true son was all-important, the only one that counted; and she constantly reminded Abraham of this. Yet Sarah was not thoroughly content.

With the birth of Isaac, a new and more profound rivalry disturbed the relationship of Abraham and his family. He already had a son and heir in Ishmael. Everyone knew Ishmael would succeed his father as head of the family—it was taken for granted. Of course, Isaac would bring joy to Abraham and Sarah in their old age, everyone thought, but the right of the first-born belonged to Ishmael. Very soon, however, Abraham's attitude toward Isaac became apparent. The Bible specifies that there was greater celebration over Isaac than Ishmael. Abraham gave a big party when Isaac was weaned (21:8) at the age of eighteen months or two years,[19] but it is not recorded anywhere that he had done the same thing for Ishmael, although his birth had also been an important occasion in the life of the family.[20] To the consternation of the entire camp, Ishmael dropped into second place.

Since breast-feeding was an obligation of the mother to the baby she brought into the world, weaning was a significant occasion among Biblical cultures. A child was generally breast-fed until he began to consume foods eaten by adults, and was self-sufficient to this degree. Weaning, tantamount to the final severing of the umbilical cord, called for a celebration, for it indicated that the mother had fulfilled her biological debt to the infant. Weaning also signalled the end of the ban on sexual intercourse for the parents. Among some primitive cultures, other signs prevailed—teething, sitting, and the like. Then the mother reverted from the active feminine role with her child to the passive feminine role with her husband, until the next baby came along.

It is claimed that under this system the primitive mother was under little strain because her functions as mother and as erotic companion did not conflict. At the time of weaning the child was temporarily separated from its mother to forget the breast, and the mother began to concentrate more on her own and her husband's satisfactions and pleasures than upon those of her child. It thus followed that competition between father and child for the mother and wife was non-existent or at a minimum, since there was a complete understanding about the mother's role. On the other hand, it is contended that our present-day familial setting leads to competition between father and child. The modern mother resumes her role of erotic partner in a relatively short period of time after giving birth, and at the same time is called upon to give her infant constant care and attention. The demands of the child tap her mental, physical and emotional energies. She not only devotes her days to his care, feeding and training, but she is alert to his cries at night as well. Her motherhood involves an ever-present awareness of her child.

On the surface it would seem that the child, being the more helpless of the two, would shut out the husband, giving rise to competition between father and child for the mother's attention. Actually, however, this is not true. After childbirth a woman is more erotic than before. The experience of giving birth, the total submission to her function in conceiving and unburdening herself of her child in the helpless throes of labor, strips her of her inhibitions. She becomes freer sexually and more able to express her need of her husband's approval and support through her submission to him in love-making. Therefore, when a mother uses her child as an excuse to avoid intercourse with her husband, the problem is probably an emotional one. She may not have wanted the child; she may fear another pregnancy; she may feel that she is not getting the support and approval from her husband that she needs for her strenuous role of motherhood. If competition does occur between father and child, the solution is not to revert to the primitive separation of mother from child or wife from husband, but to recognize and satisfy the emotional needs of both parents.

The "weaning" mentioned in Scripture may refer to Isaac's thirteenth birthday, when the religious duties of manhood became incumbent upon him.[21] This feast, then, would be the forerunner of the *Bar Mitzvah* celebration of our own day, when a Jewish lad of thirteen formally accepts his religious responsibility.[22] There was no such celebration on behalf of Ishmael, perhaps because Abraham no longer lived with Hagar after their son was born. Or, since Ishmael was not circumcized until he had reached age thirteen (17:25), and since he was conceived and born before Abraham had entered into the covenant of circumcision, it is possible that he did not merit this celebration. It would seem that the *Bar Mitzvah* ceremony was not practiced until after circumcision was introduced as a religious rite.

The sudden and total demotion of Ishmael from heir to step-child must have been a bitter pill for Hagar. All at once Ishmael had traveled the gamut from number one son to the child of a slave. And on the birth of Isaac, Hagar's own position suffered. Hagar must have entertained unkind thoughts toward Isaac, and identified him with his detested mother. Because of him she was once again reduced to the status of a slave. Her motherhood and her suffering no longer stood her in good stead. She could have spared herself all this trouble.

An appalling struggle between Sarah and Hagar must have followed the birth of Isaac. Since Hagar had more to lose, she unquestionably put up a stubborn fight to win Abraham's affections, if not for her own sake, then on behalf of Ishmael. Although Sarah had reared Ishmael for about thirteen years and no doubt was fond of the boy, now that she had her own child she abandoned Ishmael. The sight of him offended her. He might have made her feel guilty for rejecting him so completely, after giving him her love and devotion prior to Isaac's birth. Now she regarded him as a threat to Isaac. It made her unhappy just to see Ishmael and Hagar in the camp. And Hagar's tactics to attract Abraham's attention to Ishmael must have infuriated Sarah. On the other hand, every time Abraham smiled at Isaac, it must have caused Hagar great unhappiness. Every look, every expression that passed between the women was charged with resentment, and Abraham was caught between them. He was torn between his two wives and his two sons. He had already shown that he really loved only one of his wives, but his children were another matter. He was bewildered and Sarah knew it. She could see his conflict every time Ishmael showed him affection. How could Abraham ignore him? His love for Ishmael was not obliterated with Isaac's birth. How could it be? Ishmael was still his son. No, Sarah realized, Abraham loved them both. So she decided to help Abraham come to a decision.

The relationship between Isaac and Ishmael could not have been wholesome. Every child's development is affected by all change that he encounters, which includes the birth of a sibling.[23] The older child will resist this type of change because he does not wish to lose gratifications he has enjoyed until then. The new baby in the house deprived Ishmael of a certain amount of his parents' time and attention, and he reacted with an antagonism to Isaac, the source of his deprivation. Sarah had discarded him totally, and Abraham neglected him to some great measure. Dependent upon his parents for love and security, Ishmael felt deprived of both. Isaac was their love, their delight.[24]

Unprepared for this abrupt change, Ishmael felt rejected by both Abraham and Sarah. They withheld more from him than from a child born under ordinary circumstances. They spoke curtly and harshly to him, and they became overly strict and domineering. With one swoop, Ishmael reverted from a wanted to an unwanted child. Nagged, scolded and even whipped, he dared not approach Sarah, and spoke to Abraham with trepidation. When he attempted to show them affection, they pushed him away and told him not to annoy them. Regardless of how well he might have performed, they gave him little or no praise. He was to be seen as little as possible, and heard not at all. Ishmael must have soon realized he could expect only hurt from them. Consequently, he tried to avoid them as much as he could. He felt hatred and loathing for them. And because he really loved Abraham and Sarah, he felt guilty. Feeling betrayed when the only mother he knew brought another child into the family, Ishmael must have attacked Sarah either physically or verbally, or both. And believing all adults were like his parents, Ishmael also became rebellious and antagonistic toward strangers, manifesting his aggressiveness in theft, murder and depoiling women. Such behavior could only earn Sarah's utter contempt for him. She had done so much for him, Sarah thought, and this was how he repaid her.

The malignant conflict between Sarah and Hagar aggravated the rivalry of their sons. Squabbling and bickering between Isaac and Ishmael was constant and vicious, and the two mothers not only did not alleviate the situation, but were the "traumatizing impulses" assaulting their children. Recent studies on mother psychology lead to the general conclusion that a child's development reflects the influence of the mother. More and more, psychologists regard the mother as the dynamic force, and the child as the image of its mother, duplicating her views and emotional characteristics.[25] Judaism recognized the influence of the mother long ago, when it was ruled that a child born of a Jewish mother (even though her mate be of another faith) be regarded as Jewish.[26]

Ishmael's immediate reaction to the presence of Isaac—jealousy—paral-

leled Sarah's response to the threat of her rival, Hagar. Abraham's love
and attention abruptly stopped coming his way and were diverted to Isaac.
His loss was Isaac's gain. Like a child who cares nothing for his toy
until he sees it in another child's hands and wants it back, Ishmael was
jealous. He not only wanted to have his father's love again, but he wanted
to take it away from Isaac. His hostile behavior betrayed that he was
anxious and worried, and deeply hurt.

To convince himself that Abraham loved him more, Ishmael continuously challenged Isaac, and may have provided the pressure that
elevated Isaac's behavior. In a story in the Midrash, Ishmael claimed he
was more beloved because he was circumcized when he was thirteen years
of age, whereas Isaac countered that he was more beloved because he was
circumcized when he was merely eight days old. He could have protested
if he had wanted to, Ishmael said, whereas Isaac was only a baby and
could not refuse. Isaac replied that Ishmael was required to lend only
three drops of blood, but if God desired that Isaac cut off one of his
limbs or be slaughtered, he would not refuse.[27]

One day while they were in the field, Ishmael shot arrows at Isaac,
pretending to play with him.[28] Under guise of play, Ishmael expressed his
resentment of Isaac and his desire to dominate him. Like parents everywhere who observe older siblings playfully pinch a younger child, Sarah
sensed an undercurrent of something more serious than childish bickering.
Ishmael proved himself a cruel brother,[29] and Sarah realized that he
really wanted to hurt Isaac, or even kill him!

Furthermore, Sarah realized, Ishmael was unhappy about his inheritance. As the only son, he had expected to acquire all of Abraham's
wealth; but now that Isaac had arrived, he would have to share this
wealth, and Isaac would inherit the double portion. Ishmael hated Isaac
for it.[30] The Rabbis recognized the potent implications of jealousy when
they declared that Ishmael acted toward Isaac as Cain had toward Abel,
wanting to be rid of him.[31] Mortido, the tension which lends force to
the destructive urge,[32] is not rare. By eliminating the threatening force,
it is a means of survival.

Finally the full impact of Ishmael's behavior drove Sarah to take a
stand. In addition to all the conflicts she had observed between him and
Isaac, now she saw Ishmael becoming a social misfit, a delinquent. Sarah
saw Ishmael "making sport." She could understand that he would mock
Isaac, but he went further and mocked the people who rejoiced at Isaac's
birth, saying that he was the first-born and would receive the double
portion of inheritance. "Making sport" has an additional connotation, with

far more serious implications. To understand the kind of "sport" Ishmael indulged in (21:9), one must compare the Hebrew word employed in this instance with the one used when Abimelech, the Philistine king, saw "Isaac sporting with Rebekah his wife" (26:8). It was then that Abimelech realized that they were husband and wife. In both instances the Hebrew work is *m'tzachaik,* which conveys a rather vivid picture of what Ishmael was doing. The same Hebrew word appears again when Potiphar's wife accused Joseph (33:17) of trying to copulate with her. In another context this verb could also denote idolatry (Exodus 32:6). Sarah knew that Ishmael had ravished maidens, seduced and dishonored married women and committed murder; she also saw him worship idols.[33]

In the face of all this, Sarah found Abraham's indecision intolerable. She sensed his disillusionment in Ishmael, and she was impatient for him to act. To help him come to a decision, Sarah announced unequivocally: "For the son of this bondwoman shall not be heir with my son, even with Isaac" (21:10).[34]

From the time Isaac was born, Ishmael presented a behavior problem. But was it inevitable that it reached such serious proportions? When parents are too occupied, as Sarah and Abraham certainly were on the arrival of Isaac, an older child may misbehave, not because he really wants to be bad, but merely to regain his parents' attention. He will risk censure or even punishment to assure himself that he is still loved. To a child, it is far better to get a whipping than to be ignored. Sometimes a child will misbehave in order to test his parents, to find the limits to which he can go without restraint or punishment. Again, his object is to determine that his parents care about him. Before Isaac was born, Ishmael was over-indulged. His parents were as indifferent to his excessive freedom and over-supply of material things as other parents are negligent in the opposite extreme. Ishmael could not be certain they really cared. After Isaac was born, Ishmael was ignored, which was also equivalent to being unloved. For Ishmael, misbehaving was not merely a device to gain attention or to establish limits of behavior, it was his only means of asserting his existence. Rejected by the mother who had formerly loved him, and shunted out of reach of his father's affection, his loss was almost tantamount to the loss of all life, and the loss of all hope. If he had not reacted as violently as he did, he might have lost not only his parents but his self. At least he clung to his identity. If ever his father reaffirmed his love, Ishmael could change.

It was Abraham's fault that Ishmael became a problem child, the Rabbis maintain.[35] It appears that Abraham did not discipline him adequately. As so often happens with an only child, Ishmael was especially vulnerable to the development of behavior difficulties, because he had enjoyed excessive attention.[36] Being the sole heir, he was overprotected, spoiled and egotistical. When Isaac was born, he was deeply hurt that he was no longer the center of interest.[37] Abraham attempted to train Ishmael to perform good deeds, but inconsistent discipline vitiated his efforts.[38] This is the general consequence of lax disciplinary practices. In addition to assuring a child he is loved, discipline in the home enables children to develop a clear conception of right and wrong and helps them anticipate the varying consequences of their behavior. Erroneous disciplinary practices may seriously retard the healthy development of personality and character. When children are not conditioned to obey legitimate authority, the results are generally disastrous,[39] as Abraham learned too late. Ishmael brought idols into the house, toyed with them and worshipped them as he saw others doing. He also constructed pagan altars, caught locusts and sacrificed them.[40] It is difficult to believe that such practices could take place in Abraham's house, yet they did because Abraham found it easier to be permissive than to be strict. Abraham's negligence did prove disastrous. Ishmael became depraved, but when Abraham realized it, he was powerless to undo his mistakes. As a result, Abraham's love turned to hatred and he ceased to think of Ishmael as his son.[41]

Abraham's treatment of Ishmael poses the question as to the type and extent of discipline necessary to maintain a stable home. Discipline is essentially of two types—the permissive approach and the authoritative approach. The course adopted by parents distinctly influences their child's emotional development.

It is difficult to discipline a child when parents place greater emphasis upon the welfare of the child than upon the welfare of the family as a whole. Overlooking their own rights as individuals and mates, such parents accommodate themselves to the child's requirements. They ignore the fact that the child is only one segment of the family triangle—father, mother, child.

In the truly permissive home children are noisy, resistant to control, and aggressive in challenging the parents' wishes. It is disconcerting to chat on the telephone while a child beats a drum, and one is frequently distracted as the children dart from one room to another. All this puts a heavy burden on the nerves and energy of the parents, and they have little opportunity to relax in quiet privacy. If the living room is not in perfect order when guests drop in, it doesn't matter. At the same time, practical precautions are taken; valuables and breakable objects are stored away or placed out of reach and the furniture is protected by slip-covers. In effect, the house is adapted to the child, rather than the child to the house. Noise, wear and tear, clutter and the like, simply take their place in the parental expectation of what life with children is like. In the permissive environment, it is the parents who are disciplined. They feel that these are merely temporary inconveniences, but have long-lasting benefits. Parents who can accept this philosophy and practice it consistently find it less nerve-wracking and very helpful to the child.

In the authoritarian home, however, the child must constantly adapt himself to the rules and preferences of his parents. Authoritarian parents subconsciously feel that the furniture and orderliness are more important than the children. They demand strict obedience to the rules that have been established for their household, rationalizing that they aim to develop a sense of discipline and responsibility in their children. Homes where such child-rearing is the accepted mode usually produce over-anxious or over-compliant adults.

Many child psychologists agree that a combination of both schools of thought is possible, and recommend some form of permissive child-rearing. This is not to suggest that all limits and restrictions in the home be abandoned. A child who is permitted every liberty and satisfaction is not being trained to tolerate the frustrations and deprivations which he will experience in life.[42] Freedom for the child is important if he is to learn for himself and gain confidence in his own values, but freedom does not require the absence of all parental control. Rather, the family relationship should be balanced, which calls for discipline on the part of the child as well as the parents. The child who learns to abide by the family's rules of behavior, as well as those of society, is able to adapt to his environment with a minimum of difficulty.

Regardless of the type of discipline parents decide to use in rearing their children, it must come naturally and be adapted to the philosophy with which the parents are comfortable, or it will harm them and their offspring.

According to the Rabbis, it would seem that Abraham's household was permissive. Also, it would appear that he was a failure as a father. On the one hand, he spoiled Ishmael by indulging his every whim so that he became uncontrollable and even defied him. Then, by demanding that Ishmael move at once from a permissive atmosphere into an authoritarian one, he expected too much of him.

Sarah precipitated a crisis in the continuous struggle for Abraham's

love. Having stated her unyielding opposition to Ishmael's inheritance
rights, she seized the psychological advantage and presented convincing
arguments against Hagar and her evil son. She ordered Abraham to divorce
Hagar,[43] and to drive her and Ishmael out—to banish them. Twice she
called Hagar "bondwoman" (21:10) to impress upon him, the husband
and father, their lowly status, thus betraying that she was motivated
greatly by hatred and hostility. Intermingled with these negative feelings
was Sarah's attitude of overprotection and oversolicitousness of Isaac,
as if to compensate for some past misdeeds or unwholesome thoughts.
She may have felt guilty because she gave her affection to Ishmael before
Isaac was born. It is also possible that while she was carrying Isaac she
felt hatred toward him because he might cause her death. To counterbalance these feelings, when Isaac was born Sarah showered him with affection and with excessive protection. She was his champion at all times and
under all circumstances. This attitude persisted throughout her life, for
Sarah was never able to effect a separation from Isaac. She was unable
to let him gain his independence or grow away from her. "Smother love,"
oversolicitousness and overprotectiveness, made Sarah the first exemplar
of "momism." Even her death was caused by the thought that Isaac was
being harmed.[44] Driving Hagar and Ishmael away was part of this pattern
of overprotection.

Abraham was not ready to comply with Sarah's request, however, for
it was forbidden to drive out the offspring of a handmaid.[45] He was
responsible for Hagar and Ishmael; he owed them his protection and
assistance. He also hesitated because he was in a turmoil; he was confused.
As wicked as Ishmael was, and though there were moments when Abraham
abhorred him, he was still his son.[46] How could he send him away? Besides,
he may have wondered, now that Sarah had everything she wanted, was
such drastic action necessary? The last time Sarah complained about
Hagar, she was miserable because she was barren and in dire need of
understanding. But now she had no problem. Abraham could not understand why his women did not get along. They did in other families, why
not in his?

Finally, for the sake of his mission, and with the Lord's guidance
(21:12), Abraham disowned Ishmael, an action permitted by the Code
of Hammurabi,[47] and sent him and Hagar away. He did not delegate this
responsibility to anyone else, but carried it out himself. He arose early
in the morning, gave his wife and son water and food, and sent them
on their way. The Bible makes it a point to specify that he gave Hagar
and Ishmael a pitcher of water, although he surely gave them more than

one ewer of water. The pitcher, not the water, conveyed a message to the people. In those years it was the function of slaves to carry pitchers of water. Through this means he broadcast Hagar's and Ishmael's servile status so that Ishmael could not subsequently claim that he was Abraham's free-born son and dispute Isaac's right as his heir.[48]

The moment of departure must have been a tragic experience for all three. Although Abraham felt estranged from his son and Hagar, he must have shared their anguish. Ishmael might have pleaded for one more chance. Perhaps he suddenly realized he had not behaved properly and promised to change, if only Abraham would allow him to stay. And Hagar, supporting her son's pleas, might have added that she would keep after him, she would make Ishmael a credit to Abraham. Although Hagar had been informed that Ishmael would be reared in the wilderness (16:12) and she should have expected something like this to happen, she was inconsolable. Abraham remained adamant. For the sake of the future, he refused to give ground. Again he ordered them to leave. All her years of suffering were as nothing compared to this. Hagar's face was a stony mask of hurt and disbelief as she took her son's hand and departed.

Following this, Ishmael developed into a thoroughly evil adult. Reared in an atmosphere replete with emotional tensions, he had already suffered psychic damage. Then divorce, which is what Hagar's banishment amounted to, had an enormous traumatic effect upon Ishmael, bringing buried anxieties to the surface. The emotional blow shattered the family structure, his concept of his parents, and his emotional identification with them.[49] It destroyed the last vestiges of family stability for him, and with it all sense of security.

The divorce was especially harmful to Ishmael because Abraham did not adequately prepare him for what was to take place. Abraham disliked what he did, and must have shown it in many ways, but he failed to soften the blow for Ishmael. There are four guiding principles[50] to be followed in broaching the subject of divorce to children. Abraham did not and could not use any of them. At no time did he break the news to Ishmael. He dealt solely with Hagar. Secondly, he could not explain to Ishmael that the entire arrangement had been a mistake from the beginning. On the contrary, Abraham's union with Hagar was regarded as a fine solution by all until Isaac was born. Thirdly, he could not assure Ishmael that he was not to blame, for he was the precipitating cause of the divorce and undoubtedly knew it. This probably heightened Ishmael's guilt-feelings for the trouble he had caused his parents, especially his mother. And, fourthly, he did not assure Ishmael of his love despite the separation, differentiating between him and the deed. The consequences of Abraham's omission were manifested in Ishmael's subsequent behavior.

Studies[51] have shown that there is a high proportion of delinquency among children who have experienced one or more household changes, for such an unsettling experience makes excessive demands upon the child's powers of adaptation. Fragmentation of the family is the most potent single factor in producing the problem child. Parents ought to be concerned about it, because it raises fears and doubts in the child's mind "regarding parental understanding, affection, protection, and the relationship to the authoritarian world." Being exiled from home made Ishmael conclude once and for all that his father was truly unconcerned about him, a feeling which had persisted since Isaac was born. In order to develop wholesome ideals, a boy needs a warm relationship with his father. He has an intense desire to be exactly like him and, without realizing it, will unconsciously copy his father's behavior traits. This accounts for the belief that the child has inherited his father's traits. Through emotional identification with the father, the son matures along positive lines. Where no such relationship exists, the growing child will usually seek substitute anti-social pleasures and gratification. Having no close ties with his father, or, for that matter, with his erstwhile mother, Sarah, or with his brother, Isaac, Ishmael was conditioned by all the factors of family life that lead to delinquency. This led the Rabbis to conclude that as Ishmael grew, so did his cruelty.[52] He sat at the crossroads and robbed and molested passersby.[53] Any time a parent gives up on a child, or merely infers it by such an innocuous statement as, "You'll never amount to anything," the results are not favorable. Giving up on any human being does not lead to happy results.

As a result of this action, Abraham suffered deep feelings of guilt and self-hate. Just how righteous was he? How could he have disowned his own son? How could he have been cowed by Sarah, he who dared stand up to the Lord Himself for the sake of justice? Was he really righteous when he permitted Sarah to deal so harshly with Hagar when she was pregnant, so harshly that she had miscarried?[54] He wondered whether Sarah might not have exaggerated Ishmael's faults in order to express her scorn for Hagar and to make Isaac's position more secure.

Then he thought of Isaac. Yes, he was a lovely child; a kind, gentle and obedient son. Truly proud of him, Abraham admitted that God did keep His word. Isaac was inwardly strong,[55] but he was dominated by his mother. Sarah did everything for him. She had made him so timid, so retiring, that he seemed to have no mind of his own—a personality unbecoming to the future patriarch of his camp. Abraham was in great torment as he wondered if he had failed in the upbringing of this son, too.

Abraham often thought of Ishmael, for an only child is hardly ever dethroned by later children,[56] and he spoke of him to Sarah. She counseled him to forget Ishmael, and advised him to put these thoughts out of his mind, but they would not be stilled for long. Approximately three years after the expulsion, in an attempt to mitigate his sense of guilt, he told Sarah that he was going to visit Ishmael to see how he was faring.[57] Sarah proferred her usual objections, that Abraham might reconsider and invite Ishmael to return,[58] that he would give the impression of visiting Hagar, and that even Ishmael might misunderstand the purpose of his visit. All to no avail. To appease her, however, Abraham acquiesced in one condition, that he would not dismount from his camel when he arrived there. Either he still loved her sufficiently to make such a promise, or he made it to keep peace at home.

Upon arriving at Ishmael's camp, he met his son's Moabitish wife. He asked for Ishmael, and his daughter-in-law told him that he had gone with Hagar to gather fruit and dates in the desert. He asked her for bread and water, but she replied that she had none. He instructed her to tell Ishmael upon his return, "An old man from the land of Canaan came to see you, and said, 'Change the threshold of your home for it is neither good for you nor worthy of you.' " Ishmael understood the intent of this message when he heard it, and he divorced his wife. Then Hagar got him an Egyptian wife, named Petumah, from her father's house.

About three years after this incident, Abraham visited Ishmael a second time, once more promising Sarah that he would not dismount when he arrived. Again, Ishmael was not at home. His new daughter-in-law told him that Ishmael had gone with Hagar to herd the camels in the desert. He proceeded to ask her for food and she immediately fed him. In violation of his promise to Sarah, he dismounted from his camel and prayed to the Lord on behalf of his son. When Ishmael returned, his wife told him what had happened. At that moment Ishmael knew that his father's love had hovered over him all this while.

Although these visits had assuaged Abraham's guilt feelings, he was not completely rid of them. Remorse for his earlier deeds persisted. He sought respite from the recurring pangs of self-reproach; the need for atonement overwhelmed him. And then it came to him: proper atonement for the mistreatment of Ishmael would be the sacrifice of Isaac. Like Abel, Abraham would sacrifice the best that he owned, his most beloved possession, as an oblation. It would clear away the guilt of the act and expiate for capitulating to Sarah. Besides, Sarah also had some atoning to do. She would pay with the life of her son for what she was instrumental in doing to another mother's son. One would neutralize what was merci-lessly done to the other. And he would perform the second deed as he did the first. As he "arose up early in the morning" (21:14) to banish Ishmael, so he "rose early in the morning" (22:3) to conduct Isaac to Moriah.

An additional motivating factor[59] which might have impelled Abraham in this direction was the fact that Isaac was born when he was one hundred years of age. Since Isaac was Abraham's exact image,[60] Abraham might have been alarmed to see himself reincarnated in his son, a belief that prevailed among some primitive tribes. Although he was anxious to have a son, now that Isaac had arrived Abraham felt supplanted, a paralyzing thought to such a powerful and active man. Possessing all his father's attributes in addition to youth, Isaac destroyed his absolute supe-riority. Abraham had passed his prime and now his powers as husband and leader of the tribe were on the decline. Abraham was jealous of Isaac and felt compelled to eliminate him in order to relieve the immo-bilizing fear that gripped him. Moriah was the answer. It provided him with time to think, away from Sarah and local influences. Its lofty peak would elevate his thoughts. From its vantage point high in the heavens he would see the meaning of his anguish.

Abraham masked his feelings and did not reveal his plan to Sarah. Instead, he told her that he was taking Isaac to study at the school of Shem and Eber.[61] He did not necessarily distort the truth. He entertained in his mind the philosophical understanding that what he and Isaac were to go through was equivalent in importance to study, the highest ideal among the Jewish people. During the night preceding their de-parture, Sarah kept Isaac with her in her tent, clinging tenaciously to him, kissing and embracing him. In the morning, before they left, she instructed Abraham, "Neglect him not,"[62] and urged him not to keep Isaac away from her for too long. She had forebodings about the voyage, however, and said to Isaac, "Who knoweth if I shall ever see thee again after this day."[63]

Isaac obediently cooperated with his father in his contemplated act because he also had misgivings and feelings of guilt. Since he had been guilty of an error of omission in not protesting Ishmael's expulsion, he decided that he would not protest his own sacrifice. He felt that he should have spoken on his brother's behalf, even if it were to no avail. His mother was a determined woman, Isaac realized, and he had kept still to avoid crossing her. In making him dependent upon her, she had stifled his best impulses and he subconsciously hated her for it. His silence at this moment would expiate his earlier silence.[64] He did make one request of Abraham, however. To balance his extreme attachment to Sarah, Isaac harbored concomitant rebellious feelings against his father. He implored Abraham to gather his ashes after he had been consumed by the fire, and to place them in Sarah's tent. Whenever she came into it, Isaac anticipated, she would burst into tears and exclaim, "This is my son who was slaughtered by his father."[65] He would thereby repay both of them. These feelings added to his guilt, however, since he knew he should not entertain hostile feelings toward his parents. Moriah offered proper atonement on all scores.

Isaac fleetingly rebelled inside, momentarily overcome by the urge to save himself. The wicked angel, Samael, taunted him saying that if he were sacrificed all his fine clothes would be given to Ishmael.[66] Also, he overheard an argument between Ishmael and Eliezer, the two "young men" (22:3) Abraham took along on the journey.[67] When Isaac was sacrificed, Ishmael said, he would be restored as Abraham's heir. Eliezer countered that Abraham had driven Ishmael out "as a woman divorced from her husband" and therefore he had no claim to the estate. He, Eliezer, had been Abraham's trusted servant long before either of the sons were born; he would be Abraham's heir.[68] Nevertheless, Isaac did not attempt to escape. He did hope, however, that when he said "My father" (22:7), Abraham would have compassion upon him and would call the sacrifice to a halt. He also felt that by not helping (22:9), he would induce Abraham to give up the idea.[69] When he finally realized that nothing swayed Abraham's resolve, Isaac resigned himself to his fate and said, "Father, I am a young man and afraid that my body may tremble through fear of the knife and I will grieve thee, whereby the sacrifice may be rendered unfit, and it will not count as a real sacrifice. Therefore, bind me very securely."[70] Justice had to be served.

During the three day journey upon which they had embarked, Abraham struggled desperately within himself. Was this the proper atonement? How would God view this action? These three days of soul-searching afforded him the opportunity to rethink his decision. Not until he held the knife in his hand and was ready to slay Isaac did he, through faith, resolve his conflict and abandon the sacrifice. In the stress of his family relation-ship, Abraham had lost sight of his purpose. His mission to establish a new nation and a better way of life had demanded the acts for which he was now prepared to make atonement. The course he had followed with

Hagar and Ishmael suddenly became justifiable, and Abraham's guilt left
him. Sarah, too, was vindicated for her relentless pursuit of Isaac's primacy
over Ishmael. The purpose of all his suffering, Abraham concluded, was
embodied in Isaac. He had chosen his younger son to carry on his mission,
and had done only what was necessary to develop in him the strength and
fortitude for the task. If he were to end Isaac's life now, leaving Ishmael
to succeed him, he would destroy the meaning of his own life. At Moriah
Abraham found affirmation and fulfillment of his suffering.

Though Abraham decided against killing Isaac, he still felt he should
draw a little blood from him as a token punishment,[71] but he decided
against this too. Isaac's life was spared, and father and son came away
from Moriah spiritually purified. Abraham must have been impressed with
Isaac's ready acquiescence to his plan. Isaac could have objected, run away,
or done something else to forestall his death. After all, he was thirty-seven
years of age.[72] But he did not. Isaac's behavior proved he had achieved
the self-control and discipline he would need to submerge himself for
the sake of an ideal. At that moment Abraham must have acknowledged
that Sarah's contention was sound—outside influences would have corrupted
Isaac. When he married Keturah (25:1), or when he remarried Hagar,[73]
as some believe, Abraham did not find it grievous in the least to send
away the additional children he had with her. Although they were mere
babes, he did not wish to test the possibility, however remote, that they
might remain to threaten Isaac's continuing spiritual development.

The act at Moriah, as far as it had gone, served its purpose admirably.
Soon thereafter, Isaac went and fetched Hagar.[74] Now that Isaac's position
as heir was no longer in dispute, Hagar was able to return and live at
peace in Abraham's household. She knew her son lacked the qualities
required to lead men to his father's ideal. His virtues, as even his mother
must admit, did not include self-control. Hagar was ready to concede that
being the first-born was not sufficient reason for Ishmael to inherit the
spiritual legacy of Abraham.

From his observations of Abraham and Isaac at Moriah, Ishmael understood what had transpired.[75] His behavior altered too. He must have
accepted Abraham's right to flout primogeniture. Perhaps he was even
grateful that he had not been put to the test as Isaac had. Ishmael repented,[76] as the Lord had told Abraham he would,[77] and he came from
the outermost recesses of the wilderness to pay honor to his father when
he died.[78]

CHAPTER FIVE

Twins in Her Womb

(Genesis 25:24)

I

GENESIS 25:28 states quite bluntly, "Now Isaac loved Esau . . . and Rebekah loved Jacob." These four personalities have been the source of much discussion and speculation. What kind of people were Isaac and Rebekah? Were they parents who were partial toward one of their children? It is not surprising that they were, for this is not an uncommon attitude. Such behavior, as ancient as family life itself, is a modern phenomenon as well. Scripture paints a graphic picture of Isaac and Rebekah, who each showed partiality to one of their twin sons, Esau and Jacob.

The main basis for drawing characterizations of them is the incident in which Jacob snatched the blessing away from Esau under their father Isaac's nose, so to speak, at Rebekah's suggestion and with her active assistance. This particular event seems of such paramount importance that scant attention is paid to the remainder of the narrative except for the scene where Esau barters his birthright for a mess of pottage. As a consequence, two camps have been formed. One exonerates Rebekah and Jacob and views the accusation of conspiracy against them as unjust and false, bordering on libel. The other condemns them mercilessly, expressing sympathy for Esau, the wronged, and indignation over the underhanded manner in which Isaac was duped.

On our initial introduction to Isaac in the previous chapter, he was a child born to aged parents, indulged, smothered with affection, and cherished because he fulfilled their long yearning for an offspring. His half-brother, Ishmael, and the mother of Ishmael were exiled so as not to corrupt him. As a child, Isaac must have been docile and submissive, as he was in his silent acquiescence to the sacrifice of his life. He even carried the wood that was intended to reduce him to ashes. And when he was to marry, his father sent his trusted servant, Eliezer, to his family in a distant area with instructions to bring him a wife. Arrangements were

made without consulting Isaac as to whether or not he wanted to marry
at all. It appears that he was so dominated and obedient that he never
rebelled, or even suggested that he would have liked to exercise his own
judgment or make his own choice in matters vital to his future.

Isaac remained true to this type and characterization throughout
his life. He never fought a battle as his father did when he freed Lot
from Chedorlaomer and his compatriots (14). When the occasion arose
to stand up for his own rights in a life and death situation, Isaac backed
down (26:18f). Securing water for his family, servants and flocks was
vital, yet "he removed from thence, and digged another well" (26:22) in
order to avoid a fight. Instead of providing forceful leadership to protect
those under his wing, he retreated to another locale. Having been over-
indulged, he was ill-equipped to deal with anxieties produced by unpre-
ventable frustrations and deprivations of everyday life. Isaac's character
had been molded in such a way that he turned from situations that would
tend to cause him apprehension.[1] No, Isaac was not Abraham—nor was
he like his son, Jacob. Jacob saw the girl he wanted to marry and, like
a gallant lover, he was ready and willing to serve seven years and then
seven more to make her his own. On the contrary, Isaac never worked
nor fought for what he wanted. Anything he could not get easily he did
not want. Unlike Abraham and Jacob, Isaac never left home to travel
into distant lands. He lived a quiet, dispirited life with his parents as
long as they lived.

Further insight into Isaac's character lies in the verse, "And Isaac
digged again the wells of water, which they had digged in the days of
Abraham his father" (26:18). Children generally like to strike out for
themselves, to display their independence, but Isaac did not. The wells
that Abraham had dug had been stopped up by the Philistines. Isaac not
only re-dug the same wells, but he called them by the same names his
father had used. Why, one may ask, didn't Isaac strike out on his own
and dig brand new wells—wells that would be attributed to him?

Since water is most essential to the survival of nomads, finding wells
is the first responsibility of the sheikh. Isaac, therefore, was in constant
search of water, as well as food, for his family, servants and livestock.
Basically, Isaac was using good judgment. It is quite feasible that in
his wanderings Isaac recalled his childhood, the wells his father had dug,
and perhaps his own participation in the effort. He remembered how
successful his father had been. Why not search out the same wells, he
asked himself? He found them, but they had been plugged up; so Isaac
instructed his servants to clear them. He would use the same water his

father had used to supply the needs of his entourage and quench his own thirst.

There may be still other motivating factors that led Isaac to pursue this course of action. There must have been a feeling of security in retracing his father's footsteps. Why should he speculate about finding water when he had a sure thing? His father had already found water in these wells. Why shouldn't water continue to fill them? Why pursue possibilities in other locations when results have already been displayed here? Regardless of the fact that these wells had been stopped up, Isaac reasoned, they would still be easier to work than starting anew in unbroken soil. Moderately certain of success, Isaac would not gamble with failure.

His decision to re-dig these wells may have also been prompted by an emotional drive. Isaac worked them out of respect for his extraordinary father. Excavating his father's wells and drinking their water had sentimental value as well as the value of sentiment itself, which is a spiritual quality. They brought back cherished childhood memories long forgotten, fond associations no longer existent. Restored to usefulness, these wells may have recalled unpleasant episodes as well. Thoughts of Ishmael must have flashed through his mind, of how his half-brother had been mistreated because of him. Yet, regardless of their nature, Isaac's memories were realistic, warm, part of his being. Though these wells may have been inferior to new ones that he might have unearthed, the memories they summoned were more significant and pithy.

Sentiment also motivated David who saw from the cave of Adullam a host of Philistines swarming over the valley of Rephaim and the town of Bethlehem. Looking down at the place of his birth, David was overcome with depressing feelings of loneliness. He recalled the years of his youth spent happily with his many brothers in his father's house. Concentrating on these reminiscences, David suddenly developed a strong craving—he yearned for a drink of water. "Oh that one would give me water to drink of the well of Bethlehem, which is by the gate!" (II Samuel 23:15). At that moment, even one sip of this water seemed urgently necessary to him. Three of his chiefs understood David's longing and the thoughts which led him to say what he did. Realizing the depth of his need, these three devoted confidants crossed the lines of the Philistines to bring him water. They jeopardized the battle and endangered their lives, not only to quench his thirst, but to refresh his youthful memories, to buoy up his spirit, and to fortify him to withstand the rigors of his entangled life.

Everyone can multiply such instances. In our adult lives, songs that we sang and recitations that we memorized during childhood suddenly erupt into our consciousness, causing us either to squirm in embarrassment or to experience a feeling of warmth and gladness pervading every limb. Though such thoughts seem trivial, in this fleeting instant we are at home again with a significant past.

Thus we can comprehend Isaac's actions in unplugging his father's wells. They tell us something further about his personality. An arch conservative, Isaac was neither a daring spirit nor the adventurous type. He did not display the faith evidenced by his father, for he had a fear of the unknown from which faith had freed Abraham. Whatever had worked for his father Isaac was ready to try too, even to pretending that Rebekah was his sister, as Abraham had said about his mother. Except for the lack of initiative, Isaac made his life a carbon copy of his father's, imitating him at important moments of his own life.

On Sarah's death, Isaac experienced acute grief and mourned his mother excessively. Three years after Sarah had died, Isaac was still incapable of reconciling himself to his loss. Preoccupied with the memory of his mother, he suffered a deep and lingering melancholia. According to one Hebrew source,[2] Sarah expired when she was informed that Isaac was to be sacrificed on Mt. Moriah, but before she could be told that it did not actually occur. A second source[3] states that it was Isaac himself who told his mother everything that had happened from beginning to end—that Abraham had taken him on a long journey, bound him up on an altar, and prepared to slay him. Except that an angel had intervened, he continued, he would have been slain. Upon hearing this, Sarah cried out, and died before her voice trailed away. Accordingly, Isaac bore a strong sense of guilt because he contributed to his mother's death.

Isaac's melancholia and immense grief were the result of a deep dissatisfaction with himself.[4] In his earlier unhappy relationship with Ishmael, a vital moral issue was involved and Isaac knew he had not been equal to it. One episode of despair heaped upon another sharpened his super-ego or punishing conscience to the point of near total loss of his self-respect. He blamed himself for what had happened; he lost his capacity to love and his interest in the outside world. He kept to himself, walking alone in the fields (24:63). Distraught, Isaac became masochistic, depreciating himself before the Almighty and pleading that He afflict him with further suffering.[5]

All this was modified, however, with the coming of Rebekah. She possessed a completely different type of character and personality. She was a fiery, independent, purposeful female, who made her own decisions and did not rest until she brought them to fruition. Our introduction to her promptly portrays her determination. When Eliezer asked her for water, she quickly replied that she would give him water and also his camels, and she set about the task without hesitation. Scripture narrates, "She hastened, and emptied her pitcher into the trough, and ran again unto the well to draw, and drew for all his camels" (24:20). One might expect a girl from a rich family to order a servant to draw the water, but Rebekah was not afraid to soil her hands; she fetched the water herself. A moment later, when Eliezer asked her whether he and his caravan might secure lodging at her home, she was not flurried. She replied immediately, without first asking her father, Bethuel, "We have both straw and provender enough, and room to lodge in" (24:25). She offered the food although Eliezer had not asked for any. When Eliezer met Rebekah's family, he requested her hand in marriage for Isaac, and showed them the will Abraham had written making Isaac heir to all that he possessed.[6] The details met with their satisfaction. Eliezer thereupon wanted to leave the following morning. Rebekah's mother and brother, however, wanted her to remain at home for another ten days, but agreed to let her decide for herself. Again without hesitation, she replied, "I will go" (24:58). She displayed a sense of the daring which she retained throughout her life. She went out into the unknown as Sarah had done when she followed Abraham. She evinced no doubts. Her straightforward reply seems to indicate that she was ready, and perhaps even anxious, to leave her home. She had been waiting for something like this to happen. Now that the moment had arrived, why tarry? Besides displaying a resolution Isaac had never demonstrated, Rebekah was certainly more free than he, and more free than the women of her day. They were opposites, and perhaps this was a good basis for a lasting and contented marriage. Eliezer might have understood that Isaac, who was so indecisive, needed a wife like Rebekah that he could depend on, as he had depended upon his mother. This might help explain why he set up such stringent requirements as to the girl's character. Isaac needed a wife who was exceptionally kind and understanding, but spirited. Such a person, Eliezer may have felt, was "appointed" (24:14) by God Himself for his master's son.

It may seem rather unusual for a young girl, especially in those days, to make a decision on a moment's notice, and by herself, that she would leave with a total stranger to marry a man whom she had never seen. Knowing she had a mind of her own, one might imagine she would have queried Eliezer extensively about her intended spouse and about his family. That she did not, suggests that Rebekah lived in an unhappy environment. A further indication of this was that her family did not make these inquiries either, nor did her father request that she remain ten days longer with the family, as did her mother and her brother, Laban (24:55). There may have been a rift between father and daughter. The Midrash, on the other hand, explains that Bethuel died suddenly during the night because he wanted to keep Rebekah from going.[7] Either her family was swayed by the money offered, or Rebekah was so unhappy at home that she was eager to leave under any circumstances,[8] perhaps overcoming an Electra complex.

Apparently Eliezer was justified in his conclusions concerning Rebekah. This marriage was successful from the first, despite an initial encounter which must have been mortifying. Upon returning home, Eliezer told Isaac all that there was to relate about his experience with Rebekah's family, and especially about Rebekah (24:66). Isaac was pleased with what he heard. Before Isaac married her, however, Abraham required a test. Since all slaves were suspect of obscenity and immorality,[9] including the trusted Eliezer, Abraham thought Eliezer might have robbed Rebekah of her chastity on the way home. He therefore advised his son to extract her virtue with his finger. If she was still a virgin, it would indicate that the Lord Himself wanted her to be his. Isaac obeyed his father and the matter was settled to the satisfaction of both.[10] Although this lack of faith and trust was a poor basis on which to start married life, there was no further mention of this incident and their marriage was a success. Isaac loved Rebekah and Rebekah was good to, and good for, Isaac.

Though he had been depressed when they married, Rebekah exerted such a tremendous influence upon Isaac that he was able to forget the loss of his mother, overcome his terrible loneliness, and regain his ability to love. The attention and devotion Rebekah showered upon Isaac assuaged his feelings of guilt and self-deprecation. She became his prop and support. By filling his need, she led him toward self-acceptance. The example of this relationship became the precedent for the law of grief universally accepted by psychiatry: when death claims a loved one, a substitute must be found to replace the lost relationship. Although Isaac was a man of forty, conservative and set in his habits, while Rebekah was only a young girl, she was a remarkable wife for him. She enabled him to incorporate Sarah, thereby diminishing his grief, and she was like a mother to him, as Sarah had been.[11] This was what Isaac needed. Eliezer's choice was excellent.

Life was not easy for Rebekah, however. She found fulfillment with Isaac, but she was unhappy because she was unable to conceive. She must have identified herself with her mother-in-law in this respect, fearfully wondering if eventually she would be compelled to make the same heart-breaking suggestion Sarah had made to Abraham. "Go in, I pray thee, into my handmaid; it may be that I shall be builded up through her" (16:2). Like Sarah, barrenness must have made her feel incomplete, worried and anxious. If she remained childless, what did the future hold for her?

As in all patriarchal families, when Rebekah married Isaac she joined the camp ruled by his father. And what she saw there must have troubled her. She observed that Abraham, who had married Keturah after Sarah's death, rejected the children he had with her, as he had rejected Ishmael. Excepting only Isaac, Abraham sent all the others away. If Isaac should marry a concubine and have children before she had her own, would he follow primogeniture and send away her sons? Or, if she bore a son who was superior to the oldest, would Isaac have the courage to upset tradition as Abraham had done? Rebekah wondered about the fate of her unborn children. Would none of her sons remain at home, or only one?

Finally, after Rebekah had been barren for twenty years, Isaac took her to Mt. Moriah where he had been bound, and he prayed for a family.[12] When Rebekah did become pregnant, they both rejoiced, but happiness was short-lived for Rebekah. She learned that she was carrying twins, and should they both be boys one would have to be sent away. Rebekah suffered from self-recriminations. She felt she had failed Isaac. By placing him in the predicament of having to choose between his sons, she would add to his anxieties. She knew Isaac was not inclined to send anyone away. He was so timid that throughout his life he had never hurt, much less killed, even an animal. The decision would therefore fall to her. Like Sarah, she would have to expel one son; but Rebekah would be the mother of both. And this would not be the end of it. If she should give birth to more children, she would compound Isaac's suffering, as well as her own and that of the children themselves. As she approached her delivery, Rebekah's apprehension mounted with each passing day.

These were the forces and the characteristics of Isaac and Rebekah as they embarked upon parenthood with all its familial complications.[13]

Even before they saw the light of day, Esau and Jacob, the fraternal or two-egg twins born to Isaac and Rebekah, were unlike in appearance and were hostile and antagonistic to each other. Two-egg (dizygotic) twins are marked by rivalry and lack of mutual sympathy as compared to one-egg or identical (monozygotic) twins, who usually are affectionate, submerge their individual personalities in the pair personality, and look so much alike that even friends have difficulty in telling them apart.[14] Jacob and

Esau were born fighting and competing, and the course of their lives continued in this vein. Jacob cursed the mischance that placed him in the inferior position of the younger son. Although he and Esau were twins, Esau left the sanctuary of the womb first, but with the hand of Jacob clutching his heel, as though he had striven to attain the rights of the first-born, even in the unknowingness of infancy. And, as they grew and matured, they developed into personality types diametrically opposed to each other. Esau had a bent for hunting; Jacob for the quiet life of a shepherd. Their very occupations indicated the difference in temperament.

This twin relationship and that of the only other set of twins recorded in all of Scripture, Perez and Zerah (38:27-30), have led some to conclude that the Jewish people have regarded the birth of twins as a tragic event. Beyond the Book of Genesis, no other such births are recorded, but it does not seem feasible that no more twins worthy of mention were born. Curiously enough, the births of these two sets of twins are described in almost identical fashion. Each set fought to leave the darkness of the womb first. Whereas Esau and Jacob lived in turmoil, the Perez-Zerah incident was also drenched in violence. Prior to their birth, there was the death of Er and Onan; incest; Tamar playing the part of a harlot; Judah's deception of Tamar in withholding Shelah as her husband; and the threat to Tamar of a shameful death. Evidence that giving birth to twins is hereditary[15] might corroborate the contention of the Rabbis that Cain and Abel were born with twin sisters. The lower position accorded females in that early period may explain the omission of the twin sisters in Scripture, while the births of twin boys warranted a detailed description. Twinning may have been quite common, but since the biblical authors saw mainly evil in twin births, they may have intentionally eliminated any further mention of them. In maintaining that competition between twins is keener than between children born singly, modern psychology supports their view. Twins share all vital moments in growing up, with a corresponding loss of individuality and attention. And their relationship is tinged with greater guilt, for they cannot achieve the perfect harmony others attribute to them.[16]

Primitive peoples commonly regarded the birth of twins as abnormal and a portent of evil.[17] They claimed that one child was usually born impotent or sterile, or both—that one twin absorbed the reproductive powers of the other. And because they believed no man can father more than one child at a time, they concluded a woman who gave birth to twins had been unfaithful.[18] Such attitudes probably prevailed among the ancient Jewish people too, as they may still prevail in some cultures.

But since the Jews elevated procreation to the category of *mitzvah,* an obligation, they may have regarded twinning as a curse and an evil. There is no scientific basis for this conclusion, however, as there is none for the contention that twins are not as bright mentally as children born singly.[19]

Primitive peoples also viewed twinning with antagonism because twin pregnancies were more apt to result in abortions, in the weakening of one embryo, and frequently in mutilation resulting in the deformity of one or both of the children. When carried to their term, twin pregnancies were great hazards to the life of the primitive mother and often led to obstetrical complications. Early peoples viewed twinning as unnatural because they regarded it as a reversion to the animal or litter type of bearing. Such a birth took the human aspect away from the children and the father felt no pride in his offspring. Mothers of twins were in disfavor until they next gave birth to a single child.[20] Happily, this attitude no longer prevails in our society. On the contrary, today mothers are generally proud of giving birth to twins. Such a mother takes on added joy and an aura of glamour.[21]

There is yet another cogent and plausible explanation for the negative attitude of the early Hebrews and other peoples, toward twinning. They undoubtedly found among twins a high proportion of left-handed individuals (left-handedness is about twice as prevalent among twins as among the general population)[22] which was a decided disadvantage to a people often at war. A soldier raising a spear or drawing a sword with his left hand, while the one beside him did the same with his right hand, must have caused many a collision and wasteful casualty. Since right-handed people are the majority, the Hebrews assumed that the left-handed were "abnormal." Then, as now, to be different was to be suspected and rejected.

The Book of Judges (20:15-16) tells of seven hundred left-handed Benjamites who were proficient soldiers. That Scripture makes a point of their left-handedness would indicate that this was an exceptional situation. To avoid impairing the fighting efficiency of their warriors, the Benjamites established a unit of only left-handed men sensibly converting their disadvantage into an asset. Excepting this one group, left-handedness must have been frowned upon. Oddly enough, the only other left-handed person mentioned in Scripture was also a member of the tribe of Benjamin. "Ehud the son of Gera, the Benjamite, a man left-handed," the Book of Judges relates (3:15). It would seem that the tribe of Benjamin was prone to left-handedness and to twinning. Being a Benjamite might have been considered a disadvantage.

The Hebrew word for "left-handed" is *'itar yad y'meeno* which literally means "incapable in the use of his right hand." Their language thus conveys the thinking of the early Hebrews. They regarded left-handed people as having lost the natural use of their right hand due to disease, or as the result of an accident, or for some other reason. In other words, they regarded them as crippled. Their discontent with twinning is thus more readily understandable.

Esau and Jacob, once grown, are depicted with their differentiating temperaments and features. Esau was physically superior to his younger twin, as one twin is usually stronger, healthier, and more energetic than the other.[23] But apparently this was his only strength. Although physically inferior to his twin brother, Jacob was more alert. He was a more profound thinker than Esau, and could overlook issues of the moment in favor of taking a long range view. Since he was no match for the robust Esau, Jacob fortified his personal esteem through scholarship. The parents of the twins responded to their differences by taking sides between them. Isaac's favorite was Esau; Rebekah's was Jacob.

The taking of sides might serve as another explanation for the twins' differing personalities.[24] Because Jacob felt rejected by his father, he was forced to regard Isaac as stronger and superior to himself to justify his rejection. He behaved as he thought Isaac expected him to behave, curtailing his masculine activities and suppressing his initiative and individuality. He resorted to solitary tent dwelling and devoted himself to study and to herding sheep. But repressing his antagonism toward his father did not diminish it. On the contrary, Jacob's consciousness of wanting to hurt his father nurtured an inner aggressiveness. Despite his father's rejection of him, or perhaps because of it, Jacob was determined to assert his masculinity. Esau, on the other hand, did not feel rejected by his father. He expressed his masculinity fully by becoming an expert hunter, a man's activity. But feeling rejected by his mother, Esau turned his love toward his father and assumed a feminine attitude toward him. Esau cooked venison for Isaac and waited upon him as a wife would. Another intimation that Esau felt rejected by Rebekah and had homosexual tendencies[25] is found in his poor relationship with the opposite sex and his mistreatment of them on various occasions.[26]

Scripture relates that Isaac sided with Esau "because he did eat of his venison" (25:28). No reason is given for Rebekah's choice. Perhaps Esau's appearance at birth repelled her. One must question whether the reason proffered by the Bible was sufficient to sway Isaac. Could food have meant that much to him? Was Esau a better culinary artist than his mother? Surely Rebekah prepared tempting and wholesome food, far

superior to anything Esau could have cooked for Isaac. Was Isaac influenced in Esau's favor merely because he filled his stomach? It does not
seem likely, but there are more plausible explanations for Isaac's choice,
which account for parents generally having favorites among their offspring.

Since Esau was the older, though only by minutes, Isaac was drawn
to him for that reason. In primitive cultures, the first-born was thought
to possess special qualities inherited from the father, and in greater measure than the later children. Virginity in males, therefore, was highly
valued, since the first son was regarded as the first of the father's strength
(49:3). This was undoubtedly one of the bases for primogeniture, and
for the earnest hope that the first-born would be a male, an attitude still
prevalent today. This had little significance for Rebekah, but Isaac considered Esau the best that was in him.

Also, most fathers take pride in their son's athletic abilities. Esau was
the outdoor type; he was rugged and muscular, having a typical mesomorphic physique. Isaac preferred Esau because he saw in him that which
he personally lacked. He was able to identify himself closely enough to
experience vicariously, through Esau's moments of glory as a hunter, what
he had been unable to accomplish himself. Isaac might have encouraged
Esau's aggressive behavior. Compelled by fear of his mother to be excessively cautious, Isaac might have derived a substitute thrill out of
Esau's riotous living. Rebekah's sympathy, however, embraced her weaker
son. He was not a robust child, but a "tent dweller." He spent his time
with books and devoted his energies to study.[27] As mothers frequently
do, Rebekah felt that Jacob needed protection and she was ever ready to
shield him. A quiet, restrained and homeloving child, Jacob was manage-
able, like his father. Rebekah could retain control and derive pleasure from
Jacob, while providing the protection she felt he needed.

Another reason parents take sides is that they favor the child who
shows them more attention, and Esau doted on Isaac. When he brought
his father venison, he would say, "Father, this is especially for you,"
and Isaac was impressed. The Midrash pictures Esau as thoughtful and
considerate of Isaac. Whenever he went hunting he brought the choicest
edible parts of the animal to Isaac[28] and attended upon him in royal
robes.[29] Later, when he decided to kill Jacob, Esau was prepared to wait
until after Isaac's death (27:41) to spare his father the knowledge that
one of his sons killed the other. It was Esau's over-solicitousness of his
father that caused Isaac to make the same mistake Abraham had made with
young Ishmael. Neither Abraham nor Isaac was critical enough of the

behavior of the oldest son. They closed their eyes to the faults of the
first-born and were too lenient. Lacking discipline, both Ishmael and Esau
fell into depravity as adults.[30] The Midrash calls attention to this error.
The Rabbis maintain that a father who disciplines his son is more loved
and more honored by his son than a father who does not.[31]

Rebekah was convinced, however, that Esau was taking unfair advantage of his blind father. She recognized the deceit that Isaac could not
see. Partial to Esau, Isaac could not admit, even to himself, that his child
was capable of committing a great wrong. Rebekah was saddened to see
that Esau was as cunning at home as he was in the field.[32] She heard
Esau ingratiate himself to Isaac by asking: "Father, how does one tithe
salt?" "How does one tithe straw?"[33] when he was aware that these items
were not subject to tithing. His false piety was designed to convince Isaac
that he was a most devout and religious son. Unable to perceive the craftiness of these queries, Isaac was impressed. This angered Rebekah and
she determined to help Jacob all the more, not only out of love and
concern for Jacob, but to punish Esau's deceit.[34]

Rebekah also learned that her oldest son ensnared married women and
violated them, and yet when he attained his fortieth birthday he compared
himself to Isaac, saying, "As my father was forty years old when he
married, so will I marry at the age of forty."[35]

It was common knowledge that Esau was frequently promiscuous,[36]
and that he tortured animals and trussed together deer and birds that he
captured.[37] People wished him luck when he hunted, for they knew that
if he did not bag any game he robbed and plundered instead.[38] Esau
behaved like an irresponsible psychopath, and his physical structure conformed to that of delinquents recently studied.[39] On the average, they
are heavier than non-delinquents and frequently of mesomorphic build.
They tend to be physically solid, closely knit, large and muscular. In
comparison to non-delinquents, they have greater strength and more vitality.
Their physical characteristics often include wide shoulders and chest, a
tapering torso, heavy arms, strong neck, and usually a small face. Ishmael
and Esau seem to have been homologous in physique, as they were in
behavior. Like other delinquents, their approach to problems was direct,
and they were extrovertive and sadistic. Also adventurous and unconven-
tional, they harbored life-long resentments, and were non-submissive to
authority. Tradition relates that Abraham lived five years less than Isaac
so that he would not know that his grandson, Esau, had raped a betrothed
maiden and committed murder.[40] A similar tradition circulated regarding
Isaac's blindness; God made his eyes weak so that he would not see

Esau's wickedness and would be confined indoors, where no one could point him out as Esau's father.[41]

At another time, Rebekah overheard Jacob ask Esau whether he wished to be buried in the Cave of Machpelah. "Do I want burial!" he exclaimed. "Give me money and take the burial for yourself, but you must heap up much money for it."[42] Esau's irreverent dismissal of the honored burial place shocked Rebekah. Sarah had been tenderly laid to rest in the Cave of Machpelah, and Abraham had instructed that he should be buried there, and his successor Isaac, and Isaac's wife. This, then, would be her own resting place, and Rebekah was hurt to know that her son would callously offer to sell his right to share it. She heard Esau make fun of Isaac's spiritual ideals at every opportunity, while he continued to cater to his father. For many years Esau openly urged Jacob to marry one of the girls of the land, as he had done.[43] Esau was insincere, and Rebekah knew it. But all this was trivial in the face of one particular act in which Esau participated. Rebekah saw Esau sell his birthright to his younger brother for a mess of pottage.

Many have used this incident to castigate Jacob and portray him in a poor light. They argue that it was heinous of Jacob to take advantage of Esau when he was dying of hunger. It would be helpful, however, to analyze this situation more closely, viewing it objectively rather than emotionally.

Scripture describes Isaac as a very wealthy man (26:12-14). He owned many servants and certainly had an abundance and variety of food in the camp. When Esau returned home from a day in the field, he could have asked the servants to prepare some food for him, and they would have done it without question. Instead, when he saw Jacob preparing lentils, Esau asked him for some. Abraham had died that day, and lentils were the traditional food symbolizing mourning and immortality.[44] Jacob was willing to give him some, but for a price.

Jacob was grieved by his grandfather's death and conscious of the change in his father's status. Isaac had become the patriarch that day, and Jacob began to understand the meaning of heritage. Abraham's legacy to Isaac was a way of life. But after Isaac, what then? Would Esau live as Abraham had lived? Could he change that much? Jacob realized that Abraham's immortality was an uncertain thing in Esau's hands. Knowing how little Esau valued the birthright, Jacob subtly belittled him. Yes, he toyed with him, he would give him some lentils—in exchange for the birthright.

Esau could have refused. If Jacob would not give him some, he could have asked the servants to prepare a meal for him. Instead, he replied to

Jacob's proposition directly: "Behold, I am at the point to die; and what profit shall the birthright do to me?" (25:33). Jacob was right. The birthright meant nothing to Esau. Satisfying his appetite of the moment meant more to him than his future—he had no appreciation of the spiritual. Watching this scene, Rebekah rebelled against all of Esau's pretenses. He was misleading Isaac too much and she could not tolerate it. Her affection and loyalty gravitated toward Jacob, whose temperament and values were opposite to Esau's. Because Jacob controlled his passions in order to secure the future, Rebekah felt he deserved her support.

Maurice Samuels' argument, however, is well taken. He observes that Jacob's ignobility is predicated upon the assumption that not a morsel of food was in the entire camp, that only Jacob's lentils were available. This is a rather far-fetched assumption, but for the sake of argument let us admit to it. Esau asked Jacob for some of his food lest he die. If Jacob was the scoundrel that some believe him to have been, and if he was anxious for the birthright at any price, there was no need to make a deal with Esau. He could simply have let Esau starve to death and the birthright would have been his by virtue of inheritance. Judging Jacob harshly is therefore unfair. Besides, Scripture states that "Esau despised the birthright" (25:34). Why is Esau described as despising the birthright if he sold it only under duress? It is because Esau was not under compulsion to sell that Scripture states "Esau despised the birthright."

Rebekah saw all this. Like any mother who sees her children virtually every waking moment, she knew her sons well. Her affections had always been drawn to Jacob, the docile and well-behaved child. Both had attended school until they were thirteen years old,[45] but Jacob continued his studies, whereas Esau, unknown to his father, worshipped idols.[46] And the more Rebekah saw Jacob immerse himself in study, the more deeply she loved him.[47] Now she saw that Jacob was not as docile as she had imagined; he was capable of indignation. Although Jacob was enraged by his brother's attitude, she saw that he controlled his temper in order to steer clear of trouble.

After having witnessed the bartering of the birthright, the apprehension that had disturbed Rebekah before the birth of her twin sons swelled into fear. The spiritual heritage of Isaac and Abraham meant nothing to Esau. Rebekah knew it and Jacob knew it. Esau must have known it, too, for he had offered to sell both the burial and the birthright. The rights of the first-born would have cost him too dearly, and in strange coin. The power of a patriarch was no bargain when the price was responsibility to the growing camp founded by Abraham. The honor of leadership paled against the self-discipline it would demand. No, Esau preferred the material pleasures of the moment to the intangibles of the spiritual, but to admit it even to himself would have signified weakness.

Too occupied in his younger years, and blind in his advanced age, Isaac had never observed his sons in their daily pursuits. Since he did not know them, he drew his conclusions from their attentions to him. Jacob, the introvert, kept to himself and his studies and resolved his conflicts by intro-spection.[48] Isaac did not see his true piety nor was he familiar with his deeds. But Esau, the extrovert, always had something to say. And where his father was concerned, Rebekah realized, he usually said what Isaac wanted to hear. She suddenly realized that Esau was misleading himself as well as his father. His pretended piety would soon trip him in the role of patriarch. He was ill-suited to bear his father's great heritage and furthermore he did not really want it. After Isaac's death Esau would continue to violate the ideals for which the tribe existed. Then it would be a only a question of time before his leadership would be challenged. With alarming clarity Rebekah saw Esau's future filled with strife. Unless something was done to avert it, his violent death seemed a certainty. Rebekah was equally convinced that Jacob truly deserved both the birth-right and the blessing that accompanied it. If ever a showdown came, she decided she would do everything in her power to divert the legacy of the first-born from her older son to the younger. Rebekah was not overly ambitious, nor did she reject one son in favor of the other, as some claim; but in order to give each son the opportunity to live in the best possible way, she did encourage flouting the law of primogeniture. With the same spirit and determination that won her a proposal of marriage to Isaac, she prepared to manipulate her sons' destinies.

There is yet another possibility to explore in the Isaac-Esau relation-ship, one which may have been obvious to Rebekah. Perhaps Isaac knew his children far better than we have surmised. If Isaac ranked Esau far below Jacob in ability, then he may have gone out of his way to make him feel wanted. He extolled his one forte—he was a mighty hunter like Nimrod[49] (10:9)—and he praised his venison. Rebekah could not have failed to observe his solicitous behavior toward Esau, and certainly she knew Isaac's undiscriminating taste in food. She capitalized on these two facets of Isaac's personality to implement her plan. Isaac ate the vile-tasting meat of the kid,[50] and thought it was venison because he believed Esau served it to him. Rebekah was right, for when Esau later returned with venison, Isaac asked him: "Who then is he that hath taken venison, and brought it to me, and I have eaten of all before thou comest?" (27:33).

The Rabbis relate that Esau asked his father what he actually ate, and the reply indicates they understood his extravagant praise of Esau's venison. "I do not know," Isaac said, "but I tasted in it the taste of bread, the taste of meat, the taste of fish, the taste of locusts, and the taste of all the delicacies in the world."[51]

Isaac felt he could not hurt his son by failing to recognize the one talent that he possessed. He went too far, however. Despite the fact that Esau had married two Hittite women who "were a bitterness of spirit to Isaac and to Rebekah" (26:34-35), and despite the fact that Abraham had instructed him to give the birthright to Jacob,[52] Isaac lacked the courage to make Esau the Ishmael of the family. He believed Esau unfit for the blessing, and it was within his power to withhold it, but Isaac shrank from making the decision. The problem became acute when Isaac told Esau that he would bless him, in accordance with the rule of primogeniture. Rebekah's earlier fears proved well founded, for she knew her husband well. To rectify the situation Rebekah mapped a daring offensive which would challenge this rule.

When Rebekah proposed to Jacob that he pose as Esau, he rebelled, for tradition holds deceiving one's father tantamount to idol worship.[53] He could not flatly disagree with his mother, however. He respected her too much for that, and he did not want to hurt her. So he argued with Rebekah, comparing his smooth skin to Esau's hairy frame. He said to her, in effect, "Mother, please forget it. Esau and I are so different, Father will easily detect the ruse. Then, instead of a blessing, I'll receive a curse, and you will be blamed for it." Rebekah persisted, "Upon me be thy curse" (27:13). If Isaac should uncover their scheme, Rebekah stood ready to accept all the blame. When a person is evil, she assured Jacob, his mother is cursed, since evil is attributed to poor upbringing.[54] Besides, she argued, she was already cursed by Esau's behavior, so "upon me be thy curse" too. Still unable to convince Jacob, she threatened to go to Isaac and declare Jacob the righteous son and Esau the wicked one. Under constraint, and to prevent her from doing this, Jacob did his mother's bidding "bowed down, and weeping."[55]

Since Jacob had no way out, and perhaps even enjoyed the prospect, he fell in with his mother's plot. And it worked! But it was not easy for this mild-mannered, retiring individual to go through with it. Perspiration broke out all over him and his heart pounded. His conscience urged him to leave his father's room before the deception went any further,[56] but he persisted and won the blessing away from Esau. To Jacob's surprise and utter relief, when Isaac became aware of the misrepresentation, he was ready to accept the outcome. Isaac did not argue about the scheme with Rebekah, nor did he reproach Jacob. It seemed that Isaac was also relieved. By seizing the initiative, Rebekah had brought about Isaac's unexpressed wish and released him from responsibility for it. Once the break with primogeniture was made, Isaac did not bequeath the greater share of his possessions to Esau. The sons themselves decided upon the division of their inheritance.[57] This may have assuaged a subconscious guilt Isaac felt for passively allowing a major change to take place, when he, the patriarch, should have been the prime mover. Or he might have wanted to assure Esau that he had not totally abandoned him. Esau also accepted the result with no outward show of emotion. When Isaac apologetically informed Esau of what had transpired, he replied simply, "and he (Jacob) shall be blessed" (27:33). Jacob had expected a more emphatic response to the bizarre plot, but he was thankful that it did not materialize.

To render a deception complete, the individual's five senses—sight, hearing, touch, taste and smell—must be duped. Isaac was blind, and Rebekah deliberately controlled the three senses within her power. To cope with the sense of smell, she "took the choicest garments of Esau her elder son" (27:15); to overcome the sense of taste, she "made savoury food, such as his father loved" (27:14); to deal with the sense of touch, "she put the skins of goats upon his hands, and upon the smooth of his neck" (27:16). Hearing depended on Jacob's voice, and this almost gave him away.

Jacob comes in for his share of castigation for this act as well as his mother. But, again, let us examine the situation in another perspective.

Esau's claim that he was "robbed" reflects his lack of intelligence more than Jacob's alleged lack of honesty. Esau should have understood that the birthright and the blessing were inseparable; the blessing implemented the birthright and gave it official sanction, like an oath of office. He knew he had sold the birthright to Jacob, but if he was simple-minded he may have thought it was irrevocably his because he was older. Esau could not have persisted in this misconception if he comprehended the relationships within his immediate family. He must have known Abraham designated Isaac, Esau's own father, for both the birthright and the blessing, revoking them from the older Ishmael. Therefore, if he had no intention of letting the deal stand, he could have eaten the lentils and then told Jacob the contract was off, that he was not serious about it. Certainly Jacob would not have argued with him about it. Since Esau said nothing, he apparently accepted Jacob's terms with respect to both the birthright and the blessing. Why, then, should Esau have claimed that he was robbed? In this light, Jacob cannot fairly be accused of stealing something for which he had paid a price, meager though it was.

After the sale of the birthright, an even greater hostility ensued between the brothers. The full impact is felt in the verse "And Esau hated Jacob" (27:41). He was filled with hatred, hostility and vindictiveness.[58] This is the first time that the word "hate" is used in their relationship. Esau did not hate Jacob after selling him his birthright, but now that he lost the blessing, he did. Either Esau was not fully aware of the consequences of his sale or he was a simpleton. Regardless, losing the benison filled him with such a passionate hatred of Jacob that he planned to kill him. When Cain killed Abel, he reasoned, God did nothing drastic to him. But Cain had misjudged the situation, Esau realized, for Adam eventually begot another son who inherited the world with Cain. Esau would outdo Cain; he would kill his father first and then Jacob, thereby inheriting the entire estate.[59] But he soon dismissed this thought.

Rebekah learned of Esau's plan. Since she loved both sons, even though she could not feel close to Esau, she did not want either of them hurt. Although Jacob did not display his prowess as Esau did, he was strong enough to lift the stone off the well for Rachel. Rebekah believed that Jacob was physically capable of dealing with Esau if attacked by him, and could possibly kill him. Then Esau's sons would avenge their father's death by killing Jacob. In this event, Rebekah would suffer a double loss. Or a more immediate prospect was the possibility that, if Esau tried to kill Jacob, they might mortally wound each other. In counseling her beloved Jacob to leave home, Rebekah pleaded, "Why should I be bereaved of you both in one day?" (27:45). Her relationship with Esau was more than superficial, as evidenced in the verse, "And Rebekah took the choicest garments of Esau her eldest son, which were with her in the house" (27:15). Although he had two wives, Esau left his clothes with his mother. And not once did he blame his mother for his loss of the blessing. The strong attachment between them enabled Rebekah to identify with Esau, too, and to exclude herself from her own plot against him. When she advised Jacob to flee to her brother Laban, to remain with him until Esau's anger abated, she added, "And he forget that which *thou* hast done to him" (27:45).

Rebekah's diplomacy must be admired. She first advised Jacob, in the interest of safety, to go to her brother, Laban. Then, withholding the fact that she had already counseled Jacob to leave (27:42-45), she spoke to Isaac. If Jacob should remain at home, she explained, he might marry a Hittite woman, and such a marriage would render her life meaningless.

Isaac did exactly what Rebekah hoped for. He called Jacob to him and instructed him to go to Paddan-aram, to his mother's family, to choose a wife (28:1-2). Rebekah's discreet manipulation of Isaac averted a tragedy. It is interesting to note that in their conversation Isaac did not reprimand Jacob for spiriting the blessing away from Esau. He could hardly preach fairness to Jacob, when he was guilty of unfair partiality toward Esau. So Isaac did not mention the incident.

Rebekah miscalculated in this instance, however. It was her only error. When she urged Jacob to leave, she said, "and tarry with him a few days, until thy brother's fury turn away . . . and he forget that which thou hast done to him" (27:44-45). She anticipated that Esau would forget this experience quickly and that Jacob would be gone only a short time. She misjudged, however, for she never saw Jacob again. Furthermore, her fears were realized. She, not Isaac, sent her son away.

After this incident, Esau's behavior pattern did not vary. In order to mollify his father's opposition to Canaanite daughters-in-law, Esau married Ishmael's daughter, Mahalath (28:8-9). He wanted Isaac to believe that he married his cousin because it would please him, but the Rabbis suggested an additional motive for his marrying Mahalath.[60] Esau presumed that by marrying Ishmael's daugher he would gain an ally in his dispute with Jacob over the birthright. Since Ishmael had experienced a similar relationship with Isaac, Esau expected his father-in-law to come to his aid. Esau hoped that Ishmael, because of his daughter, would express his repressed resentment against Isaac by killing Jacob. As a blood kinsman to Jacob, Esau would then be "compelled" to kill Ishmael, thereby inheriting the fortunes of both Ishmael and Isaac. In offering this hypothetical motive, the Rabbis left unexplained a serious obstacle to its realization. How could Esau have hoped to obtain his father-in-law's estate when Ishmael's sons had inheritance rights? The possibility of further bloodshed would seem unlimited.

Some believe, however, that Esau sincerely meant to reform.[61] Perhaps he did, since he never again complained of being treated unjustly. His grudge against Jacob seems to have vanished. He might have finally accepted his limitations and realized that he was not cut out for the blessing.

II

Upon leaving home, Jacob was beset by fear of the future. He felt a kinship with Cain for, like his ancestor, he became a wanderer because of rivalry with his brother. In the field where he slept on his first night away from home he had a dream. Jacob envisioned a ladder extending

from heaven to earth with angels running up and down on it (28:12).
According to Freud, ladders, steps, or staircases unquestionably designate
an act of copulation. He finds the comparison facile since the rhythmical
pattern of coitus is reproduced in ascending and descending stairs.[62] This
interpretation, however, is at variance with the intent of the Midrash,
which claims that Jacob had never had any thoughts regarding sex.[63]
According to Freud, Jacob's dream indicates that he had repressed his
sexual drives. And, after the sublimated sexual experience of his dream,
Jacob readily succumbed to Rachel's physical appeal.

Although the father of modern psychology differs with the Midrash,
other psychiatrists support the contention of the Rabbis that the ladder
symbolism is not necessarily sexual in implication. Seeing Jacob's dream
as an unconscious preparation for the future, Adler would interpret the
ladder as the steps Jacob would take toward asserting himself in his new
environment. Jung would have found in it the progressive realization of
his unconscious wisdom, his ability to transcend his present spiritual limitations. Wolff and Fromm would have found a synthesis of both the
behavioristic and the spiritual, as well as the sexual, for Jacob's subsequent
growth to the ultimate role of patriarch did proceed on all three levels.
Dr. Marshall L. Fisher, formerly of the Charlotte (N. C.) Mental Health
Clinic, prefers to interpret dreams involving ladders as a subconscious
desire to climb heights, to elevate one's standing, and thereby one's
self-esteem. This view could readily explain Jacob's dream of a ladder.
A fugitive from a complex and potentially explosive situation, Jacob
for the first time faced an uncertain future alone. His dream suggested at
least the possibility that he could ascend from his insignificant position.

At first, Jacob did not fare well. He trusted his crafty uncle, who
exploited him and milked every ounce of usefulness out of him. It was
after fourteen years of virtual servitude that Jacob first utilized his ingenuity, but he finally outmaneuvered his wily kinsman. Having assumed
the responsibilities of a family (and Jacob was blessed with many children)
circumstances forced him to alter his personality. Jacob overcame many
obstacles and acquired flocks and herds. But, when his mother's maid,
Deborah, came to summon him home, he claimed that he was in no position to leave.[64] His parents were growing old, she told him, and wanted
him to return to Canaan to look after them and to take up his duties
on Isaac's death. Jacob protested that Laban refused him permission to
leave (30:25-26). Besides, Jacob complained, such a trip would be a
hardship for his wives and their many small children, and he was too
poor to outfit a caravan with provisions for such a journey.

Jacob's reluctance to break away was in fact an unwillingness to go home. After fourteen years, the scars were still tender. Isaac had originally favored Esau, and Jacob still felt insecure in relation to his father. But the heaviest blow had come from his mother on the day of his departure. Rebekah had contrived the plot and urged his participation, yet she allowed the full responsibility for it to fall ultimately upon him. Resentment of his parents deterred Jacob from returning until six years later, when he detected the plot of Laban's sons to kill him. Then he was compelled to flee with his family and possessions.

Twenty years had elapsed since Jacob left his parental home. Now he was returning to his family as a conquering hero. He was a man of means —far more successful than he could have imagined when he was a fugitive. His moment of glory, however, was abruptly dispelled. Messengers from Rebekah brought him the appalling news that Esau and a company of four hundred men were approaching. To steady himself, Jacob inquired about his parents' health. His mother was still looking out for him, he learned, for she had also sent advice. She suggested that he take counsel with himself and consider what he would do when he and Esau met. "When he cometh up to you, supplicate him, and do not speak roughly to him, and give him a present from what you possess, and from what God has favored you with. And when he asks concerning your affairs, conceal nothing from him, perhaps he may turn from his anger against you, and you will thereby save your soul, you and all belonging to you, for it is your duty to honor him, since he is your elder brother."[65] Seized with anxiety and distress, Jacob wept bitterly. Beneath his mother's genuine concern and thoughtfulness lay the assertion of his guilt as it had twenty years before. But Jacob's hurt and resentment of his mother were overshadowed by the impending encounter with his brother. Since he could not know Esau's intentions, he decided to follow Rebekah's advice.

Jacob tried to avert what he thought could be the fatal showdown. He sent a message to Esau stating, "If you are prepared for peace, I am with you; and if for war, I am ready for you."[66] He included God's name in this notice,[67] thereby advising Esau to tread lightly since the Lord was on his side. Furthermore, he informed Esau, he was no longer the retiring person who left home; he was more self-assertive.[68] The message which was meant to impress Esau of his stature also bolstered Jacob's estimate of himself.

That night an unknown assailant accosted Jacob and they wrestled until day-break. They fought to the finish; there was no surrender. Nor could Jacob call upon anyone for assistance. If he would prevail, he must do it alone. Jacob left the field of battle in victory. Victory, however, often exacts its price. Jacob was crippled; he limped upon his thigh" (32:32).

Although the actual identity of Jacob's adversary is unimportant, it is commonly agreed that Jacob wrestled with himself that night. He contested with his past, and his future was at stake. Jacob faced a great crisis in his life. It was a moment of decision! He thought he had successfully buried his past experiences with Esau. For years he had hardly thought of his older brother, but the moment he heard his brother's name the entire past came alive to torment him. The tensions of the past were as real as if they had just erupted. The day of reckoning had arrived; he was to face Esau on the morrow.

Without doubt Esau had been wronged, and Jacob admitted his part in the conspiracy. His experiences after leaving home put his actions in clearer perspective. At his Uncle Laban's home he was exploited, like Esau, in an underhanded and conniving manner. His agreement with Laban called for seven years labor in exchange for Rachel's hand in marriage. At the end of the term, Laban surreptitiously gave him Leah and required him to labor seven additional years for Rachel. In a conversation the Rabbis report having taken place on the morning after the marriage to Leah, she forcefully brought to his attention the parallel between Laban's deception of him and his own treatment of Isaac. Throughout the night, the narrative relates, Jacob called her "Rachel" and Leah answered him. In the morning, when he found that it was Leah, he exclaimed, "You are a deceiver and the daughter of a deceiver!" Leah retorted, "Is there a teacher without pupils? Did not your father call you 'Esau' and you answered him? So did you call me and I answered you."[69] From that moment, Jacob lived with guilt.

The memory of this conversation recalled to Jacob his many misdeeds in relation to Esau and the birthright. He had lied and deceived his blind and trusting father; he had shrewdly taken advantage of his own brother. He had not deterred his mother from going through with the plan when she said, "Thy curse be on me." An unselfish son would not have permitted his mother to place herself in such jeopardy. His protest was too weak. He argued against the plan, not because he found it morally indefensible, but because he was afraid it would fail. He followed through with it because he really wanted the blessing. Now Jacob's only defense was that he did not comprehend at the time all that was involved.

His cousins had accused him of appropriating their father's wealth, complaining, "Jacob had taken away all that was our father's" (31:1).

They went further and clamored, "Of that which was our father's hath he gotten all this wealth" (31:1). Laban's resentment and jealousy of his prosperity reminded him of his own displeasure with Esau for possessing the birthright. And, just as he was angry at Laban for the way he had been treated, having complained to his wives, "Your father hath mocked me, and changed my wages ten times" (31:7), Jacob could understand Esau's feelings toward him. Jacob finally realized that Esau was thoroughly justified in hating him.

Jacob felt a compulsion to make up with his brother and beg his forgiveness. He knew that regret could not erase his misdemeanor, nor could penitence on the Day of Atonement undo his wrong against him.[70] Unless he personally sought Esau's forgiveness—face to face—his confession would remain forever locked within him, incapable of communication, and understanding could never flow between them. Jacob wanted to feel whole again, to regain some measure of self-acceptance. But how would Esau respond? Would he greet him as a brother, or as an enemy? Feelings of insecurity cropped up again and Jacob sought a way to avert his brother's wrath. While he lived with Laban he was compelled to rely upon his cunning. He had learned intrigue and furtiveness, but now he wanted to deal with his brother in a wholesome and straightforward manner. He felt he had to undergo a transformation. In his inner turmoil, Jacob punished himself severely. How could he avoid it as he looked at the naked truth? In this crippling experience, the spiritual confrontation of self, Jacob saw himself as an inferior human being. He had never acted, but only reacted to the people around him, as if inanimate or incapable of setting himself in motion. For the first time in his life Jacob was fully aware of his responsibility to himself. He deliberately chose to risk a meeting with Esau, and assumed the responsibility for the consequences. In resolving to commit an act of his own, Jacob discovered his freedom and the meaning of his life. He was finished with solitude, escape and retreat, with waiting for others to make the first move. His freedom acquired worth in the commitment to meet his adversary, or his brother, or whatever might come, not defensively but on his own terms. Conserving his life was no longer enough; Jacob had discovered how to live it. By substituting action for inertia, Jacob became a different person. He attained a deeper and more profound personal insight together with a new and more meaningful name, Israel. His new attitude marked his psychological rebirth.[71] He underwent a conversion.

While recognizing his limitations and his halting gait, Jacob discovered that he could move forward on the strength of his new insights and inner God-given energy. When he first met Esau, Jacob followed his mother's advice. He bowed down before him seven times and soothed him with humble words. He abashed himself before his older brother, calling him "my lord" eight different times. But then Jacob noted Esau's ambivalence. If Esau was forgiving, why did he have a force of four hundred men with him (33:1)? But if he still sought vengeance, why did Esau kiss him (33:4)? Originally Esau intended to attack Jacob, but when he saw his brother his hostility turned to reconciliation.[72] Jacob was relieved to learn that Esau no longer carried the grudge of many years ago. On the contrary, his attitude was quite the reverse. Esau clearly relinquished his claim to the blessing by saying, "My brother, let that which thou hast be thine" (33:9).[73]

Esau's change of heart followed the usual pattern of cases where bitter hatred engenders thoughts of injuring or killing a sibling or a parent. Feelings of hatred are gradually submerged and disappear, and are replaced by tenderness and delicate sentiments toward the hated persons. This change serves to undo all the harm they had conceived or wished upon them.[74] This would explain why Esau, after wishing for his father's death (27:41), married a girl more acceptable to Isaac (28:8-9).

A most valuable and important psychological truth is depicted in the events leading to the meeting of Jacob and Esau—the need to face our inadequacies, to encounter ourselves, and to forge a new and more adequate mode or pattern of behavior. Jacob's life, like that of all humans, consisted of a mixture of the base and the noble. It is essential that man recognize this and establish a Jacob's ladder reaching from the lowest strata of human personality to the noblest traits of which man is capable. Grappling with the experience of emotional rebirth, Jacob personified man's struggle for mastery of himself.

At the same time, Jacob realized something even more valuable. In acquiring the birthright he had compromised with the ethical. His goal was not to attain the material wealth of his father; rather he sought the spiritual heritage and the privilege of transmitting it to future generations. Now he recognized that he could not occupy his lofty position with a breach of honor standing between him and his brother. Jacob was ashamed of himself; he realized that he was morally lame.

At this point, some people lose their courage and back away from personal responsibility. Such a person will acknowledge his faults and admit that he knows how to rectify them, but upon the slightest excuse will continue in them. Jacob stood firm, however, a mature man who had earned the right to become his father's spiritual heir. Because he did not flee coward-like when he faced the agonizing truth about himself, Jacob became Israel in the full sense of the term—a true child of God and a leader of the people to be called by his name, "the children of Israel."

Although Jacob had gone through a transformation and although Esau had greeted him with kindness and consideration, the rapprochement was not genuine. The memories of the past were not wholly erased. Awareness of their capacity to hurt each other incurred mutual distrust and suspicion, an attitude their children adopted from their fathers' example, and one which still limits mankind's capacity for cooperation. When Esau suggested that they travel together, Jacob proposed that Esau go on ahead because he was encumbered with family and flocks. In reality, Jacob wanted to stay away from him, for he was still not convinced that Esau had no intention of harming him.[75] It is also possible that Jacob still suffered from guilt and wished to avoid being reminded of it every time he looked at Esau. The reconciliation lacked depth; each brother had matured in his own way, but remained unable to fathom the other.

Another valuable insight is that a handicap is not necessarily a hindrance. Jacob's progress, his future, did not come to a halt because he limped. Jacob continued to grow after this experience, attaining an emotional maturity and a spiritual growth beyond his reach in his youth. Only when one discerns his own weakness can he elevate himself into maturity. Jacob acknowledged his dependence upon his mother, and went on to new relationships; he admitted his fear of his brother and by confronting him bravely he was not compelled to fight. Like Jacob, no man needs to dissipate his energy in anti-social or unproductive tactics. When he accepts his limitations he no longer needs to defend and maintain them. He can forget his figurative limp and approach new and worthier goals with a steady step. Great personalities throughout history, as well as countless unsung heroes, have attained nobility not only in spite of their handicaps, but often because of them.

CHAPTER SIX

He Loved Rachel More Than Leah

(Genesis 29:30)

JACOB'S family life was in constant turmoil, not only in regard to his struggle with his brother and the partiality of his parents, but also concerning his marriage relationships. It began on a doleful note when his uncle and intended father-in-law, Laban, deceived him by giving him a wife for whom he had not bargained. As a result of this duplicity, Jacob found himself married to two sisters. This was not an unusual situation in a polygamous society, but the circumstances under which Rachel and Leah became his wives were most unusual.

When Jacob ran away from home, Esau ordered his son, Eliphaz, to pursue him and to kill him. Influenced by Isaac's teachings, however, Eliphaz was reluctant to kill his uncle. But since the poor were regarded as dead,[1] he decided to obey his father by seizing all of Jacob's possessions. So Jacob arrived at his Uncle Laban's house with nothing but the clothes on his back. His poverty thus contributed to Jacob's peculiar situation, for having more than one wife was a sign of affluence.

On Jacob's first encounter with his cousin Rachel at the well where she had come to water her father's flock, he fell in love at first sight. He kissed her (one of the few instances recorded in the Bible of a man kissing a woman) and soon thereafter asked her father's permission to marry her. Since he had nothing to offer Laban as the price for his bride, Jacob agreed to terms that were not exceptional at the time—he would render seven years labor for Rachel's hand.[2] It has also been suggested that if Rachel was too young for marriage, seven years might have been stipulated to give her time to mature.[3]

Although he was a pauper and no longer young (his age is placed at seventy-seven),[4] Jacob impressed his uncle favorably. Rachel and Leah also accepted him without reservation, for Rachel was willing, even eager, to marry him and Leah was prepared to defraud her sister to become his

98

wife. And so it happened. On Rachel's wedding night, Laban substituted her older sister, or older twin sister.[5] When Jacob protested, Laban announced it was not their custom to give the younger daughter in marriage before the older (29:26). He might have gambled that Leah would marry long before Rachel's seven-year betrothal would culminate in marriage; then he could have kept his bargain without violating the privilege of the first-born. Or Laban might have kept silent about the right of the first-born in the initial bargain in the hope that Jacob could be tricked into serving him another seven years for Rachel.[6]

Rachel knew her marriage would be an affront not only to her older sister but also to the customs of her people, and she warned Jacob that Laban would resort to treachery to prevent it. To avoid a misunderstanding when he confirmed his agreement with Laban, Jacob cautiously specified "for Rachel, thy younger daughter" (29:18): for Rachel—not for Leah; thy daughter—not some other woman from the market place; younger—you are not to exchange their names.[7] In addition, Jacob and Rachel devised signals so that he would recognize her in the dark on their wedding night:[8] Rachel would touch his right toe, his right thumb, and the lobe of his right ear.[9] Then, when Jacob saw that all the candles had been extinguished before his bride entered the chamber, he became alarmed and accused Laban of trickery. Decency required it,[10] Laban explained, and Jacob was satisfied, secure in the belief that he had covered every loophole.

Laban's promoting one sister over the other could be expected to cause bitterness, but no harsh words passed between the sisters at that time. Rachel was ambivalent. She was torn between her desire to marry Jacob and her duty to obey her father and to honor her older sister. Could she rebel against a system that took no cognizance of her rights? Yes, she could have called a halt to the subterfuge, but at the last moment she decided to submerge her own desires and to aid Leah. She felt that she should have been a bride before Leah, and that if she sent the warning "Beware, you are being deceived," Jacob would have refrained, but Rachel accepted the inferiority attributed by primogeniture to the younger child. "If I am not worthy that the world be built through me, let it be built up through my sister,"[11] she thought. Against her own interests, Rachel became an active participant in the ruse perpetrated against Jacob. To spare her sister embarrassment, she divulged to Leah the signs upon which she and Jacob had agreed.[12] Her sympathy for her sister's feelings led one commentator to suggest that Rachel hid beneath the nuptial bed and replied when Jacob spoke, so that Leah's voice would not betray her.[13] In renouncing her bethrothal, Rachel displayed great restraint and perhaps even greater sensitivity to her sister. Without her help, the switch obviously could not have been made.

To sustain the deception, Rachel allowed her maid to take the place of Leah's. According to custom, the daughters' handmaids became part of their dowries; the older handmaid went in marriage with the older sister, and the younger handmaid with the younger sister. So Laban gave Zilpah, who Jacob knew to be Rachel's handmaid, to Leah as her marriage portion. When Jacob saw her he was none the wiser.[14]

Throughout it all, Leah did not object to taking part in the deception. When Jacob called her "Rachel" on their wedding night, she answered him, assuming her sister's identification[15] (if we cannot accept that Rachel was actually in the room with them). Leah was prepared to do anything that would make her Jacob's wife, for she, too, was fighting predetermination.

Mingling with the people at the crossroads, Leah had overheard some gossip that concerned her. Her father, she learned, had agreed to allow Rebekah to marry Isaac on the condition that if Rebekah bore sons they would marry his daughters—the older son to the older daughter and the younger son to the younger daughter. Leah inquired of travelers how Rebekah's older son conducted himself and was distressed to learn that Esau was a robber and a murderer, a villainous character. She sought information about the younger son and when she learned that he was a "quiet man dwelling in tents," she cried, "My sister and I came from the same womb; shall Rachel marry the righteous Jacob and I the wicked Esau?" What did it avail her that she was born before her sister? Leah prayed the Almighty to spare her such a marriage; she felt she did not deserve to be bound to a man like Esau.

Rachel may have pitied Leah, for apparently she lacked much with which to attract a husband. She must have been physically weaker than Rachel, who was robust enough to care for the flock, and whatever natural beauty she had was marred by her excessive weeping. She fasted and bemoaned the fate her father had arranged for her until her eyesight was impaired (29:17) and her eyelashes dropped from her lids.[16] Also, Esau was long overdue in making good his mother's pledge; the insult must have hurt Leah as much as the anticipated injury. Rachel may have realized that tricking Jacob offered Leah her only prospect for marriage.

Although neither Rachel nor Leah dared rebel against their father's strict adherence to primogeniture, they knew that the Hebrews had begun to take exception to the rule. Jacob's father had superceded his older brother, and Jacob's presence in Laban's household was the result of such a rebellion. Leah must have realized that the chicanery they were about to employ to enforce her rights might work to her disadvantage. Nevertheless, she displayed an air of optimism, and willingly risked unfavorable consequences. Unfortunately, things did not work out as well as she had hoped. Her marriage to Jacob did not put an end to her weeping, for Jacob hated her and treated her with disdain (29:33). His aversion for her began the morning after the wedding, and he regarded her as an enemy.[17] Jacob called her "a deceiver and the daughter of a deceiver," but Leah retorted, "Is there a teacher without pupils? Didn't your father call you 'Esau,' and you answered him? So did you call me and I answered you."[18]

The bride of one night was humiliated when Jacob arranged the next morning to marry Rachel. Laban softened the blow somewhat when he required Jacob to live with her a week before taking Rachel, and he insisted that Jacob work another seven years for her. Leah had Jacob for a week, but knowing he would leave her for Rachel in a matter of days made it a joyless honeymoon.

Jacob was infuriated when he realized that he had been tricked into marriage with a woman who not only held no appeal for him but who was pledged to his brother. He had left home in mortal fear of Esau. Now, unwittingly, he had added fuel to his brother's hatred. Esau would be enraged[19] and the breach between them could never be repaired. Jacob determined to divorce Leah, but when he learned that she had become pregnant,[20] he decided against it. The happiness he found with Rachel eased his anxiety about Esau—he was, after all, far away—and with Rachel to share his life, he felt he could tolerate Leah.

Jacob treated Leah with patience and understanding and did not deny her conjugal relations—she bore him four sons, one soon after the other (29:32-35)—and he granted her an equal voice in the family's affairs. In the privacy of a field where they could not be overheard,[21] Jacob consulted both his wives when he learned that Laban threatened his life (31:5). He was relieved when both agreed to return to his native land with him (31:13-16); Leah's feelings in the matter counted too. She also had her say when Jacob showed anxiety before his meeting with Esau. Along with Rachel and the handmaids, Leah quarreled with him and reproached Jacob for taking them from the safety of their father's house and exposing them to danger.[22]

Leah's troubles did not cease, however, with Jacob's change of heart regarding divorce. The women turned on her, accusing her of leading a double life. She pretended to be righteous, they declared, but she was not, for a righteous woman would not have deceived her husband.[23] Nor would a righteous woman deny her sister the man she truly loved. Identifying with Rachel's romantic aspirations to marry Jacob, the women were so sympathetic that they maligned Leah. She was a gadabout, they said, who liked to go out and have the men look at her.[24] If this were so, then Ezekiel's statement, "as the mother, so her daughter" (16:44), would be borne out by the behavior of Dinah, Leah's daughter.

Despite the fact that Rachel had willingly helped to deceive him, Jacob held her blameless. Since she had apprised him of Laban's trickiness, he must have understood that she was more or less compelled to cooperate with her father's plan. He had simply failed to anticipate every contingency. Laban should have told him at the outset that the older daughter must marry before the younger. Set forth at the last moment, the excuse was obviously contrived. Jacob exonerated Rachel and agreed to work another seven years to make her his wife, but this time he married her before his servitude began.

Jacob made no secret of the fact that he loved Rachel so deeply that no one could displace her (29:30). She was outnumbered by Leah and her many children, but Jacob found ways to elevate Rachel's position.[25] Her couch always stood in his tent,[26] and even though she was barren, she remained his favorite. As Abraham had never criticized Sarah for her lack of children, Jacob saw no reason to demote Rachel. While having children is one of the goals of marriage, it was not paramount to Jacob. Rachel's unique response to him was more important than whether or not she could bear children. It was Rachel he loved; everything else was secondary. For the rest of her life, she remained the chief spouse of her household.[27]

When she did give birth, her children were Jacob's favorites, and he gave her grandchildren, Joseph's sons, Ephraim and Manasseh, equal status with Joseph's brothers. They became founders of two of the twelve tribes, filling the places of Joseph, their father, and Levi, whose descendants became the caretakers of the Temple and the line of the priesthood.

When Rachel died at the early age of thirty-six[28] or forty-five,[29] Jacob was deeply affected. But, although he is quoted in the Midrash as having said that her death was more grievous to him than all the calamities that had befallen him,[30] Scripture does not mention that he mourned for her. Instead, Jacob shared her joy in the fulfillment of her life's aim (35:16-20). Bearing his children had meaning and value to Rachel (30:24); therefore her death, while giving birth to Benjamin, had meaning, and even value, for Jacob. Separation could not diminish his love for Rachel, nor alter her image. He contemplated her presence in a vividly real and satisfying relationship, adding a new dimension to his spiritual growth. He had tasted of love—the years they had shared were part of his exist-ence—and death could not negate her being. Jacob gratefully accepted the happiness he had known, and did not complain that it came to an end. His reconciliation foreshadowed that of Job, who said, "The Lord gave and the Lord hath taken away; Blessed be the name of the Lord" (1:21). Her premature death did not perceptibly drain his emotional reserve. Be-cause her life had meaning to him, Rachel's death left her unique value intact.

Jacob's love for Rachel was evident in his meeting with Esau and his four hundred cohorts. His entire family was in danger as Jacob faced the possible annihilation of his wives and children and the looting of his possessions. Therefore he arranged his family and flocks in such a way that if one segment was attacked, the remainder could escape. When he presented his wives and children to his brother, he placed the more beloved further to the rear.[31] He first introduced the handmaids and their sons, then Leah and her children, and lastly, Joseph and Rachel (33:6-7). It is interesting that Joseph preceded Rachel, the only child placed before his mother. Rachel was pregnant with Benjamin at that time, and Joseph may have feared the sight of Esau would frighten her.[32] Or, having heard his uncle had a roving eye, Joseph hoped to prevent his notice of his mother.

Jacob's statement and the genealogical table of Jacob's family also indicate that the authors of Scripture recognized the spiritual value of Jacob's deep love for Rachel. With reference to Joseph and Benjamin, Rachel's sons, Jacob said, "My wife bore me two sons" (44:27), as if he had only one wife. And the genealogy does not refer to Jacob's other spouses as "wife," but lists "the sons of Rachel, Jacob's wife, Joseph and Benjamin" (46:19). In addition, Jacob expressed his greater love for her son over all his other children, by making a coat of many colors for Joseph, something he did not do far any of the others. (37:3).

Yet, although Rachel was his dearest wife, she was not the one to be buried with him in the Cave of Machpelah. Jacob's family was on the road, traveling to a new watering place in Ephrath, when Rachel unex-pectedly died in childbirth. Jacob was unprepared for the decision that confronted him. He could have proceeded to the burial place of the patri-archs and their wives to bury Rachel in the place of honor. But, even though Rachel had been his true mate both physically and spiritually, Leah still lived. She was his first wife. To preclude her from the honored resting place would have caused her to lose face in the eyes of her family and her people. Taking away all hope of acceptance would have embittered Leah, and to what avail? Rachel was dead, and nothing could tarnish his memory of her. Out of deference to Leah and her people, Jacob fol' lowed the principle of primogeniture. Since it was so important to them that they had resorted to a ruse to make Leah his first wife, Jacob buried his beloved Rachel beside the road to Ephrath. Leah would lie by his side for the eternal sleep even though he felt guilty about it. In fact, this act preyed on Jacob's mind for the remainder of his life. He considered his culpability so great that he was impelled to excuse his behavior (48:7). In requesting that Joseph promise to bury him in the Cave of Machpelah, he recognized that he was asking for a consideration he had not extended to Rachel.

Although no overt hostility between the sisters was evident, it smol' dered unseen. Leah must have begrudged Rachel her beauty and the accident of birth that determined she would marry Jacob, the more genteel of the twins. Knowing that Jacob was willing to work another seven years for her, that all his labors were to the end that he could marry Rachel, must have affected Leah adversely, too. No one, it seemed, was really interested in her or in her welfare. Rachel, on the other hand, grew envious of Leah, because she was unable to conceive (30:1). Barren for several years, Rachel felt unfulfilled as a woman and feared that Jacob was slipping from her; having a child would hold him. She might also have rationalized her emotional need for a child: *her* child would per' petuate Jacob's fine qualities which seemed to be lacking in Leah's children. Furthermore, she envied Leah's good deeds. Regardless of what the women were saying about her, she reasoned that Leah would not have borne children if she were not righteous.[33] Rachel was jealous of Leah on several scores.

Rachel's view, however, was one'sided. She concentrated on the selfish benefits of parenthood without considering the difficulties involved. Par' enthood includes caring for sick children and dealing with the endless succession of problems inherent in growing'up. Rachel overlooked the trying moments and the heartaches. Leah, whose motherhood Rachel envied, learned with anguish that her twelve'year'old daughter had been raped.[34] It may have been childish curiosity that drew Dinah to town to see a chorus of dancing and singing women. Or Dinah may have exposed herself to danger, imitating the bravado of her six brothers to overcome her feeling that being a girl was an inferior condition. No matter why Dinah came to town, Leah could not have controlled what happened there. Shechem seized the child and violated her in both natural and unnatural ways.[35] Jacob learned of her abduction and sent twelve servants to rescue her, but Shechem brazenly mauled her before their eyes and drove them off.[36] Rachel's envy of Leah's parenthood could not have taken into account such shocks as this.

Although some post-biblical authors portray Rachel as denying that she envied Leah,[37] psychology supports the biblical assertion that she did (30:1). A common character trait, envy of others stems from a feeling of being neglected and the victim of discrimination.[38] Envy also compensates for one's denied hostility toward another. It was only natural for Rachel to envy her older sister. Many experiences seemed to justify it. When Jacob sent her betrothal presents, her father took them from her and gave them to Leah. It irritated her to see Leah handle them, but she said nothing. She feared that if she made an issue of it her father would prevent her from marrying Jacob.[39] This treatment at the hands of her father led her to conclude that Laban preferred Leah to her. Then Laban actually gave Leah to Jacob in her place. And, as this situation developed, Rachel's jealousy gave rise to hostility and the impulse to hurt. She almost permitted Leah to be found out by Jacob—it would have demolished Leah—but at the last moment she repressed her hostility and came to Leah's rescue.

Jealousy is also a form of striving for power, and usually involves the element of envy. One who envies the success of others develops an overwhelming feeling of helplessness. Rachel saw Leah abounding with children. She envied her and imagined that Leah was more secure because of this, more self-confident and happier than she. Although Leah was really miserable because of Jacob's attitude toward her, Rachel was nevertheless exceedingly unhappy and developed an oppressive attitude of inferiority. Her estimation of herself kept diminishing, and she was dissatisfied with her life. She felt that because she was barren she was of lesser worth. She was overly sensitive, though Jacob had elevated her above Leah and had made it clear to everyone that she was his most beloved and his principal wife.

In an emotionally charged situation, the person most involved is generally too subjective. There is an inverse ratio between the degree of subjectivity in the individual and his ability to view himself objectively; the extent to which subjectivity obscures objective reality measures the neuroticism. Rachel must have become neurotic over her inability to conceive. To the world she was obviously Jacob's favorite, but in her own eyes she was neglected and mistreated by him. She suffered from envy

not because of what she herself did or did not accomplish, but in comparison with Leah's successes.[40] Leah not only had many children, but
she had loyal children. Observing all this, Rachel felt that she was losing
Jacob's love and that she might eventually lose Jacob too. Thus, Leah
and her family were a potential danger to Rachel and her jealousy was
a striving for the power to hold her husband. The birth of each of
Leah's children cut Rachel to the quick, filling her life with bitter frustration; her suffering became insurmountable. Equating childlessness with
death,[41] she demanded of Jacob, "Give me children, or else I die." If
he wanted to, she told Jacob, he could certainly enable her to bear children,
just as he had made the sheep bring forth their young.[42]

Jacob, for the first and only time, lost his temper with Rachel, retorting,
"Am I in God's stead, who hath withheld from thee the fruit of the
womb?" (30:2). He had nothing to do with her sterility; she should
address her petition to God.[43] Rachel was confounded by his outburst.
She said, "Did your father speak thus to your mother? Did he not pray
that she be blessed with children?" "I have children," Jacob replied,
"whereas my father had none." She persisted, "Your grandfather, Abraham,
had children, yet he girded up his loins by Sarah." Hard pressed, Jacob
challenged, "Can you do what my grandmother did? She brought her
rival into her home; she gave Hagar to Abraham." "If that is the obstacle," Rachel said, "behold my maid, Bilhah. Go in unto her . . . and
I also will be builded up through her."[44]

When a person feels inadequate, the most common reaction is to
degrade and reproach others, shifting all blame to them.[45] When Rachel
said to Jacob, "Give me children," she was vindictive, telling him, in so
many words, that he was inadequate in regard to her. She projected her
failure onto him, claiming that he was not the man he was thought to be.
Perhaps subconsciously she enjoyed the intimation that he was incapable;
she could tear down his manliness at no cost to her own self-esteem.
Jacob retaliated, pointing out that she alone was responsible for her condition, and dealt her a decisive blow when he suggested that she give
him Bilhah. For the sake of children—for the value they would impart
to her and for the security they would lend to her position in the home—
Rachel was willing to follow Sarah's example.

But Rachel did not suggest that Jacob marry her handmaid, as Sarah
did. Rachel was too proud to admit defeat—to admit that she was not a
complete woman. Coming from Jacob, it must have been a staggering blow
to her ego. Also, she must have felt that such a suggestion might alienate,
rather than please Jacob. He already had four sons, two more than his

father. Why should he assume responsibility for an additional wife? But when Jacob made this proposal himself, she accepted it immediately. He reassured her that her position was secure, that he loved her whether or not she had children. Leah's many sons did not affect his feelings toward her. If the assurance was insufficient for Rachel, however, and she really wanted children, then she could give him Bilhah in the hope of experiencing motherhood through her.

Adopting the child of another woman would permit Rachel to sublimate her feelings.[46] It would afford the opportunity to gratify her maternal yearnings, and to satisfy her narcissistic pride through the personal influence she would exert on the adopted child. Although the adoptive mother does not experience the uterine development of the child, she is nevertheless capable of becoming a real parent emotionally. This is expressed in the verse, "Thou art My son, I have given birth to you today" (Psalms 2:7), which is regarded by some as the basis for legal adoption. As her relationship evolves with the child, caring for him and making it possible for him to survive and thrive, the adoptive mother experiences in some measure the feeling of a natural mother in the early pre-natal relationship.[47] In full accord with this, the Rabbis many years ago stated that "who brings up children is called the parent, not who gives birth."[48] The love the adoptive mother gives him and his constant contact with her make the child truly her own. She absorbs him wholly into her self-system, and her love for him is as deep as though she had given birth to him. Within a relatively short period of time, it no longer occurs to her that she did not actually bear him, especially when the child is adopted at a very early age.

Since it was believed at that time that when a woman's handmaid conceived her fertility passed on to the wife, who would also become pregnant,[49] Jacob's suggestion stilled Rachel's qualms. The knowledge that Sarah eventually had a son of her own, after a similar experience, eased her tensions. Rachel must have found comfort in the promise that her shame might be removed.

As a result of Jacob's union with Bilhah, two sons were born. When the second one came, Rachel significantly named him Naphtali, because "with mighty wrestlings have I wrestled with my sister, and have prevailed" (30:8). Rachel betrayed that she was engaged in a fierce competition with Leah, that she was waging war with her sister. Although Jacob loved her more than Leah, it was insufficient. She felt that Leah was superior to her. It is comparable to a conversation that reputedly took place between Peninah and Hannah, the two wives of Elkanah (I Samuel

1:2). Hannah, being the beloved of Elkanah, but barren, was taunted by
Peninah, "Of what value is it that Elkanah loves you? You are no more
than a dry tree. I know that he will love me, because he delights to see
my sons standing around him like the planting of an olive-yard. Therefore, Hannah, do not boast of your beauty. If you wish to boast, boast
of your children. And, when women are unable to bear, then love becomes
of no account." Peninah then reminded Hannah, "Of what profit was it
unto Rachel that Jacob loved her? If not that she eventually did have
children, surely his love would have been of no purpose."[50] Now Rachel
finally felt fulfilled and victorious. She could lift her head high. Her
sister had nothing on her.

Rachel regarded this turn of events as a reward. Whereas at first she
was disheartened that she herself could not bear children, now she was
rewarded through her maid for allowing Jacob to marry Leah first.[51]
Naphtali's birth gratified Rachel immensely.

The spirit of envy and competition between the sisters took hold of
Leah too. When she stopped bearing after her fourth son, perhaps because
Jacob stopped living with her, she gave her servant, Zilpah, to him. And,
when Zilpah bore a son, Leah named him Gad because, she said: "Fortune
is come!" (30:11). She was showing up her sister. When Zilpah gave
birth to a second son, Leah was ecstatic, exclaiming, "Happy am I! for
the daughters will call me happy" (30:13), and she named him Asher,
meaning "praise." Leah rationalized that she deserved praise for giving
Zilpah to Jacob. Sarah and Rachel gave their handmaids to their husbands
because they had no children. Leah had children, however, and she nevertheless gave her handmaid to her husband without feelings of jealousy.[52]
Some contend that she deceived Jacob into marrying Zilpah by putting
her garment on her, leading Jacob to conclude that he was with her, not
with her handmaid.[53] This would further prove that Leah was intensely
jealous of Rachel. She would deceive Jacob a second time and exploit
her handmaid in order to entrench her position.

The rivalry between Rachel and Leah infected their children, who
naturally took sides, each with his own mother. Leah held the deep affection of her oldest son, Reuben, who greatly respected her and to whom
she was somewhat partial. Despite her difficult situation, Leah must have
presented a jolly appearance, displaying a sense of humor, as she did
when Zilpah gave birth to Gad. According to Jacob's understanding of it,
this name means "a troop" (49:19). Gad was Jacob's seventh son and,
when she said "a troop is come,"[54] Leah must have felt she had a small
army of defenders. Such an attitude sets well with children and must

have contributed to their unity and loyalty to their mother. Leah was also lavish with praise of her sons, pointing out Reuben's superiority to her father-in-law's first-born son. Esau voluntarily sold his birthright and yet he hated Jacob. On the contrary, she claimed, although Joseph usurped the benefits of Reuben's birthright, yet Reuben did not hate him.[55]

When Rachel died, Jacob felt the immediate need to replace the lost relationship. As much as he respected Leah's rights, there was no emotional bond between them. In an effort to retain the emotional security of Rachel's love, he substituted not Leah, but Bilhah, Rachel's handmaid. First, Jacob elevated Bilhah and Zilpah from the status of concubines to legitimate wives,[56] although he had promised Laban that he would not mistreat his daughters by taking other wives (31:50). They were, however, daughters of Laban born of a concubine[57] and not bondwomen,[58] so Jacob felt that this did not violate his agreement. Then Jacob placed Bilhah's bed in his tent, thereby making her his main wife.

Leah met this affront with stoic silence, but her oldest son expressed her sentiments and, incidentally, his own. "Is it not enough for my mother to be humiliated during her sister's lifetime?" Reuben exclaimed. "Must she be made to envy the dead?" He thereupon disarranged the beds, putting Leah's bed in Jacob's tent in place of Bilhah's.[59] He justified his action on behalf of his mother, while he demonstrated the he, too, had a stake in the matter. As the eldest son of Jacob's first wife, he served notice that he was Jacob's rightful heir. The issue of primogeniture had been clouded by the aura that surrounded Rachel. Now that she was dead, he had no intention of allowing Bilhah to give birth to more competitors.[60]

In order to separate Bilhah from his father, he even attempted to throw suspicion on her purity. Jacob learned, however, that he had no cause to suspect her.[61]

That a more than competitive spirit prevailed between Rachel and Leah is displayed in the incident of the mandrakes. Playing in the field, Reuben found some mandrakes. He would not taste them or keep them for himself, but set out to bring them to his mother.[62] As he neared the house, Rachel aggressively took the mandrakes away from him. Reuben's cries brought Leah to the scene. Still considered love-charms in the East, mandrakes, or "love-apples," are believed to make barren women fertile and impotent men potent. "Give me, I pray thee, of thy son's mandrakes," (30:14) Rachel said. Leah's retort indicates how bitterly she really felt toward her sister. "Is it small matter," she shouted, "that thou hast taken away my husband? And wouldst thou take away my son's mandrakes also?" (30:15). Conveniently overlooking the fact that Jacob did not want to marry her at all, Leah openly accused her sister of taking her husband away, when the reverse was true. In her limited view, the only right was the right of the first-born, and Leah attributed to her sister that of which she was guilty. Besides, giving the mandrakes to Rachel would relinquish an advantage to her competitor. Rachel would be able to conceive.

Leah's angry accusation indicates that Jacob flouted the rules relating to marital relations which a man with two wives accepts upon himself. The law which is in effect today among the tribes of the Syrian-Arabian desert, and which was probably in force in Jacob's day, requires that the husband alternate between his wives, spending one night with one wife and the next one with the other, even if he does not love one of them. He may, if he wishes, sleep in his own tent, but he is definitely not allowed to sleep with the wife he prefers if it is not her turn. Because of Jacob's great love for Rachel, he did not alternate with regularity between Rachel and Leah, as custom required. This must have angered Leah to the point of accusing her sister of taking her husband away from her.[63] It was Leah's prerogative to complain to her family about it, but she didn't. Or, if she did, they did not help her.

To placate Leah, and in her determination to have the mandrakes, Rachel was ready and willing to barter a night with Jacob for them. Leah could have him for an evening of love (30:15). Rachel must have been a desperate woman, indeed, to be willing to go to such lengths to extricate herself from the shame of childlessness. Natural means had been of no avail, so she resorted to artificial devices. Leah insisted, however, "Jacob is mine, for I am the wife of his youth." Rachel replied, "Boast not and vaunt not thyself; for he espoused me before thee, and for my sake he served our father fourteen years. . . . For thou art not his wife, but in craft were taken to him in my stead. And my father deceived me, and removed me on that night, and did not suffer Jacob to see me. . . . Nevertheless, for the mandrakes I will hire Jacob to thee for one night."[64] The pleasure of attacking Leah this way must have given Rachel some relief from her unhappiness.

There was truth in Rachel's words, and certainly mandrakes were as nothing compared to a night with her husband, so Leah agreed to the bargain. Co-wives had the right to trade among themselves for a night with their husband, without consulting him;[65] but, if the husband chose to ignore the arrangement, the neglected wife could not enforce it.

The braying of Jacob's donkey outside her tent brought Leah running to him. Without giving him a chance to wash his feet,[66] she insisted,

"Thou must come in unto me; for I have surely hired thee with my son's mandrakes" (30:16). At first, Jacob refused.[67] Her invitation was immodest, but Jacob could understand it. According to the customs of her people, not only Leah's self-respect was at stake, but also Laban's. And Jacob still remembered his father-in-law's determination to enforce a bargain according to his own standards. Prodded by a guilty conscience and his fear of Laban, Jacob agreed to abide by the arrangement of the two sisters. Following this incident, Jacob then resumed the conventional custom. After her sixth son was born, Leah said, "Now will my husband dwell with me, because I have borne him six sons" (30:20). Jacob gave her the attention due her, and Leah was content as long as he complied with custom. Some Rabbis comment that Rachel was not buried beside Jacob in the Cave of Machpelah because she slighted Jacob by giving him up so readily for the mandrakes.[68]

Although hard feelings existed between the sisters because of their husband, they were of an ambivalent nature. When Leah became pregnant a seventh time, she dropped her attitude of competition with Rachel and prayed that she would give birth to a girl. It had been foretold that the Lord would raise twelve tribes from Jacob. She already had six, and each of the two handmaids had two sons. If she would now give birth to a seventh son, then Rachel could never be on a par even with the handmaids.[69] Though the sisters vied with each other, each was nevertheless considerate of the feelings of the other. Even before Rachel had given birth to Joseph, Leah prayed with Jacob and the concubines that Rachel's barrenness be removed from her.[70] She was truly compassionate. How different she was from Peninah, who, in similar circumstances, treated Hannah shabbily and "vexed her sore, to make her fret, because the Lord had shut up her womb" (I Samuel 1:6).

In any event, the deal that was made between the two women seems to have benefited them. Leah got her husband back, and Rachel conceived and gave birth to Joseph (30:22-24), after having been married for fourteen years. It is ironic that Joseph, born as a consequence of Reuben's mandrakes, inherited the double portion of the first-born.

Rachel's reaction can be understood from her own words, "God hath taken away my reproach" (30:23). She felt vindicated on a number of scores. When she became pregnant, she gave the lie to those who maintained that she was barren because she was not a pious woman. Sarah had also been accused of this when she was unable to conceive. This turn of events stilled the idle talk.[71] By giving birth, Rachel escaped another disgrace. She feared that when Jacob decided to return to his homeland, her father would detain her because she was childless. He could not restrain his daughters who had given birth from going, but the barren he could. She was also afraid that Laban would marry her off to a heathen,[72] or perhaps even to Esau if she remained at home.[73] Now that she had a son of her own, her reproach and her fears were eliminated.

When the family secretly left Laban's household, Rachel stole her father's *teraphim.* It is possible that Rachel took the idols either because she could not tear herself away from home, or because she wanted to aggravate her father. It would seem that the latter is closer to reality. It was believed that the *teraphim,* idols which Laban consulted, supplied him with whatever information he sought. Without them he could not learn where they had gone and would not be able to overtake them. It would seem that Rachel did not want to see her father again. If she still harbored resentment against him and desired to hurt him, she aimed well. As Laban had stolen her right to be Jacob's first wife, she stole the symbol of his power. Rachel felt her right to free choice was innate, and she realized the inefficacy of *teraphim* in the determination of her fate.

Rachel exhibited resentment of her father in her untruthful excuse for not standing when he came into her tent (31:35). Laban did notice that Rachel was ill at ease, as if she were trying to hide something, and he became suspicious. After searching Leah's and the handmaids' tents, he searched her tent a second time, and again found nothing.[74] It has also been suggested that Rachel stole the *teraphim* to be able to pacify him by returning them should he succeed in catching up with them.[75]

The fact that Rachel was able to conceive and give birth would indicate that she had suffered from functional infertility, not sterility.[76] Though it is claimed that she was sterile,[77] the evidence does not bear this out. The same would hold true for Sarah and Rebekah. A permanent and unalterable condition, sterility renders a woman biologically incapable of producing a child. In infertility, which means "non-producing," there is no demonstrable organic or physiological pathology to explain the inability to conceive. Such a condition may be temporary and often responds to treatment. Functional infertility has been shown to be related to emotional problems in the life of the individual.[78] If psychotherapy succeeds in uncovering the psychological reasons for this condition, infertility may disappear.

Many women who appear eager to have children and who are sorely disappointed if they are unable to bear, actually have an unconscious wish not to have offspring. It is possible that Sarah, Rebekah and Rachel had hidden reasons for suppressing their fertility. Whereas these attitudes and feelings do not always result in infertility, they may manifest themselves in difficult pregnancies and in obstetrical difficulties in childbirth. Pain is an expression of protest and sometimes results from a deeper repression. The difficulty a woman experiences while pregnant and during childbirth has been found to be in direct proportion to the degree of resentment, guilt, and other disturbed attitudes concerning the fulfillment of this aspect of her feminine role. It is well known that a woman's conflicting attitudes influence to a marked degree the regularity of her menstrual cycle, as well as the degree of distress or comparative ease of this physiological female function.

Although Rachel manifested a desire unto death to have children, it is quite possible that actually she was in conflict about it. She may have felt that becoming pregnant would detract from her beauty; she would be unattractive to Jacob during that nine month period. Like many women who are unable to bear, Rachel may have been unconsciously gripped by fear, which is the most frequent cause of infertility.[79] This kind of fear may be due to the reproductive function with its concomitant discomfiture and pain and the danger it poses to life itself. She may have believed that she had injured her body when she herded and watered the sheep, and she feared pregnancy for that reason. It is also possible that Rachel may have had an aversion to the sex act, or she may have been troubled by a sense of shame at having a child because this reveals that which has taken place in the bedroom. She may have unconsciously been saying to herself and to others, "Though my couch is in Jacob's tent continuously, we do not indulge in sexual relations."[80] When such an ungainly attitude prevails, these women gratify their desires to become mothers by utilizing the sexual service of other women.[81] Rachel may have feared the responsibilities of motherhood and of raising a child. Or the possibility of bearing a lifeless or malformed offspring might have lurked in her unconscious as just retribution for her death wishes toward Leah. Finally, Rachel might have found her relationship with Jacob so gratifying and fulfilling that she feared a child would change the status quo. If she experienced such overwhelming satisfaction in expending her motherliness in her love for Jacob, she may have felt he would be deprived by a child; so, unconsciously, she concluded Jacob did not really care for her to conceive.

Rachel also seems to have suffered excessively during menstruation. In many women, no demonstrable reason can be found for the difficulty. When Rachel's father came into her tent to search for his lost teraphim after Jacob had fled from his house, she used as her excuse for not rising that she "cannot rise . . . for the manner of women is upon me" (31:35).

That Laban accepted it, without asking her to move just a little, might indicate that she had suffered severely from it in the past and that he was aware of it. Her excuse apparently was not new to him. Also, when she gave birth to her second son, Benjamin, her pains were extreme for "she had hard labour" (35:16). Furthermore, it took about twelve years for her to become pregnant the second time.[82] She had difficulties in this phase of her life, which might give insight into her attitudes on this dimension of her existence.

Whereas such a disturbance may damage a woman's self-esteem, causing her to regard herself as inadequate and worthless, it may also be an almost entirely unconscious and disguised expression of the desire to frustrate and humiliate the mate.[83] It is quite possible that Rachel harbored resentment against herself for allowing Leah to marry Jacob, and her transferred resentment against Jacob was expressed in her refusal to give him a child.

Another possible reason for unconscious infertility is a desire to avenge one's mother for horrible treatment received at the hand of the father.[84] It is conceivable that Rachel observed with fear the primal scene of her parents and viewed it as a struggle in which her mother seemed to be getting the worst of it. Her mother died when she was quite young,[85] and she might have blamed her father for this. Her mother is not mentioned or even alluded to in Scripture. Rachel's infertility might have been a refusal to submit to her mother's fate. As such, it was a form of rejection of her femininity and inherent motherliness which could be equated with death itself.

Still another possible explanation is that Rachel wanted to remain a child herself and did not want to surrender that role to a baby. If she wanted to be cared for and protected like the baby she had been, she was emotionally unprepared to accept the responsibility of motherhood.[86] She was psychologically infantile. Only when this role no longer suited her, could she outgrow it and became a mother. The birth of Joseph not only satisfied the basic human drive to bear a child, but this experience concurrently gave birth to a true adult emotionally.

Faith in the power of the mandrakes and the adoption of Bilhah's two sons had favorable therapeutic effects upon Rachel. By removing the sting of her earlier traumatic experiences, they enabled Rachel to conceive and become a mother in her own right. And Jacob, prompted by the awful realization that Rachel was the only one of his four wives who was barren, may have become emotionally ready for her to have a child. Emotional maturation affected Rachel and Jacob even as it does couples today who find themselves expectant parents after many years of childless mar-

riage. They may have yearned for a child for many years, but subconsciously erected psychic barriers to conception. Whatever motivated them
to avoid parenthood vanished after therapeutic experiences, and with it
their infertility. Or, as they outgrew their infantilism and accepted their
mature roles in marriage, the meaning of having offspring became real
for them. Or, having become convinced that they would under no circumstances be able to produce a child, they let their guard down, so to
speak, and became parents.[87] Samson, for instance, was born at a time
when his parents had given up all hope of ever having children.[88]

A comparable phenomenon often takes place after a child is adopted,
or even before, while the couple is discussing arrangements with an appropriate agency. Their unconscious fears, guilt feelings, neurotic beliefs and
hesitations seem to disappear. "Perhaps the warming-up of the parents
toward the adopted child releases formerly suppressed maternal and paternal feelings" which "limber up the temporarily unbalanced endocrine
system. When the emotions begin to supply the needed stimuli, it may
be that the glandular apparatus related to reproduction begins to function
smoothly again, and hence pregnancy results."[89] This can happen, however, only when the emotional factor or factors have engendered a hor-
monal imbalance which is capable of being reversed.[90] After such an
occurrence, many couples explain that the adoption was responsible for
easing their tensions, which enabled them to produce a pregnancy. Adoption diminishes their anxiety and relieves the inhibiting psychogenic factors
sufficiently to make conception possible. A woman who was about to
adopt a child and found herself pregnant, explained it this way: "During
the first three years of marriage, we were tense at every coitus, trying to
avoid conception; during the following five years, we were tense trying
to achieve it. Only in the last six months had we given up all attempts
and become free from anxious attention."[91] Conception came when they
had spontaneously attained a state of relaxation. This came about when
they relinquished the idea of having their own child, and knew that
adoption was imminent; they surrendered to the seriousness of the ultimate.
There are others, however, who put these instances in the category of
"chance."[92] Still others, whose infertility was caused by a fear of failing to
be a good parent, were able to conceive after they had adopted a child
and found that they were equal to this responsibility. Some women are
unable to bear children because of extreme guilt toward their mothers.
Such a woman must first have a symbol that the child does not belong
to her, but may be thought of as her mother's; an adopted child serves
as the symbol. Original conception on her own may be fantasied as in-

cestuous and matricidal. If this interpretation disappears with the adoption, she may be free to have a child of her own.[93]

Sarah adopted Ishmael not for the child's sake, and not primarily for her own satisfaction, but for the purpose of propagating the ideal for which she and Abraham had left home. Rachel's reasons for adopting Bilhah's offspring, however, were entirely self-centered. The child and his feelings were of little, if any, importance. Rachel's needs were the only considerations, and adoption filled them admirably. The adopted children masked her feelings of inferiority and restored what she believed was a disintegrating marriage. With pride in a child of her own, she overcame the neurosis concerning her childlessness and was better able to cope with the rivalry of Jacob's other wives who had children. Although the avowed attitude of adoption agencies today is that adoption serves the child, the frankly mother-centered adoption prevailed until very recently.

Rachel was well prepared for the adoption, having waited for conception to take place and for the nine month period that followed. For her, the family came into existence with a child; the interrelated bonds between her and the child and her husband created the family. It is to Rachel's credit that she was able to establish a healthy relationship with her adopted children. She became a real parent by making them emotionally her own, by establishing a mutually beneficial relationship between herself and them. When Naphtali was born, she loved him exceedingly. She pampered him and kissed him frequently. She would say to him, "May I have a brother of thine from mine own womb, like unto thee."[94] She made him feel that he was very dear and precious to her, that he was an admirable example and pattern for the children she herself would like to bear.

In this respect, Rachel and Leah were quite different from Sarah. Neither of them abandoned the children of the handmaids, whereas Sarah had forsaken Ishmael. Sarah insisted that Ishmael be driven from home, but in Jacob's household the sons of the handmaids were given equal status with the wives' sons. Rachel and Leah apparently were able to lose almost immediately the awareness that these boys were not of their own flesh, and they accepted them wholeheartedly. Perhaps this was understood by the people who bestowed a blessing upon Ruth when they said, "The Lord make the woman who has gone into thy house like Rachel and like Leah" (Ruth 4:11). Because the adoption did not serve Sarah's own needs, she was unable to incorporate Ishmael. She never accepted him unconditionally, which is the attitude of mature motherhood. A constant reminder of her insecurity, Ishmael was not an expression of love between Abraham and herself. Sarah was ready to desert him as soon as her own son was born, and when he became a behavior problem she severed herself from the role of his parent.

While the rivalry that prevailed between Rachel and Leah was not as intense as that displayed by the brothers of the Book of Genesis, it was an equally dramatic episode in the revolt against primogeniture. Unlike their male counterparts, nowhere does Scripture state that the sisters hated each other, nor did they manifest their envy and jealousy in overt destructive behavior. If Scripture only implies that sisters are more devoted to each other, or are better able to control their animosity, it does applaud their freedom to govern their lives. Although Leah accepted the superiority attributed to the first-born by primogeniture, she employed the concept to effect her escape either from predetermined marriage or from spinsterhood. Still, Leah was unable to transcend her function as childbearer to find a higher meaning to her life, because she married Jacob essentially to escape. Rachel's commitment to life was a positive, rather than a negative motivation. Her struggle to surmount her limitations portrayed the dynamic spirit of a free woman.

CHAPTER SEVEN

The Sons of Jacob Were Twelve

(Genesis 35:22)

I

THE envy and jealousy that prevailed between Leah and Rachel was reflected in the relationships of their sons and became magnified in intensity to hatred. Their maternal loyalties divided the twelve brothers, and the uncertainty which had come to surround the succession to leadership excited disaffection among them. In the ensuing struggle for Jacob's favor, their enmity found expression in violence.

As Leah's position as Jacob's first wife had never been secure, neither was Reuben, her oldest son, certain to succeed the patriarch. Each first-born of Jacob's four wives, Leah, Rachel, Zilpah and Bilhah, had equal claim to the rights inherent in their position in the family. Thus there were four first-born sons contending for favor. While it was natural for the brothers to divide into cliques, a breach developed that finally isolated Joseph from all his brothers. This most damaging "rift within the lute" was created by Jacob himself.

Although Jacob had suffered because of his parents' favoritism, he fell into the same pattern by showing extreme partiality to Joseph. It is often observed that parents treat children as they themselves have been treated, whether with extreme harshness or extreme partiality. Parenthood provides an opportunity to express revenge, long displaced and deferred, for the indignities suffered at the hands of irrational authority —like a boy after a fraternity "hazing" whose first thought is of next year, when he will be in authority and another willing victim will seek his approval. And, odd as it may seem, these parents rarely recognize the hate implied in their behavior. On the other hand, the child who is loved irrationally, or unconditionally, feels the stranglehold of possessive love, and upon attaining parenthood himself becomes the possessor, instead of the possessed, in the only manner he knows.

Beyond this, Jacob had a personal need to love Joseph and to translate this love into action. The first child of his beloved Rachel, Joseph was most precious to him. Although Benjamin was younger than Joseph, and also Rachel's son, Jacob loved Joseph as if he were the only son to grace his old age.[1] As comely in his father's eyes as Rachel, Joseph was a consolation to his father after her death;[2] he personified Jacob's love for Rachel. But Jacob also saw in this son reflections of himself. The lad's vivid imagination recalled his own youthful dreams of leadership, and of the satisfactions that would be his. Of all his sons, Joseph most resembled Jacob.[3] He was more interesting than his older brothers and responded more freely to affection. Jacob identified himself in body and spirit with Joseph and, in indulging Joseph, he indulged himself. It was immature and selfish love, but Jacob found satisfaction in it. Disregarding both the comparative merits of his other sons and the human imperfections of Joseph, Jacob loved him unconditionally and unwaveringly. Most parents tend to alternate their preference, favoring one child one year and another the next, even if only slightly.[4] Jacob's love for Joseph, however, remained constant.

Jacob "loved Joseph more than all his children . . . and he made him a coat of many colors" (37:3). The result, as in his own youth, was an emotionally charged relationship. His special gift to Joseph signified Jacob's love and protection, which he denied his other sons, and indicated that he was to assume leadership of the tribe when Jacob died. Jacob's blind love of Joseph cut the ten brothers deeply and convinced them that Joseph alienated them from their father. "When his brethren saw that their father loved him more than all his brethren, they hated him, and could not speak peaceably unto him" (37:4). Even when Joseph inquired about their well-being, they would not answer him. The mere sight of him made them angry.[5]

Jacob permitted Joseph every liberty, while he held the rest on a tight rein of discipline. Joseph was allowed to attend school until he was seventeen years of age,[6] but the others worked with the flocks as soon as they were able. They also attended to Jacob's personal needs, rotating this chore among them, while Joseph was exempt from menial work of any kind. While they were sweating in the fields, Joseph lounged about in fine clothes studying, and he was always close to Jacob. Having been raised in this fashion, Joseph found it difficult to grow up. Helplessness was gratifying; the temptation to continue in this pattern was strong. Immaturity was the best method of getting his own way and of holding Jacob's love; being dependent was his most effective tool. By the same token, because of his favored position in the family, he bore the brunt of his brothers' resentment, which normally decreases with each successive baby. Unlike the young in other families who are adopted as a sort of mascot, Joseph never gained his brothers' acceptance.

Since younger children profit most from their parents' greater maturity and from the model and teaching of older siblings, Jacob considered Joseph more prudent than all his brothers.[7] For this reason, Jacob entrusted the laws he had learned from Shem and Eber to Joseph alone.[8]

Jacob's favoritism damaged the other sons' individual self-esteem and collective ego. They could neither excuse their father's partiality, nor could they accept it. Their hero had let them down. How could he play favorites with Joseph? It was unfair. They were hurt and they wanted to retaliate, but what could they do to Jacob? He was impregnable. They could not express their resentment against the patriarch—he could have banished any of them at will—so they displaced it. Rather than hate Jacob, they hated Joseph without reservation.

Joseph, too, gave his brothers reason to hate him. Though he was a scholar, he was immature, spoiled and self-centered. He pencilled his eyes, curled his hair, and walked with a mincing step.[9] These traits earned his brothers' disdain. But Joseph was fully aware that Jacob held him above and apart from his brothers, and he exploited his position at every opportunity. He tattled to Jacob, embroidering his tales with false accusations; he belittled them and cast doubt on their most innocent motives; and he held over them a fearsome threat of supernatural power—his dreams. For all this his brothers repaid him with unremitting hatred.

Yet, although he enjoyed Jacob's unequivocal indulgence, Joseph would have preferred acceptance within the fraternity. He was excluded from the salty camaraderie of brothers who were men. His life of ease did not remove the stigma of being rejected, and he felt hostility toward those who belonged. With his lies and fantastic dreams he achieved self-aggrandizement; he equipped himself with unique and remarkable qualities with which to compete with his older brothers.

Once Joseph tended the flock with his brothers, but he stayed with them only thirty days. Unfamiliar with his tasks, and unaccustomed to the constant movement of the shepherds and exposure to the elements, he fell ill. Also, fear of leaving his father for an extended period may have induced illness. Benjamin might monopolize his father's time in his absence and win Jacob's love, a prospect Joseph could not endure. But when he was returned to his father, Joseph told a story that effectively obscured his own inadequacy. The sons of the handmaids squandered and wantonly destroyed the flocks, he told Jacob. He accused Gad and Asher,

Zilpah's sons, and Dan and Naphtalı, Bilhah's sons, of slaughtering the choicest animals of the herd. Not content to assert that they consumed some animals without the permission of Reuben, the eldest, or of Judah, the acknowledged leader, Joseph accused them of eating flesh torn from living animals. The accusation was baseless (even the kid whose blood was smeared on the coat of many colors was slaughtered according to ritual)[10] although Joseph did see Gad kill a lamb. Actually, Gad had saved the lamb from the claws of a bear that attacked in the night, and when Gad saw that the lamb would not survive, he slaughtered it.[11] But Jacob believed whatever Joseph told him. To satisfy his need to feel superior and victorious, to compensate for his physical inferiority, and to further ingratiate himself with his father, Joseph alienated himself even from the sons of the handmaids, who had formerly been his friends (37:2). Although he had once offered his services to them as though he were their slave,[12] his unpunished lies hurt them now as much as their father's one-sided love. Gad, particularly, was infuriated. He hated Joseph and longed for the chance to retaliate.

Joseph again displayed immaturity when he incited friction among his brothers. He accused Leah's sons of mistreating the four sons of the handmaids. They called them slaves, he claimed, while Joseph professed that he treated them as brothers.[13] When he falsely accused them of casting eyes upon the Canaanite girls, he deepened his alienation from the six sons of Leah.

Joseph's dreams irritated and infuriated all his brothers. At first they refused to listen, but finally they gave in.[14] He told them that he dreamed they were binding sheaves in the field and their sheaves bowed down to his. His brothers "hated him yet the more for his dreams, and for his words" (37:8). When he told them his second dream, regarding the sun, the moon and the stars, "his brothers envied him" (37:11). Because they recognized the dreams were self-centered and flaunted his importance in their faces, they listened with growing hostility as he recounted still others. He and they gathered fruit; theirs rotted, but his remained sound.[15] Their children would set up idols, he foresaw; and all his brothers would prostrate themselves before him five times.[16]

Already denied their father's love for reasons beyond their control, the sons of Leah and the handmaids accepted the implication of Joseph's dreams. They were ordinary people with ordinary tastes, who derived satisfaction from the performance of their daily tasks. Joseph, however, was different—so different that he posed a threat. He was important; they were insignificant. With the retelling of his dreams he engendered feelings of worthlessness in them,[17] and aggravated their long-standing envy and hate. The future he imagined for himself in such grandiose terms dispelled the power of their physical strength and endurance; his dreams displayed a superior power. As their self-esteem and sense of security were increasingly threatened, they responded with fear and with anger. They felt compelled to injure Joseph, the threatening force, and to prove their own superiority in order to obtain the love and esteem that Jacob withheld from them.

Their aggressive feelings produced at the same time feelings of guilt and anxiety. They could not attack Joseph directly. With Jacob's unquestioning support, Joseph was too powerful, too dangerous a person to hurt. The fear of Jacob's dictatorial power held them in check; he could punish them severely. So the brothers repressed their hostility, and contented themselves with trading stories of the injustices they had suffered, sympathizing with each other and savoring the anticipation of revenge.

The brothers' opportunity for direct aggression finally presented itself when Joseph came to visit them at a distant camp site, far from the protection of their father. Jacob was aware of the animosity that prevailed among his sons. They did not hide their feelings, nor were they spiteful or sullen, but they openly displayed their distaste for Joseph, and Jacob knew it.[18] Striving to mitigate the hostility among his sons, Jacob on this particular occasion sent Joseph to "see whether it is well" with his brothers (37:14). They had gone to Shechem to revel there and, because he had had no word from them, Jacob was worried.[19] Also, he thought the brothers would welcome an expression of concern and interest from Joseph, unaware that they were beyond conciliation. Joseph, however, had misgivings and feared the mission would have unpleasant consequences, but he said nothing and went as he was told.[20]

Although rivalries existed among the brothers too, having a common target united them. When they saw Joseph coming, the brothers were startled. "Behold," they said with biting sarcasm, "this dreamer cometh" (37:19). It was as if they had been discussing their grievances against him when he materialized before their eyes. Their first impulse was to rise as one and kill him. Calling him a name and poking fun at him gave vent to their hostility, but it did not touch Jacob, the real target of their resentment, nor did it allay their unexpressed fear. Only violence could restore their feeling of superiority. They discussed the feasibility of inciting dogs against him,[21] but decided against it. This "catharsis of aggression"[22] reduced the desire to harm him directly in all but Simeon and Gad, whose hatred of Joseph was extreme. These two approached Joseph with intent to kill him. Joseph threw himself at the feet of each one and begged for pity.[23] When they knocked him to the ground, he pleaded: "Pity me, my brethren, have mercy upon Jacob our father. Lay not your hands upon me to shed innocent blood, for I have not sinned against you. And if I have sinned, chastise me, my brethren. But lay not upon me your hands, for the sake of Jacob our father."[24] Joseph realized how closely Jacob identified with him—whatever hurt him would hurt his father—but he ignored, or he chose to forget, that he personally had offended his brothers. He implied, however, that he was not to be held guilty for his father's favoritism. After all, he pleaded, it was Jacob who set him apart. Didn't they know that he wanted to be one of them even at this moment? Zebulun was touched by Joseph's wailing and pitied him. He cried convulsively, imploring his brothers not to kill Joseph. When Simeon and Gad, who had remained unmoved, were about to carry out their impulse to kill him, Joseph hid behind Zebulun and begged his brothers to come to his rescue.[25]

Reuben and Judah joined Zebulun in speaking out against murder (37:22, 26-27). Reuben suggested "let us not slay him, but let us cast him into one of those dry pits, which our fathers digged and found no water."[26] Throwing Joseph into a pit would express their hostility, if only indirectly. Their desire for direct aggression had been mitigated, so the brothers agreed to go along with Reuben's proposal. They stripped Joseph bare,[27] and Simeon and Levi threw him into a pit swarming with snakes and scorpions.[28] Then Simeon told his brothers to pelt him with stones.[29] He took sadistic delight in inflicting pain upon Joseph.

Once Joseph was in the pit, Reuben left for home, for it was his turn that day to attend his father.[30] Also, as the first-born, the affairs of the household were committed to him and demanded his attention.[31] Reuben had acted to prevent murder by suggesting the pit, and he planned to return and rescue Joseph, but he may have been glad to have an excuse to leave. If Reuben was ambivalent about Joseph's fate, he knew he could not be blamed for what happened in his absence.

When Joseph was cast into the pit, he called out to them: "O my brothers, what have I done unto you and what is my transgression? Are you not afraid before God? Am I not flesh of your flesh, and bone of your bone? Jacob your father, is he not also my father? O Judah, Reuben, Simeon, Levi, my brethren, deliver me, I pray you, from the dark pit into which you have cast me. Ye are children of Abraham, Isaac and Jacob, who were compassionate with the orphan, gave food to the hungry, water to the thirsty, and clothed the naked. How, then, can you have no pity for your own brother, your own flesh and bone? And, though I sinned against you, have pity for the sake of my father. O that my father knew what my brothers are doing to me, and what they said to me!"[32] To shut out the sound of Joseph's cries and the accusation of his words, they removed to the distance of a bow-shot from the pit.[33]

After their meal, the brothers decided, they would pull him out of the pit and kill him. When they had finished eating and were about to say grace, Judah asserted his leadership and remonstrated with every argument at his command. "We seek to take the life of our brother. Shall we bless God? We do not bless; we blaspheme His Name."[34] Citing precedent, Judah counseled, "Let us follow the ancient paths. When Canaan sinned, was he not cursed to be a slave?"[35] Pragmatically, he continued, "What profit is it if we slay our brother and conceal his blood?" Judah could find no meaning to murder—there were other ways to be rid of Joseph. "Come," he concluded, "let us sell him to the Ishmaelites, and let not our hand be upon him." The brothers agreed that the Ishmaelites would take him to the ends of the wilderness and he would be lost among the peoples of the earth.[36] It was sufficient to sell Joseph into slavery; he would trouble them no more.

Before the brothers could sell him to the Ishmaelites, seven Midianite merchantment passing by were attracted to the pit by Joseph's cries. They dragged him out and decided to take him along on their journey. When the brothers saw Joseph in the possession of the Midianites, they accused them of stealing him. Joseph was their slave, the brothers claimed, who had been placed in the pit for disobedience, and they demanded his return. The brothers threatened to kill them, but the merchantmen refused to release Joseph, contending they had found him in the wilderness and that he belonged to them.

The Midianites were ready to do battle, when Simeon sprang at them and with great prowess threw them all to the ground. Simeon would not allow his victim to be spirited away. Terrified, the Midianites said, "Didn't you cast him into the pit because he was rebellious? What would you do with an insubordinate slave? Sell him to us, for we are ready to pay any price you want."[37] The brothers agreed to sell Joseph and the price was set, when the Midianites unexpectedly withdrew their offer and refused to buy him. They thought Joseph had been mutilated when they saw that he was circumcized. The Ishmaelites had come along during the bargaining, however, and they were ready to consummate the deal. So the brothers sold Joseph to the Ishmaelites for the price agreed to by the Midianites,[38] twenty pieces of silver (37:28), or thirty pieces of gold,[39] or five shekels[40]—in any case enough to purchase shoes for themselves and for their wives and children. They would not buy food with the money because it was the price of their brother's blood, but they would convert it to shoes, the totem for their brother, and walk on them. Symbolically they reduced Joseph to a position beneath them. Now what would become of his grandiose dreams of ruling over them?[41]

Returning from his duties at home, Reuben went to the pit to rescue Joseph and restore him to Jacob. He called Joseph, but there was no reply. He went down into the pit, fearing that Joseph had died there, but there was no trace of his body. When Reuben climbed out he tore his clothes as a sign of mourning, and cried out, "What answer shall I give my father, if Joseph be found dead?"[42] Jacob would hold him, the oldest son, responsible. Reuben returned to his brothers, who told him that they had sold Joseph, that they had tried to retrieve him to rectify their error, but that the merchantmen were gone and Joseph with them. Now that Joseph was gone, they wanted him back. Confused by the cross-currents of their emotions, they experienced the peculiar anxiety of "I can't live with you, and I can't live without you." With the money, Reuben tried to overtake the Ishmaelites, but he, too, failed to find them[43] and returned to his brothers to contemplate their next move. Before all else, they vowed never to divulge to anyone what they had done with Joseph. They pledged them-selves to secrecy; whoever would break it would be killed.[44]

Then they needed a plausible explanation of Joseph's disappearance for their father. They could make Jacob believe he had been killed by a wild beast, Dan suggested. They could tear Joseph's coat of many colors and dip it in the blood of a kid, which looks like human blood.[45] Jacob would never know. Simeon disagreed. He had taken Joseph's coat when they stripped him and now he refused to give it up. He was angry because he had been overruled and Joseph was still alive. He had fought the Midianites so that he could kill Joseph himself, and then lost his opportunity when his brothers agreed to sell him. Simeon wanted to keep the coat, to abuse it in place of Joseph if he pleased. When they threatened to tell Jacob that Simeon alone committed the evil deed, he gave up the coat.[46] So they took the garment, the symbol of their father's preference of Joseph; they tore it and dipped it in blood, symbolically rending the special relationship between Jacob and Joseph. They felt they had released their father from Joseph's grip. Having fulfilled their aggressive wish, although indirectly, they felt their self-esteem restored.[47] Successful in dealing with Joseph, the brothers had delivered a double blow. They eliminated the tattler and dreamer from their midst and, at the same time, delivered a crushing defeat to their father. By making Joseph the scapegoat, they also symbolically attacked the partial, all-powerful, patriarch.

Naphtali or Judah[48] took the torn and bloody coat to Jacob and asked him to identify it. Jacob recognized it and was so overcome with grief that he fainted. When he was revived, he identified it as the coat he had made for Joseph.

To gather more details, Jacob called his other sons to him. When they confirmed what he had been told, Jacob fell into deep lamentation. He recalled Joseph's willingness to go in spite of the hard feelings that existed between him and his brothers, and he blamed himself for sending him where harm would befall him.[49] But the brothers denied having seen him since they had left home.[50] Then Jacob expressed how much Joseph meant to him, saying: "How sweet was thy life to me and how bitter is thy death! Would God I had died for thee, O Joseph, my son, for now I am distressed on thy account. . . . Arise, arise, from thy place, and look upon my grief for thee. Come and count the tears that roll down my cheeks. . . . None had died a death like thine since the world did stand."[51] Hearing this must have hurt the brothers—they may have wondered if Jacob would suffer as much on hearing similar news about one of them. Perhaps they were glad Joseph was gone.

Yet, when they saw the extent of Jacob's grief, they regretted what they had done. Judah was grief-stricken. He placed his father's head upon his knees and wiped away his tears, while he himself wept violently. Jacob's sons and their wives tried to comfort him. They arranged a great memorial service and they wept and mourned over Joseph's death and over their father's sorrow,[52] but Jacob refused to be comforted.

That month Jacob suffered a triple tragedy. Bilhah, who had taken her mistress' place after Rachel's death, had died the same day that the news reached Jacob about Joseph. Dinah died soon thereafter.[53] Jacob fell into a deep melancholia and refused to accept Joseph's death as a fact. Somehow aware that the loss of Rachel, Bilhah and Joseph were all one to him, he subconsciously felt the burden of guilt. He grieved not only because he had lost those he loved, but because he had loved them selfishly and caused them to be the objects of bitter hatred. If there had been violence, Jacob felt that he was to blame. He was inconsolable.

When Jacob recovered somewhat, he told his sons to search for Joseph's body, so that he might bury it. He wanted to resolve his doubts about Joseph's fate. He also instructed them to look out for beasts of prey. "Capture the first beast you meet," he ordered them, "and bring it to me alive." Jacob indulged in displacement or substitution of aggression. Since the original culprit was not available, he determined to transfer his hatred and wreak vengeance upon another animal.[54] Subconsciously, however, Jacob transferred his resentment of Joseph to an innocent animal. His guilt for having loved Joseph unconditionally was so great that he was subliminally provoked with Joseph for it. Destroying the animal compensated for his hostility toward Joseph, and helped Jacob to emerge from his melancholic state. He still did not accept Joseph's death as fact, however. Suspicion and guilt disturbed him continuously—suspicion that his sons had done violence, and guilt that the responsibility for it was his.

II

The peculiar relationship between Jacob and Joseph affected each of the other sons so deeply that they sold Joseph into slavery. But as soon as the sale had taken place they regretted what they had done. They pursued the Midianites hoping to redeem Joseph, and when they were unable to overtake them they suffered remorse. The pleasure derived from their treatment of Joseph[55] was followed by a backwash of recrimination and guilt, culminating in various psychogenic illnesses.

Of all the sons, Jacob's favoritism toward Joseph hurt Simeon most. Being the second son of Leah may have contributed to his neurotic tendencies, as it placed him one step below the privileged position of Reuben, the first-born. He was subjected to the hostility of Reuben, to whom Simeon's birth constituted an emotional threat. But love and status were not reserved for Reuben—they were arbitrarily conferred upon Joseph. He had many reasons to envy Joseph, but most of all Simeon envied him their father's love. And the more Joseph flourished under this love, the more damaging it was to Simeon. It disturbed him mentally and physically,[56] and gnawed at his peace of mind. Unwholesome feelings roused him from sleep, leaving him confused and physically weakened. He wanted to destroy Joseph; and, if he had not been sold, Simeon would have killed him. Simeon was so angry at Judah for having suggested the sale, that he harbored ill-feelings against Judah for five months.[57]

Although Simeon wanted to hurt Judah, he was unable to express his anger because his right hand was "half-withered" for a week.[58] By losing the strength in his hand Simeon restrained himself psychologically. He resolved the psychic conflict of loving Judah and yet wanting to hurt him by curbing the expression of hostility with a paralyzing disability in his right arm. The ancient authors understood what we call conversion hysteria, in which psychic conflict brought about by unresolved problems or repressed emotions is converted into hysterical symptoms,[59] a concept later developed by Freud. Unless these emotional conflicts are expressed and relieved, they may induce physical disorders.

Simeon's ailment illuminates his personality. Generally, a person who suffers this reaction is emotionally outgoing and receptively elastic, one to whom love and kindness mean a great deal. Regarding himself as helpless and infantile, he yearns for emotional closeness, yet is frightened by it. His greatest fear is that of "rejection, abandonment, injury and, frequently, bodily frustration." His physical defects appear during a situation of distress and, once the stress subsides, disappear. By means of the symptom, he erects a defense against distress and "expresses help-lessness, punishes himself, and seeks forgiveness, love and support. . . . Weakness of the arm may mask fantasies of murder, of being hurt, of being tied and injured."[60] Thus Simeon hated Joseph for depriving him of Jacob's love; he was disposed to hurt Jacob and unwilling to spare his feelings in relation to Joseph; and he wanted to injure Judah for pro-tecting Joseph,[61] but his disabled arm restrained him.

Dan was similarly affected by Jacob's unconditional love of Joseph. Although he was the first of Bilhah's sons, and grew up in Rachel's care, he was insecure in relation to Jacob. His real mother was a handmaid and became a true wife to Jacob only after Rachel's death. By that time, Joseph had diverted Jacob's affection from him and shattered whatever aspirations of leadership he might have had. While Simeon sensed the futility of competing with Joseph—their father's love was irrational and could not be swayed—Dan naively took a quantitative view of his father's affection. If he disposed of Joseph, he concluded, Jacob would again have love enough for him. With the others Dan resolved to kill Joseph, and he lent support to his brothers' aggressive actions. When they failed to complete the murder, however, Dan was satisfied to see Joseph sold into slavery.[62] Dan seems to have been spared both remorse and psychogenic illness. Once set in the direction of hatred and murder, he did not stop to reconsider. He felt no remorse for the sale of Joseph; his purpose had been accomplished and he suffered no conflict about it.

Gad, like Simeon, hated Joseph violently, and Gad also suffered a psychogenic illness. The first-born of Zilpah, Leah's handmaid, he grew up in an atmosphere of resentment toward Rachel's household. Everyone respected his bravery and initiative—it was he who guarded the flock at night. He was infuriated, therefore, when Joseph convinced Jacob that he squandered the flock for his own gratification. After this, Gad wanted to kill Joseph. He refused to look at Joseph or to hear anything about him until the opportunity arose to dispose of him.[63]

For lack of a better explanation, Gad and the people of his day believed that hostile and aggressive feelings emanated from a person's liver. Gad felt that he had transgressed in hating Joseph and in expressing the aggres- sion that resulted in selling him into slavery. He reasoned that suitable punishment would affect the source of evil. Accordingly, he internalized his aggression in self-punishment, developing a liver ailment. He suffered from this functional disorder for eleven months. When his father prayed for him, Gad achieved self-acceptance and became more objective in his estimate of Joseph. When a person is hated, he came to realize, whatever he does is subject to criticism. Hatred enlarges even inconse- quential faults and errors in the eyes of the antagonist. And a person who is hated, Gad finally admitted, is deemed to be wrong even when he is right.[64] The insight Gad attained into the underlying cause of his illness eliminated the symptoms of internal self-punishment and restored his health.

Everyone recognized Simeon's and Gad's deep-seated hatred of Joseph. When they cast Joseph into the pit, Zebulun and Judah kept guard over it. They feared that Simeon and Gad, and possibly Dan, might jump into the pit and murder Joseph.[65]

Although Reuben had reason to feel more hostile toward Joseph than any of his brothers, because there was also the problem of the birthright between them, he interceded on Joseph's behalf. He disguised his true feelings with sympathy and solicitude, a practice oldest children often employ to push jealousy beneath the surface of consciousness. Reuben submerged his jealousy, which he considered bad, beneath an attitude of self-sacrifice.[66]

Reuben was caught in the vise of a double conflict. Like his brothers, he was deprived of Jacob's love and he resented both his father and Joseph. Yet Jacob expected a great deal of Reuben, for he was the first-born of Leah and the rightful heir. Responsibility rested on Reuben for certain household affairs, as well as for the actions of his younger brothers. When the fateful crisis came, Reuben wanted to express his hostility toward Joseph, but was restrained by the knowledge that Jacob would hold him accountable.[67] He labored under the responsibility of the oldest son, but was denied its rewards.

Unsuccessful in eliciting love from Jacob, Reuben's resentment mani- fested itself in an act of aggression that troubled his conscience until he died. When he was thirty years old,[68] Reuben observed Bilhah bathing, and he was disturbed by a sexual desire for her. According to one version, Bilhah later became intoxicated while Jacob was away visiting his father.

She fell into a deep sleep naked in her chamber. Reuben saw her there and was overcome with passion; he had intercourse with her without waking her. Another version relates that Reuben hid one night and entered Bilhah's room to find her sleeping alone. She awoke while he was having relations with her and cried out. Bilhah attempted to hold him until someone might come, but she released him and Reuben fled. She pitied Reuben and told no one about the incident. But when Jacob returned and wanted to be with her, she felt compelled to reveal what Reuben had done. Jacob's anger never completely left him;[69] when he blessed Reuben from his death-bed he reminded him of his sin (49:4).

After his intemperate act with Bilhah, Reuben was overcome with guilt and shame. He had fallen from grace in his father's eyes by violating his wife, and he had caused Bilhah to lose her husband, for Jacob never slept with her again.[70] When the men of Shechem possessed his sister, Dinah, Simeon and Levi destroyed the entire village. His own act was more vile, Reuben felt, because it involved his father's wife. He was unable even to look at Jacob's face.[71] In attempting to absolve himself, he abstained from strong drink, ate no meat, and permitted no tasty food to cross his lips.[72] This did not give him the release he sought, nor did it bring him self-reconciliation. He suffered from an abdominal illness for seven months.[73]

In addition to his severe sense of guilt, Reuben was in conflict concerning his status as the first-born son. Responsibility was not what he wanted.[74] He longed for a sheltered existence; he longed to be loved. Reuben repressed this dependent attitude successfully, concealing it from himself. Becoming ill, he subconsciously felt, disqualified him for leadership—his health would not permit it. Furthermore, it was already apparent that Jacob's attachment to Joseph might upset the customary succession. Hadn't Jacob relegated Leah to a secondary role? If he would be displaced, Reuben would provide an excuse for it. His illness justified giving the birthright to someone else. Compromise was the way out.

It would appear that Reuben suffered from a psychogenic disturbance generally caused by excessive worry, fear, quarrels, and other types of reverses. When emotional tensions occur in a conflict situation, one can avoid his problem by concentrating upon the symptoms of his ailment. Improvement is possible with a change of environment, rest and release from the situations which are causing the disturbance.[75] These maneuvers, however, are merely stop-gap measures which do not resolve the underlying cause of the upset.

Reuben nearly died, but he recovered from the acute phase of his

illness when his father comforted him and prayed for him.[76] He construed
this to mean that he was forgiven and that Jacob loved him again. It
satisfied his need for dependency, but he felt that he must constantly guard
against sinning again.

Still, Reuben was obsessed with the need to expiate his guilt regarding
Bilhah. His self-image was so distorted that he felt unworthy to be one
of Jacob's sons.[77] Joseph's dream of the sun, the moon and the eleven
stars had a special meaning for him; Reuben experienced genuine relief
that Joseph had included him. Overjoyed, Reuben felt that he owed Joseph
a debt of gratitude.

Joseph's appearance at his brothers' camp in the wilderness created a
real crisis for Reuben. Like his brothers, he hated Joseph and would have
found satisfaction in eliminating him from the family scene. But Reuben's
need for expiation was greater than his need for aggression. And his
need to escape from the burden of responsibility was greater than either
of these. Suddenly realizing that Joseph was valuable to him, Reuben
resolved to do everything in his power to return him to Jacob.

First Reuben asserted his leadership. Speaking with great compassion
and appealing to their conscience, he attempted to convince his brothers
to give up the idea of harming Joseph. When they would not relent, he
suggested that they need not kill him personally. If they would simply
cast him into the pit, he would perish. If they agreed, Reuben planned
to return to the pit with rope and help Joseph escape during the night.[78]
He would return him to Jacob and atone for his sin against his father's
wife.[79]

Ambivalence vitiated Reuben's resolution; he went too far, and he
stayed too long. In his absence, Joseph was sold to the Ishmaelites and
Reuben was left with his burden of guilt and incompetence.

While Gad and Dan, the first-born sons of the handmaids, were aggressive and hostile toward Joseph, and thereby toward Jacob, their younger
brothers were relatively benign. Little is said about Asher, but Naphtali
is characterized as an affectionate son, ever ready to execute his father's
commands.[80]

Of the remaining four of Leah's six sons, the younger two are depicted
as basically gentle personalities to whom violence was repugnant. Issachar
was a pure and virtuous person who never had relations with any woman
other than his wife.[81]

Zebulun, a fisherman, was compassionate. Until they went to Egypt,
he provided his entire family with fish and frequently shared his haul with
poor strangers. He gave according to their needs and sympathized with

those in distress. If the strangers were old or sick, he prepared the food himself.[82] Like the rest, Zebulun suffered remorse after the sale of Joseph, but he escaped psychogenic illness. He was the only one who committed neither direct nor indirect aggression against Joseph, except that he did not tell Jacob the truth when the bloody coat was returned to their father.[83] But the experience was deeply ingrained in his character. Zebulun, who was so touched by Joseph's plea for mercy, could never see a naked man without feeling great compassion for him. Reversing the original act, he would take a garment from his father's house and give it to the needy person.[84] This specific atonement for the mutilation of Joseph's coat helped Zebulun maintain his emotional stability.

Levi must have been a formidable personality and influential among his brothers. They regarded him as their wise man and religious counselor,[85] since Jacob had taken him to Isaac for instruction in the laws of the priesthood. They accepted his authority concerning sacrifices, first-fruits and free-will and peace offerings.[86] But, although Jacob fostered Levi's leadership in this respect, and thus set the precedent for separating leadership into two categories, one secular and one religious, Levi had one fault which rankled Jacob. Levi had an explosive temper which led him and his brothers into violence. In a frenzy of righteous indignation over Dinah's enforced prostitution, Levi and Simeon destroyed the people of Shechem, and some of their brothers joined them in the blood-letting. In his last words, Jacob cursed their anger, "For in their anger they slew men" (49:6). Levi should have known that the defense of his family's honor did not justify wholesale murder.

Another issue fixed Levi in opposition to Jacob. He was intensely loyal to his mother, Leah, and adopted her attitude of rejection. His mother was denied the honor she deserved as first wife; his brother, Reuben, was losing the rights of the first-born; and his own judgment and leadership ability were overshadowed by Joseph. In Levi's eyes, Joseph's special niche in the family was an affront, not only to him, but to justice, and he responded with the fervor of a visionary who will set the world aright with his sword. In the name of justice he would destroy his own brother. Levi never lost his zeal for righteousness, and was always ready to fight for it. With maturity, Levi learned to control his temper,[87] but his descendents destroyed their own brethren with equal zeal for worshipping the Golden Calf (Exodus 32:25-29).

Although Jacob's attachment to Joseph was an emotional one, he was objective in his relationships with his other sons. He knew Reuben was "unstable as water" (49:4), but he discerned merit in Levi and Judah which he fostered with special recognition. He selected them to accompany him to visit their grandfather,[88] perhaps because they offered the best protection on a hazardous journey, or perhaps to have an opportunity to observe them closely—to get to know them better. For Levi, the trip was an educational one. Beneath his furious temper, Jacob saw a power to be harnessed and directed. The religious instruction Isaac gave him ultimately served this purpose, and established Levi as his brothers' religious leader.

For Judah, however, recognition was never made explicit until just before his father's death, when Jacob accepted him as spokesman for the group (49:8-10). Until then, Judah never really knew where he stood. Judah was confident that his leadership would secure his family against internal and external threats, yet the future loomed uncertain for lack of his father's approval.

Regardless of the special status of any of them, his brothers regarded Judah as their chief. Judah's stature is implicit in the quick acceptance of his suggestions. When Judah spoke, his brothers listened, and they were accustomed to following him. It was Judah who warded off the immediate murder of Joseph by suggesting his sale to the Ishmaelites. He placed himself at the edge of the pit to guard against an outburst of violence, knowing that the most hot-headed of his brothers would hesitate to challenge him. In support of his argument, Judah knew how to offer cool logic, the kind of unemotional appeal that left his brothers' self-esteem intact and offered them a practical course of action.

Since Jacob had flaunted primogeniture in regard to his wives, and he was apparently prepared to by-pass Reuben, Judah must have wondered why Jacob did not acknowledge and sanction his position of leadership. The bitter pill that caught in his throat, and in the throat of each of them, was simply that he was born of the wrong mother. As Leah was unloved, so were her sons. On the basis of his father's actions, Judah concluded that his ability would be wasted. He became disturbed by the possibility that Jacob might choose Joseph to succeed him, and that the future of the entire family might be precarious.

After the sale of Joseph, when Jacob and his sons were in the throes of remorse, the brothers turned on Judah, blaming him for their misfortune. Judah was stunned by the accusation. If not for him, he argued, they would have committed murder. He had asked them, "What profit is it if we slay our brother and conceal his blood?" And now they laid the sin at his door![89] They reminded him that he had also said, 'Come sell him to the Ishmaelites," and they followed his advice. "Had you said,

'Come let us return him to his father,' we would have heeded you," they reproached him.[90] They had accepted Judah's leadership because he dis-played qualities which entitled him to the position, but he proved a disap-pointment when he led them to disaster.[91]

Subconsciously, Judah had given advice that could not effect Joseph's deliverance. Since going away or traveling is unconsciously equated with death,[92] Judah's suggestion to sell Joseph contained meaning similar to the conscious expression of his brothers. The loss of his father's love impaired his natural leadership qualities, although Judah was convinced that he acted in the best interests of the family. Now his brothers considered him incapable of adequate leadership. They deprived him of his role and ex-cluded him from their fellowship. To escape the frustration that confronted him, Judah resorted to nomadism,[93] leaving home to seek a new life (38:1).

When he left his family, Judah visited Hirah, an Adullamite. There he met Shua, or Bathshua (38:2), a Canaanite maiden. Bathshua was beau-tifully adorned and plied him with wine, while her father displayed the considerable gold of her dowry. Judah wanted to discuss the marriage with Jacob first because he knew it would displease his father, but they overcame his resistance and he married her.[94] Again, while intoxicated, he slept with Tamar, his daughter-in-law.[95]

Judah's excessive drinking would indicate that he faced deeply dis-turbing problems and suffered unresolved conflicts. He had been deposed from leadership and ostracized by his family. His brothers treated him unfairly, he felt. He tried to help, and was punished for it. Drinking made him feel capable of leadership—still a strong and well-functioning person in complete control of his destiny. Alcohol induced a deceptive feeling of virility and maturity, while subconsciously he knew he had failed the test of responsible leadership. Like running away, drinking was another attempt to escape this conflict. Marriage without his father's ap-proval produced further conflict, and the subsequent death of two of his sons shattered his equanimity. Alcohol obliterated his consciousness of failure and strife; drinking was his symbolic act of suicide.

Judah's legacy to his sons reveals the guilt and shame his drinking engendered. He counselled them against it. Drinking disturbs the mind with filthy thoughts, he cautioned them, and causes one to lose respect for himself and for his fellowman. He pointed out, however, that if one can maintain a measure of modesty and reasonable discretion it is all right to imbibe.[96] The early Hebrew authors understood that alcohol reduces inhibitions and that excessive use of it leads to greater difficulties than those the drinker seeks to escape. Bilhah also drank to overcome her failure to take Rachel's place. Since Reuben had already expressed the resentment of Leah's sons by removing her bed from Jacob's tent, she had reason to be on her guard. If she had not imbibed so much, Reuben might have never found the opportunity to defile her.

Later, Judah exhibited an increased sense of responsibility. When Tamar proved he had fathered her twins, Judah admitted it (38:25-26). Subsequently, his brothers returned Judah to the helm and Reuben followed his example by confessing his act with Bilhah.[97]

Although the interaction of Jacob and his twelve sons culminated in the sale of Joseph, many incidents emphasize Jacob's merit as a father and portray his sons favorably. Except for the incident of the sale, the ancient Hebrew sources say,[98] Jacob's sons had a good upbringing—they were virtuous, deficient in nothing, possessed great understanding and were devoted to one another.

Unlike Abraham and Isaac, who were indulgent, Jacob was a stern father. He kept track of their whereabouts, even when his sons were full-grown men. If they did not report to him, he sent to inquire about them. Neither Abraham nor Isaac were intimately involved in the lives of their sons, and Ishmael and Esau grew wantonly destructive, indulging in theft, rape and murder. While the twelve sons of Jacob were aggressive and hostile, they were not altogether without control. Jacob held up standards of behavior, and if they fell short they judged themselves by his guide. The detailed record of Jacob's role as a father reflects the early Rabbis' recognition of the value of discipline.

His sons treated Jacob with great respect, especially Judah who was devoted and obedient. Judah captured deer and personally prepared them for Jacob, and he honored his mother, Leah, and his aunt, Rachel.[99]

Ultimately, the relationships among the twelve brothers were mutually beneficial. They interceded for each other, as when Dan came to Judah's assistance in a battle and saved his life.[100] After the incident in Shechem, Dinah was too ashamed to leave the city. Simeon promised to marry her, which he did,[101] and he and Levi took revenge on her behalf. The other brothers joined them in the battle, regarding this as their affair too.[102] When Jacob complained that Simeon's and Levi's actions had made him "odious unto the inhabitants of the land" (34:30), Judah came to their defense. "Did Simeon and Levi kill the inhabitants of Shechem for nothing?" he asked Jacob. "It was because Shechem violated our sister that my brothers destroyed the city. Now, why are you afraid and why are you distressed? Why are you hard-hearted toward my brothers? . . . And now cease and do not be afraid. Pray for us to the Lord, for He will give our

enemies into our hands."[103] Credit must also be given to Reuben and
Judah, who interceded for Joseph at the pit. Reuben confessed his act
with Bilhah to protect his brothers from being accused and stigmatized by
his offense.[104] And Judah reproved him for his behavior,[105] as only an
interested brother would.

The remorse they felt after the sale of Joseph remained with the
brothers. They suffered from a compulsive need for punishment. When
guilt feelings oppressed them, punishment gave them relief. They may
have derived masochistic pleasure from their guilt. When the brothers
suffered illnesses induced by psychological tensions, and when they were
accused of being spies, they regarded it as punishment (42:21-22). Simeon
was not sad when he was held as hostage for Benjamin. His suffering was
justified atonement.[106] On their way home, when they found their money
in their sacks, the brothers concluded that their appearance of guilt was
the Lord's visitation upon them (42:28). And again, when Joseph's goblet
was found in Benjamin's sack and they all returned to Egypt, Judah
attributed the failure of their mission to God's punishment for their sins
(44:16).

III

Joseph's demotion, when his brothers seized him and threw him into
the pit, was as complete as it was sudden. Stripped of the symbol of his
favored position, his immunity was gone. Without his father to protect
him, he was helpless. Until that day, he had been the king-pin at home.
His brothers would not have dared to lay a hand on him. Now they ignored
his pleas for mercy; nor were they moved by his urging to spare their
father grief. He had lost every vestige of personal power and emerged
from the pit a common slave. For the first time in his life he was alone
and at the mercy of strangers. If his brothers could be so cruel, what
could he expect from slave traders? Joseph was terrified.

Joseph learned that the Ishmaelite caravan was taking him to Egypt.
The knowledge that he would be so far away from his father shattered his
sense of security and he wept convulsively. One of the Ishmaelites, seeing
him cry, thought that Joseph found riding uncomfortable. He lifted him
off the camel and permitted him to walk. But Joseph continued to weep,
"O Father, Father."[107] He begged them to return him to Jacob, but they
laughed at him. Since he was a slave, they ridiculed him, how could he
know who was his father.

Their route passed Ephrath, where his mother, Rachel, was buried. He
ran to her grave, threw himself across it, and cried, "O Mother, Mother,
thou didst bear me. Arise! Come forth and see that thy son has been

sold into slavery with none to take pity on him. Weep with me over my misfortune, and observe the heartlessness of my brethren. Rouse thyself from thy sleep. Rise up and prepare for the conflict with my brethren, who stripped me even of my shirt, and sold me as a slave . . . and without mercy tore me from my father. Accuse my brethren before God, and see whom He will find guilty. Awake and see how my father is with me in his soul and in his spirit, and comfort and ease his heavy heart."[108]

Joseph believed that Jacob suffered with him, that their souls and spirits were intertwined. He identified with his father because of the similar course of their lives. Their mothers had difficulty in conceiving and each bore two sons, suffering severely in childbirth. Both Jacob and Joseph were born circumcized, were shepherds, and had prophetic dreams. Jacob was hated by Esau, and Joseph was hated by his brothers.[109] Although he wept for his father and hoped that Jacob would be comforted, thinking about Jacob relieved his fears and helped Joseph face the future. If his life continued to parallel his father's, he would also emerge victorious.

Losing the protection of his father promoted Joseph's emotional development. Now that he was among strangers and had no ally, he quickly learned to weigh his actions against the possible consequences. It was the beginning of responsibility. Out of deference to his brothers, he did not tell the Ishmaelites his true identity.[110] Formerly a talebearer, ready to cause his brothers trouble, he was silent now. It could serve no useful purpose to malign them. To avoid incriminating his brothers, Joseph said he was a slave whenever he was asked about his parentage. The Ishmaelites threatened him with death, and Potiphar, his Egyptian master, had him stripped and flogged for concealing his background, but Joseph did not betray his brothers.[111] A eunuch, sent by Potiphar's wife to purchase Joseph from the Ishmaelites, paid eighty pieces of gold for him, but reported that he had paid one hundred pieces of gold. Joseph was aware of the deception, but said nothing. He did not want to see the eunuch harmed.[112] Furthermore, since he could not know what his own fate would be, he enlisted a friend by his silence.

Well-educated and well-bred, Joseph impressed Potiphar as a likable young man. He was not cut out for slave work,[113] Potiphar maintained, and he treated him as one of his family. He provided instruction usually given only to a free man and fed him better than his other slaves.[114] Under these favorable conditions, and no longer obliged to contend with the envy and jealousy of his brothers,[115] Joseph made significant strides. Whereas he had formerly been favored unconditionally, he now learned that he could earn favor through his own merit. He developed his capabilities and won his master's confidence to such an extent that Potiphar entrusted his entire household to him.[116]

Joseph's new-found personal integrity was soon severely tried. Potiphar's wife, Zuleika, tried to seduce him. Joseph's good looks and the fact that Potiphar had been castrated[117] may have combined forces to arouse her. She showed him off before guests and took special delight in merely having others look at him. At a banquet, she provided knives for the women to peel citrons and called Joseph to stand before them. Sharing Zuleika's infatuation, the women feasted their eyes on Joseph and cut their fingers with the fruit knives.[118] Zuleika employed extreme forms of conniving and trickery to break down Joseph's resistance, but he rejected her advances. She threatened him with death, had him beaten, and offered him large sums of money. She promised to be subservient to him[119]—he would be her lord—but Joseph refused to approach greatness in an underhanded manner. He would not indulge in compromise formation or in counteract-ing,[120] nor would he rationalize that a religious act could atone for immoral behavior. Zuleika visited him at night, pretending to regard him as a son, embracing him and baring herself before him. She feigned illness, and gave him presents. She studied his religion as a pretext to be with him frequently, proposing to abandon idol worship and to persuade Potiphar to do the same, if he would only satisfy her desire. Joseph informed her that God prefers purity. Before her husband she flattered Joseph and praised his chastity, while secretly she coaxed him not to fear Potiphar because he was convinced of Joseph's virtue. When none of these tactics succeeded, she threatened to kill Potiphar, to hang herself, to throw her-self from a cliff. She failed in all these attempts.[121] When Joseph discouraged suicide with the argument that Potiphar's concubine would beat her chil-dren and obliterate her memory, she regarded this as evidence Joseph loved her.[122] The training Jacob had given him proved a source of strength, however. Joseph went into his room, fasted, and prayed that God would deliver him from her tentacles.[123]

Just once, Joseph almost weakened. Preoccupied with building a new life for himself, he seldom thought of his father and his brothers. But when he did, he experienced again the trauma of his plunge from power. The unbearable helplessness of his first separation from his father returned and, with it, the need to display his superiority over his brothers. Zuleika caught him at such a moment. He would take her, and all the wealth and power she offered him. He would show his brothers. By winning the favor of so prominent a woman he would compensate for the humiliation to which they had subjected him. But his family was too much on his mind. The images of Jacob and Rachel suddenly appeared before him and he became impotent, or he ejaculated before he could begin the act. He imagined their feelings if they learned what he was about to do; he remembered that this was the same building in which his great-grandmother had been held captive by Pharaoh.[124] He thought of Potiphar, who trusted him. And he thought of Reuben, who had lost his birthright because of an immoral act. If Jacob should learn that he had committed adultery, wouldn't he withhold the birthright from him, too?[125] As in a dream, the image of his parents aroused his moral sense and he refrained from indulging in what they had conditioned him to regard as abhorrent. His illicit passion left him and he ran out of the house. Now Joseph's humiliation was complete. Instead of superiority, he had demonstrated his weakness. He threw himself on the ground and clawed the earth in despair.[126]

Soon Joseph dared to return to the house. Zuleika caught him by his garment and demanded, "Lie with me." Joseph looked about and saw that "there was no man there" (39:11). Again, he was tempted to take her; but as he was about to succumb, the thought of God sobered him. What would God expect of him? Joseph knew—and found himself wanting. There was no man there—not even himself. If he were a man, could he use this foolish woman to wield power over his brothers? He could not. As Joseph was about to leave her a second time, Zuleika clutched his garment and swore she would kill him if he left her now. Like her castrated husband, Joseph frustrated her. Zuleika pressed a sword against his throat, but Joseph rushed away before she could slash him, leaving his garment in her hands.[127]

In his moment of self-discovery, Joseph became aware that hostility toward his brothers still rankled him. Then he realized that he had used his father, as he had almost used Zuleika, as an instrument of power over his brothers. More than ever, Joseph wanted to prove himself his brothers' equal, to be regarded by them as a man; but he realized for the first time that the love of a powerful person could not give him strength. If he would ever be strong, he must find strength in himself.

Zuleika's scorn was evident in her version of what happened. Now she accused Joseph of molesting her. On her word, Potiphar had him flogged without mercy. He would have had Joseph killed, but Zuleika advised against it, suggesting that Joseph be put in prison until he could be sold to recoup the money spent for him. He remained there for twelve years. With Joseph under her control, Zuleika still nourished the hope that he would submit.[128] Asenath, Potiphar's adopted daughter, had seen

Joseph retreat from Zuleika and she told her father about it.[129] Although she convinced him of Joseph's innocence, Potiphar felt constrained to imprison him. He told Joseph, "I must do this lest a stigma fall upon my children."[130] Joseph continued to minister to Potiphar's needs, spending time in his house, even though it meant that he would run into Zuleika frequently.

Zuleika did not give up. She sent word to Joseph in prison that she would cause him greater duress unless he obeyed her, but he remained undaunted.[131] She went personally and threatened to blind him, to have him languish there in chains, to sell him to a distant land, but he was adamant.[132] She went so far as to place an iron fork under his neck to force him to look at her, but he didn't.[133] When every threat failed, she promised to obtain his release if he would only grant her wish. Zuleika continued to visit him from time to time, but to no avail.[134] She had to be content with embracing, kissing and fondling his garment, which she had kept.[135] She indulged in fetishism, turning for erotic satisfaction to his coat which could neither reject nor humiliate her. By achieving mastery over this inanimate totem of her desire, she safeguarded herself against the mortification she felt each time Joseph refused her.

Even in prison, Joseph continued to mature—proof that he had learned to get along with people. Tests have shown that younger children often work out real life situations more successfully than older ones.[136] Both the chief butler and the chief baker had made Joseph their confidant and told him their dreams (40:8, 16), with the result that the people around him, and Joseph himself, came to appreciate his extraordinary insight into the needs and problems of others. Because he was cooperative and conscientious, his jailer was disposed to be kind to him, and the chief butler recommended Joseph to the Pharaoh as an interpreter of dreams. It was this ability that finally placed in Joseph's hands the power to which he had aspired all his life. As chief advisor to the Pharaoh and viceroy of all Egypt, Joseph was second to none. He had come to accept as God's will all that he had endured since he last saw his father. If his brothers were a villainous lot, and his father had foolishly caused him years of misery on account of a coat—it no longer mattered. The present was rich and satisfying—besides wealth and position, he had a wife and two sons. Joseph severed himself from the past when he named his first son Manassah, saying, "God hath made me forget all my toil, and all my father's house" (41:51). He believed the past was forgotten.

When famine struck and spread as far as Canaan, travellers poured into Egypt in search of food. Joseph knew that his family would be

affected by the famine and that they would probably come to Egypt for
food, too. He could have easily communicated with them to offer assistance. Instead, revealing a trace of malevolence, he decided to wait for
them to come to Egypt. To make certain that their arrival would come to
his attention, Joseph ordered every traveller entering Egypt to purchase
food to furnish his name and the names of his father, grandfather and
grandmother. He stationed extra guards at the gates of the city to record
the information and he purused the list every evening. With all these
precautions, Joseph expected to know when his brothers arrived.[137] As
he reviewed the lists each night, Joseph became more and more hopeful
that he would see his father and brothers again, especially his younger
brother, Benjamin. Nostalgia for his boyhood filled him with thoughts
of his family. Although he was uncertain what he would do when he
found them, Joseph wanted to see them once more.

Except for Benjamin, who remained at home with his father, the
rest of the brothers journeyed to Egypt to purchase food. They also anticipated a reunion, for they knew Joseph had been taken there, and it
weighed heavily on their minds. Their hostile feelings toward Joseph
had subsided, and they confessed to each other that they regretted what
they had done to him. They planned to search for Joseph and to show
him brotherly love if they found him. If he were a slave, they resolved
to ransom him; and, if his master should refuse to sell him, they would
risk their lives to free him by force.[138]

On the day they arrived, Joseph saw his brothers' names on the list.
He ordered all food stations except for one closed the next day. He left
the names of his brothers with the manager of that depot and commanded
that they be brought before him when they appeared.[139] The alert continued for several days, but there was no sign of the brothers. Unaware
that they were searching for him in every part of the city, Joseph became
impatient, even angry, and sent servants to look for them. They were
found and forced to surrender their shoes before they were brought
before the viceroy. As they lay prostrate before him, the Egyptians spat
upon them and put them to shame.[140] Joseph realized that they did not
recognize him—he had been a beardless youth when they sold him—but
he recognized each of them (42:8).[141]

Joseph still believed that he had never meant to harm his brothers,
even with his evil reports to his father. In his legacy to his children, it
was evident that he did not regard himself as someone special in his youth,
even though his brothers knew how much Jacob loved him. As he felt
that he had never acted maliciously toward his brothers and had always

honored them,[142] Joseph instructed his sons to honor each other. Nowhere is it stated that Joseph hated his brothers as they hated him. Since he could have revealed himself at once and spared them debasement, however, his behavior disclosed the extent of his ambivalence. His nostalgia was heavily laced with hostility long denied expression. Having been exposed to an extraordinary amount of sibling rivalry, Joseph harbored antagonism toward his brothers that time alone could not erase. As they bowed before him, he grasped the opportunity to retaliate.

Joseph asserted that all others who came to buy food did so without delay, while they lingered for three days wandering all over the city. He accused them of being spies. Although they declared their innocence and explained that they were looking for their brother, not the youngest one who remained at home with their father, but the one who had been kid-napped by an Ishmaelite caravan on its way to Egypt, Joseph persisted in doubting them. Perhaps he was gratified that they had been looking for him. To discover their attitude, Joseph asked what they would do if they found their brother a slave held for a high ransom. They said they would pay it and redeem him. What would they do, he continued, if his master refused to give him up? When they replied that they would kill him and carry off their brother, even if it meant their deaths,[143] Joseph turned and accused them of coming to slay the inhabitants of the land. He knew that they had massacred the people of Shechem, he told them, but they would not have the chance to do the same in Egypt.

Still professing that he believed them to be spies, Joseph demanded that one of them fetch the young brother from home to corroborate their story. The brothers refused, saying that one man could not take enough grain to feed all their families. If they were detained, their wives and children and their aged father might die of hunger. Surely Joseph under-stood their distress, but with utter disregard for his starving family, and for no apparent reason, Joseph had them imprisoned for three days (42:17). Finally he relented a little. He would permit them to deliver the grain, provided they would return with Benjamin, and he would hold one of them hostage. While Joseph did long to see Benjamin, he enjoyed his brothers' obvious discomfiture.

In his presence the brothers expressed the opinion that their misfortune was punishment for their treatment of Joseph (42:21). Reuben reminded them that they had another wrong to expiate—the wrong against their father, who was grieved by their deed (42:22).[144] Since they accepted his toying with them with such pious resignation, Joseph persisted in tor-menting them. He decided to keep Simeon as the hostage, since he, together with Levi, had advised that Joseph be put to death. He dismissed Levi because he feared the wrath that had destroyed Shechem.[145] Also, since Simeon was the least popular among the brothers, Joseph did not expect them to resist his detention as violently as they would if he held Levi, their wise man and priest.[146] Besides, Joseph had a particular grudge against Simeon, for he remembered all too clearly that he was the one who had lowered him into the pit.[147]

The brothers agreed to Joseph's demand and Simeon found himself bartered for their freedom. He turned and accused them, "What you did to Joseph, now you do to me!" He associated his predicament with the sale of Joseph, and felt that his detention was justifiable punishment for his part in it.[148] The brothers replied, "What can we do? Are the members of our household to die of famine?"[149] They saw him bound and taken to prison.

As soon as Simeon was out of sight of the rest, Joseph released him. Forgiving Simeon, he ordered him fed stuffed poultry and that he be dressed well and treated with great kindness.[150] Simeon had acknowledged his guilt, and Joseph was satisfied.

Having purchased their grain, and having heard Joseph impress them once more to return with Benjamin, the brothers departed. On the way, Levi opened his sack to feed his donkey and found his money.[151] Trembling with fear, they all concluded that appearing guilty was the Lord's visitation upon them (42:28). Although they could not understand the presence of the money that marked them as thieves, they punished themselves, acknowledging their guilt in relation to Joseph. With every step toward home, their crime increased in magnitude. They faced the double dilemma of rescuing Simeon by turning over Benjamin, and of winning their father's cooperation without reopening the subject of Joseph's disappearance. As they struggled to solve these problems amid the urgency of the famine, Judah and Reuben found relief in reminding the others that they had advised against the mistreatment of Joseph.

When Jacob heard what they had encountered and what was expected of them, he refused to let Benjamin go. Intuitively, he blamed them in one breath for the loss of both Joseph and Simeon. Now they proposed to take Benjamin, his only link with Rachel. She had died on the roadside, and Joseph had died on the way to his brothers. If Benjamin should suffer the same fate, Jacob would lose forever the feeling of Rachel's presence which her sons gave him, and he himself would die of grief.[152] He could not give up Benjamin, for "if harm befall him . . . you will bring down my gray hairs with sorrow to the grave" (42:38). In desperation, Reuben offered to have his sons killed if he failed to bring Benjamin back. His guilt was so great that he would have sacrificed the lives of his own sons to atone for the lives of Joseph and Benjamin. But Jacob thought Reuben a fool. Didn't he know his sons were also Jacob's grandsons?[153]

Judah stepped in to prevent the situation from deteriorating. Having lost two sons himself, he understood his father's behavior and advised against arguing the issue with him. Eventually Jacob would consent, he predicted. When their food gave out, another journey would be impera-tive.[154] His judgment proved correct, for soon the family suffered from hunger again. Jacob castigated his sons for revealing that they had a younger brother, and ordered them to purchase food from the viceroy, but without Benjamin. Judah protested the reproach, and informed Jacob that the viceroy already knew everything about them, even the kind of wood of which their beds were made.[155] It was possible that Benjamin might be taken from them, he admitted; it was also possible that he might not. He advised his father not to concern himself with the doubtful.[156] Judah extolled the viceroy's might, his vision and understanding, and his administrative ability.[157] And, measuring his father's anguish against his own when Er and Onan had died, Judah pledged himself as surety for Benjamin's safety[158]—he would renounce his position in the world to come if a third son should be lost to Jacob. Finally, Judah refused to go to Egypt without Benjamin. Each of them was equally involved in the welfare of the others, he asserted. If Jacob failed to act to avoid the risk of personal loss, it would influence not only the future of Benjamin, but that of Simeon and, eventually, of all the rest. It was better that one life should be risked, he said, than that they should all certainly die.[159] Under the added weight of responsibility to the group, Jacob resigned him-self to the bitter choice and consented to Benjamin's going. He gave them gifts and a letter for the viceroy, and double money to provide against a rise in prices since their first trip. He blessed them, and they departed.[160] Once more, Judah's leadership had been decisive.

Joseph's masquerade, begun in a wave of nostalgia, had by now swept his family to almost total despair. He had forced his brothers to grovel before him and execute his every whim, and he had brought grief to his ailing and aged father. He knew Jacob's suffering when they were sep-arated was as great as his own, yet Joseph did not hesitate to take Simeon from him, and now Benjamin. Joseph employed the same displacement mechanism that made him the victim of his brothers' aggression in lieu of his father. His weapon—withholding food—betrayed his all-encompassing hostility. Although he believed he had transcended his limitations in his new life in Egypt, Joseph had remained unreconciled to his past. Subconsciously, he still blamed his father for the fate that befell him, and he wanted to cause him anguish. But, with each encounter with his brothers, Joseph became more involved emotionally. His conflicting desires for aggression and for reconciliation fought for expression.

Overjoyed to see Benjamin, Joseph saw in him the loving images of his father and mother,[161] and his conflict was eased. Through his steward, he invited his brothers to a Sabbath meal,[162] another tie with his parents. At first, they refused the invitation. They suspected a ruse to capture them on account of the money they had found in their sacks, and they feared that the food would not be ritually prepared.[163] They offered to return the money, but the steward assured them that he had received their payment. Then Simeon, who had grown fat while he was being held,[164] was brought to join them. They listened with wonder as he told them that he had been treated with kindness and released from prison after they had left the city, and that he had been entertained with splendor in the viceroy's house.[165] When Joseph came into the room, Judah took Benjamin by the hand and presented him, and they all bowed before him. Then Judah gave Joseph his father's letter. Deeply moved, Joseph spoke to Benjamin and blessed him, but he was unwilling to display his emotion before his brothers. He quickly left them and, when he returned from weeping in his chamber, he had washed his face and composed himself to preside at the meal.

Since the meal was prepared in their presence according to ritual regu-lations, the brothers finally agreed to eat with the viceroy.[166] As he seated them with elaborate ceremony, they marvelled that he knew so much about them. His winecup told him whatever he wanted to know, he said, as he attributed to the cup facts that he either knew or overheard. He placed Judah at the head of the table, saying that he was king. Reuben, the first-born, he seated second, and the others he assigned according to their dignity and age,[167] except Benjamin, whom he placed next to himself. Since he had no brother born by his own mother, and since Benjamin had none, therefore Benjamin would sit next to him, Joseph explained.[168] No doubt Joseph enjoyed his little joke on them. He and his wife, Asenath, and their two sons gave Benjamin their portions of food,[169] and they all drank much wine for the first time in twenty-two years (43:34). Joseph had abstained from drinking because he grieved over the fate of his father,[170] and his brothers had done likewise because they regretted the evil they had done to Joseph, but they permitted themselves to share the viceroy's cordial mood.

Joseph was beginning to consider revealing himself to his brothers, but his hostility was not yet spent. Even while they were dining together, he was planning to put them to a test. To provide an excuse to seize him and take him away from his brothers, Joseph would conceal his winecup in Benjamin's sack. If they would risk their lives to fight for Benjamin, then he would know they had repented, and he would reveal himself. But, if they forsook Benjamin, then he would let them go without making his true identity known.[171]

Next morning, before they had gone far, Joseph sent Manasseh, his steward, to overtake them and recover his silver goblet. Manasseh charged them with the theft. Certain that it could not be substantiated, the brothers decreed death for the culprit if he be found among them, and bondage for the rest. Manasseh reduced the penalty to comply with Joseph's instructions. Only the thief would be a bondman; the rest would be set free. The brothers watched as each man's sack was searched. From the eldest to the youngest, each was absolved in turn until, horrified, they saw the cup in Benjamin's sack. They shouted at him, "You are a thief and the son of a thief. You are your mother's son. Thus did your mother shame our father." They were referring to Rachel's theft of her father's idols. Their attack on him and on his mother's memory suddenly illuminated for Benjamin the mystery of his only real brother. He retorted, "Have we he-goats here? Have we here brothers who sold their brother?"[172]

They rent their clothes and returned to Egypt. On the road back, the brothers mistreated Benjamin and accused him, but he suffered their blows and abusive words in silence.[173] Benjamin was preoccupied, trying to understand why he was the key to the success or failure of his brothers' errand to buy food. He sensed that he occupied much the same position as Joseph before his disappearance, and he wondered why his brothers sometimes stopped talking when he approached. Suspicion ploughed up memories of questions unanswered, of fearful looks and attitudes of guilt. Benjamin saw his brothers with new and sharper vision, and hoped for a clue to explain their strange predicament.

While the others abused Benjamin, Judah did not. They were willing to sacrifice Benjamin to appease the viceroy and gain their freedom, but Judah refused to compromise himself again.[174] During all the years since the sale of Joseph, Judah had been trapped in guilt. He had exiled himself, he had attempted to drown the memory in drink, he had dedicated himself to serve his father, but awareness that he had failed to live up to his best self had stripped his deeds of value. Judah felt he had lived as a coward. Now he faced a choice again. He could abandon Benjamin and take his freedom, or he could return to Egypt and fight for him. Even with the aid of his brothers, his chance of surviving the might of the viceroy was slim; but to abandon Benjamin was equivalent to abandoning himself. This latest crisis was not only punishment for what he had done to Joseph (44:16), but also an opportunity to invest his life, or his death if necessary, with meaning. Prepared to return with them, Judah turned to accompany the Egyptians, leaving his brothers confused by the action of their leader. He appeared to be going to certain death, yet they followed him, begrudgingly at first, and full of fear. But the example of Judah's commitment inspired his brothers to rally behind him. He roused them to action, declaring, "Be brave, demean yourselves as men, and let each one of you show his heroism, for the circumstances demand that we do our best."[175] They rallied to his leadership and stood solidly behind him when they returned to Egypt. When the viceroy had Benjamin locked in a room, Judah broke down the door;[176] in response to his unequivocal assertion of leadership, his brothers would destroy all of Egypt, if Judah told them to. Although they would not speak while they were in the presence of the viceroy—"for it is not seemly for us to interfere. . . . It is fit for a king to contend with a king"[177]—they stamped their feet on the ground and they raged. They supported Judah as long as he acted as a leader. Judah found himself free at last to exploit his capacities to their limit, without reservation. He grasped the full meaning of responsibility to himself, and to those who looked to him for leadership, when he remarked that even a king, should he live immorally and unethically, would be stripped of his position.[178]

Joseph did not hold court that day, but remained at home so that his brothers would not be exposed to shame in public.[179] When they were brought into his preseice, Joseph ordered the Egyptians to leave the room. He was prepared to reveal himself to his brothers and face a final showdown. They might decide to kill him, but Joseph felt confident they would not.[180]

Although he felt kindly toward them, his hostility came to the fore again. At the same time that he emphasized his own power to "divine," Joseph played upon their guilt with double-edged accusations. He told his brothers that Benjamin stole his cup in order to perform magic with it, to learn the whereabouts of his brother.[181] When they refused to return to their father without Benjamin, Joseph provided a ready-made excuse for them. "Your first brother, who did not steal and did not trouble you,

you told your father was torn by animals. This one, who did steal and did trouble you, go tell your father he, too, was torn by animals."[182]

Judah became Joseph's adversary in verbal combat. He told Joseph that two of his brothers destroyed a city because of a female; on account of a son, he threatened, they would definitely do so.[183] He argued many points with Joseph and even accused him of wanting to detain Benjamin as a slave to commit sodomy on him.[184] Impressed by Judah's forcefulness and the support of his brothers, Joseph retaliated by asking Judah why he was the spokesman. "I see in my cup that there are greater among your brothers than you, and you are a babbler."[185] Showing no anger, Judah agreed with Joseph that his brothers were greater than he.[186] Judah calmly disregarded the attempt to make him look ridiculous; he was determined to rescue Benjamin and nothing could deflect him from his purpose. He stalked Joseph until he reached his heart.[187] "What do you want with Benjamin? If greatness, I am greater than he; if strength, I am stronger than he. It is better that I be a slave, instead of him, than to bring grief to my father." With mention of his father's grief (44:34), Judah unwittingly cut deep. Joseph burst into hysterical weeping (45:2) and found it difficult to control himself since there was no other outlet for his tension,[188] but he managed to stay.

Weary of this cat and mouse game, Joseph felt drained of hostility and wanted only to be accepted by his brothers. To focus attention once more on himself, he demanded, "Where is your brother? Where is he?" He then upbraided them, "Why do you speak falsely? Didn't you sell him to me and I bought him from you? I will call him and he will answer me." He then cried out, "Joseph, the son of Jacob! Joseph, the son of Jacob!" The brothers looked in all directions. "What do you see?" Joseph asked. As they searched the corners of the room, he said, "I am Joseph, your brother" (45:4).[189] They would not believe him, even when he spoke to them in Hebrew and showed them that he was circumcized.[190] They wanted to kill him for causing them shame and suffering, but they were too heavily burdened with guilt to approach him.[191]

Now that this was out of his system, Joseph's attitude underwent a momentary change. He was sorry to see his brothers in distress. He tried to calm them, saying, "Now be not grieved, nor angry with yourselves, that you sold me hither; for God did send me before you to preserve life" (45:5), but they would not be calmed. He embraced Benjamin and wept upon his neck, and Benjamin cried too (45:14). He kissed them all in turn and wept over each of them, although there is no indication that they also cried (45:15). Seeing Joseph's tears settled them and they spoke to him (45:15) for the first time since he revealed his identity. Joseph's violent sobbing convinced them that the wound they had caused him was healed, and they no longer had reason to fear him (45:3). They saw that his tears drained away his anger and hate and reduced his tension.[192] As Joseph became more relaxed and affable, they became reconciled to him.[193]

The description of this emotional crisis in the lives of the twelve brothers, both in Scripture and in other early Hebrew sources, reveals a most sophisticated insight into human behavior. In this reconciliation, as in the reconciliation of Jacob and Esau, the brothers cried at the termination of their long-standing enmity (33:4) and friendship took over. The number of incidents of crying recorded in Scripture underscores the different attitudes regarding tears in the East and the West. Whereas Orientals display their tears openly and do not consider crying a form of weakness, we suppress what we consider a feminine trait, only to have tears appear in the disguised form of allergies and other psychogenic illnesses.

The Hebrew authors do not suggest that Joseph or Jacob or Esau shed "tears of joy." Like many students of psychology today, they found other reasons for shedding tears on happy occasions.[194] Happy events awaken other thoughts, which do cause tears. Happiness restored produces guilt and the feeling that one is unworthy of the present joy. If one had exercised kindness instead of cruelty and harshness, happiness would not have been lost in the past. Thus Joseph and Jacob and Esau cried at their reconciliations because they were reminded of the bitter hatred that had prevailed in the past. This is called "the inner dialectic of human behavior,"[195] which holds that the flow of feelings is generally regulated by the expression of opposites, preventing expression in exhausting bursts and thereby maintaining emotional equilibrium. Funerals, for instance, recall weddings; sickness recalls health; old age recalls youth; and happiness recalls sadness.

Another explanation for tears on a happy occasion can be derived from the use of the Hebrew word vayishawkayhu in the reconciliation of Jacob and Esau. It means "and he kissed him" (Esau kissed Jacob), but it is written with a number of dots above it. To the ancient Rabbis the dots denoted an impulse to bite Jacob, but Esau checked himself. Long before modern psychology, they recognized that a kiss is a disguised bite.[196] Because he felt the reconciliation was not genuine or complete—an undercurrent of hostility persisted that must be controlled—Esau wept. Despite his show of forgiveness, Joseph also felt that he could not wholly forgive his brothers. Compulsive talk after he revealed himself (45:4-13) must have had a cathartic value, but it was insufficient to completely eradicate his hostility. Joseph's tears and his barbed remarks indicate that he was not fully reconciled, although he wanted to be. Tears also reveal regret for the lost years he could have shared with his family, when he could have given kindness and love, but did not.[197]

Still another theory for crying takes into account the universal awareness that happiness is only temporary, and death is inevitable. One weeps for the sad end which is sure to come.[198] Related to this is the phenomenon called the "delay of affect."[199] While one is concerned about the future—as long as the wished-for happy solution has not taken place—one suppresses his sadness. When the wish is fulfilled, the inhibition is lifted and one permits himself the discharge of the repressed sadness.

Tears reduce the sense of insecurity that follows an injury to narcissistic feelings. They are wet and warm and strikingly similar to amniotic fluid. Almost identical in the content of sugar, protein and sodium chloride, tears on the skin may be reminiscent of the uterine existence.[200] Thus, when Joseph confronted the full scope and force of his hostility for the first time, his self-image was shattered. No longer able to pretend that his attitude toward his brothers and his father was without malice, he felt estranged from himself. He had lost the security of self-knowledge and was forced to evolve a new concept of himself. The warmth and moisture of his tears must have momentarily relieved his insecurity.

Whether any or all of these theories are operative, tears serve, at the same time, as a protective reflex action. "Happiness can be painful if it is too intense" because of the tensions built up in achieving it. Crying relieves the pressure and reduces the suffering.[201] Joseph and his brothers, and Jacob and Esau, were so overjoyed by the turn in their personal relationships that crying was the quickest and surest way of easing their pain.

Perhaps because he was impressed by Judah's stature, Joseph immediately reinforced his own. Indulging his vanity, he described his greatness to his brothers, and instructed them to hasten to Jacob and tell him: "God hath made me lord of all Egypt" (45:9). He slyly alluded to their tendency to fight among themselves when he added, "See that ye fall not out by the way" (45:24). The attitude of condescending superiority that characterized his youth reappeared in their new relationship, the difference being that now his bragging corresponded with the facts. Joseph had the upper hand now, and he had no intention of relinquishing it. He gave his brothers two changes of clothing, one for the weekdays and one for the Sabbath, but to Benjamin he gave five changes of clothing. In wielding his undisputed authority arbitrarily, he resembled his father and his grand-father, who had also shown favoritism,[202] overlooking the injunction that distinctions should not be made among children on the basis of the father's preference.[203] Without recognizing it, Joseph readily repeated the pattern for which he held his father blameworthy. Jacob did arrive at the realiza-tion that he resembled Isaac but he was an old man when it came to him. It seems that one does not always learn from personal mistakes; something more is needed. Through insight and depth of understanding, one must recognize and acknowledge his error.

Joseph's attitude toward his brothers did change considerably. The dramatic unfolding of his identity coupled with the act of forgiving his brothers served as a form of catharsis. He told his brothers, "Ye meant evil against me; but God meant it for good" (50:20). He was content to let bygones be bygones, and he made plans to insure their future welfare.

When Joseph presented his brothers to Pharaoh, he selected the weakest among them so that Pharaoh would not be tempted to retain them as warriors.[204] He introduced them as shepherds, since the Egyptians, who regarded cattle as sacred, kept away from such people. Pharaoh, never-theless, invited them to settle in Egypt, but gave them the outlying district of Goshen, away from the populace (47:6). Pharaoh was pleased with the turn of events in Joseph's life, but not all of his ministers agreed with him when he invited Joseph's brothers to settle in Egypt. Many of them protested, saying, "If one of the sons of Jacob came hither, and he was advanced to a high position over our heads, what will happen to us when ten more come hither?"[205] The seeds of anti-Semitism already existed. They forgot that Joseph saved Egypt when it was besieged and supplied the country with food.[206] But Joseph succeeded in securing land for his family.

The brothers themselves admitted that Joseph bore them no malice.[207] Though most antagonistic toward him, Simeon praised Joseph for not reproaching them for selling him into slavery. Simeon was especially grate-ful that Joseph loved him as the rest of the brothers.[208] Joseph loved them as himself, glorified them even more than his sons, and he made them wealthy. Joseph not only refrained from upbraiding them, but he comforted them. He did not hurt them in any manner, but their suffering was his. He regarded their children as his children, and his own children as their servants. He was not arrogant with them, but regarded himself as the least among them.[209] When his family settled in Goshen, Joseph provided them with food, drink and clothing, and he entertained his father and his brothers daily at his own table.[210] Whatever he gave his brothers he gave

with a liberal spirit.[211] He drove the wrong his brothers had done him
from his mind, and he begged his father to pray for them.[212]

His excessive generosity suggests that Joseph still suffered from the
feeling that his brothers rejected him. Even in their distress, he envied
the bond that united them and excluded him. He exhibited the extreme
protectiveness, cloying sweetness and over-eagerness to please that frequently disguise jealousy and rivalry. By giving all and demanding nothing
in return, he still hoped to win their love. The same need had motivated
his youthful bragging and self-aggrandizement, but Joseph had matured
in his struggle from slavery to eminence. He was capable now of turning
his attention outward, of concentrating on the needs and desires of others.
He had learned that he was nothing except what others recognized him to
be through his actions.

As a result of the manner in which Joseph treated them, Simeon and
Levi became Joseph's champions and were violent with anyone who wanted
to harm him. They welcomed the opportunity to protect him from new
threats, because in this way they could undo the harm they had wished
upon him in the past.[213] When Pharaoh's son became enamored with
Asenath, Joseph's wife, he attempted to induce Simeon and Levi to kill
Joseph. Simeon was so angry that he wanted to kill the Egyptian prince,
but Levi stopped him, advising that they must not repay evil with evil.
Then Levi addressed Pharaoh's son with the moral authority that earned
him the priesthood. Nothing could persuade them to kill Joseph, he
told him; and then he gave the Pharaoh's son a choice. If he did anything
to harm Joseph, Levi warned him, he would kill him; but, if he would
abandon his plan, Levi told him he need not be afraid.[214] Levi stood ready,
as always, to defend his family's honor, but he had learned temperance.
As long as the deed had not been committed, he offered the alternative
of refraining. His morality was not aimed at punishment, but at the preven-
tion of destructive behavior.

Pharaoh's son, however, did not give up the plan. He tried to induce
the sons of Bilhah and Zilpah to kill Joseph. He lied to them about a
conversation he overheard between Joseph and his father. He claimed that
Joseph said he awaited the death of Jacob to kill them because they had
been the most brutal. The sons of the handmaids experienced again the
deep sense of insecurity of their youth. The implication that they were
still inferior because of their mothers' lowly station rekindled their hatred
for Joseph. Dan and Gad wanted to believe this about Joseph, and agreed
immediately to the proposal to kill him. Insisting that they must stand
together to repel the danger that threatened them, they enlisted Naphtali

and Asher to join in the plot.[215] It was agreed that they would kill Joseph, and the Pharaoh's son would kill his own father to eliminate the possibility of punishment. He would obtain Asenath for his wife as well as the throne. When their attack failed, Simeon wanted all the plotters killed. As extreme in his feelings about defending Joseph as he had been extreme in his aggression against him, Simeon was unwilling to make any concessions. Asenath, however, was charitable toward her misguided brothers-in-law, and Levi added his counsel to prevent violence against them. Since their attempt was abortive and they learned they were being used as pawns, he felt they would not repeat their error.

The understanding and maturity which was reflected in Joseph's treatment of his brothers also entered into his new relationship with his father when Jacob came to live nearby. Joseph avoided being in constant attendance upon his father. He did not want to give him the opportunity to inquire into how he came to Egypt, so Joseph was hardly ever alone with him. If Jacob should learn what had happened, he would curse his brothers, Joseph feared.[216] He instructed his brothers never to tell Jacob what they had done to him, but advised them to say only that he had been violently kidnapped by Canaanite merchantmen who sold him to Ishmaelites. Joseph told this much to Benjamin, too, but he never personally told him the whole truth.[217] Jacob, however, pressured him to reveal what had taken place, and Joseph finally told him, but he begged Jacob to pray that God would forgive his brothers. For saying this, Jacob embraced him and kissed him for two hours.[218]

Joseph's attachment to Jacob and reverence for him never left him. Their lives continued to reflect a repetitive pattern. Both were forced into exile by their siblings, and Jacob became a servant to Laban while Joseph served Potiphar. Both their masters were blessed by God; both married outside of Palestine; both were wealthy; both extracted promises to be buried in Palestine; and both put an end to famine when they came to Egypt.[219]

Only two years of the seven-year famine had passed when Jacob came to Egypt, but the famine ceased then. The remaining five years were remitted until after Jacob died.[220] Even as viceroy of Egypt, Joseph manifested his love and respect for his father. He readied his own chariot to meet him,[221] and ordered everybody to meet Jacob with him.[222] He wore Pharaoh's royal crown, lent to him for the occasion.[223] Out of respect, he descended from his chariot when he was about fifty ells from his father and walked the rest of the way on foot.[224] To keep Jacob from a too sudden meeting with him, he sent his older son ahead, and then his younger son. As each son approached, Jacob thought he saw Joseph. In this way Joseph prepared him gradually to see him face to face.[225]

The reunion of his sons in Egypt brought peace to Jacob and he was content to die in their midst. All twelve survived him, and they and their children held fast the promise of the new nation conceived by Abraham. Jacob blessed his sons before he died, acknowledging both their merits and their weaknesses, and charged each one with the responsibility for his own tribe in the future. His own legacy to them was encumbered neither by the custom of primogeniture nor by the tradition of Abraham and Isaac. Jacob made his belief in the concept of individual merit vividly explicit; the younger son who displayed greater potential worth was given the nod. The right of the first-born was forfeit by Reuben's actions—his behavior with Bilhah betrayed that he was "unstable as water" (49:3-4). In his stead, Jacob elevated not one, but three of his sons to the role of leadership. In each case, he acknowledged the self-image held by that son and deferred to by all the others. Levi, whose influence among his brothers was his moral leadership, was to become the progenitor of the priesthood, but Jacob condemned his vindictiveness at Shechem and implied that morality could not exist without charity. Thus, for the first time, a distinction was made between the spiritual and the secular.

To Judah his father bequeathed the secular leadership, for the reason that he exercised it already. His ability to find the heart of a matter and to initiate appropriate action—whether words or warfare—held the respect of his brothers. Jacob knew that Judah had accepted the responsibility of leadership; therefore he blessed his discerning mind, his vigor and physical grace, and the dispassionate temperament that denotes a good ruler.

Jacob's jubilant praise of Judah contrasts with the gnawing doubt that marred their relationship after Joseph's disappearance. Never able to accept Joseph's death as a fact, Jacob looked to Judah, as the leader of his sons, to allay his suspicions. But Judah's behavior misled him. Jacob misconstrued attentiveness for atonement, and labored many years under the impression that Judah had killed Joseph.[226] It was only when he learned how assiduous Judah had been in securing Benjamin's safety that Jacob realized his error. He gave Judah the honorable task of building a school and a dwelling in Goshen to compensate for the injustice he had done him. And it gave him great joy, before he died, to acknowledge Judah's merit.

To Joseph, Jacob gave a double blessing and a double portion in his inheritance. He blessed Joseph twice—once by blessing his sons, Manasseh and Ephraim, and once directly. By adopting each of Joseph's sons as his own, and by giving each of them an equal share with his own sons, he endowed Joseph with the double portion ordinarily reserved for the first-born.

The principle of primogeniture had value for Jacob—he agreed that one son might be superior to the others, but he disagreed that it was necessarily the first-born. And, in addition to recognizing the value and merit of each son, he reserved to himself the freedom to express his love without regard for the proprieties of the social order in which he lived. Thus, his unconditional love for Joseph found its fullest expression in Jacob's final blessing. Every good of which Jacob was heir from his forefathers, and every good of which he could conceive in limitless space and time, he wished to be the portion of his favorite son. And all this Jacob bestowed without excuse, for Joseph had withstood every test and "abode firm." Whether Joseph was strengthened by his father's love or by the hand of God, his ultimate maturity justified Jacob's emotional preference for him. To the end, Jacob saw Joseph as a "prince among his brothers," and neither Joseph nor his brothers ever denied his eminence.

Jacob's death occasioned a new readjustment for the brothers. Joseph respectfully placed his body upon an ivory couch ornamented with gold, studded with gems and surrounded by draperies.[227] He observed the mourning customs to the fullest extent. The anger and hostility he felt toward Jacob for causing the disruption within the family[228] found release with his tears. He wept over his father and lamented the empty years of their separation (50:1).

The brothers, however, did not cry over Jacob. They were fully reconciled to their past relationship with him—both Joseph and Benjamin had been restored to him—but the funeral raised doubts in their minds as to the future. Jacob had instructed that he be buried in Palestine in the Cave of Machpelah, an arduous journey from Egypt. Levi was not to carry his bier, he specified, because he was to carry the Holy Ark; and Joseph was not to carry it, because he was a king.[229] The procession, swelled to great numbers by the Egyptians who paid homage to Joseph's father, and by the charioteers and horsemen who protected them along the way, testified to Joseph's power. The brothers' guilt and insignificance combined to undermine their sense of security, and they became apprehensive that Joseph would still even the score with them.

After the burial, when they passed the pit into which they had cast him, Joseph kneeled and said, "Blessed be God who permitted a miracle to come to pass for me here."[230] The brothers interpreted these words to mean that he would take revenge on them. When they returned to Egypt, they also observed that he had given up entertaining them at his table. They regarded this, too, as a sign of hatred. Actually, Joseph had stopped the invitations out of respect for them. While Jacob was alive, he complied with his father's wish that he sit at the head of the table, although Reuben was the oldest and Judah the leader. Now Joseph was reluctant to flaunt his position; and yet, as the ruler of Egypt, he could not yield his place. He therefore decided not to have his brothers at his meals.[231] But the brothers' guilt and insecurity demanded appeasement, so they contrived a way to reassure themselves.

The sons of Bilhah were sent as emissaries to Joseph with a message purported to have been spoken by Jacob. Before he died, they claimed, Jacob commanded them to tell Joseph to forgive his brothers.[232] Joseph knew his father had not spoken this order, and he wept (50:17) because they betrayed their lack of trust in him and in his affection.[233] He was hurt to find he was still suspect, and angry with himself for failing to overcome the hostility which undermined his earlier protestations of good faith. He assured his brothers again that he would do them no harm, and sought to win their acceptance with a number of appeals. He had stopped inviting them, he explained, not because of enmity, but out of consideration for their feelings. They had been compared to the dust of the earth and the beasts of the field, he reminded them. Could these be exterminated? They had been likened to the stars, he said, and who could destroy them? If ten stars had wanted to destroy one star and failed, could he then, being one star, destroy all of them? In a most diplomatic fashion, Joseph maintained his supremacy while establishing his unity with them. He compared them to the body and himself to the head. If the body is removed, of what value is the head? They had no reason to fear him for he had no intention of becoming his father's opponent. What his father begot, he would not destroy. Above all, he told them, they had given him status. He had been regarded by the Egyptians as a slave. They affirmed that he was of noble birth. If he were to kill them, the Egyptians would claim that they were not his brothers after all, and he would lose their trust. In this fashion he comforted them.[234]

Jacob's death removed the barrier to reconciliation for the twelve brothers. Their common loss permitted the discharge of their guilt in rela-tion to their father—the brothers' guilt for the grief they had caused him in his lifetime, and Joseph's guilt for having wanted to forget his father and his entire family. They drew together in common need for each other. Now that Jacob was dead, a bond of devotion developed among his sons.

Grateful for the dynamic interplay with them that gave impetus to his growth, Joseph loved his brothers even more after his father's death.[235] If anyone sought to do them evil, he counselled his children, treat them well.[236] Through suffering, Joseph surmounted the wall that alienated him from his father and his brothers and attained the full realization of self that enabled him to love others.

CHAPTER EIGHT

He Set Ephraim Before Manasseh

(Genesis 48:20)

IN Egypt, Joseph married Asenath, the foster daughter of Potiphar and Zuleika, who bought him from the Ishmaelites. While the Bible takes little note of her, a number of legends in Hebrew literature concern Asenath. Perhaps her character aroused speculation because she married such an extraordinary personality, and because Jacob bestowed an unpre-cedented blessing on their two sons, Manasseh and Ephraim.

Asenath was only a young child when she interceded to prevent Potiphar from hanging Joseph. Asenath swore under oath that Joseph was innocent of molesting Zuleika. Potiphar believed the child and recanted.[1] Although he was unaware of it, Asenath had saved Joseph's life.

Years later, when Joseph was viceroy of Egypt, Asenath was among the girls who threw gifts to attract his attention as he passed. Having no other gift, Asenath took the gold amulet from about her neck and threw it to him. From the inscription on the tab, Joseph learned that the child of his former master was a member of his father's household. Asenath had become a beautiful young woman. She was as slender as Sarah, as beautiful as Rebekah, and as radiant as Rachel,[2] the Rabbis say. Because Joseph wanted to marry her, he inquired into her background and uncovered a fascinating tale.

Joseph learned that Asenath was the daughter born to Dinah as a consequence of her ill-fated experience with Shechem. Her uncles (Joseph's brothers) wanted to kill her when she was born because she would remind them of Dinah's enforced prostitution. But Jacob would not permit the child to be killed, insisting that she was innocent of blame. Instead, he inscribed God's Name and her parentage on a golden flower and tied it around her neck. Then he abandoned her at the Egyptian border, select-ing a place where he was confident she would be found. Potiphar was walking near the city's wall with his servants when he heard Asenath cry and had her brought to him. When he learned from the inscription on her necklace that she was from the household of the great Hebrew patriarch, he decided to raise her as his own daughter.

At first Asenath refused when Potiphar proposed that she marry Joseph. Although Joseph had become the most influential man in Egypt, she declined to marry a vagabond and former slave, the son of some unknown Canaanite herdsman. Perhaps she rationalized that such a handsome and popular figure might reject her. She had been blinded in one eye,[3] and undoubtedly felt inferior. But when she realized that her deformity made no difference to Joseph, she regretted having maligned him and agreed to marry him.[4]

Their two sons, Manasseh and Ephraim, were born during the years of plenty, for during the famine Joseph refrained from marital relations.[5] Like Noah and his sons, Joseph avoided cohabitation when general calamity endangered mankind.

The boys were well-educated in Egyptian culture and became favorites of Pharaoh's court.[6] Joseph and Asenath, however, also taught them the Hebrew language and trained them in the knowledge of the One God; they were a Hebrew family.

Of the two, Manasseh receives far more attention in Hebrew literature than his younger brother, Ephraim. According to the Rabbis, Manasseh was Joseph's aide, and often served as his father's deputy. When Joseph's brothers first came to Egypt, the guard who took their names was their nephew Manasseh,[7] and when they failed to appear at the storehouse for several days, Manasseh was sent to find them.[8] In order to conceal his identity, Joseph spoke to his brothers through an interpreter—Manasseh.[9] And it was Manasseh who subdued Simeon when he resisted being taken as a hostage,[10] and who, by a great show of strength, caused Judah to moderate his tone before Joseph.[11] Matching Judah in feats of strength, he threw an exceedingly heavy stone into the air, caught it in his left hand and, by merely sitting on it, turned it to dust.[12] On another occasion, Manasseh's hand on Judah's shoulder allayed Judah's fury.[13] At Joseph's request Manasseh gathered an army to intimidate Joseph's brothers when they threatened to destroy Egypt.[14]

As the steward of Joseph's house, Manasseh brought the brothers into the palace when they returned with Benjamin, and he prepared the meal in their presence, according to ritual regulations.[15] At his father's command, he placed Joseph's cup in Benjamin's sack, and pursued his uncles to return them to Egypt.[16] And it was Manasseh who informed Joseph of his father's illness.[17]

Ephraim, however, was the silent one. The lack of detail in both Scripture and the Rabbis' writings suggests there was nothing distinctive about his activities. He displayed no talent, no achievement.

Serving as Jacob's nurse, Asenath was the first to realize that Jacob was dying. She sent an urgent message to the palace, suggesting that Joseph come and bring their two sons for Jacob's final blessing.[18] When he was told that they were coming, Jacob sat up in bed, making a determined effort to show that he possessed all his faculties. When he blessed his grandsons, no one was to question whether it was the act of a senile, irresponsible old man.[19]

When Joseph arrived, Jacob confided that a problem confronted him: if he would bless Joseph's two sons there would be fourteen tribes instead of twelve as foretold. He could not exclude the sons of the concubines; they deserved the same consideration as those of his other wives.[20] Time was short, and a decision had to be made. Still burdened with guilt for denying Rachel the honored burial, Jacob wanted to affirm his belief in individual freedom before he died. He had buried Rachel beside the road out of deference to primogeniture, a system that did violence to his beliefs; he would not be bound by it now. Freedom won out. He determined to elevate Joseph's two sons to an equal position with Reuben and the others, conferring the double portion on Joseph's heirs, rather than on his own first-born. This would compensate for denying Joseph's mother; it would win Joseph's forgiveness; and it would acknowledge Joseph's greatness (47:12). By eliminating Joseph as a tribe in favor of his two sons, and by consecrating Levi to God as the priest,[21] Jacob felt he could treat each son in accordance with his God-given potentialities while the number of tribes remained at twelve. Jacob was satisfied that his decisions, freely made, were in accord with the Divine promise.

As he was about to bless them, Jacob felt the Divine spirit leaving him. He questioned whether Joseph had married Asenath according to law. Joseph replied that they had been married with a proper ceremony and showed Jacob their marriage contract. Jacob called his grandsons to him, hoping Divine inspiration would return, but it did not. This was not the propitious moment for the blessing, so Joseph decided to bring them back later. Before he took them away, however, Joseph proved to Jacob that his sons had been circumcized.[22] Leaving Jacob, Joseph entreated God to return the holy spirit to his father, and he told his sons to pray, too, because "high station (and) worldly honors are but for a time."[23]

They returned and Jacob said, "Ephraim and Manasseh, even as Reuben and Simeon, shall be mine" (48:5). Joseph became concerned.

His father was showing a preference for the younger son. Joseph felt there was no reason for this because both had studied Torah with Jacob,[24] and both had attended his needs during his seventeen years in Egypt. Anxious and alarmed lest Manasseh lose his birthright, Joseph placed them before Jacob so that his right hand would rest on Manasseh's head and his left hand on Ephraim's head (48:13). Jacob crossed his hands, placing his right hand on Ephraim's head and his left hand on Manasseh's head (48:14). Astonished, Joseph blamed Jacob's poor eyesight (48:10). He attempted to transfer his father's hands so that they would rest on his sons' heads as he felt they should (48:17), and advised his father of his mistake. Three times he tried to influence Jacob in favor of Manasseh,[25] but Jacob plainly told him that he knew what he was doing and refused to move his hands. Although Manasseh was the older, Ephraim would be the greater (48:19), Jacob said, and he bestowed an additional blessing upon Ephraim.[26]

Joseph's consternation can be readily understood. Because he had been favored over his older brothers, Joseph had incurred their jealousy and enmity; he did not want to see a rift between Ephraim and Manasseh. Jacob was sowing the seeds of strife among his grandchildren as he had among his sons, and Joseph was most unhappy about it.

Joseph later realized that he reached the height of his development, not in spite of, but because of, the strife he experienced with his brothers. But he was unable to apply the same principle to his sons. Like many parents who wish to protect their children from suffering, he failed to appreciate its value to their emotional and spiritual growth. His concern for his sons also masked his own ego striving. Manasseh was everything a father could hope for in a son—handsome, strong and masterful in every situation. If Ephraim should be tested and found wanting, Joseph would have suffered acute embarrassment.

Jacob's ego, however, was not involved. His life was over and he was content that he had lived it well. Now his concern was for those who would live after him. As he considered his two grandsons, echoes of his own youth spoke a challenge. Reliving his own experience in these boys, Jacob saw in Manasseh his own powerful older brother, Esau; in the gentle and retiring Ephraim, Jacob saw himself. Jacob sympathized with the grandson who was akin to him, and he identified the blessing with the turning point in his own life. By giving Ephraim the opportunity to expand his limitations, Jacob justified his behavior toward Esau. The deed declared the conviction that had unlocked his own possibilties—he deserved the blessing more than Esau. So Jacob blessed his grandsons and his sons "fittingly." First he deprived Reuben of his birthright by giving the double portion to Joseph, through his sons. Then he blessed the younger Zebulun before the older Issachar (30:18-20; 49:13-15), and the younger Asher before the older Naphtali (30:8-13; 49:20-21).

The Rabbis who wrote long ago that Ephraim was given the birthright because of his modesty and humility, understood Jacob's intent.[27] Aware that he was withdrawn, introvertive and physically weaker than Manasseh, Jacob felt that Ephraim would be unable to manage himself in the competitive life unless something was done to help him. Jacob decided to stir him up. By making the extrovertive and powerful Manasseh jealous, Jacob put pressure on Ephraim, producing the immeasurable dynamic force of necessity. Forced to compete, Ephraim would develop. When he told Ephraim he would become the head of an academy,[28] Jacob held a high goal before him, one that would test his resourcefulness.

Co-mingled with Jacob's objective appraisal of Ephraim was the subjective association of guilt with Ephraim's name. The name Ephraim reminded Jacob of Ephrath and his lingering guilt after he buried Rachel there. Believing that Joseph might still resent his mother's unceremonious burial, Jacob thought that honoring Ephraim would obliterate and atone for his behavior at Ephrath.

Ephraim did survive, and the greatness foretold by Jacob was reflected in the future generations of his tribe, if not in his own lifetime. At the dedication of the Tabernacle, the prince of Ephraim was honored to present his gift before the prince of the tribe of Manasseh (Numbers 7:48-54).

CHAPTER NINE

Who Made Thee A Ruler
and A Judge?

(Exodus 2:14)

T HE only other sibling relationship encountered in the remaining four books of the Pentateuch differs from those found in Genesis. In early childhood Moses was separated from his older brother and sister, and when they were reunited they were all adults. Despite several dramatic episodes of tension between them, Miriam, Aaron and Moses were more relaxed in relation to each other. They displayed a higher degree of mutual respect than the brothers and sisters described earlier and shared a deep and genuine devotion.

Perhaps the fraternal bond was forged by the difficult circumstances under which they were born. Their names reflect the extremity of the Israelites in Egypt. The Hebrew name Miriam means "bitterness";[1] the Egyptians enslaved the Jewish people when she was born. Aaron means "woe unto this pregnancy";[2] during the months prior to his birth Pharaoh ordered the midwives to kill the newborn Jewish boys.[3] Moses' name tells that he was "pulled out of the water," where his mother had placed him to escape death at the hands of the Egyptians. Although his parents had named him Jekuthiel,[4] and he had nine other names,[5] he was called Moses all his life. The names of the children were constant reminders of the trying conditions under which they were brought into the world.

It is to their credit, and to the continuous benefit of mankind, that Miriam, Aaron and Moses were able to rise above their predicaments. They liberated their enslaved people, and bequeathed to the world the concept of protest against social injustice. And, playing key roles during the earliest national beginnings of the Israelites, they introduced the concept of representative self-government through law. They transformed a mass of abject slaves into a people who contributed much to world civilization.

It is impossible to analyze all of the forces that produced their qualities
of superior leadership, but many details gleaned from Hebrew writings
portray the dynamic evolution of their personalities. Their parents, Amram
and Jochebed, were influential leaders among the slaves. Their example,
both positive and negative, undoubtedly influenced the developing attitudes
of their children.

Miriam, the oldest of the three,[6] enjoyed no childhood. At the age
of five she accompanied her mother and assisted in her duties as a midwife.
Miriam cared for the baby and fed it while Jochebed attended to the
mother.[7] The two midwives, Shiphra and Puah (Exodus 1:15), were
Jochebed and Miriam, respectively.[8] When Pharaoh decreed death for new-
born Hebrew boys, he attempted to make the midwives amenable to
his wishes with amorous proposals. Although he threatened them and
their households with death by fire, they refused him.[9]

Instead of murdering the male babies as he ordered, Jochebed and
Miriam supplied the basic needs of the mothers and the children. If a
family was poor, they collected food and water from the rich to keep
the children alive.[10] In the interest of preserving life, mother and daughter
alike defied the most powerful man in the realm, the Pharaoh himself.

Miriam was a precocious child. At one time, when she and her mother
appeared before Pharaoh, she blurted out, "Woe be to this man when
God visits retribution upon him for his evil deeds." For her audacity,
Pharaoh would have killed Miriam but Jochebed appeased him. "Pay no
attention to her," she said, "She is but a child and does not know what
she is saying."[11]

Nor did Miriam reserve her forwardness for Pharaoh. She was just
as outspoken with her father, Amram. His reaction to Pharaoh's decrees
was irrational; to foil his plan, Amram divorced Jochebed. Since the Hebrew slaves recognized him as their leader, all the men followed Amram
and they, too, divorced their wives. There would be no more infant
victims for the Pharaoh!

Miriam confronted her father with his illogical defense. His decree,
she charged, was more severe than Pharaoh's, and more thoroughly destructive of the Jewish people. Pharaoh's decree involved only the male children,
while her father's stamped out both the male and the female. Furthermore,
there was some doubt that Pharaoh's decree could be enforced, while the
Hebrews could definitely destroy themselves in anger. What chance had
the midwives to save a few babies if they had never been conceived?

Impressed by the wisdom of Miriam's argument, Amram remarried
Jochebed, and all the other Israelites did the same. This explains the

statement that Amram "took to wife a daughter of Levi" (Exodus 2:1), when he already had two children, Miriam and Aaron—he remarried her.[12] And when he did, both children were overjoyed.[13] The separation of their father and mother had broken up their home. In addition to external threats, the loss of guidance and strong leadership at the head of the family must have had a debilitating effect upon the children and depressed them. The reunion of their parents dispelled their insecurity and reconstituted them as a strong family unit once again.

When Moses was born, Miriam's maturity again appeared to exceed that of her father. She attended the birth and helped Jochebed care for him and successfuly hide him for three months. Amram began to fear that both he and the baby would be killed if Moses was discovered. Amram agitated to get the baby out of the house, to abandon him. If the Egyptians suspected the birth of a baby, they would come to search the house, and bring an Egyptian child with them. They would make the child cry, on the theory that another infant in the house would hear and join in the wailing.[14] Claiming that he would rather entrust his son to Divine Providence,[15] Amram refused to risk his own life any longer on behalf of the baby.

Since parents are generally ready to imperil their lives for their children—and Amram was regarded not only as the head of his household but also as the fearless leader of his people—his attitude reveals to what extent the conditions of slavery distorted the meaning of their lives.

The existing circumstances required that Jochebed become overly concerned with Moses. Caring for the infant required constant vigilance, lest he cry out and be discovered. It was necessary to enlist both Miriam and Aaron to provide the continuous attention Moses required, and the life of the entire family revolved around the baby. Jochebed developed an overwhelming attachment to her infant son, and Amram was clearly left out. Jochebed, not he, hid Moses for three months (Exodus 2:2). Amram wanted no part of him. He may have felt that he was in an unfair competition with his son for Jochebed's attention; and Amram was getting none of it. Even the other children were primarily concerned with the baby's fate. Amram was ambivalent, feeling both love and hate for his offspring. He wanted a wife and the only way he knew to deal with the matter was to get rid of the child. Hate won out over love, and Amram ordered Jochebed to abandon the baby.

Rather than risk divorce again, Jochebed obeyed her husband. She had the other children to consider; if the baby were discovered, she would lose both husband and son. In preparing the little ark in which she would set him adrift, Jochebed displayed her strong attachment for Moses. She built a canopy into it, because she felt she "may not be worthy to be present at his marriage canopy."[16] Although she was prepared to be sep- arated from him, no matter how it grieved her, she could only conceive of Moses as living. He would grow up, and marry. For abandoning her son, it was she who was unworthy to live.

When Moses was placed in the water, Miriam wept[17] and "stood afar off, to know what would be done to him" (Exodus 2:4). She was concerned about her brother. Yet, more was involved. Miriam had been instrumental in bringing her parents together again, and Moses was born as a result. If not for her, Jochebed would not have suffered her present anguish, and Miriam may have felt guilty. Furthermore, Miriam had prophesied that her mother would bear a son who would be the savior of Israel. After setting Moses adrift, Jochebed had turned on her, venting her hostility with a slap on the head. "Where, now, is your prophesy?" her mother cried.[18] So Miriam stood by to see what would happen to her brother and her prediction. She was concerned with his future, for she felt that she and all her people were involved in it.

Pharaoh's daughter, Bithiah, came to the river while Miriam watched. It was her custom to remain in the palace,[19] but Bithiah was drawn to the water by the heat that scorches Egypt and by a depressing illness. Her illness, the ancient authors seemed to sense, was psychogenic. She bathed in the river to relieve her pain,[20] and also to find solace in nature for her aching heart.[21] Bithiah was childless, and bathing in the Nile, the source of life to the Egyptians, held the promise of motherhood and an end to her depression. When the infant was brought to her, Bithiah touched him, it is told, and she became well.[22] The sudden change in her condition convinced Bithiah that her prayers had been answered. She saw that Moses was circumcized[23] and knew that he was a Hebrew child (Exodus 2:6) abandoned on the river by a desperate mother, but she loved him exceedingly and defied her father's decree by adopting him. The great river, she felt, had given her a child of her own. As being rescued from water in a dream is symbolic of birth, Bithiah regarded Moses as though she had actually given birth to him herself.[24]

Miriam observed from a distance all that transpired. She saw that Moses refused nourishment from all the Egyptian women brought to nurse him,[25] and that this was her opportunity to salvage a tragic situation for her family. Miriam came forward and offered to call a Hebrew woman (Exodus 2:7). Bithiah agreed and Miriam fetched Jochebed to nurse him. No one was the wiser when Bithiah instructed Jochebed to keep Moses and to nurse him. Thus Moses remained with his own mother and she raised him for two years.[26]

No mention is made of Amram during this time. Although his confidence in Moses' future was vindicated—he was safe and sound and a bright future lay before him as the adopted son of Pharaoh's daughter—it is likely that Amram felt guilty about his actions. He may have decided not to interfere where Moses was concerned, or he may have felt more neglected than before. In place of secrecy, now royalty dictated the care of his son. Moses and Jochebed undoubtedly received special favors and Bithiah and her entourage must have visited Moses frequently, but this could hardly enhance Amram's importance in the family circle. With Jochebed raising a future member of the royal household, baby Moses continued to overshadow his father in occupying her attention.

Miriam and Aaron saw their brother given preferential treatment, but apparently they were not hurt by it. He was given the best of everything, while their early childhood had been marked by hardship, but they did not feel deprived. They had no reason to be jealous of Moses. Because of him, their lot improved. They enjoyed a certain notoriety because of Moses' high connections, and they attained a new and greater importance because of his presence. Well-established as a young adult in her parents' eyes, Miriam made herself Jochebed's indispensable assistant. And while he may have been deprived of his mother's attention, Aaron was amply compensated by the warm and intimate relationship he developed with his father. Amram retained the stature of leadership with Aaron, and the boy enjoyed accompanying him among the populace. Both Miriam and Aaron accepted Moses' privileged position without jealousy. They understood the life-and-death seriousness of the arrangement, and their emotional security with relation to their parents was not in jeopardy. For all intents and purposes, Moses was the child of Bithiah.[27]

Although Bithiah felt genuinely maternal toward Moses, she felt constrained to convince others that he was her real son.[28] Therefore, before she took him from Jochebed, she pretended to be pregnant. No one in the palace was fooled, though, for Moses was a lusty two-year-old when he was taken there to live. Her father and the royal magicians knew that he was a child of the Hebrew slaves,[29] but they winked at the truth. This child from the river had transformed Bithiah from a sick and melancholy wretch into a happily doting mother. Bithiah was less trouble to her father and husband than she had been for years, and other matters demanded Pharaoh's attention. So young Moses was permitted to remain and he was treated like a wanted child. Bithiah hugged and kissed him and loved him as if he were her own. Pharaoh also found the little fellow appealing, and showered affection upon him.[30] The servants and all the Egyptians with whom he came in contact liked Moses. He was raised as a prince and educated in science and other subjects deemed necessary for the elect.[31] It was even suggested that Moses might become Pharaoh's successor.[32]

Bithiah must have told Moses that he was an adopted child, and that he was a Hebrew. Believing, as she did, that her ruse had worked, she warned him not to disclose it to anyone. She described the dire consequences that might ensue if he divulged the story of his origin. As an added precaution, she kept him close to her, always under her watchful eye. A possessive mother, Bithiah kept Moses from leaving the palace until he was a young man. She may have feared he would go to the Hebrews, and cast his lot with theirs.

Bithiah's neurotic behavior and psychogenic illnesses may have stemmed from her resentment that she was a woman.[33] If she had been a man, she could have inherited her father's throne, instead of Moses or any other offspring that she might have had. Such a feeling could have caused her inability to conceive. Her illness masked her unwillingness to become pregnant, and provided a sufficient excuse both to herself and to her husband. Adopting Moses gave her the benefits of motherhood without acting like a woman. To assuage her guilt for her negative attitudes, Bithiah developed an overly-protective attitude toward Moses, crushing his attempts to assert his initiative, his independence and his masculinity. Such a mother is jealous of the friends her son may make, both male and female, and seeks to prevent his alliance with anyone.

To avoid Bithiah's displeasure, Moses was compelled to suppress his masculine tendencies and to accentuate his passive traits. Yet she must have teased him for being a sissy, as all possessive mothers do. To prove his masculinity, Moses finally rebelled against Bithiah's crippling domination. Once he expressed his defiance and asserted his independence, Moses stifled his passive impulses and behaved in the opposite way—he "went out" to see the very people she had prevented him from visiting (Exodus 2:11,13).[34] His possessive mother had made him feel so unbearably powerless and weak that only opposing her could make life tolerable. He needed a sense of power and strength. Going out to his people engendered a feeling of belonging. Among them, he felt alive and a tower of might.

Handsome and of remarkable size—one legend asserts that he reached fifteen feet in height[35]—Moses was wise beyond his years. He had only one defect, an impediment of speech (Exodus 4:10). According to legend, this deformity resulted from a childish prank. Moses took the crown from Pharaoh's head and placed it on his own; or, in another version, Pharaoh playfully put the crown on Moses' head and Moses threw it to the floor and stepped on it. Seeing portents that Moses would seize Pharaoh's kingdom, the court magicians counseled that Moses be killed. Bithiah prevented this, but not before Jethro, a high priest, suggested a test to determine whether Moses knew what he did. A brilliant gem and a live coal were placed before Moses. If he reached for the gem, it would prove that he acted knowingly, and he would be put to death. If he innocently reached for the red-hot coal, he was not to be held responsible and would be spared. When the two objects were placed before him, Moses put forth his hand to take the precious stone, but an "angel" pushed his hand to the coal. From the threatening attitudes of the adults around him, Moses must have perceived that he faced a choice between two evils; he chose the lesser one. With a glowing fragment seared to his flesh, Moses put his scorched fingers to his mouth and burned his tongue. The injury left him slow of speech and tongue.[36]

Aware that he was a Hebrew, and that he had been raised two years in a Jewish home, the subconscious memory of that experience must have lingered with Moses. Since Jochebed was his real mother, the impression his nurse made upon him was ineradicable, and the warmth he associated with her drew him to his family and his people. He was able to break away from Bithiah because he felt that a greater kinship awaited him. The first time Moses left the palace, "he went out unto his brethren" (Exodus 2:11).

As Moses moved among his enslaved people for the first time, he saw conditions that shocked him deeply. He saw gross inequality. Great burdens were placed upon small people and light burdens upon large people; he saw a man's burden on a woman and a woman's burden upon a man; he saw the burden of a youth on an old man, and vice versa. Out of compassion, he rearranged the burdens, pretending his purpose was to help Pharaoh. On other occasions he helped slaves struggling under their burden of clay.[37] Again, claiming to extend their usefulness, Moses secured one day of rest for them. Without rest, he warned, the slaves would die.[38]

On the way to Goshen to find his parents,[39] Moses ran headlong into the plight of the slaves. Moses stopped at the roadside to hear the complaint of Dathan, who was bruised, bleeding and laboring under a heavy burden. Dathan explained to Moses that he was a Hebrew officer and not supposed to do this heavy work. He was in charge of ten fellow slaves, but his Egyptian taskmaster had demoted him, beat him, and tried to kill him—and all for no fault of his, he cried. At daybreak he had gone to drag his ten men out to work, and returned home to find the taskmaster leaving his house. His wife, his beautiful wife, he wailed, had been forced to have intercourse with the taskmaster.[40] Misjudging Moses' sympathies because of his princely bearing and Egyptian dress, the taskmaster beat Dathan to unconsciousness to silence him. Moses believed that he was dead, or that he had been beaten so severely that he could not survive.[41] He waited, but no one came forward to avenge the outrage. The apathy of the slaves sickened him as much as the brutality. Still, Moses hesitated, hoping that the Egyptian might repent. But as his rage mounted, death could be the only end;[42] Moses killed the Egyptian (Exodus 2:12).

Although Moses had acted on Dathan's behalf, Dathan taunted him after he recovered, and later conspired to betray him.[43] A mock scuffle with Abiram created an occasion to be taken before Pharaoh. When they told Pharaoh that Moses was dishonoring him, Pharaoh was indifferent. But when they declared that Moses had killed an Egyptian, Pharaoh issued an order for his arrest, and Moses was condemned to be beheaded.[44]

In the intervening years, Moses had helped Egypt win its war against Ethiopia,[45] but now it did not stand him in good stead. It would seem that Pharaoh seized the pretext to get rid of him. In a land where slavery flourished and human life was cheap, the life of one taskmaster could not have been more significant than a prince of the realm. But when Pharaoh learned that Moses defended the Hebrews, he realized where Moses' sympathy lay. Now he knew that his daughter's son did not share his thoughts or his loyalties; Moses hated those of whom Pharaoh was fond, loved those whom Pharaoh rejected, and pitied those to whom Pharaoh was relentless and inexorable.[46] Pharaoh concluded that he must dispose of him, but Moses escaped (Exodus 2:15).

From Egypt, Moses fled to Ethiopia, where he found the king, Kikanos, encamped with his army outside his own capital. When war had erupted between Ethiopia and the nations of the East, Kikanos led the army into the field, leaving Balaam and his two sons to guard the capital. Victory was won, and Kikanos returned only to find the city barricaded against his entry. On Moses' arrival in camp, Kikanos appointed him commander-in-chief of his forces. Kikanos soon died, after blockading the city for about nine years, but Moses and his forces recaptured the capital. The Ethiopians crowned Moses king and gave him Kikanos' widow, Adoniah, as his wife. Moses accepted her for appearance's sake; she was his wife in name only. Moses reigned justly and wisely until Adoniah's son was grown, when she began to agitate against him. He was a foreigner, she argued, for he still dressed like an Egyptian, and she persuaded the Ethiopians to place her son on the throne that had been his father's. They gave Moses gifts and sent him away with great honor. Afraid to return to Egypt, Moses headed for Midian.[47]

Arriving there, Moses stumbled upon another violent scene. Like Jacob, Moses met his future wife at a well. Some girls, who he later learned were the daughters of Jethro, had brought their sheep to water there, but rough shepherds harassed them with insults and interferred with their task. The thirsty animals were thrown into confusion, and the girls lost control of their flock. The men seized them and were about to carry them off to rape them,[48] when Moses came to their rescue (Exodus 2:17). He overpowered the shepherds and arraigned them in a lengthy address. Awed by his prowess and his voice that rang out like a prophet's, the shepherds humbled themselves before the girls and watered their flocks to make amends.[49] Speaking for her sisters, the comely Zipporah thanked Moses for his assistance. He replied gallantly that it was the Egyptian he had killed whom they should thank. If not for him, Moses would not have fled from Egypt and would not have been there when he was needed.[50]

Moses inquired why the shepherds were so hostile. Jethro, he learned, had relinquished the priesthood when he realized the futility of believing in idols. His people excommunicated him and permitted no one to work for him. As a result, Jethro was compelled to employ his daughters to care for his flocks. When she presented him to Jethro, Zipporah described Moses as an Egyptian, probably because of his clothing. Moses did not protest and assert his Hebrew origin, as did his ancestor, Joseph, who publicly proclaimed that he was a Hebrew. It is interesting that Joseph was eventually buried in Palestine, while Moses was not.[51]

Impressed by her honesty and piety and by her good deeds,[52] Moses fell in love with Zipporah. He requested her hand in marriage and cited as qualifications that he had escaped from Egypt and that he had ruled Ethiopia. Apparently Jethro was frightened by Moses' career of controversy —he had enemies enough of his own. Alienated from his own people by his religious rebellion, and ambivalent about his Egyptian heritage, Jethro was insecure and confused. He felt that Moses could only bring him more suffering. Rationalizing that he was helping the Egyptians and Ethiopians, Jethro attempted to resolve his own anxiety. Without warning, he imprisoned Moses without food or water and left him there to die. And Moses would have died if Zipporah had not taken pity on him and secretly fed him.[53]

Jethro finally released Moses and gave him permission to marry Zipporah, but the conditions he specified again reflected his dilemma. Moses
could marry Zipporah, he declared, providing half their children were
raised as Egyptians and the other half as Israelites. Moses agreed and
also promised that he would not take his wife and children away against
Jethro's will, as Jacob had done in leaving Laban. Moses respected Jethro
for his courage in breaking with the idolatrous customs of his people, but
he realized that Jethro was an old man now, too old to change his attitudes
completely. He also realized that Jethro leaned heavily on Zipporah. Her
quiet strength and devotion—the motherly qualities that appealed so
much to Moses[54]—gave Jethro security. Moses felt that no conflict would
result from Jethro's terms. To raise half of their children as Egyptians
could mean only a national identification; Jethro would not want his
grandsons to be taught the beliefs that he had repudiated. So Moses
agreed,[55] and he and Zipporah were married. Later, when Moses almost
died of remorse because his son Eliezer had not been circumcized, Zipporah
proved that she was the kind of wife he needed. She came to his rescue
again by circumcizing the boy herself.

Moses settled into an uncomplicated pastoral life, tending Jethro's
flocks in an almost idyllic absence of strife. He took care that the herd
did not consume or despoil the property of others,[56] and he lavished tender,
even loving, care upon them. When a kid wandered from the flock in
search of water, Moses gently carried it back to the herd on his shoulders.
To save the tender grass for the young, he restrained the full-grown
sheep from grazing before the smaller ones.[57] Although Jethro was not
averse to criticizing him in this period,[58] Moses respected his father-in-
law. Years later, when they met in the wilderness after the liberation,
Moses bowed before him and kissed him and Jethro, recognizing his
worth as well as Aaron's, called Moses the sun, and Aaron the moon.[59]

But Moses began to feel a growing dissatisfaction. His life was monot-
onous—grazing the dumb animals day after day—and meaningless. Anyone
could do it. With each succeeding day he became more restive. Could he
remain a shepherd forever? He recalled his life in the palace of the Pharaoh
and the circumstances under which he had killed a man. He had escaped
and served as commander-in-chief of the Ethiopian army, and he had
ruled that country for forty years. But his brethren in Egypt still wal-
lowed in slavery. Moses had seen their misery and the depravity to which
their suffering reduced them. He contemplated their situation often and
he was not at peace.

Moses began to feel that the Lord had spared his life for a purpose, and that all his experiences had meaning. He could not live out his life on a rocky hillside tending a flock of sheep while his people were slaves. He felt he must act on their behalf. But what could he do? Jethro treated him like a son; Moses could not leave him. Encumbered with a family and pledged to remain with his father-in-law, Moses felt trapped. His life demanded a purpose; he searched for something to liberate him from his freedom.

With Jethro's flocks, Moses found solitude in the wilderness. There, in the stillness of the mountainside, he contemplated every rock and bush and blade of grass, considering its form, its function, its origin, its possibilities—the meaning of its existence. While nature seemed to stand still, a sudden disturbing awareness drew his attention to a bush. It appeared to burn before his eyes, but was not consumed. Moses felt uneasy. The apparition was unreal. Any other bush would fall into ashes. Standing unchanged in the midst of flames, the bush denied the meaning of existence. His disquiet swelled into an overwhelming awareness of himself. Moses realized that he was standing unchanged in the midst of a life that demanded change. Like the bush, he was alive but not living. And his life would have no meaning until he could unite with something outside himself, changing the other and himself. His search for meaning in all things led Moses to confront his Maker, and to discover the meaning of his existence.

God's voice spoke to him "from out of the midst of the bush and said, 'Cast thy shoes from off thy feet, for the place whereon thou standest is holy ground'" (Exodus 3:5); to seek the meaning of his life was to seek God. Then, reminding Moses that he was descended from others who had sought God—Abraham, Isaac and Jacob, and his own father—implying that everyone who ever lived sought meaning for their lives, God recalled His afflicted people in Egypt. "Come now, therefore, and I will send thee unto Pharaoh, that thou mayest bring My people the children of Israel out of Egypt" (Exodus 3:10).

The trap that held Moses in a meaningless existence suddenly vanished. God had shown him that he could draw on the past from which he sprang, combined with the present which unfolded at every moment, to become himself. The possibility did exist that he could lead his people out of slavery into freedom so that they, too, could "serve God upon this mountain" (Exodus 3:12). God's offer to make him His personal messenger revealed the opportunity Moses had failed to discern: that he could marshall his strength, his mind and the totality of his experience for a great purpose.

With the ineradicable consciousness of God, Moses found the meaning of his existence.

Holding before him his newly discovered life goal, Moses cast about for the means to achieve it. In agonizing self-appraisal he took account of his weaknesses. "Who am I, that I should go unto Pharaoh, and that I should bring forth the children of Israel out of Egypt?" (Exodus 3:11). Moses felt he did not know enough about God yet to be a spokesman on His behalf. And he questioned his acceptance by the people. "They will not believe me, nor hearken unto my voice" (Exodus 4:1). He was not eloquent enough, he feared, to convince them that they were not unalterably destined to be slaves. Could he cope with the untold thousands— the sick, the old, the pregnant women, the little children—and provide them with food and drink? The distance from Egypt to Canaan was not great, but the journey would be replete with hardship. The Israelites might turn on him and kill him, if the Egyptians did not kill him first. Should he risk his own safety? Could he love them enough? Perhaps they were not worth it.[60]

Moses' doubts betrayed a deeper anxiety. In reality he was questioning whether he was worthy of the enormous authority the mission entailed. He recalled his own rebellion against those who held authority over him, and wondered whether the Jewish people might not also rebel. Would he, entertaining such grave doubts, be capable of wielding his power and authority effectively and with gentleness? Or, forced to mask his inadequacies, would he become stern and harsh—a different sort of person from the peaceful shepherd he thought himself to be?

In recognizing his inadequacies, Moses discovered his strength. He was not alone. He had a brother in Egypt who could share the burden of responsibility with him. Aaron, he realized, was not a slave, for the entire tribe of Levi had been exempt from servitude.[61] He was a priest who knew the glory of his forefathers; the people would listen and understand when he spoke about God; Aaron would serve as spokesman. And forty years on the throne of Ethiopia had taught Moses to govern. Together they would attempt the great mission which Moses came to see as his duty to God. What he lacked, would be provided; what he could not foresee, would be revealed. He was certain that slavery was not God's will for man. He was equally certain that living for himself was meaningless and cowardly. Moses was now prepared to commit himself to freedom for all mankind. His aggressive energy, dormant, internalized, and utterly repressed during the years he lived in Midian, would find an outlet in activities on behalf of the larger group. He would devote himself to humanity, to existence in the broader scope.

First, he went to Jethro. Moses felt he owed him much, even to the point of risking his life for him,[62] and he could not consider leaving without Jethro's permission. Jethro tried to dissuade him from taking Zipporah and their sons, but Moses argued that laws would be given at Sinai by which each man could govern himself, and that his sons should be present. Jethro acquiesced when he learned about the Ten Commandments.[63] Perhaps he felt that he would like to be there, too. Such laws would have spared him the years of groping since he abandoned idolatry. Jethro released Moses to his higher commitment and told him, "Go in peace."

Although he had assumed the responsibility of leading his people to freedom, Moses dallied on his way to Egypt. He had fled because of the malicious caviling of the Israelites there, and he wondered if they deserved his help.[64] He lost heart and felt that the time had not yet arrived for their redemption.[65] And he was apprehensive about Aaron. He had not seen him since he was a child; perhaps he assumed too much. Aaron had been living and working among the Hebrews in Egypt. Would he welcome Moses' coming to take over the leadership,[66] or would he feel that Moses was encroaching on his province?

Moses' misgivings about Aaron were dispelled when he arrived. Aaron ran to meet him and kissed him when they met (Exodus 4:27). He inquired where Moses had spent all the years of their separation and rejoiced when he heard the events of Moses' life and his mission in returning. Moses' conviction in the rightness of his purpose and his renewed faith in himself filled Aaron with respect; he treated Moses as his master.[67] On his part, Moses was equally impressed with his brother.

When Aaron learned of his marriage and saw Zipporah and their sons, he told Moses bluntly that he had underestimated the problem. "Great enough is our sorrow through those who have been in Egypt from the beginning, and you bring more to the land."[68] Moses realized that Aaron's assertion was correct and that he had much to learn about suffering. He sent Zipporah and his sons back to Jethro,[69] and he accepted Aaron's qualifications to serve as High Priest. Although Aaron was older and might have resented Moses for his privileged treatment in childhood, apparently he did not. Aaron had learned compassion from Amram during the years when he was often in his father's company, and he was eager to see his people freed from their misery. When Moses came forward with the promise of accomplishing this, Aaron was ready to do whatever was required of him, even though the order came from his younger brother.

His people meant more to him than personal position. Without envy or jealousy they prepared to save their people. Each imparted his wisdom to the other; in the knowledge of the Torah they were equal.[70]

Together Moses and Aaron apprised the elders of their aspirations. The people listened, and "they believed." Then, having the approval of the elders, Moses and Aaron called on Pharaoh and asked a small favor— only that the slaves be permitted a three-day respite for prayer (Exodus 5:3). To their consternation, the effect of their visit was to make the plight of the Israelites worse. Their request was not granted. And to discourage further appeals, the issue of straw was withheld; henceforth the slaves would be forced to scrounge for the straw to make their quota of bricks, and the quota would be no less. At every turn the Israelites were confronted with brutality. An Egyptian who found a slave attempting to gather straw in his field would break the man's thighs.[71] At this time the attitude of the Israelites toward Moses and Aaron was made clear by Dathan and Abiram. "You are responsible," they said, "for the widespread stench now issuing from the Israelite corpses used as bricks for building. . . . We are in the quandary of the poor sheep that has been dragged away by a wolf. The shepherd pursues the robber, catches up with him, and tries to snatch the sheep from his jaws, and the wretched victim, pulled this way by the wolf and that way by the shepherd, is torn to pieces. Between you and Pharaoh, this is what Israel faces."[72] Suffering from inferiority feelings engendered by a continuously degraded and joyless existence, the Israelites viewed Moses' interference as a threat. They were roused to defend whatever small measure of security they had; they were content to be sheep, if they could be safe.[73]

Moses was deeply shaken by the increased suffering of the Israelites. When his entreaties to Pharaoh brought only greater cruelties upon Israel, he implored God, "Tell me if Thou wilt now deliver them or not." He had done what he believed God wanted him to do to effect their freedom, but they were farther from that goal than ever. Wanting desperately to understand the present, and to know what the future held, Moses addressed his questions to God. "Why is this people more enslaved than all the preceding generations? Because our father Abraham displayed doubt, saying, 'Whereby shall I know that I will possess (the land)?' are his children therefore slaves? If so, then Esau and Ishmael should also have been subjected, and the generations of Isaac and Jacob, rather than my generation. Should Thou ask, 'How does it concern thee?' then I will ask 'Why hast Thou sent me?'" Moses was conscious of the insolence of his words[74] and he softened his tone as he continued. "Thy Name is great, mighty and revered in the entire world, but the wicked Pharaoh, though he has heard Thy fame, still deals arrogantly with Thy people. . . . I know that one day Thou wilt deliver them, but what about those who have been immured in the buildings?"[75] Moses could not restrain himself from demanding to know more than he could perceive. The patriarchs did not demand to know His Name and they did not search after His characteristics, but Moses asked, before he embarked on his mission of deliverance, "What is Thy Name?"[76] Throughout his life Moses continued to question God; but he also questioned himself. In so doing, he extended his understanding, his endurance, and his faith.

Egypt was beset by plagues, and still the Israelites remained slaves, but Moses was not disheartened. Pharaoh's broken promises, even his threat to kill him, left Moses undismayed. As chaos and destruction engulfed the land, Moses became more confident that the Israelites would be freed. It was increasingly apparent that slavery was destroying Egypt. When the final plague came upon the Egyptians, the entire people was seized with dread. Pharaoh and Bithiah went to look for Moses to ask him to pray for them and their people. The death of the first-born meant that Bithiah was doomed. Frantically they searched for Moses and when they found his home Pharaoh shouted to him. Moses called back, "Who are you, and what is your name?" "I am Pharaoh," he replied, "who stands humiliated." Toying with Pharaoh, as Pharaoh had so often done with him, Moses asked, "Why do you come to me yourself? Is it the custom of kings to linger at the door of common folk?" Pharaoh ignored the sarcasm. In need now, he begged Moses to come outside and to intercede with his Lord on their behalf. Moses replied that he could not leave the house until morning, since no Israelite was permitted outside during the plague. But Pharaoh continued to plead, "Come, at least, to the window," and Moses did.[77]

Then Bithiah spoke and reproached Moses. "Is this how you repay me?" She reminded him that of all his names he was called Moses because she had saved him from the water.[78] Moses knew she was right, but he asked whether any of the plagues had affected her. She admitted that none had. He told her that although she was the first-born,[79] she would remain untouched. Her security was of no advantage to her, she cried, when her father, his household and his servants were in danger. Moses pointed out that saving him from the river had not justified the enslavement of the rest of the Israelites. All the difficulties of the Egyptians had come upon them, he said, because they had obstinately refused to obey the Lord.[80]

Moses again addressed Pharaoh. "If you would spare Bithiah, proclaim

unto the children of Israel, 'You are free; you are your own masters
and no longer my slaves; you are under the authority of God.' "[81] Ready
to come to terms, Pharaoh agreed, but he insisted that they leave the
country immediately. Moses objected. They were not thieves who slink
away under cover of night. They would leave in the morning. But when
Pharaoh urged and begged them to leave and was joined by his people
in exhorting them to quit Egypt, Moses knew that the moment had
come. While the Israelites hastily loaded their possessions, Moses collected
Joseph's bones to carry them to Palestine,[82] and the Israelites left Egypt and
slavery behind them.

Even without the necessary provisions,[83] the Israelites did not hesitate
to follow Moses into the wilderness. He expressed their repressed inner
strivings. No one else had ever evinced an interest in their liberation.
Now their unexpressed hopes for salvation might be realized through
him. His outer glow of optimism and confidence gave them confidence.
His courage before Pharaoh inspired them with courage. They identified
themselves with the man who would not yield to Pharaoh's pressure but
ultimately forced Pharaoh to come to him. The personification of their
cause, Moses gave them a sense of importance and power.

In order to weld the Israelites into a cohesive group, Moses directed
their attention to the external dangers they faced. Rather than permit
them to immerse themselves in their own misery, he capitalized on their
accumulated aggressions by focusing their hostility on their enemies. He
made ordinances regulating their relationship with the Egyptians—from
the giving of the Ten Commandments to the time when Egyptians would
be admitted to the household of Israel—to remind the people that Egyptians
were their erstwhile oppressors. For their merciless and unwarranted attack
on the Israelites, Moses also marked the Amalakites as enemies to be
guarded against forever (Exodus 17:8-16; Deuteronomy 25:17-19); and
to the Ammonites and Moabites, for their lack of sympathy, Moses reserved
a share of the hostile feelings of the Jews (Deuteronomy 23:4-5).

But it was his social genius that won Moses the support of the people.
Even though he was free, the social conditions that enslaved others oppressed him. There was no place for him in such a society, so he attempted
to reorganize it. His empathy for each individual slave provided the seminal
idea of a new social frame work. In every man he saw the spark of
rebellion against predetermination and knew that together they could
melt the chains that enslaved them. He conceived the idea of a society
in which the ultimate well-being of the group evolved from the highest
development of the individual. For the community can be no more righteous

than the people who compose it. The social ideals of freedom and dignity that he held before the people lessened their long-standing feelings of inferiority and quickened their aspirations. The ennoblement of the self elevated their status as individuals and as a group. For the first time within their memory, the future held promise. Although it began slowly, the movement to re-form society gained momentum and the people accepted Moses' leadership.

For his part, Moses responded to their confidence with the deepened sense of responsibility that made him a great leader. He believed each individual should feel responsible to the group, but he knew that slaves could not rise overnight to social responsibility. As their leader, Moses felt his own responsibility exceeded that of any other individual. It was his special duty to maintain their morale on a high plane if they were not to fall into chaos. He must guide the group effectively, or lose their esteem.

The people were easily exhausted, however, by the strain of the sudden change from slavery to freedom.[84] When Moses encouraged them to sacrifice animals that the Egyptians worshipped, they obeyed fearfully. No harm befell them, but their anxiety took its toll of their meager physical and emotional resources. Diseased and crippled when they left Egypt, at times they moved against their will.[85] It was a battered and crippled host that reached Sinai.[86]

Conducting the former slaves through the wilderness and mollifying their myriad complaints taxed Moses' patience and ingenuity. He devoted his whole being to Israel, yet he often felt the sting of their reproach. At first the people accepted his leadership out of gratitude, a sense of personal indebtedness for taking them out of reach of the Egyptian taskmasters. But when they encountered hardships, they quickly forgot. Moses soon learned that leadership must rest not on loyalty to an individual, but on loyalty to the group. Fortified in his conviction to act always in the best interest of the group, Moses braced himself for the abuse he knew would come.

Before a month had passed, the people complained because they had gone three days without water. When they did find water, it was too bitter to drink (Exodus 15:23-25). Shortly thereafter they complained that they had too little food (Exodus 16:1-3); they wanted meat (Numbers 11:4). They had brought much cattle with them from Egypt (Exodus 12:38), for the Gadites and the Reubenites still had an abundance of cattle when they entered Palestine (Numbers 32:1). Apparently, Moses rationed the consumption of meat, but the people resisted his efforts to conserve it and made his administration difficult. Again they encountered a dry spell, and again the people murmured against him (Exodus 17:3). The situation became so tense, Moses feared the people would stone him. Boldly, he took up his rod—the symbol of his authority—and walked among them, and they did not molest him (Exodus 17:5).

The people had conflicting feelings about Moses. He began to direct their actions even before they left Egypt, ordering them to take lambs into their houses. Later he instructed them in great detail concerning their personal conduct to prepare them for receiving the Ten Commandments on Mt. Sinai. He prevented them from doing what they wanted to, touching off the resentment frequently directed toward a person in authority for the frustrations suffered at his hands.[87] They recognized that Moses acted on behalf of the group, and not for personal aggrandizement. They nevertheless resented him, as most benevolent leaders are resented by their followers.

The heady brew of freedom intensified their conflict about Moses. The people wanted complete freedom of thought and action but, unaware of the full meaning of freedom, they blundered into painful mistakes. They did not have all the answers, they needed direction and leadership; without it their freedom was useless. The admission that they needed Moses magnified their resentment of him. Subconsciously hating themselves for their weakness, they expressed it against Moses, as if his strength and wisdom had created their own inadequacies.

His every effort to lead them toward maturity met with resistance. The practice of incest still prevailed. Men married their sisters and their aunts from both their mothers' and fathers' families. Moses instructed them to abandon this ruinous practice in the interest of their long-term welfare as a people, but they cried out against him when they heard his orders (Numbers 11:10).[88] Unable to dislodge them from the shortsighted, self-destructive habits of the slave, Moses complained to God that the burden of these people was too great for him (Numbers 11:11-14), that he was inadequate for the task. Large groups demand too much of their leaders. Moses felt compassion for them, however, and prayed on their behalf on several occasions (Exodus 32:11-14; Numbers 14:13-20; Deuteronomy 3:23). Finally he came to understand that the generation of slaves was immature and irrational, and that they would have to die out before the Israelites would be ready to govern themselves in Palestine (Numbers 14:28-35; Deuteronomy 1:35-38). And so he decided to keep them in the wilderness two score years, until a new generation could grow up.

Although he was affected by their complaints, Moses never allowed

the people to press him into violating his basic beliefs. Expediency and
compromise of principle had no place in his thinking. Aaron did yield to
the winds of popular opinion, however, and proved himself weak in a
crisis.

When Moses failed to descend with the Ten Commandments on the
day when he was expected to return, a panic swept through the people.
Unaware of a miscalculation, they assumed that their leader had died
on Mt. Sinai. Without Moses, they felt insecure and utterly abandoned.
They were unable to conceive of the unseen God of whom Moses and
Aaron had spoken, and reverted to the slave mentality. They wanted a
god that they could see and touch, an idol such as they had seen the
Egyptians worship. They called upon Aaron to make a god for them,
a god to stand between them and the uncertainty of their existence. Aaron
was abashed. They went to Hur, Miriam's son, whom Moses had appointed
to assist Aaron in his absence, and demanded that he make a god for them.
Hur scolded them. They were ungrateful, he said, for all that Moses had
done for them; they were unmindful of the miracles by which God had
kept them alive; they were, he said, "brainless fools." Enraged by his
words and driven by fear of the unknown, the people lost all control. They
killed Hur and then, pointing to his corpse, threatened Aaron with death
if he would not make them a god.[89] Destroying their leaders, they felt,
would release them from an intolerable situation.

Aaron rationalized that God would never forgive them if they killed
their two leaders. Rather than cast the burden of such a deed upon the
people, he reasoned, he would accede to their demand, and assume the
responsibility himself. Hur was killed spontaneously, in a frenzy of hysteria,
but the people had confronted Aaron with a choice. In this critical moment he might have attained true leadership if he had dared to refuse
them, but Aaron acquiesced. He attempted a ruse, however, in the hope
that the promise he made would not be fulfilled. To obtain material with
which to fashion the idol, Aaron ordered the men to divest their wives,
sons and daughters of their jewelry. They would not willingly give up
their ornaments, Aaron felt, and so the matter would come to an abortive
end. His assumption was only partly correct. The women did refuse to
relinquish their jewels for this foolish purpose, but the men, who wore
earrings like the Egyptians and Arabs, broke off their ornaments and
brought them to Aaron (Exodus 32:2-3).[90]

When the calf was fashioned from the golden jewelry, the mixed multitude that had joined the Israelites in their exodus from Egypt said to
the people, "This is thy god, O Israel."[91] They made thirteen idols in

all, one for each tribe and one for all the people as a whole, and the people worshipped them. They used manna, which God did not deny them even on that day, as an offering to the idols.[92] The seventy elders, however, refused to worship the idols with the rest, and they were killed.[93]

Crazed with excitement, the people wanted to erect an altar for their idol, and again Aaron tried to forestall them. It would be more reverential, he told them, if he built it himself. Aaron made the suggestion hoping that he could prolong the building of the altar and that Moses might appear in the meantime. He proclaimed, "Tomorrow shall be a feast to the Lord" (Exodus 32:5), not the Golden Calf, but again his expectations were not realized. Moses had not returned on the morning of the following day, and the altar had been completed. The people began to offer sacrifices to the Calf and indulged in lewdness.[94]

Moses became openly incensed against Aaron when he came down from the mountain and saw him beating the Calf with a hammer. He concluded that Aaron was a part of this wholesale defection from God and was outraged by his behavior. Moses soon learned Aaron's true intention, however, and his anger abated when he realized that Aaron was frantically trying to prove the inefficacy of the idol.[95]

God, too, incurred Moses' anger for permitting the people and his brother to be so weak as to bring destruction upon themselves. God told Moses to go down from Mt. Sinai because "thy people . . . have dealt corruptly" (Exodus 32:7). Like one angry parent to another, Moses retorted, in a story in the Midrash, "When they sin they are mine. No," said Moses, "they are Thine, and repent of this evil against Thy people" (Exodus 32:12).[96]

When God offered to relieve Moses of the burden of leadership by destroying the people, and to make him another Abraham from whom a mighty people would emanate, Moses refused (Exodus 32:10). As in his personal life, Moses felt that all experience had meaning, and that if the people were permitted to live there was always the possibility that they could live more nobly. Despite the new low to which the Israelites had fallen, Moses remained devoted to them and to the heritage of Abraham, Isaac and Jacob. He refused the offer of the Lord to destroy them and begin anew, making him the first patriarch. He said, "If the three-legged stool has no stability, how then shall the one-legged stand?"[97]

Although he accepted once more the role of advocate of the Jewish people, Moses nevertheless recognized that as the leader of an enormous group he must be firm and impersonal. When he descended from Mt. Sinai, he ordered the destruction of the idol worshippers (Exodus 32:27) because they discarded the ideal for which they had been liberated. This, he felt, could not be tolerated. Except for this one incident, Moses never utilized force to carry out his functions as a leader, which indicates the measure of his success in this role.

But when he debated the issue of the Golden Calf with the Lord, he displayed a broad grasp of the sensitive human situation. He knew the people were fearful and emotionally immature. After more than two hundred years amidst pagan worship and practice, they could not fully comprehend the meaning of One God. In the short time that had elapsed since the exodus their experiences were too limited to alter the illogical behavior conditioned by slavery. Communication between the three—God, Moses and Israel—had been inadequate. While he was frustrated by their inability to understand his constructive efforts, Moses was not willing to abandon them. He felt he could tolerate the irritations. He understood that people feel weak and ineffectual when their leader seems lost to them and that activity relieves their anxiety. That their energy went into building an idol indicated not so much an attack upon God, or upon himself, as a need for tolerance and guidance. To fill this need, Moses directed their energies toward the construction of the Tabernacle.

When it was completed, Moses told Aaron that the Lord had appointed him High Priest.[98] Reluctant to accept this office, Aaron protested that he did not want any distinction. "What!" he told Moses, "You had all the labor of erecting the Tabernacle, and I am now to be its High Priest!" Moses was displeased with the choice since he had been fully involved in the construction of the Tabernacle,[99] but he did not lose all perspective. He assured Aaron that he was as happy as though he himself had been chosen. "As you rejoiced in my elevation, so do I now rejoice in yours."[100] Aaron was persuaded and Moses made the announcement in the presence of the newly appointed elders.[101] He then trained Aaron and his sons to perform the priestly functions in the Sanctuary, and preparations were made for Aaron's installation.

Although he had been formally brought into his office, Aaron refused to enter into his priestly activities. The horns on the altar filled him with fear. They reminded him of the Israelites worshipping the Golden Calf, and of his part in it. Aaron suffered from such severe feelings of guilt that Moses had to encourage him to step up to the altar and offer the sacrifices.[102] And when the sacrifices had been offered and the Divine Presence did not descend upon the Sanctuary, Aaron's guilt mounted. He felt certain that God's presence did not enter the Sanctuary because he was weak when the people demanded an idol. Moses sensed Aaron's frustration. He accompanied Aaron to the Sanctuary, and the prayers they offered together relieved Aaron's distressing sense of guilt.[103] In praying that Aaron's guilt would not destroy him, Moses displayed his unselfish love for Aaron (Deuteronomy 9:20).

No sooner did Aaron embark upon his new life's work, than he met with a sorrowful experience. His two oldest sons died in the Taber- nacle because they "offered strange fire before the Lord" (Leviticus 10:1) while under the influence of wine.[104]

They were arrogant young men, who refused to marry because they felt that no woman was good enough for them. Thus they flouted the command to "be fruitful and multiply." With their father, uncle, brothers and they themselves in prominent positions, their family status made them feel superior to the people.[105] This feeling so permeated their attitude that when they followed Moses and Aaron in the procession at the dedi- cation of the Tabernacle, they said, "When will these two old men die so that we may assume authority over the community?"[106] Like children who long for power adults possess, they attempted to acquire it. Earlier, they had dared give a legal decision in the presence of Moses.[107] Impressed with their own importance, they committed other insolent acts. They en- tered prohibited areas of the Sanctuary, offered sacrifices they were not instructed to offer. They officiated in improper dress, did not wash their hands and feet before entering the Sanctuary, stopped taking counsel with each other and the group. Finally, they brought a strange fire to the altar from the kitchen.[108]

The death of Aaron's sons could have marred the dedication of the Tabernacle, but Moses took control of the situation. Understanding grief, Moses did not permit Aaron to indulge in self-pity, but helped him to sublimate his personal feelings in ministering to the people. Moses kept him occupied with his duties as High Priest, so that Aaron could not brood or dwell upon his loss. Aaron accepted Moses' counsel and, for the sake of the people, controlled his grief. Aaron learned that although life is uncertain, man must be prepared for whatever loss he may sustain. He bore this heavy blow without murmur or lament and submerged himself in the duties of the priesthood. Aaron proved dedicated and proficient in his office. He cooperated with Moses in circumcising the Hebrews so that they would qualify to eat the Paschal Lamb.[109] He worked tirelessly, con- secrating in one day twenty-two thousand Levites.[110]

The elements hostile to Moses' leadership were generally held in check by the tacit understanding that he would be replaced. Since he could not serve as leader forever, they were willing to suspend their hostilities. Nevertheless, from time to time the complaints of the people swelled to open opposition, erupting in rebellion led by individiuals or groups who pushed for Moses' ouster.[111] One of the most trying episodes—enough to wilt the most resolute leader—was instigated by a man called Korah. A fancied slight over an appointment was his excuse to overthrow all the institutions Moses had founded. When Moses appointed his cousin Eliza-phan as chief of the Levite division of Kohathites,[112] Korah's envy of Moses found an outlet.[113]

Korah, it seems, was a weak individual who strove for a position of authority to compensate for his feelings of inferiority and inadequacy. When Moses elevated Elizaphan, he wounded Korah's pride and aroused his envy and hostility. Although he realized that Elizaphan deserved the honor, Korah felt he was equally deserving. He rationalized that his failure to elicit praise in the past stemmed not from his lack of achievement, but from the blindness of others who failed to discern his worth. Like a sibling who believes his brother or sister receives more affection, Korah reacted with self-hatred, which he turned against the one who rejected him, Moses. He attempted to destroy Moses' authority and seize his power, believing this acquisition would compensate for his own short-comings. He stirred up rebellion, enlisting Moses' long-standing enemies, Dathan and Abiram. The Reubenites, descendants of Jacob's first-born, joined the dissenters; they were angry because honors had been conferred upon the tribe of Judah, and not upon them.[114] Each tribe, except Levi, joined the rebellion and was represented by twenty-three men.

The consecration of the Levites was the occasion for Korah to move against Moses. When he returned home from the ceremony, Korah's wife incited him to action. Along with all the Levites, the hair on his head and body had been shaved. Who did it to him, she asked? He told her it was Moses. She remarked, "Moses hates you and he did this to disgrace you." Moses had shaved his own sons, too, Korah replied. "Moses would be willing to disgrace his own sons," she declared, "as long as he could disgrace you."[115]

Others also asked Korah who had disfigured him. He blamed Moses, and added that he had adorned his brother, Aaron, as a bride. Their hatred kindled by what they considered an insult, Korah and Moses' enemies assembled their adherents and attracted others who came to listen. They incited against him and exclaimed: "Moses is king, his brother Aaron is High Priest, his nephews are deputy high priests, and he allots to the priests the tithe, the heave offering, and many other tributes."[116] They concocted false stories to depict his love of power;[117] they accused him of immorality, and warned their wives to keep away from him.[118] Rumor and innuendo colored reality and obscured the facts, undermining the people's confidence in Moses.

Followed by the grumbling crowd, Korah confronted Moses and attempted to discredit him in public.[119] Asking questions designed to make Moses look ridiculous, Korah tried to show that the Torah contained absurd laws, and that it was not God's work, but Moses'. Moses was no true prophet, he contended, nor Aaron a true High Priest. But Korah was a true demagogue. He attacked Moses and Aaron for regarding themselves as superior to the people. They had all heard the Ten Commandments as Moses had, he said. Finally he voiced the complaint of the slave mentality. "You have laid upon us a burden that is greater than Egyptian slavery! We were better off under the Egyptians than under your rule!" The people were so incensed that they wanted to stone Moses,[120] and Moses was thrown into a tremor by the dissension.

Moses appealed to Korah to cause no schism in Israel. When Moses saw that it was useless to reason with him, he sent for Dathan and Abiram, but they refused to appear before him. The feelings these three men entertained toward Moses reflected their attitudes toward the Jewish people as a whole. When Moses carried out his duties as leader of the group, he represented the people, to whom he owed allegiance and who vested in him power and authority. The hostility the three expressed against Moses was thus a barometer of their feeling about the people generally.

Since Dathan and Abiram would not come to him, Moses went to them, hoping they would feel ashamed and retract their lies. He admonished and exhorted them to change their minds, but they became abusive and refused to be reconciled.[121] Seeing that he made no headway with them, Moses directed his warning to the other Levites who might join in the rebellion.[122] It was futile; even the Levites were hostile. Wisely, Moses averted a showdown by ordering them to appear the next day, together with Aaron. He hoped that by giving them time to reflect on their actions, to which strong drink might have carried them, they would change their tack.[123] Their energy spent, the crowd disbanded until the following day.

Confronted by the mob, Moses realized that they held the key to his power. If they refused to obey him, or simply did not cooperate, he would no longer exercise control over them. To maintain his position of leadership, and to salvage the years of personal sacrifice he had invested on their behalf, he must continue to attract and mobilize their loyalties.

If he appeared callous to their needs and feelings, or if he could no longer fulfill their expectations of him, they would lose faith in themselves and in leaders generally. As they dispersed, Moses knew that their meeting on the following morning would be crucial to their future and to the achievement of their ultimate goal.

During the night, Korah was not idle. He and his corps of delegates moved among the tribes, opening the wounds of grievances and salting them with slander of Moses and Aaron. With the bland assurance that he was not seeking a position of honor for himself,[124] Korah won them to his side. By morning not only Korah's original company, but all the people, appeared before the Tabernacle to quarrel with Moses and Aaron. But Moses stood his ground before the entire camp. His voice rang with authority as he warned them of the punishment that threatened them and of the innocents who would suffer on their account.[125] He ordered them to stop following these wicked men who would not save them but destroy them. Moses' unqualified assurance and radiantly confident countenance overawed the people. With the Tabernacle behind him, his righteousness appeared to emit rays of light (Exodus 34:29-30), while Korah was no more than a snarling cur. The loyalty of the people swung back to Moses. Only Dathan and Abiram continued to harangue and abuse him. When the people saw that Moses controlled his anger,[126] they turned their wrath on his detractors. Korah and his men were destroyed, except for Korah's three sons and On, a relative of Dathan and Abiram.[127] A few, confused by the issues and by the sudden reversal of the crowd, blamed Moses for the death of these people,[128] and the relatives of those who died sought to glorify their death, as a sort of vicarious claim to fame. Except for these few, who urged the people to set a limit to Moses' power, insisting that the public welfare and the safety of Israel demanded such measures,[129] the people accepted the discipline Moses imposed upon them and his leadership remained undisputed.

It was also in the wilderness that personal relationships took on added importance to the Israelites. Perhaps with the pressure of servitude gone, and during the long years of marking time, they attached greater significance to their personal feelings. Here jealousy and hostile feelings manifested themselves among Moses and Miriam and Aaron. The most glaring incident of this nature involved all three.

It began innocently enough when Miriam, in the company of Zipporah, heard from others that Eldad and Medad were prophesying in the camp. Miriam remarked, "Blessed are the women who behold their husbands raised to dignity." Caustically, Zipporah replied that it would be closer to the truth to say, "Woe to the wives of these men who will now have no conjugal happiness." What made her say this, Miriam inquired? The conduct of her husband, Zipporah replied; ever since Moses had returned to redeem his people he no longer knew her. Miriam understood then why Zipporah did not adorn herself with jewelry. When she had asked why Zipporah was lax about her appearance, she had answered, "Your brother is not particular about it."[130]

Miriam's resentment of Moses manifested itself now, although it may have lain dormant since his infancy. The motherly concern and loving care she had showered upon her baby brother, since it was her sole response to him, probably masked completely her intense jealousy of him.[131] As an infant, Moses was the center of attention, at first because he was in mortal danger and then because he was adopted by the royal family. Miriam may have discovered when she was very young that open rivalry brought disapproval from her parents, and that protecting Moses won their approval. She might also have made an unconscious effort to win Moses away from Jochebed, so that she could rank first with him, if not with his mother. Or, deprived of her mother's care, she tried to embody it in herself by attempting to be her own mother. Furthermore, mothering, by dominating a younger sibling, gave her a sense of power. Actually hating Moses, and forced since childhood to suppress it, she loved him exceedingly. Now that an opportunity arose to inveigh against him and portray him as a law-breaker and a recalcitrant husband, she could not keep Zipporah's comments to herself. She went to Aaron and told him what she had learned about Moses' personal life, and added, "The Word was upon me, but I did not keep away from my husband." Aaron, surprisingly, joined her refrain. He, too, may have smoldered with repressed resentment against the "baby" in the family who drew off the attention he craved. Aaron might never have derided his younger brother if Miriam had not started it. Now he replied, indignantly, "The Word was upon me, but I did not keep away from my wife. And the Word was also upon our fathers of old, but they did not separate themselves from their wives. But, he, because of his presumptuous spirit, kept away from his wife."[132] By means of this aggressive behavior, they sought to cause Moses some measure of injury.

Miriam and Aaron, close all their lives, found themselves in accord where Moses was concerned. In childhood, when Moses was the chief concern of their mother, Aaron had depended on Miriam, who must have been more like a mother to him than a sister. It was natural, then, for

Aaron to respond to her maternal demeanor. For his own good, they would go to Moses and tell him what they thought of his behavior.[133]

Moses was hurt by their meddling, but not angry. Over-protected by his own mother and by Bithiah, Moses had first discovered his great strength when he broke away from Bithiah. Perhaps Moses rejected Zipporah, who had a motherly appeal to him, because he feared that dependence upon her would render him unable to lead. Moses was unconsciously aware that he feared women. He said, "I can understand that Miriam might speak slanderously against me, since women as a rule are talkative." But he was hurt that Aaron, whose criticism when he had brought his family to Egypt had caused him to send them away, now also spoke against him.[134] He had divorced Zipporah when he sent her with their sons back to Jethro.[135] After the escape from Egypt he sent for them so that his sons could grow up among the Israelites. Although he had not fulfilled the command, "be fruitful and multiply" (1:28)—to abide by the injunction both a male and a female child are required[136]—Moses never resumed marital relations with Zipporah. He had two sons, but no daughter, and he admitted his culpability in this regard.

Moses also took into consideration the marital difficulties Miriam had experienced, and realized that she sympathized with Zipporah. When she was betrothed to Caleb, Miriam contracted a serious illness that almost destroyed her prospects for happiness. Her face was "as pale as the color of curtains" and she became an invalid, but Caleb honored his pledge. Although he was married to Bithiah, Moses' adoptive mother, he nevertheless married Miriam in spite of her condition. (Mered, another name for Caleb [I Chronicles 4:18], married Hajehudijah, which means "the Jewess," another name for Bithiah. She was given this name because she had repudiated idolatry, and anyone who does so is called "a Jew.")[136a] For the duration of Miriam's illness, which must have been a considerable time, conjugal life was denied them. But although everyone was certain she would die, Miriam recovered both her health and her beauty, and she and Caleb eventually lived as husband and wife again. Their happiness restored, Caleb treated her as though he was marrying her for the first time.[137] They were both overjoyed when they were able to bear so fine an offspring as Bezalel, who became the master architect of the Tabernacle the Israelites built in the wilderness.[138] Miriam, Moses felt, knew the blessings of marital bliss and tried to convey to him that his dedication to God did not bar him from the opportunities available to all married couples. She meant well. If he could not accept her advice, he could not hate her for it either.

Although Moses did not reprove them, both Miriam and Aaron regretted that they had exposed the one weakness in his personality. Miriam could have kept Zipporah's confidence to herself, rather than detract from Moses' real greatness. Aaron, having heard, could have stopped, rather than encouraged, her interference. Zipporah's happiness was, after all, a matter between Moses and Zipporah; and Moses' compliance with the law of reproduction, an affair concerning Moses and God. They subconsciously wanted to hurt Moses, however, as much as they consciously wanted to help him. That they both subsequently suffered from guilt is apparent in the fact that both fell ill, and the illness they contracted was then known as leprosy, the punishment ordained for those who speak ill of others (Deuteronomy 24:8-9). Aaron's leprosy lasted only briefly, but Miriam, who started the talk about Moses and was therefore the real talebearer, was punished more severely.[139]

Aaron tried to heal her—he felt doubly guilty because he was spared although he was as much to blame as she—but he failed to give her relief. In fact, the more he looked upon Miriam's leprosy, the more it increased. Distraught over his sister's condition, Aaron turned to Moses for help. "Moses, my brother, do you think this leprosy is being visited upon Miriam alone? It is visited indeed upon the flesh of our father, Amram."[140] "Brothers," he told him, "do not part only in death. Our sister, even though she is alive, has left us as though she were dead."[141] Anxious to exonerate himself, Aaron asked whether, in Moses' judgment, he or Miriam had ever done harm to any human being. No, Moses replied, they had not. "If we have done no evil to others, how could we think of doing evil to our brother? It was an error on our part. Shall we therefore lose our sister?"[142] Waxing emotional, he cried, "Alas, shall our sister, who was with us in Egypt, who intoned with us the song at the Red Sea, who instructed the women while we instructed the men, shall she now sit outside the camp?" Aaron's fervent appeal on behalf of Miriam explains the reference, "Miriam, the sister of Aaron. . . ." (Exodus 15:20). She was not called Moses' sister because it was Aaron who showed special devotion to her when she was smitten with leprosy.[143]

When he saw her, Moses was also moved to intercede on his sister's behalf. He felt she should not suffer[144] and he wept, for he knew her pain when his hand bore this disease as a sign to Pharaoh.[145] She had not intended to slander him, he realized, but had sought to help him. It was not judicious to speak of his neglect of his marital duty,[146] but she spoke of it only to Aaron—she kept it within the family. And he could never forget that she had come to his aid when Bithiah took him out of the river. He drew a circle and stood within it, declaring that he would not move from that spot until Miriam was healed. He sought God's mercy for her, urgently exclaiming, "Answer me whether Thou wilt heal her or not,"[147] and concluded by stating, "but if Thou dost not heal her, I myself shall do so."[148] He would not forsake her.

The Lord's reply links Miriam's leprosy, as punishment, to guilt, and suggests that her illness, like many forms of dermatitis observed today, was actually psychosomatic. "If her father had but spit in her face, should she not hide in shame seven days? Let her be shut up without the camp seven days and after that she shall be brought in again" (Numbers 12:14). Having suffered the punishment she felt she deserved, and having obtained Moses' forgiveness, Miriam became well.

Miriam's punishment did not diminish her eminence among the people. They were at that moment breaking camp and had already saddled their beasts of burden for the march. They waited, however, as Moses had figuratively vowed to wait within the circle, until Miriam recovered. They knew that she did not have an evil nature. As she had walked up and down along the shore to await Moses' fate, so the people waited for her, until she recovered.[149]

Divorce, as Miriam seemed to know, had a great traumatic effect not only on Zipporah but also on their sons, and ultimately Moses suffered as a result of it too. Even before the divorce occurred, Moses' sons were raised without a father, for Moses spent much time alone, preoccupied with the mission that seemed to be thrust upon him. His sons felt threatened from the earliest days of their lives. Moses was not at home for them to imitate, or to identify with. They could not learn from him "how to temper and exercise their feelings of aggression and love." Though the father's presence becomes less necessary as boys grow up, he still plays an important role. Even adults derive pleasure merely from the fact that they have parents.[150] Due to Moses' preoccupation, his sons were deprived of the example of useful reaction patterns which Moses developed from life experiences. They were denied his knowledge of life and of masculine experiences and ways of thinking and feeling.

Moses' sons had already been rebuffed and now they were being dis-carded again. They had made the long journey to Egypt with Moses to share his new life there, but instead of having a part in his mission, they found themselves unceremoniously dismissed. Moses divorced their mother and sent them home with her. They must have regarded their father as a tyrant, an unreasoning authority, wholly incomprehensible, who aroused only feelings of hostility in them.

During the estrangement, with Zipporah playing both mother and father to them, Moses' sons may have cross-identified, that is identified too much with their mother. They adopted her attitudes and developed strong attachments to her. She, in turn, might have loved them excessively, jealously attempting to keep them to herself; they may have symbolized her lost husband. The boys, at the same time, may have blamed her for the loss of their father, and found themselves in the circular dilemma of resenting their mother and fearing retribution and the loss of her love.

A backlog of such feelings added to their conflicts when Moses sent for them and the family was reunited. They construed their loneliness during the separation as punishment, for children usually blame themselves for the separation of their parents, regardless of the cause. And now, when they rejoined their father in the wilderness, they must have seen Moses as a rival for their mother, which undoubtedly led to further guilt. All told, there is ample reason to believe Moses' sons did not have a wholesome attitude toward themselves, for they were never able to rise above the ordinary and they were in no sense capable of leadership.[151]

The long years of waiting and teaching in the wilderness taxed the relationship between Moses and Aaron in every conceivable way. Each rejoiced in the achievements of the other, yet as the years passed, they each became more aware of the limitations of the other. Early in their relationship, when Moses learned that Aaron would be his spokesman (Exodus 4:16), the Lord told him that Aaron would respect and revere him. Moses, however, did not rely on Aaron alone to maintain this balanced relationship, but gathered "all the elders of the children of Israel" to bear witness to their equality.[152] It would seem there was a twinge of jealousy, but Moses and Aaron worked shoulder to shoulder, neither of them assuming airs of superiority. The ability and temperament of each one offset the limitations of the other. At one time, Moses forgot the laws he himself taught. Aaron pointed out his error, and Moses did not take exception to it. In fact, he sent an announcement throughout the camp that he had incorrectly interpreted the law and that Aaron had corrected him.[153] Moses praised Aaron, saying that he ministered services of love to his people.[154]

One notable characteristic of Moses was his quick temper. Like the rage that moved him to kill the Egyptian in his youth, his fury often exploded in outbursts against the people and even, on occasion, against God. When the people complained in the wilderness of Zin that they were without water, God told Moses to speak to the rock to bring forth water. But Moses was so angered by the tormenting complaints of the people that he shouted at them, "O, ye madmen, ye stiff-necked ones,"[155] and in his rage, instead of speaking to the rock, he struck a stone he had chosen himself.[156] When water merely trickled from the rock, the people ridiculed him. "O son of Amram! Is this water for sucklings, or babes weaned from milk?" In his fury he struck the rock a second time and water gushed forth abundantly (Numbers 20:11).[157]

As a result of this angry scene, both Moses and Aaron were condemned by God to die in the wilderness. When Aaron offered no defense for himself, Moses appealed to God, "I have sinned; wherein did Aaron sin?" Moses praised Aaron's absolute faith in God's justice, but felt that Aaron should not suffer for his error.[158] Aaron was regarded as guilty of an omission, however, since he did not attempt to curb Moses from using angry words against the Israelites,[159] nor did he reprimand him for it.

Moses might have defended his short temper on this occasion, but he did not. Miriam had recently died and all the people mourned for her. After a time, when Moses and Aaron continued to weep in their tents, the people came to Moses and said, "How long will you sit here and weep?" Apparently forgetting the advice he had given Aaron, Moses replied, "Shall I not weep for my sister, who has died?" "While you are weeping for one soul," they retorted, "weep at the same time for us all, for we have no water to drink." Amid the protestations of the people, Moses went out to see for himself. Clinging to the respite from responsibility that his mourning afforded, Moses soon found himself quarrelling with them. He felt sorry for himself and complained that he could not bear them alone.[160] He went to the Sanctuary with Aaron, but in place of offering comfort the Lord ordered him to action. "Hasten from this place. My children die of thirst, and you have nothing better to do than to mourn the death of an old woman."[161] Upset and angry, Moses lost his temper with the people because he was angry with himself. He defended Aaron, but he felt that he had been remiss in his duty.

Another story regarding this incident sharply defines the difference between the personalities of the two brothers. While Moses and Aaron were grieving Miriam's death, a mob of people gathered to protest the dearth of water. Moses saw them approaching and asked, "What do all these people want?" Aaron replied that they were coming, no doubt, to express their sympathy. No, Moses corrected him, this was no well-ordered procession, but a motley crowd. Was Aaron unable to distinguish between them? They were not coming to express their sympathy, he informed Aaron, but for some other unholy reason.[162] The interpretations

Moses and Aaron gave to the same scene differentiated them from each other.

Herein lay the basis for their distinctive character traits and for the hostility that did exist between them, although it was held in check. Aaron was the favorite of the people because of his kindness and his unlimited love of peace. Just as he built the Golden Calf to spare the people the guilt of another murder and the punishment that would follow, he was motivated always to establish peace between God and man. His own guilt for making an idol in the place of God remained with him, and he endeavored, for the remainder of his life, to atone for his sin. He went from house to house and whenever he found someone unable to recite the *Shema,* the declaration of faith in One God, he taught it to him. When he found someone incapable of entering into the study of Torah, he initiated him into it. Aaron strove not only to promote peace between God and man, but also between the learned and the ignorant Israelites, and between man and wife.[163]

Both men and women loved Aaron more than Moses,[164] for Aaron was a humble man. He was friendly, greeting first even the lowliest. While Moses felt that the law must be upheld, Aaron strove to prevent the people from sinning. He established peace between people by sitting with them until they removed all rancor from their hearts. Because he reconciled husbands and wives, male children subsequently born were often named after him.[165] At one time the people thought Aaron had attained a higher position than Moses and they rejoiced.[166]

Moses, on the other hand, felt that peace between God and man, and peace between man and man, could only follow voluntary universal adherence to law. Notwithstanding his strict judgment according to the truth of basic law,[167] Moses was a democratic leader in the sense that he encouraged the people to take part in the decisions of the group. Ever ready to welcome worthwhile suggestions, he agreed when the people requested that scouts be sent ahead into Palestine to look over the land (Deuteronomy 1:22-23). To insure an unbiased report, he sent one man from every tribe except Levi.[168] He also accepted Jethro's suggestion to institute a more efficient judicial system. It meant delegating some of his authority, but Moses readily agreed that the people were prepared for increased self-government.

Whenever possible Moses sought the cooperation of the people through their representatives, or through the elders, rather than wield his authority arbitrarily. Sharing his power was not to surrender it, because enlisting the support and loyalty of his followers and keeping open the channels

of communication actually increased his influence. He was always acces-
sible to the people. They came to his tent with their problems, and the
solutions were born out of the relationships they established. Although he
could not eliminate these negative reactions entirely, the best antidote for
the jealousy and fear which a leader's power instills in his followers was
shared responsibility, Moses realized. As the singular leader and judge
for many years, Moses aroused more fear than love in the people. He
was harsh in pointing out their sins, and when he was obliged to mete
out justice to the guilty, they did not soon forget.

His steadfastness in matters of principle, probably more than anything
else, assured the ultimate success of Moses' mission, but it cost him
dearly in emotional gratification. He saw that Aaron was adored by the
Israelites, and felt jealous and threatened. He had lived only for his
people, sacrificing wealth, position and marriage; he had surrendered the
opportunity to establish a new nation. Instead of showing appreciation to
Moses, the people gave their love to Aaron. Since infancy Moses was
accustomed to being the focus of everyone meaningful in his life. Jochebed
lavished attention upon him, Bithiah protected him, Pharaoh loved him,
Zipporah sacrificed for him. Now Aaron was the object of love and Moses
resented him for it. Moses did not overtly display hostility toward Aaron,
but defensive hostility on his part is inferred from the elaborate details
in Rabbinic literature regarding Aaron's death. With Aaron out of the
way, Moses subconsciously felt, he would regain the love he had lost. The
fantasy of Aaron's death was equivalent to destroying Aaron and served,
therefore, to ameliorate Moses' need for love and his loss of self-esteem.

The guilt which is a concomitant of the death wish is apparent in
Moses' behavior prior to Aaron's death. Aaron would die, the Lord told
Moses, and He instructed Moses to prepare Aaron for death. Although
he had wished Aaron dead,[169] Moses wept so passionately about the
impending loss of his brother that he approached the brink of death
himself,[170] which indicates the depth of his guilt feelings. Moses rebelled.
He could not be so presumptuous as to tell his older brother, "Go up unto
Mount Hor and die there." God told Moses not to tell him directly, but
to take Aaron and his son Eleazer and to go with them to the top of Mount
Hor. When Aaron questioned him about the meaning of the journey,
Moses tried to tell him of his impending death by means of allusions. But
Aaron, in his trusting simplicity, did not understand. With great finesse,
Moses finally succeeded in breaking the news gently. Engaging Aaron in
a discussion of a difficult passage in the Bible regarding creation, Moses
asked Aaron's assistance in interpreting it. They read the first chapter of

Genesis together. When they came to the creation of Adam, Moses remarked, "How is the creation of man to be called good and beautiful,
if man must eventually die!" Aaron replied, "Far be it from us not to
resign ourselves to the will of God."[171]

When they were about to enter a cave, Moses told Aaron that it
would be improper to enter in his priestly garments, because they might
become unclean. Moses took the garments from Aaron and put them on
Eleazer.[172] As they were about to enter the cave, Aaron understood the
purpose of the mission. He said to Moses, "How long, O my brother, will
you conceal the commission. . . . Even if it were to refer to my death, I
would accept it with a cheerful countenance. Far be it from us not to
resign ourselves to the will of God." Moses confessed that he had been
afraid to tell Aaron about his imminent death. He consoled Aaron, telling
him that he wished his own death could be like his, for he would have
no brother to tenderly bury him. And his sons, unlike Aaron's who would
inherit the priesthood, could never inherit his position. Moses admitted
that his sons in no way measured up to their father,[173] and that strangers
would take his place when he died.[174] When Aaron was sufficiently consoled to meet his end with equanimity,[175] Moses clothed him in shrouds
and took him into the cave. Inside, Moses bid him lie down and stretch
out his feet, which he did. And then Aaron expired. Seeing his brother
die in peace and without suffering, Moses said, "Blessed is the man that
dies such a death."[176]

When Moses and Eleazer returned to camp without Aaron, some believed that Moses had killed Aaron, while others accused Eleazer of killing
his father in order to become High Priest. Infuriated, the people wanted
to stone them both.[177] Moses saw the deep-felt sorrow expressed by the
people. Since Numbers 33:38 indicates Aaron died on Mount Hor, while
Deuteronomy 10:6 states that he died on Moserah, it is deduced that the
people retraced their steps eight stations through the wilderness to give
Aaron proper mourning rites.[178] Their reverence for Aaron was so great
that Moses feared the people might worship him. At the same time, they
were so hostile that Moses prayed he and Eleazer would be delivered
from this "unmerited suspicion."

Within one year all the siblings died.[179] Aaron died four months after
Miriam, and Moses about eight months after Aaron.[180] Aware that his
end was approaching, Moses' first concern was for the welfare of his
people. He prayed that God would appoint a leader for the people who
would know how to deal with each man according to his views,[181] a
man who would have patience with them.[182] He implored God for a good

and worthy successor.[183] When he learned that his disciple, Joshua, was chosen, he was pleased with the choice, but he was nevertheless depressed because neither of his sons was appointed to succeed him. When the Lord assured him that his brother's sons would reflect honor to his memory as if they were his own children,[184] Moses was consoled. He knew that neither of his sons was equipped to take his place.

The appointment of Joshua further elaborates upon the freedom-for-the-individual principle first encountered in Genesis. Succession to leadership was no longer confined to the leader's sons, nor even to his family, but was now open to the individual most capable of assuming office. This extends the attitude of Abraham, who announced that his servant, Eliezer of Damascus, would inherit the helm of his household (15:2). Abraham made this designation before the birth of his own sons, but Moses had two sons and bypassed them both.

Moses was thereupon instructed to induct Joshua into the office of leader (Numbers 27:20), for in Joshua, he was told, all good qualities would be found. The prophesy of Eldad and Medad would be fulfilled— Moses would die in the wilderness and Joshua would succeed him.

Moses, however, did not easily resign himself to his fate. He wanted to enter Palestine, the goal toward which he had led his people. He offered to relinquish his leadership in favor of Joshua, exchanging roles with him for the remainder of his life. He fancied that he was willing to become Joshua's disciple in order to fulfill his wish to see the Promised Land.[185] But Joshua was uneasy about his selection.

Gershom, Moses' older son, did not conceal his displeasure in Joshua's appointment. Moses would have liked to side with him, but placed the good of the people above his son's feelings. Joshua, too, was deeply agitated to find himself disrupting the loyalty of father to son. But Moses insisted that he was pleased to have Joshua take his place. "O Joshua," Moses protested, "can you believe that I begrudge your splendid future? It is my wish that you may be honored as much as I have been and that all Israel be honored like you."[186]

Joshua sensed Moses' true feelings and was reluctant to be the one to hurt him. He expressed the belief that he was incapable of leading the people, that compared to Moses he was dwarfed to insignificance. Moses instructed Joshua not to underestimate himself and persuaded him to accept the leadership. After presenting him to the people so that they might acknowledge Joshua as his successor,[187] Moses took steps to dispel Joshua's feelings of inferiority. Moses bade Joshua, who had been sitting on the floor with his other students according to custom, to sit on the bench

beside him.[188] And he honored Joshua by interrupting his discourse whenever Joshua entered the house of learning and resuming it only when he
had taken his seat.[189] Moses ordered a herald to proclaim throughout the
camp, "This man Joshua is worthy of being appointed by God as His
shepherd."[190] The Lord told Moses to place one hand on Joshua in
benediction; but to emphasize that he was pleased with Joshua's appointment, Moses placed both hands on him, and inducted him with joy as
though he were his own son.[191]

Overcoming his personal disappointments, Moses extended himself
in every way[192] to prepare Joshua for his elevation and to prepare the
people to accept him. For the last thirty-six days of his life, Moses served
Joshua from morning till evening, as though he were the disciple and
Joshua the master. Moses arose each midnight and went to Joshua's tent.
He cleaned Joshua's shoes and placed them beside his bed and he laid his
shirt near his pillow. He arranged his undergarments, his cloak, his turban,
his golden helmet and his crown of pearls. Then he fetched a pitcher of
water and a golden basin and placed them where Joshua would find them
to wash himself when he awoke. He swept Joshua's rooms and when
everything was in order he went out and ordered the herald to proclaim
in the camp: "Moses stands at Joshua's gate and announces that whoso-
ever wishes to hear God's word should betake himself to Joshua, for he,
according to God's word, is the leader of Israel."

Even at the end of his life, Moses made a concerted effort to do the
will of God. Throughout many decades Moses consciously set aside self-
indulgence in order to realize the greater meaning of his life. The fear
of God, of living less nobly than he ought to, became second nature to
him.[193]

An ancient story depicts the consciousness with which Moses transformed the evil in his nature to become a noble, exalted character. After
the exodus of the Israelites from Egypt, a king of Arabia sent an artist
to paint a portrait of Moses, so that he might have the likeness of this
great man before him. The painter returned after completing the mission,
and the king assembled those of his wise men familiar with the science
of physiognomy. He displayed the portrait and invited their judgment of
it. The unanimous opinion was that it represented a covetous, haughty,
sensual man—a man disfigured by all possible ugly traits. The king was
angry, contending that if they declared Moses to be a villain they did not
know physiognomy.

Defending themselves, the scientists blamed the artist. If he had produced a true likeness of Moses, they could not have misjudged him. But the artist insisted that his work closely resembled the subject.

Unable to decide who was right, the king went to see Moses personally, and he had to admit that the portrait was a masterpiece. Moses in the flesh was the Moses on canvas. The king was convinced that the physiognomy scientists were incompetent.

The king told Moses what had happened, and his own feelings in the matter. Moses thereupon told him, "Your artist and your experts are masters, each in his own line. . . . Unashamed, I confess that by nature I possessed all the reprehensible traits your wise men read in my picture and ascribed to me, perhaps to a greater degree than they think. But I mastered my evil impulses with my strong will, and the character I acquired through severe discipline has become the opposite of the disposition with which I was born. Through this change, wrought in me by my own efforts, I have earned honor and commendation upon earth as well as in heaven."[194]

When Moses died, only his nephew Eleazer, the High Priest, accompanied him to his tomb.[195] He was buried without elaborate processional or public ceremony. No attempt at self-effacement, this was the choice of a truly perceptive and consecrated leader.

Throughout his long career, Moses recognized the people's low threshold for sustained enthusiasm when goals do not relate directly to daily life. He also recognized their tremendous capacity for interest in, and devotion to, an individual,[196] and he harnessed this force to accomplish his goals. He saw that the people craved the reality of a flesh and blood leader who could enthrall them with the call, "Follow me." To rally a segment of the people to return to the monotheistic belief after the sin of the Golden Calf, he thundered, "Whoso is on the Lord's side, let him come unto me" (Exodus 32:26), and the tribe of Levi responded to this personal appeal.

Moses knew that many people never outgrow the need for someone to serve in the role of father or hero, that they find following a leader a profoundly satisfying experience. But he could not allow them to find this comfort in a dead leader. He feared they would so venerate him in death that they would vitiate the effectiveness of their new leader and discard the high purpose of becoming "a holy nation" consecrated to God. Even in death Moses inspired his people to reach beyond the meanings they could grasp. He shed all personal glory, therefore, in an unmarked sepulchre (Deuteronomy 34:6) and left his people free.

CHAPTER TEN

This Dream Which I Have Dreamed

(Genesis 37:6)

I

PURSUIT of the underlying theme of the early books of the Bible—the revolt of the Hebrews against primogeniture—necessarily involves an examination of the dreams presented in Scripture. Primogeniture repressed the instinctual growth of individuals and promoted rebellion, which manifested itself in dreams. People do not dream of trivial things, although it may seem that they do as they describe the ludicrous behavior and situations they have dreamed. Psychiatrists of today and the Rabbis of old contend that dreams are significant and deserve serious consideration. Freud's assertion that dreams "are not meaningless, are not absurd,"[1] rephrases an attitude that had been entertained by the Jewish people from the earliest times of which we have records. Dreams, the ancient sages have maintained, are meaningful even when false. When they suggest action in the name of God, but against His commandments, then they are a "test" from God (Deuteronmy 13:4; Jeremiah 23:25-27; 27:9-10; 29:8-9), another way to describe psychic conflict. In every instance "a dream stands upon its foundation."[2] A dream is not an empty experience because man dreams only when there is reason for it.

The Book of Genesis, in addition to all the other fascinating data it contains, records more action dreams than all the other thirty-eight books comprising Jewish Scripture combined—eight in all. There are Jacob's dreams about the sheep (31:10) and the ladder (28:10-17), Joseph's two dreams (37:2-11), the dreams of the butler and baker who were Joseph's prison mates (40:5-19), and Pharaoh's two dreams (41:1-7). No other action dreams appear in the Pentateuch and only six such dreams are narrated in the remainder of Scripture. They include Gideon's dream (Judges 7:13-15), and those described in Daniel (2; 4:1-15; 7; 8; 10:4-14). Other dreams mentioned in Scripture consist merely of conversations with no dramatizations. Like action dreams, they, too, indicate the state of the dreamer's psyche.

200

In the Bible, a dream is accepted as a direct and valid form of communication between God and man—a metaphysical bearer of messages
between the supernatural and the natural worlds. "If there be a prophet
among you," Scripture states, "I the Lord do make Myself known unto him
in a vision, I do speak with him in a dream" (Numbers 12:6). But the messages of dreams were not restricted to prophets, for as Elihu tells Job, "In a
dream, in a vision of the night, When deep sleep falleth upon men, In
slumberings upon the bed; then He openeth the ears of men" (33:15-16).
In the Bible dreams were also instructive, as in the case of Abimelech
(20:3), or when Agrippa was told in a dream that the sacrifice of a
poor man preceded his.[3]

Some biblical dreams also conveyed messages from the Almighty regarding future events. Daniel told Nebuchadnezzar after a perturbing dream:
"He that revealeth secrets hath made known to thee what shall come to
pass" (2:29). Joseph told Pharaoh the same thing. "What God is about
to do He hath declared unto Pharaoh" (41:25) as well as "shown unto
Pharaoh" (41:28). These were explicit, but hidden meanings were also
attributed to dreams. Since a message was taken for granted, each dream
recorded in the Bible was subjected to serious analysis. Although the
Rabbis were not unanimous as to the validity of dreams,[4] they believed
that not to dream was cause for alarm, and whoever did not dream once
in seven days they considered evil.[5]

A normal process which cannot be divorced from life, dreaming is
common to all people in every age. Living and dreaming go hand in hand;
only the dead are free from dreaming. But during the experience of dreaming, the individual does not perceive it as such. Upon awakening he realizes
for the first time that he has dreamed. A Chinese gentleman expressed the
inter-relatedness between these two conditions. "Last night," he said,
"I dreamed that I was a yellow butterfly. Now I do not know whether
when asleep I was a man dreaming of being a yellow butterfly, or that
I am now a yellow butterfly dreaming that I am a man."

Dreams have diverse effects upon the dreamer. They are as warm and
pleasant as they are irritating, as uplifting as obscene, as inspiring and
colorful as depressing and tasteless, as soothing as anxiety-laden. When
Jacob awoke from his dream of the ladder he was "afraid" (28:17),
the butler and baker "were mad" (40:6), Pharaoh awoke "troubled" from
nightmares (41:4, 7), Nebuchadnezzar's "spirit was troubled" (Daniel
2:1) and he was "afraid" and "affrighted" (Daniel 4:2). Dreams caused
Daniel to become "affrighted" and his "countenance was changed" (7:28),
he "fainted, and was sick certain days" and was "appalled" (8:27), and

he "retained no strength" (10:8). Enoch wept in his sleep because his dream was confusing to him; and after a dream that frightened him Nimrod's heart beat like a trip-hammer.[6] Solomon, on the other hand, awoke from his dream in good spirits. He went to Jerusalem to offer sacrifices and he made a party for all his servants (I Kings 3:15). Hearing a dream narrated, Gideon gained sufficient courage to launch a campaign immediately (Judges 7:13-15). Dreams offer consolation, deliver warnings, gratify secret longings, and offer solutions to the inner conflicts of the dreamer.[7]

Also enigmatic, dreams often contain opposites to the dreamer's conscious emotions. In them we may love those we hate or hate those we love, be content when ambitious, resistant when submissive, anxious when happy. "One man will dream of the banquet hour, but wake to lamentation and sorrow. Another will dream of lamentation and sorrow, but wake to enjoy himself in the hunting field."[8] The mood in which a person awakens from a dream may last throughout the day, and psychiatrists have cited cases in which mental disorders became evident after dreams. Expressing the dreamer's response to life in ways quite different from his waking thoughts and actions, dreams nevertheless have their own language and logic. This seeming confusion and topsy-turvy upheaval within the dreamer, like hypnosis, reveals hidden dimensions of personality.

Under hypnosis man apparently possesses intuitive insight which enables him to interpret his dreams. Fromm[9] and Wolff[10] observed that people asked to interpret their dreams while under hypnosis did so without difficulty or hesitation, while they found the same dreams utterly meaningless when they were not hypnotized. Under hypnosis, inhibitions disappear almost completely, allowing the individual to admit the true symbolism of the dream and the repressed thoughts it represents. The expression, "I never imagined it in my wildest dreams" indicates that we satisfy in dreams those desires which are nullified by reality.[11]

Each person has two opposing psychic systems functioning simultaneously at all times—the wish and the censor of the wish—and the tension between them is the primary cause of dreaming.[12] These forces are never equal (if they were we would be immobilized), but they maintain a balance by reversing their proportionate influence upon behavior during waking and sleeping. Awake, the censor dominates and often represses the wish, permitting only those wishes of which it approves to reach consciousness. Asleep, the censor is weakened, but continues to judge the content of wishes without actually repressing them. When a particular wish clashes with moral scruples, the censor will permit it to emerge as a dream wish only after imposing upon the dreamer's thought processes what it regards as safe and proper alterations and modifications. Utilizing all sorts of configurations, or "dream work," as Freud called them, the censor transforms the latent dream—the real, underlying thoughts in the dreamer's mind—into the manifest dream, which is the version the dreamer remembers. One such device is condensation, when the dreamer assembles within the same dream unrelated and irrelevant events, emotions, experiences, and fantasies of the present and the past. Displacement is another. It is the technique whereby an insignificant detail occupies the foreground of the dream, while the important theme is relegated to the background. Still another mechanism is elaboration. It composes a related and logical story out of many otherwise unrelated ideas. And there are still others. The severity and strictness of the censor can be determined by the degree and extensiveness of the "dream-disfigurements" or distortions.[13] In this fashion, the censor performs a beneficial function: it protects the dreamer from developing fears and other disagreeable emotions that his repressed desire might produce should he see it candidly, and thus keeps him from waking.[14] Yet, it is possible for dreams to completely escape the hand of the censor and to appear without modification. Then the repressed wish is regarded as so far removed from the mind of the dreamer that he disowns it; he believes he could never wish such a thing, not even in a dream. Or, if he has confronted the repressed wish on the previous day and anticipated in some form the deleterious effect of its fulfillment, then he may dream of his wish unaltered, for he has already subjected himself to psychic punishment.[15]

In his outstanding contribution toward the understanding of dreams, Freud demonstrated that dream dramatizations, the acting-out in pictorial imagery of the thoughts, conceptions and ideals latent in the unconscious, are really symbols which allude to suppressed wishes within the person's mind. An unrealized wish is a problem unsolved. Dreams fulfill them.[16] Dreams are messengers of the unconscious, integral parts of man's total personality, either repeating his waking moments or compensating for them.[17] Their function is to reveal and clarify, not to conceal, what is in the dreamer's mind, to disclose his views of himself and to preview possible solutions to a present problem. They represent reality rather than what the dreamer would like it to be or supposes it to be;[18] they mirror the self. They are merciless in that they uncover man's "deceptive morals and hypocritical affections" and display to him "the under side of his character."[19] They contain valuable communications with the self.

As a rule, dreams have their roots in the past and are wholly egotistical.

One dreams primarily of himself, his conceptions of others, his conflicts, his impulses, his view of the world; involvement with the outside world merely indicates his cultural environment.[20] These distinctions are not clearly defined in dreams, however. Transposed into language, dream symbols may disclose the secretive and complex aspects of his inner life and may well resolve the enigmas that perplex him.[21] When interpreted, symbols expose the repressed mental activity of the dreamer. The analyst, utilizing this technique, proceeds from the manifest dream to an under-standing of the latent dream. As Freud has shown, the remembrance of a dream is not generally a correct reproduction of the dreamer's innermost thoughts, but a disguise or distortion of the true dream-thoughts. Cloaked in symbols, the repressed thoughts emerge unchecked.

This should not be interpreted or lead to the inference that the un-conscious is a "demonic monster." On the contrary, the unconscious is absolutely neutral, devoid of any explosive material. It does not take sides on moral issues, nor does it possess aesthetic taste or intellectual judgment. A natural counterbalance to the conscious mind, the unconscious compen-sates when attitudes become so hopelessly false that they threaten the integrity of the individual. It mellows and tones down extreme conscious tendencies which repress basic values and endanger the self. Nebuchad-nezzar, for instance, was at the zenith of his glory when he dreamed of a tree that had grown so tall that the top of it reached into heaven and its branches and food gave shade and sustenance to all animals. In his dream, however, it was ordered that the tree be cut down (Daniel 4:7-14). This dream might well be regarded as a counterbalance to his grandiose feeling of great power.[22]

In symbolism formulated by the unconscious, the images represent for-gotten or repressed thoughts, that which one is unable or unwilling to remember consciously. It "is language in which inner experiences, feelings and thoughts are expressed as if they were sensory experiences."[23] Dream symbols have a different logic from conventional language, and there is a reason for one symbol, or one detail, to appear rather than another. Like a secret code, or hieroglyphics, symbols distort the latent thoughts and do not actually represent what they appear to. It is also recognized that a dream symbol may have more than one meaning;[24] that its meaning is not fixed and definite, but lies in its relation to the dreamer.[25] It is a language in which symbols originating in the environment stand for things which seem similar yet are different from the thoughts they express. Tal-mudic and Midrashic writings also recognized that dream symbols may connote something different.[26] If one dreams of walking in the shade of a myrtle, according to the Talmud, it has sexual content. On the other hand, if one dreams of having intercourse with his mother, the Talmud predicts that he can expect to obtain wisdom.[27] Here, a sexual dream has non-sexual implications. Symbols, in other words, serve as facades "which conceal the contents within the house,"[28] protecting the dreamer when problems and conflicts threaten him in the reality of life.

Since the fundamental interests of men are perennial and unchanging, dream symbols thousands of years old are the same as those visualized by dreamers today. They express the same meanings, with little variation. Such symbols are derived not only from dreams, but also from imagery in language, from the prejudices of a culture, and from folklore and myths. Thus the symbolism that operates in the unconscious conceptions held by groups of people widely separated in time and place is considered to have meaning common to all.

Most common are those symbols involving members of the family and the essential elements of life. A king and queen are universally regarded as symbols for father and mother; prince and princess for the dreamer himself or herself. Mother is also symbolized by water or earth or other elements from which life flows or develops. Father may be symbolized by one particular individual who has become a father figure for an entire nation, as Goethe, who appeared in the recorded dreams of many German people. Large animals or elongated objects or sharp weapons often represent the father or ancestor in dreams, as they do in the graphic arts of many cultures, past and present, while small animals, or "kids," generally symbolize children.[29] Leaving or departing may refer to death. These are merely a few of the dream symbols regarded as having the same meaning to dreamers throughout the ages.

Despite the progress that has been made toward understanding the mind of man, the dream remains largely baffling. Since it is a subconscious psychic activity, reflecting thought and emotion, it is as complex as man himself. The dream is therefore open to a great variety of interpretations. On this point, too, there is agreement between psychiatrists and the early Rabbis. Should a scholar dream of drinking wine, the Midrash states, it is a good augury. Should an ignoramus have the same dream, it betokens misfortune.[30] Regarded as one of the great dream interpreters among the Jewish people, Almoli also wrote that the same symbol may mean different things to different people.[31]

In the area of dreams, psychiatry agrees extensively with the explanations expressed by the Rabbis in the ancient Hebrew writings. Both disciplines agree that dreams induced by physical factors have lesser significance.

Rabbi Chisda, who seems to have been the psychiatrist of his day, formulated this principle which Freud expressed approximately two thousand
years later.[32] The Rabbis add that a dream observed on Saturday night
is less significant because Sabbath rest gives rise to idle thoughts which
are reflected in dreams.[33] Dreams of convenience are mentioned in Scripture
when Isaiah states, "And it shall be as when a hungry man dreameth, and,
behold, he eateth, But he awaketh, and his soul is empty; Or as when
a thirsty man dreameth, and behold, he drinketh, But when he awaketh,
and, behold, he is faint, and his soul hath appetite . . ." (29:8). Psychiatry also acknowledges that such dreams assuage the dreamer's need
by serving as substitutes for action. They prevent the dreamer from
awakening, and preserve sleep.

Another Talmudic statement corroborated by psychiatry today underscores the need to restudy early sources regarding psychic phenomena.
Rabbi Yochanan teaches that "three kinds of dreams are fulfilled: a
morning dream, a dream that a friend has about one, and a dream which
is interpreted in the midst of a dream."[34] Fromm supports this statement
psychologically.[35] In the morning, one is closer to consciousness, not as
deeply asleep as he is in the early or middle night. Both Rabbi Yochanan
and Dr. Fromm assert that when one is emerging from a deep sleep one
has clearer insight into the psychic forces within him and is capable of
better judgment. He is freer then than he is at any other stage of sleeping
or waking.[36] The same principle would operate in the dream one has about
someone else. Such a dream can come true because one often has better
judgment about another person than he has of himself. Since inhibitions
are greatly reduced during sleep, the insight of dreams is particularly
sharp and therefore has much value. In this vein, the Midrash states that
the baker and the butler each dreamed not only his own dream, but also
the interpretation of his companion's dream. The Rabbis believed that each
understood what the fate of the other should be.[37] Within this category
is the dream of Rabbi Simeon ben Yochai regarding his nephews. The
government would demand six hundred denarii of them, he dreamed,
and it occurred just as he foresaw it.[38]

The Rabbis and psychiatrists also maintain that repetitive dreams are
fulfilled, as were Joseph's and Pharaoh's. They are regarded as "expressive
of important themes" in an individual's life.[39] Such dreams are even regarded as having predictive value, perhaps because the dreamer strives
to make them come true. This might help explain the Talmudic statement,
"all dreams follow the mouth,"[40] meaning the interpretation given to
them. This conclusion is derived from the remark the butler made to

Pharaoh concerning Joseph's interpretations of his and the baker's dreams. "As he interpreted to us, so it was" (41:13). It is possible that, when an interpretation is given, the person subconsciously helps bring the explanation to fruition because of the confidence he has in the interpreter, though the butler and baker had no opportunity to do so in their particular cases. It also points to the prominent place the interpreter of dreams held among the Jewish people. Like the psychiatrist and analyst, he deciphered dreams; and like his modern counterpart, his insight commanded fear and respect.

Long ago the biblical authors recognized that a dream series, such as Joseph's and Pharaoh's dreams, can be regarded as parts of a single dream. Psychiatry, too, recognizes that a series of an individual's dreams is far more revealing than a single dream.[41] Although some things may be learned about the dreamer from a single dream, it is not until a group of dreams is available that a valid picture of the person can be gained.

Both the ancient and modern scholars agree that man's dreams are stimulated by the thoughts that occupy his mind during the day. Ecclesiastes' declaration, "For a dream cometh through a multitude of business" (5:2), is later echoed by Rabbi Samuel ben Nachmayni, who states in the name of Rabbi Jonathan, "A person is shown in a dream only that which is suggested by his own thoughts."[42] The many concerns that occupy the individual during the day come to the fore during sleep.[43] Trajan, the Roman emperor, once asked Rabbi Joshua to tell him what he would see in his dreams. The Rabbi replied that he would see the Parthians despoiling him, compelling him to do forced labor and feed unclean animals with a golden crook. Trajan thought about it all day and saw this very thing in his dreams that night. And so it happened in reality—he was defeated by the Parthians in 116 C.E. Another Rabbi, named Samuel, was questioned in similar fashion by King Shapur. Samuel told the King that he would see the Romans take him prisoner and force him to grind date-stones in a golden mill. The king thought about it all day and he saw this in a dream that night. Following this same school of thought, another Rabbi stated that a person will never see in a dream a golden date palm or an elephant going through the eye of a needle,[44] because people do not think of such things. Psychiatry acknowledges the same theory. Carl G. Jung writes that almost every dream contains details which originate "in the impressions, thoughts, or states of mind of one of the preceding days."[45] Dr. Solomon contends that dreams are a continuation of man's waking mental life.[46]

The Talmud and psychiatry further agree that an individual's subcon-

scious thoughts come relatively closer to the surface of consciousness during
sleep. The individual's subconscious finds greater expression in dreams
when conscious repressions of the day are dormant. During wakefulness
the moral censor is not willing to allow indiscretions to go by, as is
evidenced in the case of the two Rabbis, Huna and Nachman, who discussed the type of person King Saul was when he reigned. The former
commented that he was like a one-year-old infant who had not sinned.
The latter, in order to illustrate the other side of what being a one-year-
old means, said, without malice, that Saul was filthy with mud and excre-
ment. Following this discussion, Rabbi Nachman had a nightmarish dream.
Harassed by his conscience for offending the memory of King Saul in
his eagerness to demonstrate the error of hasty interpretation, he dreamed
that he cried, "I beg your pardon, bones of Saul, son of Kish." But his
conscience remained troubled and he had another nightmare. This time
he apologized by saying, "I beg your pardon, bones of Saul, son of Kish,
King of Israel." This time he felt relieved, his conscience having been
cleared by this more elaborate and all-inclusive statement. Thus, although
Rabbi Nachman was not aware during his waking moments that he was
troubled by what he had said, it came to the surface during the night. Both
these dreams were clues to his subconscious thoughts. Although he felt
he had made sufficient amends for the offense he had committed, subconsciously his mind was not satisfied until he had made what he inwardly
knew to be the proper atonement for his ill-considered remark.[47]

Recognizing that dreams express the unconscious strivings which are
barred from the mind when the individual is in more complete control of
his thoughts, the dreams in Scripture tell much about the characters who
dreamed them. Although repressed, the strivings they expressed in disguised and distorted forms were considered significant by the biblical authors, as they are by modern psychiatry. The support that science now
lends to the ancients' understanding of dreams underscores the value of
their inclusion in Scripture. The rebellion against primogeniture docu-
mented in Genesis was a rebellion against repression of the self; the
dreams recorded there exemplify the conscious and subconscious striving
of every individual to realize the self. What one aspires to become, one
dreams.

II

In order to analyze a dream adequately, it is necessary to have as
complete an understanding of the dreamer as possible. Specific knowledge of
his experiences, hopes, fears and mental processes are required. Regarding
our subjects, sufficient information concerning their backgrounds and the

situations in which they are involved is available from biblical and other Hebrew sources to make reasonable interpretations of their dreams.

Joseph's dreams—of his brother's sheaves of corn bowing down to his (37:5-7) and the sun and the moon and eleven stars bowing down to him (37:9)—can be readily identified as an ardent desire for superiority, for leadership, for lording it over his brothers. He was unhappy with them, and they with him. Joseph was Jacob's favorite and his brothers made no secret of their envy. They picked on Joseph, taking full advantage of their age and strength. Naturally, Joseph wanted to retaliate. Excluded from their companionship and always on the defensive, he resorted to tattling, but it was not satisfying. What he really wanted was to dominate all of them completely—to place them in the inferior position he occupied. Joseph hungered to bring his brothers to their knees before him, to see them stand obediently in his presence.

What he was unable to do in his waking hours, he accomplished in his dreams. The two dreams narrated in Scripture, and the one related in the Midrash, in which they were gathering fruit and his brothers' rotted while his remained wholesome,[48] all lucidly express personal ambition and aspiration. They indicate how Joseph felt about himself and convey his ardent wishes and desires. They were powerful wish-fulfillments, visions of grandiose strivings, enactments of the role he wished to play as compensation for reality.

Joseph's brothers and father recognized the intent of these dreams immediately and with facility. There was no need for Joseph to supply the unconscious thoughts which lay behind the dream content, nor to tell of what each part of the dream reminded him, which is necessary if a psychiatrist is to interpret dreams correctly. His brothers concluded immediately, without the services of an interpretor, that Joseph was hoping to dominate them. They mocked him and accused him of having delusions of grandeur. With contempt, they asked, "Shalt thou indeed reign over us? or shalt thou indeed have dominion over us?" (37:8).

When Joseph told of his second dream, Jacob came to the identical conclusion. He understood from the symbolism of the celestial bodies that Joseph was forecasting his mastery over his entire family. The most typical father-symbol, the sun,[49] represented Jacob; the moon, Rachel, his mother; and the eleven stars, his brothers. But Joseph's mother had died when she gave birth to Benjamin. Jacob rebuked Joseph, saying "Shall I and thy mother and thy brethren indeed come and bow down to thee to the earth?" (37:10). It was impossible, Jacob told him. His mother was dead and could never bow down to him; so would the rest of his dream remain unfulfilled.[50] Still Jacob understood Joseph's ambition—it was not unlike his feelings toward his own older brother and his dream of the ladder. But he lashed Joseph and made light of his dream, hoping by this tactic to improve the relationship between Joseph and his brothers. For his part, Jacob saw merit in upsetting the position of the older and younger sons within the family, but his rebuke implied his concern for the violence that might follow if accepted customs were broken. Although his actions before and after this incident contradict it, Jacob advised Joseph then that it was improper for the patriarch and matriarch and older siblings to be subservient to the younger.

Dreams with such simple and unconfusing content are quite usual among youngsters.[51] At first Joseph dreamed only of dominating his brothers, and he himself was symbolized by a sheaf. The second was bolder. He saw himself, unmasked by any symbol, and his wish for mastery was intensified to include his parents. Unwilling to permit his parents and brothers to bow before him, Joseph's internal censor concealed them in symbolic disguise, exchanging them for sheaves and celestial bodies. The distortions were not severe in these dreams, nor the censor very strict, yet Joseph was not shocked out of his sleep by the moral implications of a wish that was socially unacceptable.

Via these dreams, Joseph was symbolically fighting the repressions of primogeniture. Because he was born next to last he was tyrannized by his older brothers. What he lacked in years and physical strength, he felt, he could make up in other ways, if he had the opportunity. Unable to fight predetermination in the conscious world, he fought it subconsciously.

Cautious not to add to their grievances, Jacob discredited Joseph's dreams in the presence of the brothers, hoping they would simply laugh and forget about them. He, personally, however, "kept the saying in mind" (37:11). Jacob was not ready to dismiss them out of hand, perhaps because he himself had experienced a release from the deadening finality of primogeniture and because he recognized Joseph's great potential ability. He was not willing to see Joseph's life wasted because he was so far down the line in order of birth. He kept Joseph's wishes and hopes and aspirations in mind, silently confident that the rebellion begun by his grandfather, Abraham, would find free expression in his most beloved and capable son.

The phrase, "kept the saying in mind," may also have had an additional intent. According to Wickes, "often the dream shows the failure of a parent and not that of the child."[52] It is possible that Joseph's dream accused Jacob of failure as a parent. It disturbed him that his sons were unable to get along together. That Joseph had to resort to dreams to achieve a feeling of importance was an indication that he had failed his son in some way. Despite the love he lavished upon Joseph, and despite the gifts and the "coat of many colors" he had given him, Jacob knew something was lacking—fine gifts were insufficient. He "kept the saying in mind," resolving to promote a better relationship between his sons and at the same time to fortify Joseph's self-esteem. This may have prompted Jacob to send Joseph to visit his brothers while they were herding sheep (37:13-14). He hoped to mitigate the feelings of hatred that existed between them.

Jacob's dream at Beth-el, with the ladder reaching from earth until heaven with angels running up and down on it (28:10-15), is in the same category as Joseph's, regarding subconscious striving or wish fulfillment. The antecedents are quite clear. Having been rejected by his father, manipulated by his mother in a conspiracy to obtain the blessing, though it rightfully belonged to him as a consequence of the sale of the birthright, and forced to flee from home, Jacob longed only for a serene and peaceful future. This wish was expressed through the symbolism of the dream. Jacob yearned to attain recognition that the birthright was properly his—to free himself of the limitation of having left the womb after Esau. Jung explains this clearly, as does the Talmud.

In dealing with a patient who dreamed of stairs, Jung found the desire to climb upstairs associated with "getting to the top; making a success of life: being grown up; being great."[53] Dreams, Jung maintained, indicate the goals and aims toward which the dreamer is tending. In interpreting the meaning of a dream in which the person was going up to the roof, the Talmud said that he would attain a high position. If he dreamed of going down, he would be degraded.[54] Jacob's thoughts, understandably, paralleled those interpretations.

A pauper and alone, Jacob ranked below his brother in many ways. He could be expected to dream of becoming a wealthy man, the possessor of much land and a large family. When he dreamed of becoming the patriarch of a model family, and of God's assurance that he no longer needed to fear Esau, for "I will not leave thee, until I have done that which I have spoken to thee of" (28:15), Jacob expressed his anticipation of the future, his self-assertion, his unconscious preparation to cope with life's tensions.[55] On the other hand, while he gained a measure of confidence, it was mingled with fear. The angels were "coming down." While his dream expressed his aspiration to become a life-force promoting the idealism of his father, it was not free of the feeling of failure. He feared that life

would pass him by and he would remain a nonentity. Expressing his strivings and his reasoned morality, his dream revealed the worst and the best
in him.[56]

Wolff[57] interprets images of ascending as expressing higher spheres
of thought, and descending as a return to the primal past. Accordingly,
this would indicate that in his dream Jacob was fluctuating between thoughts
of spiritual accomplishments versus earthly attainments. Dreams generally
synthesize thoughts in which reality and imagination, past and present
experiences as well as future expectations, fall into one unit. They mirror
not only that which life denies us, but also that which we deny life.[58]

According to Freud, ladders, steps and staircases are symbols of copulation.[59] He would claim that a dream such as Jacob's has a sexual connotation because of the rhythm of climbing steps. The top of the staircase
is reached in a series of rhythmical movements and with increasing breath-
lessness, and then, with a few rapid steps, the dreamer descends to the
bottom. That Jacob saw "the angels of the Lord ascending and descending
on it" (28:12), would seem to coincide with Freud's theory, since his
interpretation is strengthened by the expression that steps are "mounted,"
a direct equivalent of the sex act. Actually, the direction of the angels
should have been reversed. They should have first descended the ladder,
since they are heavenly creatures, and then ascended it. The Rabbis infer
that Jacob had been accompanied by angels from the time he left Isaac's
house until he reached Beth-el, and that in his sleep he saw these angels
go up and others descending in their places.[60]

Freud conceded that not all dreams have sexual meaning,[61] and the vow
Jacob made upon awakening (28:20-22) would support those interpretations that do not associate the ladder with sex. If God would be with
him, sustain and clothe him, and return him in peace to his father's
house, then would his wishes and desires be fulfilled. As he lay under
the open sky, bereft of any reasonable promise that the future would be
better, the thought of living a simple, peaceful life seemed enormous and
remote. In his dream he had pictured the little that he desired in gigantic
proportions, but awake he was burdened by his feeling of insignificance
and insecurity. Measured against his present situation, his modest wish
appeared to Jacob as the highest achievement.

The same interpretation would apply to Jacob's dream in which he was
tending his father-in-law's flocks. Jacob had heard his brothers-in-law
complain that he had taken things that belonged to their father (31:1),
and Laban himself was less cordial than he had been. This was so upsetting to Jacob that he thought of leaving. He met with his wives in

the field and told them how their father's attitude had changed toward him. Although Jacob had served him faithfully, Laban had changed his wages many times. First, the speckled sheep were given him as salary; then, the streaked. His income was contingent upon the unborn flock. Preoccupied and apprehensive about his future and that of his family, Jacob was so distracted by the uncertainty of Laban's behavior that it was reflected in his dreams. Jumbled and confused, Jacob dreamed of sheep (31:10). Streaked, speckled, and grizzled he-goats, the subjects of his thoughts by day, occupied his dreams.

Not all dreams are symbolic of something else, the Rabbis realized. If a man should dream that he had intercourse with a married woman, they stated, he can only be assured of salvation if he does not know the woman with whom he supposedly consorted and did not think of her during the evening.[62] If he knew the woman about whom he dreamed, how-ever, she was not a symbol for something or someone else. Then the sex symbol was expressive of the sex wish and the Rabbis regarded it as though he did sleep with her, thereby ruling himself out of the hereafter. The reasoning was based on the assumption that his dream was conditioned by his state of mind before he fell asleep.

A similar experience affected Efraim ben Isaac of Regensburg after he ruled that sturgeon was a kosher fish. That night he dreamed that it was not. He was so preoccupied with this matter that it appeared in a dream. Giving credence to the dream, he reversed himself and banned the eating of the fish.[63] Daniel told Nebuchadnezzar the same thing. "As for thee, O king, thy thoughts came (into thy mind) upon thy bed, what should come to pass hereafter" (2:29). Before Nebuchadnezzar fell asleep, his thoughts were occupied with the future. This, Daniel informed him, was the cause of his dream.

By inference, we can surmise the events that transpired in the kingdom of Abimelech, the king of Gerar, which could have led to his dream (20:2-8). As was his practice when a desirable woman came within his borders, Abimelech appropriated Sarah for his harem. Taking an unmarried woman posed no problem for the king; but, if she were married, he had her husband killed and promptly added the luckless widow to his harem. Sarah and Abraham, however, had posed as brother and sister to avoid such a calamity. Their guise offered no escape for Sarah, but at least Abraham's life was spared.

Before he retired on the wedding night, Abimelech fell asleep upon his throne and he slept until morning. During that night, he dreamed that an angel raised his sword to kill him. Frightened, he inquired what he had done to deserve such a fate. Sarah was Abraham's wife, the angel told him, and if the king did not return her, his entire household would die.

That night a great wailing was heard all over Philistia. A man's figure with sword in hand stalked the countryside and killed whoever was in his way. Another cause for widespread alarm was that all the apertures of the body in both man and beast were closed up.[64]

When he awoke in the morning, Abimelech was in agony and terror. He told his servants of his dream. One had heard that it was Abraham's custom to pretend in strange lands that Sarah was his sister. He had done it in Egypt and the Pharaoh was afflicted when he took Sarah. He reminded Abimelech of the suffering that swept the land during the night. The pain and wailing came, he insisted, only because of Sarah,[65] and he advised the king to return her to Abraham. Others, however, counseled the king not to fear his dream because dreams reveal only lies.

The next night, God appeared to him and commanded Abimelech to let Sarah go; if he did not he would die. Abimelech protested: Abraham himself declared Sarah was his sister, and Sarah called Abraham her brother. God excused him on the ground that he had not yet trespassed with Sarah and that he was unaware that she was a married woman. By engaging Abimelech in dreams, He kept him from sinning.[66] But God questioned the propriety of his actions. Was it courteous to inquire of a stranger in his territory if his companion was his wife or his sister? One should ask a stranger about food and drink, and nothing else. Then God told Abimelech that Abraham was a prophet who knew what dangers lay before him if he had revealed the truth. Being a prophet, he also knew that Abimelech had not touched his wife. Abraham would therefore pray for him, and Abimelech would live.[67]

The following morning Abimelech reproached Abraham for the false statement regarding Sarah that brought misfortunes to him and his coun- trymen. Abraham replied that he had been afraid that he would be killed because of his wife, since the fear of God did not exist in this country.[68]

Abimelech's dream suggests that he was profoundly disturbed by his own actions. It seems to have been common practice in those days for monarchs to take women into their harems by murdering their husbands— Pharaoh indulged in this practice (12:14-15) and Rebekah had the same experience later (26:6-9). Abimelech may have conformed to the behavior expected of a ruler, but his conscience rebelled against it. He regarded him- self as a basically religious and righteous person, to which Abraham attested in acknowledging the fair treatment received at his hands (21:22-24). His rebuke of Abraham indicated his striving for a higher morality. "What hast thou done unto us? and wherein have I sinned against thee, that thou has brought on me and on my kingdom a great sin?" (20:9).

Abimelech may have sensed that Sarah was not really Abraham's sister. In observing them together, he may have surmised it. This must have preyed on his mind before he retired and he therefore dreamed about it. The dream confirmed his suspicions and kept him from indulging in a practice that could have been sinful. With God as the spokesman, a moral problem was clearly involved. Abimelech was torn between the practice of the day and what his own sense of justice dictated. He talked it out with his servants, hoping that they would help him arrive at the proper solution. His servants disagreed among themselves, however, presenting two sides to the issue. The final decision was his own; such a problem is a matter between man and his own conscience. In the final analysis, Abimelech justified himself and God agreed with him. "In the simplicity of thy heart thou hast done this" (20:6). The kings of Philistia might have had a strict moral code about violating another man's wife, for Abimelech's son went through the same experience with Rebekah and reacted in the same fashion (26:26-31). The kings of Philistia may have had higher moral standards in this matter than other monarchs of their day.

III

There are only two recognized interpreters of dreams in all of Scripture—Joseph (40-41) and Daniel (2, 4). Each had many opportunities to put his gift to proper use. Of the two, Joseph did more interpreting, while Daniel displayed a greater talent for telling the person, without being told, what he had dreamed (2:25-36). The Bible would thus seem to imply that a dream expert is born with his skill; it is innate. Joseph and Daniel, however, regarded themselves as instruments selected by the Lord to reveal the future (41:16; Daniel 2:30).

Neither Joseph nor Daniel had any training in dream interpretation. They did, however, have above-average intelligence. They were quick witted, and apparently knew how to evaluate the conditions and circumstances surrounding the dreamer. They were astute enough to pick out the significant aspects of dreams and to interpret the symbolism that was reported. It is interesting that when Joseph's ability is mentioned, he is referred to as "a Hebrew" (41:12), and in later years the Jewish people were known as able dream interpreters.[69] In our own age, some of the recognized interpreters of dreams have been Jews, such as Freud himself, Alfred Adler, Otto Rank, Theodor Reik, and others. Daniel's qualifications are described as being able "to understand all visions and dreams" (1:17) and to "answer with counsel and discretion" (2:14).

According to the biblical narrative, Joseph's dreams came true. He attained the exalted position of viceroy of Egypt, the most civilized and most powerful country of the day, and his brothers and father bowed down before him. How can the realization of these dreams be explained?

Erich Fromm claims that insight and prediction are closely related, in that the latter results from the former.[70] He states that the individual can predict or infer future events on the basis of the understanding he acquires by observation of the direction and intensity of forces in operation in the present. When one has a thorough knowledge of the underlying forces, one is able to make predictions in dreams, forecasting future events. In this category are Rebekah's dream of Esau's plan to destroy Jacob,[71] Eve's dream of Cain drinking Abel's blood,[72] and similar incidents.[73] And these predictions, Fromm maintains, are to be considered rational, with no clairvoyance involved. Jung concurs that dreams occasionally have predictive value because they express knowledge that is latent in the unconscious in advance of its being brought into consciousness.[74] Fromm maintains that, although Joseph's dreams were merely expressions of his ambition, without these ambitions Joseph would not have been able to attain the high office that he did. Joseph's dreams, therefore, were "a blend of his passionate ambition and an insight into his gifts without which his dreams could not have come true."[75]

Joseph had no difficulty in deciphering the dreams of the chief baker and the chief butler. Possessing a knowledge of local events due to the strategic position he held in Potiphar's house, he was able to put diverse bits of information together with ease. Both the baker and the butler dreamed of the number "three." Mirod, the butler,[76] dreamed of a vine with three branches (40:12) and the baker of three baskets of white bread (40:16). Joseph knew, as did all of Egypt and especially two former servants of the king, that Pharaoh was to celebrate a birthday in three days (40:20). On that day he reviewed the prisoners and granted some of them amnesty. Utilizing his intelligence, Joseph understood that both of these men were occupied with thoughts of that particular celebration. Undoubtedly both wanted not only to be pardoned and to attend the celebration, but to participate in the preparations for the festivities. The chief butler was the cup-bearer and the chief baker was the superintendent of the bakery. It was their duty to taste the food for the king before the royal meal was served. They did not want to be left out. The thoughts of the day ran through their minds at night, and found expression in their dreams.

Associating their dreams with Pharaoh's birthday party, and perceiving the needs of the two men, Joseph was able to predict with accuracy the intent of their dreams. Both men had been incarcerated either for one or ten years, and Joseph ministered or attended to them during that entire time.[77] Having an ingratiating personality, evidenced by the fact that he found favor in Potiphar's eyes (39:4), and later in the sight of his jailer (39:21), Joseph was easy to talk to. Perhaps his fellow-prisoners even confided in him. In his long association with them, it is quite possible that words slipped out in unguarded moments that indicated their innocence or guilt. Joseph acquired an understanding in depth of each of them. Taking into consideration all his observations, plus the content of the dreams and the attitudes of the men regarding them, Joseph was supplied with ample material to predict the outcome accurately.

Observing the butler's readiness to divulge his dream, and that in it he was actually pressing grapes into the king's cup, Joseph concluded that the butler was innocent. Offering the fruit of the vine to Pharaoh strongly indicated his benign feelings for the king. He was eager to serve his monarch. Joseph was therefore able to predict pardon for him. Similarly, Joseph was reasonably certain that the baker's fate would be the opposite of the butler's. The baker was hesitant in speaking, and was willing to tell his dream only after he had heard the beneficent prospects of the butler. Joseph must have surmised that he was aware of his guilt and felt that he deserved imprisonment. The suspicion was strengthened by the dream content. Unlike the butler who dreamed that he did the actual pressing of the grapes into Pharaoh's cup, the baker did not dream of doing the baking himself. Furthermore, in his dream, the food never did reach the king. It was eaten up by the birds and the baker did not make the slightest effort to drive them off. Joseph understood this to mean that he harbored malevolent feelings toward the king and was justifiably imprisoned. A further indication of the baker's feeling of guilt was that he saw birds eating bread and cakes, which symbolized himself. In Egypt, decapitated bodies were hanged exposed to public view and were the prey of birds. In his dream, the baker dreamt of the punishment due him for his transgression. By taking all these factors into account, Joseph was able to predict the baker's fate accurately.

In Pharaoh's dreams, we encounter another type—the anxiety or distressed dream. A sense of terror, of something evil about to overwhelm him, woke Pharaoh. For two years these dreams came to him with no effects, and each time the dream was forgotten by morning. The first dreams that Pharaoh remembered were the two dreams that Joseph interpreted.[78] Such a pattern, according to Freud, indicated "thinking ahead," a function of preconscious waking thought.[79] Repeated every night until it is carried out, a recurring anxiety dream expresses an intention.[80] Subconsciously, Pharaoh repeatedly attempted to frame a course of action that would avert the impending crisis, but his inability to cope with the problem compounded his anxiety. His desire to act on behalf of his country, and his expression of the knowledge that he must act, finally erupted in the nightmares that expressed his intense conflict.

Nebuchadnezzar also suffered a nightmare (Daniel 2:1), apparently even more horrible than Pharoah's. Unable to tolerate even the repressed thoughts that caused him anxiety, Nebuchadnezzar succeeded in effecting a full repression of the dream content.[81] He forgot his dream completely, a sort of "mental confiscation." Following such a dream, the dreamer remembers only that the dream was good or bad. In this instance, Nebuchadnezzar was "troubled." Another anxiety dream (4:2) escaped his confiscation; it did not awaken him, and he recited it freely to Daniel.

The Midrash[82] tells that Ahasuerus, the king in the Book of Esther, dreamed that Haman would kill him. He awoke and could not fall asleep again. Job describes such nightmares: "Then Thou scarest me with dreams, And terrifiest me with visions" (7:14). Like the Talmud, which regards them as worse than scourging,[83] psychiatrists consider that nightmares revolve around a repressed desire and express intense or maximum mental conflict.[84]

There are problems that cause deep psychological pain when the individual becomes aware of them. In turn, this awareness causes anxiety, which is expressed in the nightmare type of dream. In nightmares, repressed fears and thoughts are about to come to the fore despite all attempts to stifle them. Without protection against the threatened loss of security, the dreamer manifests distress. Faced with a situation offering more than one course to pursue, the dreamer becomes confused and his anxiety is intensified. Finally, before the repressed thought emerges completely, the anxiety rouses the sleeper. This, it would seem, is what faced Pharaoh. Unable to cope with the problem confronting him, he became confused and increasingly anxious, until he was unable to sleep.

Pharaoh's first dream (41:1-4) readily conveys the anxiety that tortured him. He saw himself standing by the Nile, the river that gave life to his land, and he saw seven "well-favored and fat-fleshed" kine emerging from it. Standing by water and coming out of water enacted the birth-phantasy;[85]

like the foetus before birth, he was surrounded by water. Whenever re-birth symbolism is seen in a dream, some sort of crisis is expected.[86] Man depends upon water for his life, but he can also drown in it. In a dream, therefore, water could signify danger.[87] And a disturbing thing did then happen. An equal number of "ill-favored and lean-fleshed" kine came up out of the river and destroyed the fat kine, symbols of prosperity that had prevailed in Egypt. In his dream, Pharoah saw his country threatened with destruction, and he awoke in terror. His dream was a symbolic expression of his own rational insight.

After satisfying himself that it was merely a dream, Pharaoh went back to sleep. But he dreamed again, this time of seven fat and good ears of corn that sprouted on one stalk, only to meet the same fate as did the healthy kine—they were swallowed up by thin and dried out ears of corn. The same thought, the loss of his country's prosperity, presented itself to him through different symbols. Again terror struck his heart and again he awoke. He satisfied himself that it had been only a dream, but he was troubled when he awoke in the morning. He could find no peace. Neither he nor his professional dream interpreters could decipher these symbols. Unable to interpret the meaning of these dreams, the magicians and wise men could not appease his agitation.

When Joseph was summoned to interpret these dreams, he had already been in Egypt a number of years and was familiar with its agricultural life. The Nile River, rising each summer and receding in the autumn, con-trolled the bountiful crops; but, should the Nile fail to perform its func-tion, Joseph reasoned, famine would strike and the people would starve. In his early life with his family, who were nomads in neighboring Canaan, the problems of securing and storing food were ever-present, and later, as overseer in Potiphar's household, he acquired a knowledge of the agricul-tural life of that area. He had been concerned daily with those factors that were vital to existence.

More perceptive than the ordinary man, and a keen observer, Joseph was aware of the weather cycles during his own lifetime and had undoubt-edly heard of events that had occurred prior to his day. There had been a famine in Canaan in the days of Abraham (12:10), and again in his grandfather's time (26:1). The former went to Egypt for food, and Isaac, who at first also wanted to go there (26:2), went to Philistia instead. Since rivers were few in Canaan, and there was no irrigation, the land was sub-ject to famine if the rainy season failed to come. And Joseph was aware that it often did. Drought and famine had occurred with some degree of regularity in the past, so Joseph could predict with almost complete certainty that another famine was soon due. And he was right, for not long thereafter famine struck in the land of Canaan (41:54).

From the biblical account, it would seem that until that time Egypt had not suffered from famine. There were no outward or evident reasons to expect it. Yet indications that foreshadowed such an event must have existed. Joseph might have heard an innocent remark here and there—from the butler and baker, from the jail keeper, or from other prisoners. It was nothing alarming, nothing to even ruffle the surface.

When Pharaoh told him his dreams, Joseph was astute enough to recognize that a dream sequence should be considered one dream. He remembered that his dreams of the sheaves of wheat and of the sun, moon and stars were accepted by his father and brothers as parts of the same thought. He used the same technique in interpreting Pharaoh's dreams, a procedure psychiatry accepts today. All dreams that occur during the same night form parts of a whole, having the same meaning and the same impulses, though the dream material is different. Also, the first of these is often more distorted than the succeeding ones.[88] The fear of famine, as exhibited in the failure of the crops, is somewhat more explicit than in the destruction of the fat kine. Joseph's awareness and intuitive or experienced knowledge again came into play. Pharaoh and his interpreters were less aware of reality than he was, or less willing to accept reality, or less intelligent in manipulating it. They needed help and Joseph was there to supply it. He assured Pharaoh that his country need not disintegrate, that he need not fear the future. All was not lost. He explained to the king that with wise management of the plenty with which Egypt was yet blessed, enough could be stored away to insure prosperity in the future. From the available evidence, Joseph reasoned that there would be another seven years of good harvests from which to siphon off the surplus for future use. Seven years may be regarded as a hypothetical period; still, Joseph offered a course of action that preserved the normal routine and at the same time prepared for the calamity he foresaw.

Freud has pointed out that when a dream is repeated, the changes that occur in the retelling are most significant.[89] On the way to the palace, Joseph must have been told the purpose for which he had been summoned. When Pharaoh retold his dreams, Joseph was struck by the additions. In his narration to Joseph, Pharaoh added that the lean kine that came out of the river were so poor, "such as I never saw in all the land of Egypt for badness" (41:19). He also added: "And when they had eaten them up, it could not be known that they had eaten them; but they were still ill-favored as at the beginning" (41:21). These are significant additions. As animals symbolize parents and ancestors to the ordinary person, to a king animals represent not only his parents but his entire kingdom, The Fatherland. The seven well-favored cows represented the bountiful prosperity Pharaoh had always known in his homeland. When he saw the seven hideous looking animals, his dream became a terrible nightmare. The symbol of Egypt became a spectre of famine. In disguised form, his fear of impending disaster confronted Pharaoh.

Like Joseph, Pharaoh may have been aware of certain factors that would affect the productivity of the land, but this knowledge was inadmissible to his conscious mind. When the repressed idea was about to overpower the censor, he tried to force it out of his mind. He was unable to face the coming destruction of his country's economy, and he did not know how to prevent it. Even when expressed in the form of kine and ears of corn, appropriate symbols drawn from his environment to express his repressed emotions,[90] the thought of a national disaster was too much for him and it broke up his sleep.

In dreams man fulfills his search for that which reality denies to him. But he also dreams of that which he would like to bring to reality in life. And when he dreams about this fulfillment, he then searches for it in reality. Under many guises, he seeks in his daily life the dream figures and the events of his dreams. In short, he seeks himself. Dreams are therefore erroneously regarded as prophetic of things that actually happen. Prophecy, however, is not involved. The events come to pass due to the dreamer's search after the dream has taken place.[91] This fits the course of events in Joseph's life. He dreamed his wish to have his brothers bow down to him. Then by applying his gift of intelligence, using what was known and inferring the unknown, perceiving his own needs and the needs of others, and having acquired the discretion necessary to get along with people, he brought this wish to fulfillment in reality. His proposed plan to keep Egypt from disaster and his appointment by Pharaoh to administer the plan, fulfilled his prediction that his brothers would some day kneel to him. There was no doubt in his mind that they would come to Egypt in search of food and that he would finally dominate them. In fact, as they stood before him, "Joseph remembered the dreams which he dreamed of them" (42:9), and he was reconciled.

Man has occupied himself from earliest times with dreams and their meanings. On the whole, there are few and minor points of departure between the early Hebrew sages and today's experts in dreams. Both approach dreams with the serious curiosity they deserve and relate them to man's endless striving to become himself.

I Seek My Brethren

(37:16)

THE meaning of their rebellion underlies the lasting worth of the biblical personalities. Whether or not they actually lived is immaterial; their life stories have become immortal through almost four thousand years of retelling. Throughout the millenia, their individual integrity remains intact; they lived and died in the same existential dilemma that confronts all humanity, but each responded to life in his own unique way. Each strained against the limitations of his environment and against the limitations of his spirit to attain the most meaningful existence of which he was capable. Not one was content with predetermined conclusions. Each existed in a state of mobility, constantly recreating his relationships with himself, with other individuals and with society. This dynamic interplay invariably produced conflict, and growth.

While "conflict" carries a negative connotation of strife, war and a divergence of interests, it is, in fact, an indispensable factor of life. Literally "striking together," conflict implies two or more forces. If man is a force—if he has the freedom to act—he strikes against other forces. He conflicts with his own incompatible desires; he conflicts with the forces of nature; he conflicts with the life-forces of other individuals and with the collective life-force of society. If he lives at all, man lives in conflict.

Tensions that result from conflict help maintain one's emotional health. An essential part of man's equipment for survival, tension activates him. He struggles to achieve equilibrium between conflicting forces when passive submission to either extreme would destroy him. Without conflict and tension, man is enervated; without the continuous need to reorient himself, he vegetates. Conditions change, and by adapting at every moment to the tension between what he is and what he ought to be man sustains his existence. Man lives not by "sitting under his vine and under his fig tree," but by striving to extend his creative capabilities.

222

Living in conflict is not without risk, however. Some individuals be-come wholly involved in one aspect of existence and remain unaware of its opposite. Under the weight of forces that have no effective counter-balance, they plunge into psycho-pathological behavior. Failure to adapt predisposes the individual to emotional breakdown—a partial end to living. He loses the ability to find compensations and no longer seeks new levels of identification; his growth is stunted. Cain, Ham, Ishmael and Esau experi-enced such malignant conflicts. Their infantile responses evidenced an imbal-ance in emotional tension, and culminated in destructive rather than creative behavior. Lacking the freedom to cope with their conflicts as they arose, these individuals had no opportunity to express their normal feelings of rebellion; their families repressed the forms of expression that could have led to their emotional growth. Turned inward, conflict distorted their self-images and resulted in social disorientation.

For all the other biblical personalities, conflict proved benign. The tension in interpersonal relationships was intrinsic to their growth and that of their groups, as it is for most people and most societies. The aim of eliminating all conflict among parents and children, and among the components of social organization on every level, is romantic. Tension is the catalyst that unites individuals and groups in new and more meaningful combinations.

The social setting evolved from Adam's small family to the nation founded under Moses' leadership. Society's basic function, protection of the individual, was apparent from the beginning, as was its corollary, cur-tailment of individual freedom. Rules of conduct established for members of the group conflicted with the individual's desire for personal gratifica-tion and limited his freedom of action. To offset the loss of freedom, the individual found compensations, inventing new avenues to self-gratification that benefited the group as well as himself. Whoever failed to adapt was in double jeopardy—from the group, which might exclude or destroy him, and from the consequence of his failure, which might destroy him together with the group of which he was a part. The tension between his need for individual freedom and his need for the protection of the group resulted in group consciousness or identification.

Like the individual, the social group exists in tension between its aspi-rations and those of other forces—tribes, nations or nature. Also compelled to adjust to changing conditions, the quality of the group's response to new experiences and new responsibilities determines its survival. If it fails to adapt, the group disintegrates. To preserve the wholeness of the group, the patriarchs fostered group identification. Given the stability assured by continuance of the group, the individual was free to work out his personal conflicts; and the individual's success in coping with his problems affected the stability of the group.

With each family that succeeded Adam's, stories of rebellion against primogeniture moved forward on the wheel of conflict like a series of lessons built one upon the other. Freedom-for-the-individual and its conflicting responsibility-to-self broke upon the awareness of the first family; freedom-for-the-individual and the conflicting responsibility-to-the-group emerged simultaneously in the consciousness of Noah. With ever-increasing complexity in family and group relationships, freedom-for-the-individual and responsibility-to-the-group ascended to their ultimate conflict and fulfillment in the most sophisticated story, that of Moses. And in dreams, freedom-for-the-individual appears in timeless and universal perspective as the irrepressible source of man's growth. Alike in human inter-relationships and in purely psychic activity, the immortal personalities rebelled against the forces of repression. And, as each individual encountered more numerous and more powerful counterforces, he surpassed his predecessors in maturity.

The process of rebellion has never ceased. Evident today in the surge of mankind toward equal opportunity, rebellion motivates the search of men and nations for identity. People long repressed are discarding concepts of predeterimned inferiority: women are seeking freedom equal to men's; dark-skinned races are grasping self-determination; new nations are emerging where group identity is new-born. And everywhere there is conflict, tension and growth.

"All nations shall stream unto the mountain of the Lord" when man will take hold of his freedom to perfect himself. In a diversity of individuality among men and nations, separate identity and mutual responsibility will exist in a state of benign tension. Each man will say to his counterpart, "I am your brother," and conversely, "Thou art my brother."

NOTES

CHAPTER I

1. BABYLONIAN TALMUD, Rosh Hashanah 9b.

CHAPTER II

1. MIDRASH RABBAH, Genesis 22:7; YALKUT SHIMONI, Genesis 38.
2. Oberndorf, "Psycho-Analysis of Siblings," *American Journal of Psychology*, 8:6, May, 1929, p. 1008.
3. IBID., p. 1010.
4. Glueck, UNRAVELING JUVENILE DELINQUENCY, p. 128.
5. Neisser, BROTHERS AND SISTERS, p. 8.
6. APOCALYPSIS MOSIS 2:2-3.
7. VITA ADEA ET EVAE 22:4-23:1.
8. MIDRASH RABBAH, Genesis 22:3.
9. IBID., Genesis 22:7; PIRKE RABBI ELIEZER 21.
10. MIDRASH RABBAH, Genesis 22:8; PIRKE RABBI ELIEZER 21.
11. YALKUT SHIMONI, Genesis 35; MIDRASH RABBAH, Genesis 22:4; ZOHAR CHODOSH, B'rayshis 19a.
12. Ginzberg, THE LEGENDS OF THE JEWS, vol. 5, p. 136.
13. BOOK OF ADAM, 1:78.
14. MIKRAOTH GEDOLOTH, Targum Yerushalmi, Genesis 4:8.
15. Menninger, A PSYCHIATRIST'S WORLD, p. 644.
16. MIDRASH RABBAH, Genesis 19:5; THE FATHERS ACCORDING TO RABBI NATHAN 1; Ginzberg, OP. CIT., vol. 1, p. 73f; 97.
17. PIRKE RABBI ELIEZER 14.
18. Ginzberg, OP. CIT., vol. 1, p. 101f.
19. VITA ADAE ET EVAE, 18:1-21:2.
20. Ginzberg, OP. CIT., vol. 1, p. 87, 93f; VITA ADAE ET EVAE 3:2-3.
21. Ackerman, THE PSYCHODYNAMICS OF FAMILY LIFE, p. 20f.
22. Oberndorf, OP. CIT., p. 1001.
23. PIRKE RABBI ELIEZER 21.
24. BABYLONIAN TALMUD, Sanhedrin 37b; MIDRASH RABBAH, Genesis 22:8; YALKUT SHIMONI, Genesis 38; PIRKE RABBI ELIEZER 2; MIDRASH TANHUMA, B'rayshis 9; THE BOOK OF JUBILEES 4-31; BOOK OF ADAM 1:79.
25. Maslow and Mittelmann, PRINCIPLES OF ABNORMAL PSYCHOLOGY, p. 375.
26. Neisser, OP. CIT., p. 8.
27. Hall, THE MEANING OF DREAMS, p. 58f.
28. Alexander and Healy, ROOTS OF CRIME, p. 283.

29. Menninger, OP. CIT., p. 338.
30. ZOHAR CHODOSH, B'rayshis 8a-8b; Ruth, 97b.
31. Maslow and Mittelmann, OP. CIT., p. 378.
32. MIDRASH TANHUMA, B'rayshis 9.
33. MIDRASH RABBAH, Genesis 22:11; Deuteronomy 8:1.
34. MIDRASH TANHUMA, B'rayshis 10; PIRKE RABBI ELIEZER 21; MID-
    RASH RABBAH, Genesis 22:8.
35. Josephus, ANTIQUITIES OF THE JEWS, I, 2:2.
36. MIDRASH RABBAH, Genesis 23:2.

CHAPTER III

1. MIDRASH RABBAH, Genesis 31:1-4, 6.
2. IBID., Genesis 30:9.
3. IBID., Genesis 44:7.
4. PIRKE RABBI ELIEZER 23.
5. SEFER HAYASHAR, (Cracow), 10a.
6. Ginzberg, LEGENDS OF THE JEWS, vol. 1, p. 147; Buber, MIDRASH
   TANHUMA HAKODOM V'HAYASHAN, Noah 6; MIDRASH TAN-
   HUMA, Noah 6, 11; Schechter, MIDRASH HAGODOL SEFER B'RAYSHIS,
   p. 151.
7. MIDRASH RABBAH, Genesis 25:2; Ginzberg, OP. CIT., vol. 5, p. 168f.
8. MIDRASH TANHUMA, B'rayshis 11; Ginzberg, OP. CIT., vol. 1, p. 147.
9. MIDRASH RABBAH, Genesis 30:7; MIDRASH TANHUMA, Noah 5.
10. BABYLONIAN TALMUD, Sanhedrin 108a-b; MIDRASH TANHUMA,
    Noah 5.
11. Ginzberg, OP. CIT., vol. 1, p. 158: SEFER HAYASHAR, (Cracow),
    10b-11a; MIDRASH TANHUMA, Noah 7; Buber, OP. CIT., Noah 10.
12. MIDRASH TANHUMA, Noah 7; Buber, OP. CIT., Noah 10; Ginzberg,
    OP. CIT., vol. 1, p. 159.
13. MIDRASH TANHUMA, Noah 11; PIRKE RABBI ELIEZER 23; TAL-
    MUD YERUSHALMI, Taanith 64b; BABYLONIAN TALMUD, Sanhedrin
    108b; MIDRASH RABBAH, Genesis 31:12; 34:7; Buber, OP. CIT., Noah 17.
14. MIDRASH RABBAH, Genesis 31:12; 34:7; MIDRASH TANHUMA,
    Noah 11.
15. BABYLONIAN TALMUD, Sanhedrin 108b; MIDRASH TANHUMA,
    Noah 9.
16. BABYLONIAN TALMUD, Sanhedrin 108b.
17. Cushing, "Psychopathology of Sexual Delinquency," Journal of Clinical Psy-
    chopathology, 11:2, April, 1950, p. 53.
18. MIDRASH RABBAH, Genesis 30:6, 8.
19. IBID., Genesis 23:3; Epstein, MIDRASH MISHLE, 31:30; Ginzberg, OP.
    CIT., vol. 1, p. 159.
20. MIDRASH TANHUMA, Noah 12; Yisro 10; MIDRASH RABBAH, Gen-
    esis 26:3; 37:7; Numbers 4:8; BABYLONIAN TALMUD, Sanhedrin 69b.
21. Ansbacher, THE INDIVIDUAL PSYCHOLOGY OF ALFRED ADLER, p.
    379f.

22. MIDRASH TANHUMA, Noah 12; TALMUD YERUSHALMI, Taanith '64b; BABYLONIAN TALMUD, Sanhedrin 108b; MIDRASH RABBAH, Genesis 36:7.
23. Conn, "Brief Psychotherapy of the Sex Offender," *Journal of Clinical Psychopathology,* 10:4, October, 1949, p. 371.
24. Ploscowe, "The Sexual Psychopath: Some Suggestions for Control;" *Prison World,* 9:4, July-August, 1947, p. 18.
25. Leppmann, "Essential Differences Between Sex Offenders," *Journal of Criminal Law and Criminology,* 32:3, Sept-Oct, 1941, p. 371.
26. Karpman, THE SEXUAL OFFENDER, p. 111; Henry and Gross, "Social Factors in the Case Histories of One Hundred Under-Privileged Homosexuals," *Mental Hygiene,* 22:4, October, 1938, p. 105.
27. Karpman, OP. CIT., p. 598.
28. IBID., p. 358-360.
29. Evans, THE CRIMINAL PROSECUTION AND CAPITAL PUNISHMENT OF ANIMALS, p. 152f.
30. Cushing, OP. CIT., p. 53.
31. MIDRASH TANHUMA, Noah 9.
32. IBID.; MIDRASH RABBAH, Genesis 32:11.
33. SEFER HAYASHAR, (Cracow), 11a.
34. MIDRASH TANHUMA, Noah 9.
35. MIDRASH CHASEROS VESAYROS, p. 50; MIDRASH RABBAH, Genesis 36:4.
36. Menninger, A PSYCHIATRIST'S WORLD, p. 233.
37. Ackerman, THE PSYCHODYNAMICS OF FAMILY LIFE, p. 180.
38. ZOHAR CHODOSH, Noah 27a; Ginzberg, OP. CIT., vol. 1, p. 165; Schechter, OP. CIT., p. 154; SEFER HAYASHAR, (Cracow), 11a; Buber, MIDRASH TEHILLIM, 29:232.
39. Gaer, THE LORE OF THE OLD TESTAMENT, p. 75.
40. Maslow and Mittelmann, PRINCIPLES OF ABNORMAL PSYCHOLOGY, p. 473; Simmel, E., "Alcoholism and Addiction," YEARBOOK OF PSYCHOANALYSIS, 1949, p. 248.
41. Simmel, OP. CIT., p. 251.
42. SEFER HAYASHAR, (Cracow), 10a.
43. Simmel, OP. CIT., p. 251; Menninger, MAN AGAINST HIMSELF, p. 24-80; Gerber, THE PSYCHOLOGY OF THE SUFFERING MIND, p. 72.
44. Simmel, OP. CIT., p. 244.
45. MIDRASH RABBAH, Genesis 28:8; BABYLONIAN TALMUD, Sanhedrin 108a; MIDRASH TANHUMA, Noah 5; Buber, MIDRASH TANHUMA HAKODOM V'HAYASHAN, Noah '6.
46. Menninger, A PSYCHIATRIST'S WORLD, p. 348f.
47. Maslow and Mittelmann, OP. CIT., p. 470.
48. MIDRASH RABBAH, Genesis 36:3.
49. James, VARIETIES OF RELIGIOUS EXPERIENCE, p. 166.
50. Selling, "Results of Therapy in Cases of Sex Deviates," *Journal of Clinical Psychopathology,* 3:3, January, 1942, p. 480; Romm, "Compulsion Factors in Exhibitionism," *Journal of Clinical Psychopathology,* 3:4, April, 1942, p. 594; Karpman, OP. CIT., p. 188.

51. Fenichel, THE PSYCHOANALYTIC THEORY OF NEUROSIS, p. 172, 331, 336, 344.
52. Selling, OP. CIT., p. 479.
53. Leppmann, OP. CIT., p. 368.
54. Bergler, HOMOSEXUALITY: DISEASE OR WAY OF LIFE, p. 89f.
55. IBID., p. 15f.
56. Karpman, OP. CIT., p. 8.
57. Ginzberg, OP. CIT., vol. 5, p. 182; BABYLONIAN TALMUD, Sanhedrin 108a; MIDRASH TANHUMA, Noah 5, 12; MIDRASH RABBAH, Genesis 28:8.
58. Odier, ANXIETY AND MAGICAL THINKING, p. 182.
59. SEFER HAYASHAR, (Cracow), 12a; PIRKE RABBI ELIEZER 24.
60. Leppmann, OP. CIT., p. 376.
61. Ferenczi, SEX IN PSYCHOANALYSIS, p. 266.
62. MIDRASH CHASEROS VESAYROS, p. 50; MIDRASH RABBAH, Genesis 36:4.
63. Ackerman, OP. CIT., p. 180.
64. Menninger, OP. CIT., p. 233.
65. MIDRASH RABBAH, Genesis 36:5.
66. IBID., Genesis 36:6; MIDRASH TANHUMA, Noah 15.
67. Simmel, OP. CIT., p. 251.
68. MIDRASH RABBAH, Genesis 23:3; SEFER HAYASHAR, (Cracow), 14b.
69. Ackerman, OP. CIT., p. 181f.
70. MIDRASH TANHUMA, Noah 15; MIDRASH RABBAH, Genesis 36:7.
71. MIDRASH RABBAH, Numbers 10:2.
72. IBID., Genesis 36:7; Buber, OP. CIT., Noah 21; PIRKE RABBI ELIEZER 23; Schechter, OP. CIT., p. 178; MIDRASH TANHUMA, Noah 15.
73. Schechter, OP. CIT., p. 178.
74. MIDRASH RABBAH, Genesis 36:5, 7.
75. MIDRASH TANHUMA, Noah 15; Buber, OP. CIT., Noah 21.
76. MIDRASH TANHUMA, Noah 15; MIDRASH RABBAH, Genesis 36:7; BABYLONIAN TALMUD, Sanhedrin 70a; Schechter, OP. CIT., p. 189.
77. Ginzberg, OP. CIT., vol. 1, p. 220.
78. PIRKE RABBI ELIEZER 23, Commentary Beur Haredal, note 64.
79. Ackerman, OP. CIT., p. 185.
80. SHULHAN ARUCH: YOREH DEAH, 240: 3, 8, 11.
81. THE BOOK OF JUBILEES, 10:14.
82. MIDRASH RABBAH, Genesis 36:6; MIDRASH TANHUMA, Noah 15.
83. MIDRASH RABBAH, Genesis 36:6; MIDRASH TANHUMA, Noah 15.
84. MIDRASH TANHUMA, Yisro 10.
85. MIDRASH RABBAH, Genesis 26:3.
86. IBID., Genesis 36:6; Leviticus 20:1; Ecclesiastes 9:2; MIDRASH TAN-HUMA, Noah 9.
87. THE BOOK OF JUBILEES 10:10-14.
88. MIDRASH RABBAH, Numbers 4:8.
89. IBID., Genesis 26:30.
90. Ginzberg, OP. CIT., vol. 1, p. 205.

91. MIDRASH RABBAH, Genesis 44:7; Leviticus 25:6.
92. IBID., Genesis 44:7.
93. IBID., Genesis 45:10.
94. IBID., Genesis 56:11; 68:5.
95. THE BOOK OF JUBILEES 8:10-30; PIRKE RABBI ELIEZER 24; Ginz-berg, OP. CIT., vol. 1, p. 172.
96. Ginzberg, OP. CIT., vol. 1, p. 171.
97 MIDRASH RABBAH, Genesis 36:8.
98. Ginzberg, OP. CIT., vol. 1, p. 171.
99. MIDRASH RABBAH, Genesis 32:6.
100. IBID., Genesis 32:8; Buber, OP. CIT., Noah 5-6.
101. MIDRASH RABBAH, Genesis 34:6.

CHAPTER IV

1. MIDRASH RABBAH, Genesis 45:2.
2. IBID., 45:1; PIRKE RABBI ELIEZER 26.
3. MIDRASH RABBAH, Genesis 45:3.
4. IBID., 47:1.
5. Finegan, LIGHT FROM THE ANCIENT PAST, p. 66.
6. MIDRASH RABBAH, Genesis 44:9, 11.
7. IBID., 45:4.
8. IBID., 41:2.
9. IBID., 39:14.
10. IBID., 41:2.
11. IBID., 45:5.
12. Bowie, GREAT MEN OF THE BIBLE, p. 22.
13. Otto, THE IDEA OF THE HOLY, p. 20f.
14. MIDRASH RABBAH, Genesis 39:15.
15. IBID., 53:6.
16. IBID., 45:6.
17. IBID., 45:5.
18. Kierkegaard, FEAR AND TREMBLING, p. 60f.
19. BABYLONIAN TALMUD, Gittin 75b.
20. Brody, PATTERNS OF MOTHERING, p. 52f.
21. MIDRASH RABBAH, Genesis 53:10, commentaries of Pairush Maharzav and Matnos Kehunah.
22. Bat Mitzvah, a ceremony for girls comparable to that of boys, is a modern innovation.
23. English and Pearson, EMOTIONAL PROBLEMS OF LIVING, p. 104f, 108f.
24. Josephus, ANTIQUITIES OF THE JEWS, I, 12:3.
25. Eissler, Freud, et al, THE PSYCHOANALYTIC STUDY OF THE CHILD, vol. 8, p. 290.
26. BABYLONIAN TALMUD, Yebamoth 23a; Kiddushin 68b; TUR, Even Ho-Ezer, chap. 4; YALKUT SHIMONI, Genesis 100.

27. MIDRASH RABBAH, Genesis 55:4; BABYLONIAN TALMUD, Sanhedrin 89b.
28. MIDRASH RABBAH, Genesis 53:11.
29. IBID., Exodus 27:1.
30. IBID., Exodus 5:1; Song of Songs 8:1:1.
31. PIRKE RABBI ELIEZER 30.
32. Berne, THE MIND IN ACTION, p. 39, 57.
33. MIDRASH RABBAH, Genesis 53:11.
34. IBID.
35. IBID., Exodus 1:1.
36. Glueck, UNRAVELING JUVENILE DELINQUENCY, p. 120.
37. Maslow and Mittelmann, PRINCIPLES OF ABNORMAL PSYCHOLOGY, p. 147.
38. MIDRASH RABBAH, Genesis 48:13.
39. Glueck, OP. CIT., p. 130-133.
40. MIDRASH RABBAH, Genesis 53:11.
41. IBID., Exodus 1:1.
42. English and Pearson, OP. CIT., p. 111.
43. PIRKE RABBI ELIEZER 30.
44. MIDRASH RABBAH, Genesis 58:5; PIRKE RABBI ELIEZER 32.
45. Finegan, OP. CIT., p. 67.
46. MIDRASH RABBAH, Genesis 55:7.
47. Bailey, DAILY LIFE IN BIBLE TIMES, p. 52.
48. MIDRASH RABBAH, Genesis 53:13.
49. Simpson, PEOPLE IN FAMILIES, p. 373; Ploscowe, THE TRUTH ABOUT DIVORCE, p. 220.
50. Despert, CHILDREN OF DIVORCE, p. 45.
51. Glueck, OP. CIT., p. 121-127.
52. MIDRASH RABBAH, Genesis 53:15.
53. IBID., Exodus 1:1.
54. IBID., Genesis 54:2.
55. IBID., Genesis 25:3; 40:3.
56. Maslow and Mittelmann, OP. CIT., p. 147.
57. PIRKE RABBI ELIEZER 30; YALKUT SHIMONI, Genesis 95.
58. PIRKE RABBI ELIEZER 30, commentary of R'dal, no. 49.
59. Wellisch, ISAAC AND OEDIPUS, p. 75f.
60. MIDRASH RABBAH, Genesis 53:6.
61. Ginzberg, LEGENDS OF THE JEWS, vol. 1, p. 274.
62. IBID., vol. 1, p. 275.
63. IBID., vol. 1, p. 276.
64. Polish, "Akedat Yitzhak—The Binding of Isaac," Judaism, 6:1, Winter 1957.
65. PIRKE RABBI ELIEZER 31; Ginzberg, OP. CIT., vol. 1, p. 280.
66. MIDRASH RABBAH, Genesis 56:4.
67. Commentary of Rashi on Genesis 22:3.
68. PIRKE RABBI ELIEZER 31.
69. MIDRASH RABBAH, Genesis 56:5.
70. IBID., Genesis 56:8.
71. Hershon, A RABBINICAL COMMENTARY ON GENESIS, p. 42.

72. PIRKE RABBI ELIEZER 31; Ginzberg, OP. CIT., vol. 1, p. 280.
73. MIDRASH RABBAH, Genesis 61:4.
74. IBID., Genesis 60:14.
75. IBID., Ecclesiastes, 3rd sec., 9:7:1.
76. BABYLONIAN TALMUD, Baba Bathra 16b.
77. MIDRASH RABBAH, Genesis 30:4.
78. IBID., Genesis 62:5.

CHAPTER V

1. English and Pearson, EMOTIONAL PROBLEMS OF LIVING, p. 112.
2. PIRKE RABBI ELIEZER 32; MIDRASH RABBAH, Genesis 58:5.
3. MIDRASH RABBAH, Ecclesiastes, 3rd portion, 9:1.
4. Freud, "Mourning and Melancholia," COLLECTED PAPERS, vol. 4, p. 152-170.
5. MIDRASH RABBAH, Genesis 65:9.
6. PIRKE RABBI ELIEZER 16.
7. MIDRASH RABBAH, Genesis 60:12.
8. IBID.
9. BABYLONIAN TALMUD, Pesachim 91a.
10. PIRKE RABBI ELIEZER 16.
11. MIDRASH RABBAH, Genesis 60:16, commentary Matnos Kehunah.
12. PIRKE RABBI ELIEZER 31.
13. Samuels, CERTAIN PEOPLE OF THE BOOK, chap. 5.
14. Newman, MULTIPLE HUMAN BIRTHS, p. 2, 11f.
15. Hirsch, TWINS, HEREDITY AND ENVIROIMENT, p. 28; Oliver, "The Hereditary Tendency to Twinning," Eugenics Review, vol. 4, p. 39-53, 154-167.
16. Neisser, BROTHERS AND SISTERS, p. 187f.
17. Newman, OP. CIT., p. 5f.
18. IBID., p. 5.
19. IBID., p. 8f.
20. IBID., p. 6.
21. Neisser, OP. CIT., p. 180.
22. Newman, Freeman and Holzinger, TWINS, A STUDY OF HEREDITY AND ENVIRONMENT, p. 39, 41.
23. Hirsch, OP. CIT., p. 26.
24. English and Pearson, OP. CIT., p. 109f.
25. MIDRASH RABBAH, Genesis 63:10.
26. IBID., Genesis 65:1.
27. IBID., Genesis 63:10.
28. IBID., Deuteronomy 1:17.
29. IBID., Genesis 65:16; Deuteronomy 1:15.
30. IBID., Exodus 1:1.
31. IBID.
32. IBID., Genesis 63:10.
33. IBID.

34. IBID., Genesis 65:6.
35. IBID., Genesis 65:1.
36. IBID., Genesis 63:10.
37. IBID., Genesis 67:2.
38. IBID., Genesis 65:13.
39. Glueck, UNRAVELING JUVENILE DELINQUENCY, p. 172, 196, 273-276.
40. MIDRASH RABBAH, Genesis 63:12; MIDRASH TANHUMA, Deuteronomy, Ki Saytzai, sec. 4.
41. MIDRASH RABBAH, Genesis 65:10; MIDRASH TANHUMA, Deuteronomy, Ki Saytzai, sec. 4.
42. MIDRASH RABBAH, Genesis 100:5.
43. Ginzberg, LEGENDS OF THE JEWS, vol. 1, p. 327.
44. MIDRASH RABBAH, Genesis 63:11, 14; BABYLONIAN TALMUD, Baba Bathra 16b.
45. MIDRASH RABBAH, Genesis 63:10.
46. IBID.
47. IBID.
48. Glueck, OP. CIT., p. 274f.
49. MIDRASH RABBAH, Genesis 37:2.
50. Samuels, OP. CIT., p. 170.
51. MIDRASH RABBAH, Genesis 67:2.
52. Morganstern, THE BOOK OF GENESIS, p. 231.
53. BABYLONIAN TALMUD, Sanhedrin 92a; MIDRASH RABBAH, Genesis 65:15.
54. MIDRASH RABBAH, Genesis 65:15.
55. IBID.
56. IBID., Genesis 44:3.
57. SEFER HAYASHAR, (N. Y.), p. 148.
58. MIDRASH RABBAH, Genesis 67:8.
59. IBID., Genesis 75:9; Esther 7:23.
60. IBID., Genesis 67:8.
61. IBID., Genesis 67:13.
62. Freud, THE INTERPRETATION OF DREAMS, p. 355.
63. MIDRASH RABBAH, Genesis 79:1.
64. Ginzberg, OP. CIT., vol. 1, p. 413.
65. IBID., vol. 1, p. 377f.
66. MIDRASH RABBAH, Genesis 75:11.
67. IBID., Genesis 75:10.
68. IBID., Genesis 75:11.
69. IBID., Genesis 70:19.
70. BABYLONIAN TALMUD, Yoma 85b.
71. Woods, THE WORLD OF DREAMS, p. 669.
72. Hertz, THE PENTATEUCH AND HAFTORAHS, vol. 1, p. 125.
73. MIDRASH RABBAH, Genesis 78:11.
74. Menninger, LOVE AGAINST HATE, p. 205.
75. MIDRASH RABBAH, Genesis 78:14; Rashi commentary on Genesis 33:14.

CHAPTER VI

1. Rashi commentary on Genesis 36:4.
2. Patai, SEX AND FAMILY IN THE BIBLE AND THE MIDDLE EAST, p. 61.
3. Lofts, WOMEN IN THE OLD TESTAMENT, p. 34.
4. MIDRASH RABBAH, Genesis 68:5; 70:18.
5. Ginzberg, LEGENDS OF THE JEWS, vol. 5, p. 318, n. 307.
6. IBID., vol. 1, p. 360.
7. MIDRASH RABBAH, Genesis 70:17.
8. Ginzberg, OP. CIT., vol. 1, p. 357; vol. 4, p. 310; BABYLONIAN TAL- MUD, Megillah 13b; Baba Bathra 123a.
9. IBID., vol. 5, p. 294, n. 159.
10. MIDRASH RABBAH, Genesis 70:19.
11. IBID., Genesis 71:8.
12. IBID., Genesis 73:4; BABYLONIAN TALMUD, Baba Bathra 123a; Schechter, MIDRASH HAGODOL SEFER B'RAYSHIS, p. 48; Ginzberg, OP. CIT., vol. 5, p. 299f, n. 202.
13. Ginzberg, OP. CIT., vol. 5, p. 310; MIDRASH RABBAH, Lamentations (Proems) 24.
14. Rashi on Genesis 30:10.
15. MIDRASH RABBAH, Genesis 70:19.
16. IBID., Genesis 70:16; 71:2; BABYLONIAN TALMUD, Baba Bathra 123a; MIDRASH TANHUMA, Vayetze 4.
17. MIDRASH RABBAH, Genesis 71:2.
18. IBID., Genesis 70:19.
19. Ginzberg, OP. CIT., vol. 1, p. 359.
20. MIDRASH RABBAH, Genesis 71:2; 96 (MSV).
21. BABYLONIAN TALMUD, Berakoth 8b; MIDRASH RABBAH, Genesis 74:2.
22. Schechter, OP. CIT., p. 504; Ginzberg, OP. CIT., vol. 1, p. 381.
23. MIDRASH RABBAH, Genesis 71:2.
24. IBID., Genesis 18:2; 80:1; MIDRASH TANHUMA, Vayislech 5-7.
25. MIDRASH RABBAH, Genesis 71:2.
26. IBID., Genesis 98:4.
27. IBID., Genesis 71:2; Exodus 14:8; Ruth 7:13.
28. Ginzberg, OP. CIT., vol. 1, p. 415.
29. IBID., vol. 5, p. 319, n. 307; SEFER HAYASHAR, (Tel Aviv), vol. 1, p. 165.
30. MIDRASH RABBAH, Genesis 97 (MSV); Ruth 2:7.
31. IBID., Genesis 78:8.
32. Ginzberg, OP. CIT., vol. 5, p. 308, n. 262; MIDRASH RABBAH, Genesis 78:10; Schechter, OP. CIT., p. 517.
33. MIDRASH RABBAH, Genesis 71:6.
34. THE BOOK OF JUBILEES 30:2.
35. MIDRASH RABBAH, Genesis 80:5; Ecclesiastes 10:8; BABYLONIAN TALMUD, Yoma 77b.
36. Ginzberg, OP. CIT., vol. 1, p. 396.

37. MIDRASH RABBAH, Lamentations (Proems) 24; SEDER ELIYAHU RABBAH 28, 148.
38. Adler, UNDERSTANDING HUMAN NATURE, p. 221.
39. MIDRASH TANHUMA, Vayetze 6.
40. Adler, OP. CIT., p. 223f; Horney, NEUROTIC PERSONALITY OF OUR TIME, p. 226.
41. MIDRASH RABBAH, Genesis 71:6; BABYLONIAN TALMUD, Baba Bathra 116a.
42. Ginzberg, OP. CIT., vol. 5, p. 296, n. 177.
43. Buber, MIDRASH TANHUMA HAKODOM V'HAYASHAN, Vayetzay 19.
44. MIDRASH RABBAH, Genesis 71:7; Buber, OP. CIT., Vayetzay 19.
45. Adler, OP. CIT., p. 223; Horney, OP. CIT., p. 228f.
46. Deutsch, THE PSYCHOLOGY OF WOMEN, vol. 2, p. 393f.
47. Schapiro, A STUDY OF ADOPTION PRACTICE, vol. 2, p. 11.
48. MIDRASH RABBAH, Exodus 46:5.
49. Patai, OP. CIT., p. 42.
50. Ginzberg, OP. CIT., vol. 6, p. 216, n. 7.
51. MIDRASH RABBAH, Genesis 71:8.
52. Schechter, OP. CIT., p. 473-4.
53. Ginzberg, OP. CIT., vol. 5, p. 297, n. 183.
54. Lofts, OP. CIT., p. 37.
55. BABYLONIAN TALMUD, Berakoth 7b.
56. Pa'aneah on Genesis 27:2.
57. MIDRASH RABBAH, Genesis 74:13; PIRKE RABBI ELIEZER 36; THE TESTAMENTS OF THE TWELVE PATRIARCHS, Naphtali 1:9-12, also states that they were sisters, but that their father was Rotheus of Abraham's family. Laban bought him and gave him Euna, his slave, as a wife, and she bore him Bilhah and Zilpah.
58. Josephus, ANTIQUITIES OF THE JEWS, I, 19:8.
59. MIDRASH RABBAH, Genesis 98:4; BABYLONIAN TALMUD, Shabbath 55b.
60. Ramban on Genesis 35:27.
61. Ginzberg, OP. CIT., vol. 5, p. 319f, n. 312; Hadar on Genesis 35:22.
62. MIDRASH RABBAH, Genesis 72:2.
63. Patai, OP. CIT., p. 44.
64. THE TESTAMENTS OF THE TWELVE PATRIARCHS, Issachar 1:10-14.
65. Patai, OP. CIT., p. 44f.
66. MIDRASH RABBAH, Genesis 72:5; 99:10; BABYLONIAN TALMUD, Nidah 31a; Schechter, OP. CIT., p. 473, 741; TARGUM YERUSHALMI, Genesis 30:16.
67. Ginzberg, OP. CIT., vol. 1, p. 367; BABYLONIAN TALMUD, Nidah 31a; Erubin 100b.
68. MIDRASH RABBAH, Genesis 72:3.
69. MIDRASH TANHUMA, Vayetze 8; BABYLONIAN TALMUD, Berakoth 60a.
70. Ginzberg, OP. CIT., vol. 1, p. 368; Schechter, OP. CIT., p. 480-1; Buber, OP. CIT., Vayetzay 17.

71. Schechter, OP. CIT., p. 480-1; Ginzberg, OP. CIT., vol. 1, p. 368.
72. MIDRASH RABBAH, Genesis 73:3.
73. Buber, OP. CIT., Vayetzay 20; Ginzberg, OP. CIT., vol. 1, p. 308.
74. Ginzberg, OP. CIT., vol. 1, p. 373.
75. IBID., vol. 5, p. 302, n. 224.
76. Schapiro, OP. CIT., p. 113.
77. Ginzberg, OP. CIT., vol. 5, p. 299f., n. 202.
78. Menninger, LOVE AGAINST HATE, p. 95-98; Franzblau, THE ROAD TO SEXUAL MATURITY, p. 176f.
79. Deutsch, OP. CIT., p. 112f.
80. Franzblau, OP. CIT., p. 182.
81. Deutsch, OP. CIT., p. 395.
82. THE TESTAMENTS OF THE TWELVE PATRIARCHS, Benjamin 1:4.
83. Maslow and Mittelmann, PRINCIPLES OF ABNORMAL PSYCHOLOGY, p. 447-8.
84. Franzblau, OP. CIT., p. 184.
85. Ginzberg, OP. CIT., vol. 1, p. 355.
86. Franzblau, OP. CIT., p. 184; Deutsch, OP. CIT., p. 397.
87. Franzblau, OP. CIT., p. 177.
88. Ginzberg, OP. CIT., vol. 4, p. 47.
89. Franzblau, OP. CIT., p. 177; English and Finch, INTRODUCTION TO PSYCHIATRY, p. 322.
90. Deutsch, OP. CIT., p. 433.
91. IBID., p. 430.
92. Schapiro, OP. CIT., vol. 2, p. 117.
93. Maslow and Mittelmann, OP. CIT., p. 423.
94. THE TESTAMENTS OF THE TWELVE PATRIARCHS, Naphtali 1:7.

CHAPTER VII

1. PIRKE RABBI ELIEZER 38.
2. SEFER HAZOHAR, Genesis 216b.
3. MIDRASH TANHUMA, Vayeshev 2; Pekuday 11; MIDRASH RABBAH, Genesis 84:8; Buber, MIDRASH TANHUMA HAKODOM V'HAYASHAN, Vayishlach 5.
4. Neisser, BROTHERS AND SISTERS, p. 10.
5. Buber, OP. CIT., Vayishlach 7; Vayeshev 12.
6. Targum Yerushalmi, Genesis 37:2.
7. Josephus, ANTIQUITIES OF THE JEWS, II, 2:1.
8. MIDRASH RABBAH, Genesis 84:8.
9. IBID., Genesis 84:7; Schechter, MIDRASH HAGODOL SEFER B'RAY-SHIS, p. 555.
10. MIDRASH RABBAH, Genesis 84:7; MIDRASH TANHUMA, Vayeshev 7.
11. THE TESTAMENTS OF THE TWELVE PATRIARCHS, Gad 2:1; PIRKE RABBI ELIEZR 38.
12. Ginzberg, LEGENDS OF THE JEWS, vol. 2, p. 5; Schechter, OP. CIT., p. 555.

13. MIDRASH RABBAH, Genesis 84:7; 87:4; MIDRASH TANHUMA, Vaye-shev 7.
14. Ginzberg, OP. CIT., vol. 2, p. 8.
15. MIDRASH RABBAH, Genesis 84:10.
16. IBID.
17. Maslow and Mittelmann, PRINCIPLES OF ABNORMAL PSYCHOLOGY, p. 14.
18. MIDRASH RABBAH, Genesis 84:9.
19. IBID., Genesis 84:13; THE FATHERS ACCORDING TO RABBI NA-THAN 34; SEFER HAYASHAR, (Tel Aviv), vol. 2, p. 187; TARGUM YERUSHALMI, Genesis 37:13; Josephus, OP. CIT., II, 2-4.
20. MIDRASH TANHUMA HANIKRAH YELAMEDAYNU, p. 42b.
21. MIDRASH RABBAH, Genesis 84:14.
22. Maslow and Mittelmann, OP. CIT., p. 67; Alexander, PSYCHOSOMATIC MEDICINE, p. 70.
23. MIDRASH RABBAH, Genesis 91:8.
24. THE TESTAMENTS OF THE TWELVE PATRIARCHS, Zebulun 2:2-3.
25. IBID., Zebulun 2:6.
26. IBID., Zebulun 2:7.
27. MIDRASH RABBAH, Genesis 84:16.
28. IBID., Genesis 84:16; 91:6; Buber, OP. CIT., Vayeshev 13; SEFER HAYASHAR, (Tel Aviv), vol. 2, p. 188; BABYLONIAN TALMUD, Shab-bath 22a; Epstein, MIDRASH MISHLE, p. 4.
29. Buber, OP. CIT., Vayeshev 13.
30. MIDRASH RABBAH, Genesis 84:15.
31. IBID., Genesis 84:19.
32. IBID., Genesis 91:8; SEFER HAYASHAR, (Tel Aviv), vol. 2, p. 188f.
33. SEFER HAYASHAR, (Tel Aviv), vol. 2, p. 189.
34. MIDRASH TANHUMA, Ki Sissa 2: Ekev 6.
35. MIDRASH RABBAH, Genesis 84:17.
36. SEFER HAYASHAR, (Tel Aviv), vol. 2, p. 189; MIDRASH TANHUMA, Vayeshev 2.
37. SEFER HAYASHAR, (Tel Aviv), vol. 2, p. 191.
38. Gaer, THE LORE OF THE OLD TESTAMENT, p. 121.
39. THE TESTAMENTS OF THE TWELVE PATRIARCHS, Zebulun 3:2; Gad 2:3.
40. MIDRASH RABBAH, Genesis 84:18; 91:7.
41. THE TESTAMENTS OF THE TWELVE PATRIARCHS, Zebulun 3:3; PIRKE RABBI ELIEZER 38.
42. Ginzberg, OP. CIT., vol. 2, p. 24.
43. THE TESTAMENTS OF THE TWELVE PATRIARCHS, Zebulun 4:6.
44. IBID., Zebulun 1:6; PIRKE RABBI ELIEZER 38.
45. SEFER HAYASHAR, (Tel Aviv), vol. 2, p. 196; MIDRASH RABBAH, Genesis 84:19; THE TESTAMENTS OF THE TWELVE PATRIARCHS, Zebulun 4:5-10.
46. THE TESTAMENTS OF THE TWELVE PATRIARCHS, Zebulun 4:11-13.
47. Maslow and Mittelmann, OP. CIT., p. 70.

48. MIDRASH RABBAH, Genesis 84:8; 95:2; Numbers 13:14; Buber, OP. CIT., Vayigash 10.
49. MIDRASH RABBAH, Genesis 84:13.
50. Ginzberg, OP. CIT., vol. 2, p. 26.
51. SEFER HAYASHAR, (Tel Aviv), vol. 2, p. 198.
52. IBID., Vol. 2, p. 198f.
53. THE BOOK OF JUBILEES 34:15-16.
54. SEFER HAYASHAR, (Tel Aviv), vol. 2, p. 199.
55. English and Pearson, EMOTIONAL PROBLEMS OF LIVING, p. 55; Buber, OP. CIT., Vayeshev 13.
56. THE TESTAMENTS OF THE TWELVE PATRIARCHS, Simeon 3:3; 4:8.
57. IBID., Simeon 2:9, 11.
58. IBID., Simeon 2:12.
59. Maslow and Mittelmann, OP. CIT., p. 439; Alexander, OP. CIT., p. 40.
60. Maslow and Mittelmann, OP. CIT., p. 442.
61. THE TESTAMENTS OF THE TWELVE PATRIARCHS, Simeon 2:6-7.
62. IBID., Dan 1:4-7.
63. IBID., Gad 2:1; PIRKE RABBI ELIEZER 38.
64. THE TESTAMENTS OF THE TWELVE PATRIARCHS, Gad 3:2-3; 5:1, 9-11.
65. IBID., Zebulun 4:1-4.
66. Ziman, JEALOUSY IN CHILDREN, p. 110-1.
67. MIDRASH RABBAH, Genesis 84:15.
68. THE TESTAMENTS OF THE TWELVE PATRIARCHS, Reuben 1:8.
69. THE BOOK OF JUBILEES 33:1-8.
70. IBID., 33:9; THE TESTAMENTS OF THE TWELVE PATRIARCHS, Reuben 3:15.
71. THE TESTAMENTS OF THE TWELVE PATRIARCHS, Reuben 4:2.
72. IBID., Reuben 1:10.
73. IBID., Reuben 1:7.
74. Alexander, OP. CIT., p. 102f.
75. IBID., p. 100.
76. THE TESTAMENTS OF THE TWELVE PATRIARCHS, Reuben 1:7-8; 4:4.
77. MIDRASH RABBAH, Genesis 84:15.
78. Josephus, OP. CIT., II, 3:1-2; PIRKE RABBI ELIEZER 38; MIDRASH TANHUMA, Vayeshev 2; MIDRASH LEKACH TOV, Genesis 37:29.
79. SEFER HAZOHAR, Genesis 185a-b; Ginzberg, OP. CIT., vol. 2, p. 12; MIDRASH LEKACH TOV, Genesis 37:30.
80. Ginzberg, OP. CIT., vol. 3, p. 206.
81. THE TESTAMENTS OF THE TWELVE PATRIARCHS, Issachar 7:2.
82. Ginzberg, OP. CIT., vol. 2, p. 205f.
83. THE TESTAMENTS OF THE TWELVE PATRIARCHS, Zebulun 1:5; 5:2.
84. IBID., Zebulun 7:1.

85. Ginzberg, OP. CIT., vol. 1, p. 175; vol. 2, p. 86; vol. 3, p. 364; MIDRASH RABBAH, Genesis 98:4; THE TESTAMENTS OF THE TWELVE PATRIARCHS, Levi 5:2.
86. THE TESTAMENTS OF THE TWELVE PATRIARCHS, Levi 9:7.
87. Ginzberg, OP. CIT., vol. 2, p. 175f.
88. THE TESTAMENTS OF THE TWELVE PATRIARCHS, Reuben 1; Ginzberg, OP. CIT., vol. 2, p. 412.
89. Ginzberg, OP. CIT., vol. 2, p. 32.
90. Buber, OP. CIT., Vayeshev 8; MIDRASH RABBAH, Genesis 85:3.
91. Buber, OP. CIT., Vayeshev 12.
92. Flugel, STUDIES IN FEELING AND DESIRE, p. 100.
93. MIDRASH TANHUMA, Ki Sissa 22; MIDRASH RABBAH, Genesis 85:3.
94. THE TESTAMENTS OF THE TWELVE PATRIARCHS, Judah 11:2; 13:4; 17:1.
95. IBID., Judah 12:3.
96. IBID., Judah 14:3-8.
97. Ginzberg, OP. CIT., vol. 2, p. 36; vol. 3, p. 455; SIFRI 76a; Buber, OP. CIT., Vayeshev 17.
98. MIDRASH RABBAH, Genesis 91:6; Exodus 1:1; Josephus, OP. CIT., II, 2:1; MIDRASH TANHUMA, Shemos 1.
99. THE TESTAMENTS OF THE TWELVE PATRIARCHS, Judah 1:4, 5; 2:2; 17:4.
100. IBID., Judah 7:6.
101. MIDRASH RABBAH, Genesis 80:11; Schechter, OP. CIT., p. 527.
102. THE TESTAMENTS OF THE TWELVE PATRIARCHS, Levi 6:5.
103. SEFER HAYASHAR, (Tel Aviv), vol. 1, p. 161.
104. BABYLONIAN TALMUD, Sotah 7b.
105. THE TESTAMENTS OF THE TWELVE PATRIARCHS, Judah 13:3.
106. IBID., Simeon 4:3.
107. SEFER HAYASHAR, (Tel Aviv), vol. 2, p. 192.
108. IBID., vol. 2, p. 193.
109. MIDRASH RABBAH, Genesis 84:6; MIDRASH TANHUMA, Vayeshev 1; Miketz 3; Buber, OP. CIT., Vayeshev 5; Schechter, OP. CIT., p. 554-5.
110. THE TESTAMENTS OF THE TWELVE PATRIARCHS, Joseph 10:6; 11:2; 15:1-3.
111. IBID., Joseph 13:3-4.
112. IBID., Joseph 16:4-6.
113. Schechter, OP. CIT., p. 581.
114. Josephus, OP. CIT., II, 4:1.
115. Ginzberg, OP. CIT., vol. 2, p. 44.
116. MIDRASH RABBAH, Genesis 86:6; TARGUM YERUSHALMI, Genesis 39:6.
117. MIDRASH RABBAH, Genesis 86:3.
118. BABYLONIAN TALMUD, Yoma 35b.
119. MIDRASH TANHUMA, Vayeshev 5.
120. Maslow and Mittelmann, OP. CIT., p. 94, 96.
121. MIDRASH RABBAH, Genesis 87:5; THE TESTAMENTS OF THE TWELVE PATRIARCHS, Joseph 3:1-2, 6-8; 4:1-2, 4-7; 5:1, 4; 7:1, 3; 9:5.

122. THE TESTAMENTS OF THE TWELVE PATRIARCHS, Joseph 7:5-6.
123. Ginzberg, OP. CIT. vol. 2, p. 45.
124. IBID., vol. 2, p. 54; Schechter, OP. CIT., p. 588-9.
125. MIDRASH RABBAH, Genesis 87:5.
126. IBID., Genesis 87:7; 98:20; BABYLONIAN TALMUD, Sotah 36b; MID-
     RASH TANHUMA, Vayeshev 9; Targum Yerushalmi, Genesis 49:24; Buber,
     MIDRASH AGGADAH, Genesis 39:11.
127. SEFER HAYASHAR, (Tel Aviv), vol. 2, 209; Ginzberg, OP. CIT., vol. 2,
     p. 54; THE TESTAMENTS OF THE TWELVE PATRIARCHS, Joseph
     8:2-3.
128. MIDRASH TANHUMA, Vayeshev 9.
129. Ginzberg, OP. CIT., vol. 2, p. 57.
130. Schechter, OP. CIT., p. 591; MIDRASH RABBAH, Genesis 87:9; THE
     TESTAMENTS OF THE TWELVE PATRIARCHS, Joseph 8:4.
131. MIDRASH RABBAH, Genesis 87:10.
132. MIDRASH TANHUMA, Vayeshev 9.
133. MIDRASH RABBAH, Genesis 87:10.
134. Ginzberg, OP. CIT., vol. 2, p. 58-9; SEFER HAYASHAR, (Tel Aviv),
     vol. 2, p. 211; THE TESTAMENTS OF THE TWELVE PATRIARCHS,
     Joseph 9:4-5.
135. MIDRASH RABBAH, Genesis 87:8; Schechter, OP. CIT., p. 590; Buber,
     OP. CIT., Genesis 39:16.
136. Neisser, OP. CIT., p. 162.
137. MIDRASH RABBAH, Genesis 91:4, 6; Ecclesiastes 9:15:2; MIDRASH
     TANHUMA, Miketz 8; Buber, OP. CIT., Miketz 17.
138. SEFER HAYASHAR, (Tel Aviv), vol. 2, p. 235; MIDRASH RABBAH,
     Genesis 91:4, 6; MIDRASH TANHUMA, Miketz 8; Buber, OP. CIT.,
     Miketz 17.
139. MIDRASH RABBAH, Genesis 91:16; MIDRASH TANHUMA, Miketz 8.
140. Ginzberg, OP. CIT., vol. 2, p. 18; THE TESTAMENTS OF THE TWELVE
     PATRIARCHS, Zebulun 3:7.
141. BABYLONIAN TALMUD, Yebamoth 88a; MIDRASH RABBAH, Genesis
     91:7; Joseph, OP. CIT., II, 6:2.
142. THE TESTAMENTS OF THE TWELVE PATRIARCHS, Joseph 10:5-6;
     11:1.
143. Buber, MIDRASH TANHUMA HAKODOM V'HAYASHAN, Miketz 17;
     MIDRASH RABBAH, Genesis 91:7.
144. Ginzberg, OP. CIT., vol. 2, p. 85.
145. Schechter, OP. CIT., p. 639; MIDRASH RABBAH, Genesis 91:6.
146. Ginzberg, OP. CIT., vol. 1, p. 175; vol. 2, p. 86; vol. 3, p. 364.
147. MIDRASH RABBAH, Genesis 91:6; MIDRASH TANHUMA, Vayeshev 4;
     TARGUM YERUSHALMI, Genesis 43:24.
148. THE TESTAMENTS OF THE TWELVE PATRIARCHS, Simeon 4:3.
149. MIDRASH RABBAH, Genesis 91:6; MIDRASH TANHUMA, Vayigash 4.
150. MIDRASH RABBAH, Genesis 91:8; Buber, OP. CIT., Vayeshev 13; MID-
     RASH TANHUMA, Miketz 8; Schechter, OP. CIT., p. 639; Josephus, OP.
     CIT., II, 6:6.
151. Buber, MIDRASH AGGADAH, Genesis 42:27.

152. IBID., Genesis 44:29.
153. MIDRASH RABBAH, Genesis 91:9; MIDRASH TANHUMA, Miketz 8; Schechter, OP. CIT., p. 641.
154. SEFER HAYASHAR, (Tel Aviv), vol. 2, p. 241; MIDRASH TANHUMA, Miketz 8.
155. MIDRASH RABBAH, Genesis 91:10.
156. IBID., Genesis 91:6; MIDRASH TANHUMA, Miketz 8; Buber, OP. CIT., Miketz 17.
157. SEFER HAYASHAR, (Tel Aviv), vol. 2, p. 242.
158. MIDRASH RABBAH, Genesis 93:8.
159. IBID., Genesis 91:10.
160. SEFER HAYASHAR, (Tel Aviv), vol. 2, p. 244.
161. MIDRASH TANHUMA, Miketz 10; Buber, OP. CIT., Miketz 13; MIDRASH RABBAH, Genesis 91:6; 93:7.
162. Ginzberg, OP. CIT., vol. 2, p. 94.
163. MIDRASH TANHUMA, Vayeshev 2.
164. MIDRASH RABBAH, Genesis 92:4.
165. Ginzberg, OP. CIT., vol. 2, p. 95.
166. IBID., vol. 2, p. 96; Buber, S., MIDRASH TANHUMA HAKODOM V'HAYASHAN, Vayeshev 6; MIDRASH TANHUMA HANIKRAH YELA-MEDAYNU 42b.
167. MIDRASH RABBAH, Genesis 92:5; Epstein, MIDRASH MISHLE, p. 5.
168. MIDRASH RABBAH, Genesis 92:5.
169. SEFER HAYASHAR, (Tel Aviv), vol. 2, p. 247.
170. MIDRASH RABBAH, Genesis 92:5; 93:7; 98:20; BABYLONIAN TAL-MUD, Shabbath 139a.
171. SEFER HAYASHAR, (Tel Aviv), vol. 2, p. 248; Josephus, OP. CIT., II, 6:7.
172. MIDRASH RABBAH, Genesis 92:8; MIDRASH TAIHUMA, Miketz 10; Schechter, OP. CIT., p. 653; Buber, OP. CIT., Miketz 13.
173. SEFER HAYASHAR, (Tel Aviv), vol. 2, p. 249.
174. MIDRASH RABBAH, Genesis 92:9; Schechter, OP. CIT., p. 656.
175. MIDRASH RABBAH, Genesis 93:6; Schechter, OP. CIT., p. 661-2; Buber, OP. CIT., Introduction 131, 146; Ginzberg, OP. CIT., vol. 2, p. 106.
176. SEFER HAYASHAR, (Tel Aviv), vol. 2, p. 249f.
177. MIDRASH RABBAH, Genesis 93:2; 5; SEFER HAZOHAR, Genesis 206a; Schechter, OP. CIT., p. 661.
178. THE TESTAMENTS OF THE TWELVE PATRIARCHS, Judah 15:2.
179. MIDRASH TANHUMA, Miketz 10.
180. IBID., Vayigash 5; MIDRASH RABBAH, Genesis 93:9.
181. Buber, OP. CIT., Miketz 13.
182. MIDRASH TANHUMA, Miketz 10; Vayigash 5.
183. MIDRASH RABBAH, Genesis 93:6.
184. IBID.; MIDRASH TANHUMA, Vayigash 5.
185. MIDRASH TANHUMA, Vayigash 5.
186. Buber, S., MIDRASH AGGADAH, Genesis 44:29.
187. MIDRASH RABBAH, Genesis 93:4.

188. Lund, "Why Do We Weep," *Journal of Social Psychology*, 1:1, Feb., 1930, p. 149.
189. MIDRASH RABBAH, Genesis 93:8.
190. IBID., Genesis 93:8, 10; MIDRASH TANHUMA, Vayigash 5.
191. MIDRASH RABBAH, Genesis 93:8; MIDRASH TANHUMA, Vayigash 5.
192. Darwin, EXPRESSION OF THE EMOTIONS IN MAN AND IN ANI-MALS, p. 177.
193. MIDRASH RABBAH, Genesis 93:12; Vitanza, "Toward a Theory of Crying," *Psychoanalysis and the Psychoanalytic Review*, 47:4, Winter, 1960, p. 67; Hunt, "The Wisdom of Tears," *Readers Digest*, October, 1955, p. 34-42; Inglis, EMOTIONAL STRESS AND YOUR HEALTH, p. 130.
194. Feldman, "Crying at the Happy Ending," *Journal of the American Psychoanalytic Association*, 4:3, July, 1956, p. 477-485.
195. Masserman, "The Conceptual Dynamics of Person, Religion and Self," *The Psychoanalytic Review*, 41:4, October, 1954, p. 311.
196. MIDRASH RABBAH, Genesis 78:9; Numbers 3:13; Song of Songs 7:5:1; Menninger, A PSYCHIATRIST'S WORLD, p. 234.
197. Feldman, OP. CIT., p. 480.
198. IBID., p. 484.
199. Weiss, "Crying at the Happy Ending," *The Psychoanalytic Review*, 39:4, October, 1952, p. 338.
200. Heilbrinn, "On Weeping," *Psychoanalytic Quarterly*, 24:2, April, 1955, p. 252, 254.
201. Feldman, OP. CIT., p. 483; Lund, OP. CIT., p. 146.
202. Ginzberg, OP. CIT., vol. 2, p. 118; MIDRASH RABBAH, Genesis 94:5.
203. MIDRASH RABBAH, Genesis 84:8.
204. IBID., Genesis 95:4; TARGUM YERUSHALMI, Genesis 47:2.
205. Schechter, OP. CIT., p. 671.
206. MIDRASH RABBAH, Ecclesiastes 9:15:2.
207. THE TESTAMENTS OF THE TWELVE PATRIARCHS, Zebulun 8:4.
208. IBID., Simeon 4:4, 6.
209. IBID., Joseph 17:4, 6-8.
210. SEFER HAYASHAR, (Tel Aviv), vol. 2, p. 267.
211. Schechter, OP. CIT., p. 693.
212. THE TESTAMENTS OF THE TWELVE PATRIARCHS, Benjamin 3:6.
213. Menninger, LOVE AGAINST HATE, p. 205.
214. Ginzberg, OP. CIT., vol. 2, p. 175f.
215. IBID., vol. 2, p. 176f.
216. IBID., vol. 2, p. 132.
217. IBID., vol. 2, p. 220f.
218. THE TESTAMENTS OF THE TWELVE PATRIARCHS, Benjamin 3:2-7.
219. MIDRASH RABBAH, Genesis 84:6.
220. IBID., Genesis 89:9.
221. IBID., Genesis 55:8; Schechter, OP. CIT., p. 688.
222. SEFER HAYASHAR, (Tel Aviv), vol. 2, p. 266.
223. Ginzberg, OP. CIT., vol. 2, p. 120.
224. SEFER HAYASHAR, (Tel Aviv), vol. 2, p. 266.
225. Schechter, OP. CIT., p. 689.

226. MIDRASH RABBAH, Genesis 95:2; MIDRASH TANHUMA, Vayigash 9; Buber, MIDRASH TANHUMA HAKODOM V'HAYASHAN, Vayigash 10.
227. Ginzberg, OP. CIT., vol. 2, p. 149.
228. Vitanza, OP. CIT., p. 74.
229. MIDRASH RABBAH, Genesis 2:8.
230. MIDRASH TANHUMA, Vayechi 17.
231. MIDRASH RABBAH, Genesis 100:8.
232. Rashi on Genesis 50:16.
233. MIDRASH RABBAH, Genesis 100:8.
234. IBID., Genesis 100:9.
235. THE TESTAMENTS OF THE TWELVE PATRIARCHS, Joseph 17:5.
236. IBID., Joseph 18:2.

CHAPTER VIII

1. Abkir in Yalkut I, 146.
2. PIRKE RABBI ELIEZER 38; Buber, MIDRASH AGGADAH, Genesis 41:45; Gaer, THE LORE OF THE OLD TESTAMENT, p. 128; Ginzberg, LEGENDS OF THE JEWS, vol. 2, p. 170.
3. MIDRASH RABBAH, Genesis 97 (MSV).
4. Ginzberg, OP. CIT., vol. 2, p. 38, 76, 170f.
5. BABYLONIAN TALMUD, Ta'anit 11a; Buber, OP. CIT., Genesis 41:50.
6. Ginzberg, OP. CIT., vol. 2, p. 77.
7. MIDRASH RABBAH, Genesis 91:4.
8. Buber, MIDRASH TANHUMA HAKODOM V'HAYASHAN, Miketz 17.
9. MIDRASH RABBAH, Genesis 91:8; Buber, MIDRASH AGGADAH, Genesis 42:23; Schechter, MIDRASH HAGODOL SEFER B'RAYSHIS, p. 639.
10. MIDRASH TANHUMA, Vayigash 4; MIDRASH RABBAH, Genesis 91:6; SEFER HAYASHAR, (Tel Aviv), vol. 2, p. 239f.
11. MIDRASH RABBAH, Genesis 93:9.
12. Ginzberg, OP. CIT., vol. 2, p. 108.
13. IBID., vol. 2, p. 110.
14. IBID., vol. 2, p. 108f.
15. TARGUM YERUSHALMI, Genesis 43:16.
16. MIDRASH TANHUMA, Miketz 10; Buber, MIDRASH TANHUMA HAKODOM V'HAYASHAN, Miketz 13; Ginzberg, OP. CIT., vol. 2, p. 99.
17. MIDRASH RABBAH, Genesis 97 (MSV).
18. Ginzberg, OP. CIT., vol. 2, p. 132; vol. 5, p. 364, n. 360.
19. Schechter, OP. CIT., p. 716; Ginzberg, OP. CIT., vol. 2, p. 133.
20. Patai, SEX AND FAMILY IN THE BIBLE AND THE MIDDLE EAST, p. 42.
21. Ginzberg, OP. CIT., vol. 2, p. 134.
22. IBID., vol. 2, p. 136.
23. IBID.
24. MIDRASH TANHUMA, Vayechi 6.
25. Ginzberg, OP. CIT., vol. 3, p. 203.

26. IBID., vol. 2, p. 138.
27. IBID., vol. 5, p. 366, n. 376; Schechter, OP. CIT., p. 720-1; MIDRASH RABBAH, Genesis 6:4; 37:7; 97 (MSV).
28. MIDRASH RABBAH, Leviticus 2:3.

CHAPTER IX

1. MIDRASH RABBAH, Exodus 1:13; 26:1; Song of Songs 2:11:1; Buber, MIDRASH TANHUMA HAKODOM V'HAYASHAN, Bo 7.
2. Ginzberg, LEGENDS OF THE JEWS, vol. 2, p. 261.
3. SEFER HAYASHAR, (Tel Aviv), vol. 2, p. 297; THE TESTAMENTS OF THE TWELVE PATRIARCHS, Levi 17:3.
4. PIRKE RABBI ELIEZER 48.
5. MIDRASH RABBAH, Leviticus 1:3.
6. IBID., Exodus 1:13.
7. IBID., Song of Songs 4:5:1.
8. IBID., Ecclesiastes 7:1:3; BABYLONIAN TALMUD, Sotah 11b.
9. BABYLONIAN TALMUD, Sotah 11b; SEFER HAYASHAR, (Tel Aviv), vol. 2, p. 297; MIDRASH RABBAH, Exodus 1:15; Ginzberg, OP. CIT., vol. 2, p. 252.
10. MIDRASH RABBAH, Exodus 1:15; BABYLONIAN TALMUD, Sotah 11b.
11. Ginzberg, OP. CIT., vol. 2, p. 251f.
12. MIDRASH RABBAH, Exodus 1:13; BABYLONIAN TALMUD, Sotah 12a.
13. MIDRASH RABBAH, Exodus 1:19; BABYLONIAN TALMUD, Sotah 12a; Baba Bathra 120a.
14. MIDRASH RABBAH, Exodus 1:20; SEFER HAYASHAR, (Tel Aviv), vol. 2, p. 305.
15. Ginzberg, OP. CIT., vol. 2, p. 265.
16. BABYLONIAN TALMUD, Sotah 12b.
17. MIDRASH RABBAH, Ecclesiastes 7:1:3.
18. IBID., Exodus 1:22; BABYLONIAN TALMUD, Sotah 13a.
19. PHILO, vol. 6, I, 4:14.
20. PIRKE RABBI ELIEZER 48; MIDRASH RABBAH, Exodus 1:23; SEFER HAYASHAR, (Tel Aviv), vol. 2, p. 306.
21. Ginzberg, OP. CIT., vol. 5, p. 398f, n. 48.
22. MIDRASH RABBAH, Exodus 1:23; PIRKE RABBI ELIEZER 48.
23. MIDRASH RABBAH, Exodus 1:20, 24; Ecclesiastes 9:2:1; BABYLONIAN TALMUD, Sotah 12a.
24. French, THE INTEGRATION OF BEHAVIOR, p. 69.
25. MIDRASH RABBAH, Exodus 1:25.
26. BABYLONIAN TALMUD, Kethuboth 60a; SEFER HAYASHAR, (Tel Aviv), vol. 2, p. 306; MIDRASH RABBAH, Leviticus 1:3; PIRKE RABBI ELIEZER 48.
27. Josephus, ANTIQUITIES OF THE JEWS, II, 9:7; PHILO, vol. 6, I, 5:19; MIDRASH RABBAH, Exodus 1:26; BABYLONIAN TALMUD, Megillah 13a; SEFER HAYASHAR, (Tel Aviv), vol. 2, p. 306.
28. Ginzberg, OP. CIT., vol. 2, p. 271; PHILO, I, 5:19.

29. SEFER HAYASHAR, (Tel Aviv), vol. 2, p. 307.
30. MIDRASH RABBAH, Exodus 1:26; MIDRASH TANHUMA, Shemos 8.
31. SEFER HAYASHAR, (Tel viv), vol. 2, p. 309.
32. Josephus, OP. CIT., II, 9:7.
33. English and Pearson, EMOTIONAL PROBLEMS OF LIVING, p. 252f.
34. MIDRASH RABBAH, Genesis 1:27; MIDRASH TANHUMA, Shemos 8.
35. MIDRASH RABBAH, Exodus 1:26; BABYLONIAN TALMUD, Berakoth 54b.
36. MIDRASH RABBAH, Exodus 1:26; SEFER HAYASHAR, (Tel Aviv), vol. 2, p. 307f; Josephus, OP. CIT., II, 9:7; MIDRASH TANHUMA, Shemos 8.
37. MIDRASH RABBAH, Exodus 1:27; Leviticus 37:2; MIDRASH TAN-HUMA, Shemos 9.
38. MIDRASH RABBAH, Exodus 1:28; SEFER HAYASHAR, (Tel Aviv), vol. 2, p. 310.
39. SEFER HAYASHAR, (Tel Aviv), vol. 2, p. 310.
40. IBID.; MIDRASH RABBAH, Leviticus 32:4.
41. MIDRASH RABBAH, Exodus 1:29.
42. IBID., Exodus 1:28; MIDRASH TANHUMA, Shemos 9; Emor 24; PIRKE RABBI ELIEZER 48; Ginzberg, OP. CIT., vol. 2, p. 280.
43. MIDRASH TANHUMA, Shemos 10; Buber, MIDRASH AGGADAH, Shemos 18:4.
44. MIDRASH RABBAH, Exodus 1:31; Deuteronomy 2:26-27.
45. Josephus, OP. CIT., II, 10.
46. PHILO, I, 8:45.
47. SEFER HAYASHAR, (Tel Aviv), vol. 2, p. 315f; Josephus, OP. CIT., II, 10-11.
48. Buber, OP. CIT., Shemos 2:16; MIDRASH RABBAH, Exodus 1:32; MIDRASH TANHUMA, Shemos 11; Hoffman, MIDRASH HAGODOL SEFER SHEMOS, p. 18.
49. PHILO, I, 10:57; Ginzberg, OP. CIT., vol. 5, p. 410, n. 84.
50. MIDRASH RABBAH, Exodus 1:32; MIDRASH TANHUMA, Shemos 11.
51. MIDRASH RABBAH, Deuteronomy 2:8.
52. Epstein, MIDRASH MISHLE, 7:14, 18.
53. SEFER HAYASHAR, (Tel Aviv), vol. 2, p. 320, 323.
54. Ziman, JEALOUSY IN CHILDREN, p. 96.
55. SEFER HAYASHAR, (Tel Aviv), vol. 2, p. 326; MIDRASH RABBAH, Exodus 1:33; 4:1-2, 4; 5:8; Buber, S., OP. CIT., Shemos 18:3; Lauterbach, MEKILTA D'REBBI YISHMAEL, Tractate Amalek, vol. 2, p. 168f.; MIDRASH TANHUMA, Shemos 20.
56. MIDRASH RABBAH, Exodus 2:2-3; Buber, OP. CIT., Shemos 12.
57. MIDRASH RABBAH, Exodus 2:2-3.
58. Lauterbach, OP. CIT., Tractate Amalek, vol. 2, p. 179.
59. IBID., Tractate Amalek, vol. 2, p. 174, 186.
60. MIDRASH RABBAH, Exodus 2:4; 3:4; Song of Songs 1:7:1-3; MID-RASH TANHUMA, Shemos 14.
61. MIDRASH RABBAH, Exodus 5:16.
62. IBID., Exodus 4:2.

63. IBID., Exodus 4:4; Buber, OP. CIT., Shemos 18.
64. MIDRASH RABBAH, Exodus 1:30.
65. Buber, OP. CIT., Shemos 4:24.
66. Ginzberg, OP. CIT., vol. 2, p. 329.
67. THE FATHERS ACCORDING TO RABBI NATHAN 27; Lauterbach, OP. CIT., Tractate Amalek, vol. 2, p. 140.
68. THE FATHERS ACCORDING TO RABBI NATHAN 27.
69. Friedman, MECHILTA D'REBBI YISHMAEL, 57b; Hoffman, MEKILTA D'REB SHIMON BEN YOCHAI, p. 86; Lauterbach, OP. CIT., Tractate Amalek, vol. 2, p. 168.
70. Ginzberg, OP. CIT., vol. 2, p. 329f; MIDRASH RABBAH, Song of Songs 4:5:1.
71. Buber, MIDRASH TANHUMA HAKODOM V'HAYASHAN, Vaera 4; MIDRASH RABBAH, Exodus 5:19.
72. MIDRASH RABBAH, Exodus 5:21; MIDRASH TANHUMA, Vaera 6.
73. Ansbacher, THE INDIVIDUAL PSYCHOLOGY OF ALFRED ADLER, p. 452f.
74. BABYLONIAN TALMUD, Berakoth 32a; Sanhedrin 111a; MIDRASH RABBAH, Ecclesiastes 7:7:2.
75. MIDRASH RABBAH, Exodus 5:22.
76. MIDRASH TANHUMA, Vaera 1.
77. Buber, OP. CIT., Bo 19: Buber, MIDRASH TEHILLIM, 113:2; Friedman, OP. CIT., 13f.
78. MIDRASH RABBAH, Exodus, 1:26.
79. PHILO, I, 4:13.
80. MIDRASH RABBAH, Exodus 18:3; SEFER HAYASHAR, (Tel Aviv), vol. 2, p. 336.
81. Ginzberg, OP. CIT., vol. 2, p. 370; Buber, OP. CIT., 113:2; BABYLONIAN TALMUD, Pesachim 94a.
82. MIDRASH RABBAH, Exodus 18:10; MIDRASH TANHUMA, Ekev 6.
83. Friedman, OP. CIT., 14a, 15b.
84. SEFER HAZOHAR II, 45a.
85. Lauterbach, OP. CIT., Tractate Vayassa, p. 86.
86. Ginzberg, OP. CIT., vol. 3, p. 212.
87. Lindgren, THE ART OF HUMAN RELATIONS, p. 188.
88. SIFRE D'BE RAV, Numbers 90.
89. MIDRASH RABBAH, Exodus 41:7; 51:8; Leviticus 10:3; Numbers 15:21; Buber, MIDRASH TANHUMA HAKODOM V'HAYASHAN, Ki Sissa 13; PIRKE RABBI ELIEZER 45; BABYLONIAN TAMUD, Sanhedrin 7a.
90. PIRKE RABBI ELIEZER 45; MIDRASH RABBAH, Exodus 41:5; Buber, OP. CIT., Ki Sissa 13; MIDRASH TANHUMA, Ki Sissa 19.
91. MIDRASH RABBAH, Exodus 42:6; Leviticus 27:8; Song of Songs 1:9; MIDRASH TANHUMA, Emor 11.
92. MIDRASH RABBAH, Exodus 41:1; Leviticus 5:3.
93. IBID., Numbers 15:21.
94. IBID., Exodus 41:7; 42:4; Leviticus 10:3; Buber, OP. CIT., Ki Sissa 13.
95. MIDRASH RABBAH, Exodus 37:2; Leviticus 7:1.
96. IBID., Exodus 41:7; Lauterbach, OP. CIT., Tractate Shirata, vol. 2, p. 4.

97. MIDRASH RABBAH, Exodus 42:5; 44:9; Numbers 16:25; Deuteronomy 5:13; BABYLONIAN TALMUD, Berakoth 32a.
98. MIDRASH RABBAH, Exodus 37:1; Song of Songs 1:7:3.
99. MIDRASH RABBAH, Exodus 37:4.
100. Buber, OP. CIT., Shemini 5; MIDRASH TANHUMA, Shemini 3.
101. MIDRASH TANHUMA, Shemini 10; Buber, OP. CIT., Shemini 5; Ginzberg, OP. CIT., vol. 3, p. 179f.
102. IBID., vol. 3, p. 183f.
103. IBID., vol. 3, p. 184.
104. MIDRASH RABBAH, Leviticus 20:9; Esther 5:1; Song of Songs 5:1:1.
105. IBID., Leviticus 20:10.
106. IBID.
107. IBID., Leviticus 20:6.
108. IBID., Leviticus 20:8, 9; Numbers 2:23.
109. IBID., Song of Songs 1:12:3; 3:7:4.
110. IBID., Lamentations 23; Ecclesiastes 12:7:1.
111. Menninger, LOVE AGAINST HATE, p. 267.
112. Buber, OP. CIT., Korah 3.
113. MIDRASH TANHUMA, Korah 4; BABYLONIAN TALMUD, Sanhedrin 110a; Josephus, OP. CIT., IV, 2:2; Buber, OP. CIT., Korah 8.
114. Ginzberg, OP. CIT., vol. 6, p. 99, n. 563.
115. MIDRASH TANHUMA, Korah 10; BABYLONIAN TALMUD, Sanhedrin 110a.
116. MIDRASH RABBAH, Numbers 18:4; Buber, OP. CIT., Korah 6; MIDRASH TANHUMA, Korah 3; SEFER HAZOHAR, III, 49a.
117. MIDRASH RABBAH, Numbers 18:4; MIDRASH TANHUMA, Korah 3; Buber, OP. CIT., Korah 6.
118. MIDRASH TANHUMA, Korah 10; MIDRASH RABBAH, Numbers 18:20; BABYLONIAN TALMUD, Moed Katan 18b; Buber, OP. CIT., Korah 22.
119. MIDRASH TANHUMA, Korah 2; Buber, OP. CIT., Korah 4.
120. MIDRASH RABBAH, Numbers 18:4.
121. IBID., Numbers 18:4, 12; MIDRASH TANHUMA, Korah 3, 8; Buber, OP. CIT., Korah 6; BABYLONIAN TALMUD, Moed Katan 16a.
122. MIDRASH TANHUMA, Korah 6.
123. MIDRASH RABBAH, Numbers 18:7; BABYLONIAN TALMUD, Sanhedrin 52a; MIDRASH TANHUMA, Korah 5; Buber, OP. CIT., Korah 10.
124. Buber, OP. CIT., Korah 19; MIDRASH TANHUMA, Korah 7.
125. MIDRASH RABBAH, Numbers 18:11; MIDRASH TANHUMA, Korah 7; Buber, OP. CIT., Korah 6.
126. MIDRSH RABBAH, Numbers 18:12; MIDRASH TANHUMA, Korah 8; THE APOCRYPHA, IV Maccabees 2:17.
127. BABYLONIAN TALMUD, Sanhedrin 109b-110a; MIDRASH RABBAH, Numbers 18:20; Buber, OP. CIT., Korah 24.
128. Josephus, OP. CIT., IV, 4:1.
129. IBID.
130. SIFRI 17b.
131. Neisser, BROTHERS AND SISTERS, p. 137.

132. THE FATHERS ACCORDING TO RABBI NATHAN 9; MIDRASH TANHUMA, Tzav 13; MIDRASH LEKACH TOV, Numbers, p. 206; Schechter, AVOS D'REB NOSON BISHTAY NUSCHAOS, 43:122.
133. SIFRI, Numbers 100.
134. MIDRASH RABBAH, Deuteronomy 6:11.
135. IBID., Numbers 13:20; Buber, MIDRASH AGGADAH, Shemos 18:2; Lauterbach, OP. CIT., Tractate Amalek, vol. 2, p. 167; Friedman, OP. CIT., 57b; Hoffman, OP. CIT., p. 86.
136. BABYLONIAN TALMUD, Yebamoth 61b-62a; Shabbath 87a.
136a. IBID., Megillah 13a.
137. IBID., Sotah 11b-12a; MIDRASH RABBAH, Exodus 1:17.
138. MIDRASH RABBAH, Exodus 1:16; 40:1; 48:4.
139. IBID., Ecclesiastes 5:5:1; BABYLONIAN TALMUD, Shabbath 97a; Buber, OP. CIT., Bamidbar 12:10; MIDRASH TANHUMA HAKODOM V'HAY-ASHAN, Metzorah '6; MIDRASH TANHUMA, Tzav 13; THE FATHERS ACCORDING TO RABBI NATHAN 9; PIRKE RABBI ELIEZER 54; SIFRI 18a.
140. SIFRE D'BE RAV, Numbers 105.
141. PIRKE RABBI ELIEZER 54.
142. THE FATHERS ACCORDING TO RABBI NATHAN 9.
143. MIDRASH RABBAH, Genesis 80:10; 100:7.
144. THE FATHERS ACCORDING TO RABBI NATHAN 9; Buber, MID-RASH TANHUMA HAKODOM V'HAYASHAN, Metzorah 6; ————, MIDRASH AGGADAH, Bamidbar 12:13.
145. MIDRASH RABBAH, Deuteronomy 6:13; THE FATHERS ACCORDING TO RABBI NATHAN 9.
146. MIDRASH RABBAH, Deuteronomy 6:14.
147. SIFRE D'BE RAV, Numbers 105; SIFRI 18b.
148. THE FATHERS ACCORDING TO RABBI NATHAN 9; MIDRASH RABBAH, Deuteronomy '6:13.
149. SIFRE D'BE RAV, Numbers 106.
150. English and Pearson, OP. CIT., p. 91.
151. THE FATHERS ACCORDING TO RABBI NATHAN 17.
152. MIDRASH RABBAH, Song of Songs 1:10:1.
153. IBID., Leviticus 10:5; 13:1; 18:1; Numbers 9:47; Deuteronomy 8:10; THE FATHERS ACCORDING TO RABBI NATHAN 1:3; 26:111; BABYLONIAI TALMUD, Zebahim 101a-b.
154. Ginzberg, OP. CIT., vol. 3, p. 457.
155. MIDRASH RABBAH, Numbers 19:9; Song of Songs 1:6; MIDRASH TANHUMA, Chukas 9.
156. MIDRASH RABBAH, Genesis 5:7; Numbers 19:9; MIDRASH TANHUMA, Chukas 9; Buber, MIDRASH TANHUMA HAKODOM V'HAYASHAN, Chukas 29-30; THE FATHERS ACCORDING TO RABBI NATHAN 1; Numbers 31:14.
157. MIDRASH RABBAH, Numbers 19:9.
158. IBID., Numbers 19:9; MIDRASH TANHUMA, Chukas 10; Buber, OP. CIT., Chukas 32.

159. Ginzberg, OP. CIT., vol. 6, p. 109, n. 619; MIDRASH LEKACH TOV, Numbers, p. 245.
160. Ginzberg, OP. CIT., vol. 3, p. 317.
161. IBID., vol. 2, p. 228; vol. 3, p. 310.
162. IBID., vol. 3, p. 308.
163. TANNA D'BE ELIYAHU, chap. 13, p. 1081.
164. Buber, OP. CIT., Chukas Addendum 2; BABYLONIAN TALMUD, Sanhe-drin 6b; Yoma 71b; PIRKE RABBI ELIEZER 17.
165. THE FATHERS ACCORDING TO RABBI NATHAN 12.
166. Ginzberg, OP. CIT., vol. 3, p. 323.
167. THE FATHERS ACCORDING TO RABBI NATHAN 12.
168. Ginzberg, OP. CIT., vol. 3, p. 263.
169. SIFRI 30a.
170. Ginzberg, OP. CIT., vol. 3, p. 322.
171. IBID., vol. 6, p. 111, n. 636.
172. IBID., vol. 3, p. 324f; Buber, OP. CIT., Chukas 40; Chukas Addendum 2.
173. Buber, OP. CIT., Tzav 12; THE FATHERS ACORDING TO RABBI NATHAN 34.
174. Buber, OP. CIT., Chukas 40.
175. Ginzberg, OP. CIT., vol. 2, p. 326, 328; vol. 4, p. 201.
176. Buber, OP. CIT., Chukas 40; MIDRASH TANNAIM 206-7.
177. Buber, OP. CIT., Chukas 41; MIDRASH RABBAH, Numbers 20:20; MIDRASH TANHUMA, Chukas 17; SIFRE D'BE RAV, Deuteronomy 305.
178. Lauterbach, OP. CIT., Tractate Vayassa, p. 85f.
179. SIFRE D'BE RAV, Deuteronomy 305.
180. BABYLONIAN TALMUD, Taanith 9a.
181. MIDRASH RABBAH, Song of Songs 1:7.
182. Buber, MIDRASH AGGADAH, Bamidbar 27:20.
183. SIFRE D'BE RAV, Numbers 138.
184. IBID., Deuteronomy 305.
185. MIDRASH TANHUMA, Vaeschanan 6.
186. IBID., Behaaloschah 12; Buber, MIDRASH TANHUMA HAKODOM V'HAYASHAN, Behaaloschah 22; BABYLONIAN TALMUD, Sanhedrin 17a; MIDRASH RABBAH, Exodus 41:1; Numbers 15:9; Ecclesiastes 9:11; SIFRI 17a.
187. SIFRE D'BE RAV, Numbers 141.
188. IBID., Numbers 140; Deuteronomy 305; BABYLONIAN TALMUD, Moed Katan 16b; Baba Metzia 84b; Sanhedrin 17a; THE FATHERS ACCORDING TO RABBI NATHAN 6; MIDRASH TANNAIM 180.
189. SIFRE D'BE RAV, Numbers 140.
190. Ginzberg, OP. CIT., vol. 3, p. 399.
191. Buber, MIDRASH AGGADAH, Bamidbar 27:23; SIFRE D'BE RAV, Numbers 141; SIFRI 30b.
192. Ginzberg, OP. CIT., vol. 3, p. 436f.
193. BABYLONIAN TALMUD, Berakoth 33b.
194. Ginzberg, OP. CIT., vol. 2, p. 275f; Philo, VITA MOSIS 1:6; MIDRASH ELIYAHU 8.
195. Ginzberg, OP. CIT., vol. 3, p. 330, 445.
196. Tead, THE ART OF LEADERSHIP, p. 48f.

CHAPTER X

1. Bergson, THE WORLD OF DREAMS, p. 19; Sharpe, DREAM ANALYSIS, p. 67.
2. MIDRASH RABBAH, Genesis 68:10; 74:7; Leviticus 1:13; Ecclesiastes 3:14. Not all of them agree with this statement.
3. BABYLONIAN TALMUD, Berakoth 14a.
4. IBID., Gittin 52a; Berakoth 55a; Sanhedrin 30a; Nedarim 8b; Taanith 24b; THE APOCRYPHA, Sirach 34:2; MIDRASH RABBAH, Lamentations 1:1:17.
5. BABYLONIAN TALMUD, Berakoth 55a.
6. Ginzberg, LEGENDS OF THE JEWS, vol. 1, p. 130, 204.
7. Freud, THE INTERPRETATION OF DREAMS, p. 353f.
8. Woods, THE WORLD OF DREAMS, p. 59.
9. Fromm, THE FORGOTTEN LANGUAGE, p. 128.
10. Wolff, THE DREAM—MIRROR OF CONSCIENCE, p. 59.
11. IBID., p. 35.
12. Freud, OP. CIT., p. 144.
13. Ginzberg, OP. CIT., vol. 1, p. 145f.
14. IBID., p. 267; Ferenczi, SEX IN PSYCHOANALYSIS, p. 104; French, THE INTEGRATION OF BEHAVIOR, vol. 2, p. 106.
15. Freud, OP. CIT., p. 266f.
16. IBID., p. 134; Ferenczi, OP. CIT., p. 101.
17. Wolff, OP. CIT., p. 109.
18. Jung, MODERN MAN IN SEARCH OF A SOUL, p. 6.
19. Jung, COLLECTED PAPERS ON ANALYTICAL PSYCHOLOGY, p. 375.
20. Freud, OP. CIT., p. 322f; Woods, OP. CIT., p. 632; Sharpe, OP. CIT., p. 14.
21. Jung, COLLECTED PAPERS ON ANALYTICAL PSYCHOLOGY, p. 281; ————, MODERN MAN IN SEARCH OF A SOUL, p. 19-21.
22. MIDRASH RABBAH, Ecclesiastes 1:1:1.
23. Fromm, OP. CIT., p. 7.
24. Jung, COLLECTED PAPERS ON ANALYTICAL PSYCHOLOGY, p. 218, 221, 308; Freud, OP. CIT., p. 353.
25. Wickes, THE INNER WORLD OF CHILDHOOD, p. 308.
26. BABYLONIAN TALMUD, Berakoth 56a-57b; MIDRASH RABBAH, Lamentations 1:1:14.
27. BABYLONIAN TALMUD, Berakoth 57a.
28. Jung, OP. CIT., p. 373.
30. MIDRASH RABBAH, Genesis 89:8.
29. Ginzberg, OP. CIT., vol. 2, p. 254. Pharaoh had a dream in which a kid was interpreted to refer to a child.
31. Trachtenberg, JEWISH MAGIC AND SUPERSTITION, p. 240.
32. IBID., p. 233; BABYLONIAN TALMUD, Berakoth 55a; Freud, OP. CIT.,
33. BABYLONIAN TALMUD, Yoma 83b.
34. IBID., Berakoth 55b; MIDRASH RABBAH, Genesis 89:5.
35. Fromm, OP. CIT., p. 128-9.
36. IBID., p. 33.

37. MIDRASH RABBAH, Genesis 88:2; BABYLONIAN TALMUD, Berakoth 55b.
38. MIDRASH RABBAH, Leviticus 34:12.
39. BABYLONIAN TALMUD, Berakoth 55b; Fromm, OP. CIT., p. 129.
40. BABYLONIAN TALMUD, Berakoth 55b; MIDRASH RABBAH, Genesis 89:8; Buber, MIDRASH AGGADAH, B'rayshis 40:8.
41. Hall, THE MEANING OF DREAMS, p. 71; Progoff, JUNG'S PSYCHOL- OGY AND ITS SOCIAL MEANING, p. 138.
42. BABYLONIAN TALMUD, Berakoth 55b.
43. IBID., Berakoth 56a.
44. IBID., Berakoth 55b.
45. Jung, OP. CIT., p. 299.
46. Woods, OP. CIT., p. 461.
47. BABYLONIAN TALMUD, Yoma 22b.
48. MIDRASH RABBAH, Genesis 84:10;; Ginzberg, OP. CIT., vol. 2, p. 7.
49. Ferenczi, OP. CIT., p. 264.
50. MIDRASH RABBAH, Genesis 84:11; BABYLONIAN TALMUD, Berakoth 55a-b.
51. Wickes, OP. CIT., p. 334.
52. IBID., p. 308.
53. Jung, OP. CIT., p. 220.
54. BABYLONIAN TALMUD, Berakoth 57a.
55. Adler, PRACTICE AND THEORY OF INDIVIDUAL PSYCHOLOGY, p. 217.
56. Fromm, OP. CIT., p. 109.
57. Wolff, OP. CIT., p. 289.
58. IBID., OP. CIT., p. 2f.
59. Freud, OP. CIT., p. 2, 335, 365, 370, 384.
60. Ginzberg, OP. CIT., vol. 1, p. 350f.
61. Freud, OP. CIT., p. 160n.
62. BABYLONIAN TALMUD, Berakoth 57a.
63. Trachtenberg, OP. CIT., p. 230.
64. SEFER HAYASHAR, (Tel Aviv), vol. 1, p. 92; BABYLONIAN TALMUD, Baba Kamma 92a; MIDRASH RABBAH, Genesis 52:13.
65. SEFER HAYASHAR, (Tel Aviv), vol. 1, p. 92f.
66. MIDRASH RABBAH, Genesis 52:6; PIRKE RABBI ELIEZER 21; Schech- ter, MIDRASH HAGODOL SEFER B'RAYSHIS, p. 299; Buber, MIDRASH TEHILLIM HAMECHUNAH SOCHER TOV, chap. 34.
67. BABYLONIAN TALMUD, Baba Kamma 92a; Makkoth 9b; PIRKE RABBI ELIEZER 26.
68. Schechter, OP. CIT., p. 300.
69. Trachtenberg, OP. CIT., p. 237.
70. Fromm, OP. CIT., p. 38f.
71. THE BOOK OF JUBILEES 27:1.
72. APOCALYPSIS MOSIS 2:2-3.
73. MIDRASH RABBAH, Genesis 6:5; Ecclesiastes 3:2.
74. Progoff, OP. CIT., p. 138.
75. Fromm, OP. CIT., p. 40.

76. Ginzberg, OP. CIT., vol. 2, p. 67.
77. IBID., vol. 2, p. 61, 63; Schechter, OP. CIT., p. 594-5.
78. Ginzberg, OP. CIT., vol. 2, p. 64.
79. Freud, OP. CIT., p. 580n.
80. IBID., p. 579n.
81. Ferenczi, OP. CIT., p. 127.
82. MIDRASH RABBAH, Esther 10:1.
83. BABYLONIAN TALMUD, Berakoth 55a.
84. Jones, ON THE NIGHTMARE, p. 54.
85. Freud, OP. CIT., p. 400-1.
86. Woods, OP. CIT., p. 672.
87. French, OP. CIT., vol. 2, p. 70.
88. Freud, OP. CIT., p. 333-4.
89. Woods, OP. CIT., p. 562.
90. Brill, BASIC PRINCIPLES OF PSYCHOANALYSIS, p. 165.
91. Wolff, OP. CIT., p. 300.

BIBLIOGRAPHY

Ackerman, N. W. THE PSYCHODYNAMICS OF FAMILY LIFE. New York: Basic Books, Inc., 1958.

Adler, A. PRACTICE AND THEORY OF INDIVIDUAL PSYCHOLOGY. London: Routledge and K. Paul, 1932.

————. UNDERSTANDING HUMAN NATURE. New York: Greenberg, Publisher, 1946.

Alexander, F. PSYCHOSOMATIC MEDICINE. New York: W. W. Norton & Co., 1950.

———— and W. Healy. ROOTS OF CRIME. New York: A. A. Knopf, 1935.

Anonymous. "Ambivalence in First Reactions to a Sibling." JOURNAL OF ABNORMAL AND SOCIAL PSYCHOLOGY, XLIV (October, 1949), 541-548.

Ansbacher, H. and R. THE INDIVIDUAL PSYCHOLOGY OF ALFRED ADLER. New York: Basic Books, Inc., 1956.

THE APOCRYPHA AND PSEUDEPIGRAPHA OF THE OLD TESTAMENT (ed. R. H. Charles, 2 vols.). Oxford: The Clarendon Press, 1922.

AVOS D'REB NOSON. Vilna, 1833.

BABYLONIAN TALMUD (16 vols.). Vilna: Rom, 1913.

Bailey, A. E. DAILY LIFE IN BIBLE TIMES. New York: C. Scribner's Sons, 1943.

Bergler, E. HOMOSEXUALITY: DISEASE OR WAY OF LIFE. New York: Hill & Wang, Inc., 1957.

Bergson, H. THE WORLD OF DREAMS. New York: Philosophical Library, 1958.

Berne, E. THE MIND IN ACTION. New York: Simon and Schuster, 1947.

Bowie, W. R. GREAT MEN OF THE BIBLE. New York: Harper & Bros. 1937.

Brill, A. A. BASIC PRINCIPLES OF PSYCHOANALYSIS. New York: Garden City Press, 1949.

Brody, S. PATTERNS OF MOTHERING. New York: International Universities Press, Inc., 1956.

Buber, S. MIDRASH AGGADAH. Vienna: Abraham Ponto, 1894.

————. MIDRASH TANHUMA HAKODOM V'HAYASHAN. Vilna, 1885.

————. MIDRASH TEHILLIM. Vilna, 1891.

————. MIDRASH TEHILLIM HAMECHUNAH SOCHER TOV. Vilna, 1891.

Conn. J. H. "Brief Psychotherapy of the Sex Offender." JOURNAL OF CLIN-ICAL PSYCHOPATHOLOGY, X (October, 1949), 347-372.

Cushing, J. G. N. "Psychopathology of Sexual Delinquency." JOURNAL OF CLINICAL PSYCHOPATHOLOGY, XI (April, 1950), 49-56.

Darwin, C. R. EXPRESSION OF THE EMOTIONS IN MAN AND IN ANIMALS. London: J. Murray, 1872.

Despert, J. L. CHILDREN OF DIVORCE. New York: Doubleday & Co., 1953.

Deutsch, H. THE PSYCHOLOGY OF WOMEN (2 vols.). New York: Grune & Stratton, 1945.

Eissler, R. S., Anna Freud, et al. THE PSYCHOANALYTIC STUDY OF THE CHILD. New York: International Universities Press, Inc., 1953, vol. viii.

English, O. S. and S. M. Finch. INTRODUCTION TO PSYCHIATRY. New York: W. W. Norton & Co., 1954.

———— and G. H. J. Pearson. EMOTIONAL PROBLEMS OF LIVING. New York: W. W. Norton & Co., Inc., 1945.

Epstein, B. MIDRASH MISHLE. Zitomer, 1890.

Evans, E. P. THE CRIMINAL PROSECUTION AND CAPITAL PUNISH-MENT OF ANIMALS. London: William Heineman, 1906.

THE FATHERS ACCORDING TO RABBI NATHAN. New Haven: Yale University Press, 1955.

Feldman, S. S. "Crying at the Happy Ending." JOURNAL OF THE AMERICAN PSYCHOANALYTIC ASSOCIATION, IV (July, 1956), 477-485.

Fenichel, O. THE PSYCHOANALYTIC THEORY OF NEUROSIS. New York: W. W. Norton & Co., 1945.

Ferenczi, S. SEX IN PSYCHOANALYSIS. New York: Basic Books, Inc., 1950.

Fine, B. ONE MILLION DELINQUENTS. Cleveland and New York: World Publishing Co., 1955.

Finegan, J. LIGHT FROM THE ANCIENT PAST. Princeton University Press, 1959.

Flugel, J. C. STUDIES IN FEELING AND DESIRE. London: Gerald Duck-worth & Co., Ltd., 1955.

Franzblau, A. N. THE ROAD TO SEXUAL MATURITY. New York: Simon & Schuster, 1954.

French, T. THE INTEGRATION OF BEHAVIOR (5 vols.). The University of Chicago Press, 1954.

Freud, S. COLLECTED PAPERS (tr. sup. J. Riviere, 4 vols.). London: Holgarth Press, 1950.

————. THE INTERPRETATION OF DREAMS (tr. J. Strachey). New York: Basic Books, Inc., 1955.

Friedman, M. MECHILTA D'REBI YISHMAEL. Vienna, 1870.

Fromm, E. THE FORGOTTEN LANGUAGE. New York: Rinehart & Co., Inc., 1951.

Gaer, J. THE LORE OF THE OLD TESTAMENT. Boston: Little, Brown & Co., 1951.

Gerber, I. J. THE PSYCHOLOGY OF THE SUFFERING MIND. New York: Jonathan David Co., 1951.

————. MAN ON A PENDULUM. New York: American Press, 1956.

Ginzberg, L. THE LEGENDS OF THE JEWS (7 vols.). Philadelphia: Jewish Publication Society of America, 1942.

Glueck, S. and E. UNRAVELING JUVENILE DELINQUENCY. Cambridge: Harvard University Press, 1950.

Hall, C. THE MEANING OF DREAMS. New York: Harper & Bros., 1953.

Heilbrinn, G. "On Weeping." PSYCHOANALYTIC QUARTERLY, XXIV (April, 1955), 245-255.

Henry, C. W. and A. A. Gross. "Social Factors in the Case Histories of One Hundred Under-Privileged Homosexuals." MENTAL HYGIENE, XXII (October, 1938), 591-611.

Hershon, P. I. A RABBINICAL COMMENTARY ON GENESIS.

Hertz, J. H. (ed). THE PENTATEUCH AND HAFTORAHS (2 vols.). New York: Metzudah Publishing Co., 1941.

Hirsch, N. D. M. TWINS, HEREDITY AND ENVIRONMENT. Cambridge: Harvard University Press, 1930.

Hoffman, D. MEKILTA D'REB SHIMON BEN YOCHAI. Frankfurt, 1905.

————. MIDRASH HAGODOL SEFER SHEMOS. Berlin, 1913.

Horney, K. NEUROTIC PERSONALITY OF OUR TIME. New York: W. W. Norton & Co., 1937.

Hunt, M. M. "The Wisdom of Tears." READERS DIGEST, (October, 1955), 34-42.

Inglis, B. EMOTIONAL STRESS AND YOUR HEALTH. New York: Criterion Books, 1959.

James, W. VARIETIES OF RELIGIOUS EXPERIENCE. New York: Longmans, Green & Co., 1925.

Jones, E. ON THE NIGHTMARE. New York: Liveright Publishing Corp., 1951.

Josephus, F. ANTIQUITIES OF THE JEWS (tr. W. Whiston, 4 vols.). London: Thomas Tegg, 1825.

Jung, C. G. COLLECTED PAPERS ON ANALYTICAL PSYCHOLOGY. London: Bailliere, Tindall & Cox, 1920.

————. MODERN MAN IN SEARCH OF A SOUL. New York: Harcourt, Brace & Co., no date.

Karpman, B. THE SEXUAL OFFENDER. New York: The Julian Press, Inc., 1954.

Kierkegaard, S. FEAR AND TREMBLING (tr. R. Payne). London: Oxford University Press, 1939.

Lauterbach, J. Z. MEKILTA D'REBBI YISHMAEL. Philadelphia: Jewish Publication Society of America, 1933.

Leppmann, F. "Essential Difference Between Sex Offenders." JOURNAL OF CRIMINAL LAW AND CRIMINOLOGY, XXXII (Sept-Oct, 1941), 366-380.

Levy, D. M. MATERNAL OVERPROTECTION. New York: Columbia University Press, 1943.

————. "Sibling Rivalry Studies in Children of Primitive Groups." AMERICAN JOURNAL OF ORTHOPSYCHIATRY, IX (1939), 205-215.

Lindgren, H. C. THE ART OF HUMAN RELATIONS. New York: Hermitage House, Inc., 1953.

Lund, F. H. "Why Do We Weep." JOURNAL OF SOCIAL PSYCHOLOGY, I (February, 1930), 136-151.

Lofts, N. WOMEN IN THE OLD TESTAMENT. New York: The Macmillan Co., 1949.

Maslow, A. H. and B. Mittelmann. PRINCIPLES OF ABNORMAL PSYCHOLOGY. New York: Harper & Brothers, 1951.

Masserman, J. H. "The Conceptual Dynamics of Person, Religion and Self." THE PSYCHOANALYTIC REVIEW, IV (October, 1954), 303-329.

McCann, R. V. DELINQUENCY. New York: Harper Bros., 1957.

Menninger, K. LOVE AGAINST HATE. New York: Harcourt, Brace & Co., 1942.

⸺. MAN AGAINST HIMSELF. New York: Harcourt, Brace & Co., 1938.

⸺. A PSYCHIATRIST'S WORLD. New York: The Viking Press, 1959.

MIDRASH CHASEROS VESAYROS. Jerusalem, 1899.

MIDRASH ELIYAHU.

MIDRASH LEKACH TOV. Vilna, Roninn, 1880.

MIDRASH PESIKTA RABOSI. Vienna: Joseph Keiser, 1880.

MIDRASH RABBAH (2 vols.). Vilna: Rom, 1884.

MIDRASH RABBAH (10 vols.). London: Soncino Press, 1951.

MIDRASH TANHUMA. Warsaw: G. Piment, no date.

MIDRASH TANHUMA HANIKRAH YELAMEDAYNU. Vilna, 1863.

MIDRASH TANNAIM.

MIKRAOTH GEDOLOTH (10 vols.). New York: Pardes Publishing House, Inc., 1951.

Morganstern, J. THE BOOK OF GENESIS. Cincinnati: The Union of American Hebrew Congregations, 1920.

Neisser, E. G. BROTHERS AND SISTERS. New York: Harper & Bros., 1951.

Newman, H. H. MULTIPLE HUMAN BIRTHS. New York: Doubleday, Doran & Co., 1940.

⸺, F. N. Freeman and K. H. Holzinger. TWINS, A STUDY OF HE-REDITY AND ENVIRONMENT. The University of Chicago Press, 1937.

Oberndorf, C. P. "Psycho-Analysis of Siblings." AMERICAN JOURNAL OF PSYCHOLOGY, VIII (May, 1929), 1007-1020.

Odier, C. ANXIETY AND MAGICAL THINKING (tr. J. W. Harvey). New York: International Universities Press, Inc., 1956.

Oliver, J. "The Hereditary Tendency to Twinning." EUGENICS REVIEW, IV (April, 1912), 39-53, 154-167.

Otto, R. THE IDEA OF THE HOLY (tr. J. W. Harvey). London: Oxford University Press, 1928.

Patai, R. SEX AND FAMILY LIFE IN THE BIBLE AND THE MIDDLE EAST. New York: Doubleday & Co., Inc., 1959.

Philo. ON THE LIFE OF MOSES (tr. F. H. Colson). Cambridge: Harvard University Press, 1950.

⸺. VITA MOSIS.

PIRKE RABBI ELIEZER. New York: Om Publishing Co., 1946.

Ploscowe, M. "The Sexual Psychopath: Some Suggestions for Control." PRISON WORLD, IX (July-August, 1947), 18.

⸺. THE TRUTH ABOUT DIVORCE. New York: Hawthorne Books, 1955.

Polish, D. "Akedat Yitzhak—The Binding of Isaac." JUDAISM, VI (Winter, 1957), 17-21.

Progoff, I. JUNG'S PSYCHOLOGY AND ITS SOCIAL MEANING. New York: The Julian Press, Inc., 1953.

Romm, M. E. "Compulsion Factors in Exhibitionism." JOURNAL OF CLINICAL PSYCHOPATHOLOGY, III (April, 1942), 585-596.

Samuels, M. CERTAIN PEOPLE OF THE BOOK. New York: A. A. Knopf, 1955.

Schapiro, M. A STUDY OF ADOPTION PRACTICE (2 vols.). New York: Child Welfare League of America, April, 1956.

Schechter, S. AVOS D'REB NOSON BISHTAY NUSCHAOS. Vienna, 1887.

————. MIDRASH HAGODOL SEFER B'RAYSHIS. Cambridge: University Press, 1902.

SEDER ELIYAHU RABBAH.

SEFER HAYASHAR. Cracow, 1628.

SEFER HAYASHAR. New York: Deutsch Printing & Publishing Co., 1960.

SEFER HAYASHAR (2 vols.). Tel Aviv: M. Newman, 1959.

SEFER HAZOHAR. Vilna, 1894.

Selling, L. S. "Results of Therapy in Cases of Sex Deviates." JOURNAL OF CLINICAL PSYCHOPATHOLOGY, III (January, 1942), 477-493.

Sharpe, E. F. DREAM ANALYSIS. New York: W. W. Norton & Co., Inc., no date.

SHULHAN ARUCH: YOREH DEAH (3 vols.). Vilna: Rom, 1894.

SIFRE D'BE RAV. Vienna, 1864.

SIFRI. Lemberg, 1860.

Simmel, E. "Alcoholism and Addiction." YEARBOOK OF PSYCHOANALYSIS, 1949 (ed. S. Lorand). New York: International Universities Press, Inc., 1950.

Simpson, G. PEOPLE IN FAMILIES. New York: Thomas Y. Crowell Co., 1960.

TALMUD YERUSHALMI. New York: Shulsinger Bros., 1948.

TANNA D'BE ELIYAHU. New York: Sophrograph Co., 1956.

Tead, O. THE ART OF LEADERSHIP. New York: McGraw-Hill Book Co., 1935.

Trachtenberg, J. JEWISH MAGIC AND SUPERSTITION. New York: Behrman's Jewish Book House, 1939.

TUR (7 vols.). Vilna. A. Rosenkrantz, 1900.

Vitanza, A. A. "Toward a Theory of Crying." PSYCHOANALYSIS AND THE PSYCHOANALYTIC REVIEW, XLVII (Winter, 1960), 63-79.

Weiss, J. "Crying at the Happy Ending." THE PSYCHOANALYTIC REVIEW, XXXIX, (October, 1952).

Wellisch, E. ISAAC AND OEDIPUS. New York: Humanities Press, 1955.

Wickes, F. G. THE INNER WORLD OF CHILDHOOD. New York: Appleton-Century-Crofts, Inc., 1927.

Wolff, W. THE DREAM—MIRROR OF CONSCIENCE. New York: Grune & Stratton, 1952.

Woods, R. L. THE WORLD OF DREAMS, AN ANTHOLOGY. New York: Random House, 1947.

YALKUT SHIMONI (2 vols.). New York: Title Publishing Co., 1944.

Ziman, E. JEALOUSY IN CHILDREN. New York: A. A. Wyn, Inc., 1949.

ZOHAR CHODOSH. Lemberg: Michael Poremba, 1858.

Index